Mirror for Humanity

A Concise Introduction to Cultural Anthropology

THIRD EDITION

Conrad Phillip Kottak
University of Michigan

McGraw Hill

Boston   Burr Ridge, IL   Dubuque, IA   Madison, WI   New York
San Francisco   St. Louis   Bangkok   Bogotá   Caracas   Kuala Lumpur
Lisbon   London   Madrid   Mexico City   Milan   Montreal   New Delhi
Santiago   Seoul   Singapore   Sydney   Taipei   Toronto

McGraw-Hill Higher Education

A Division of The **McGraw-Hill** Companies

MIRROR FOR HUMANITY:
A CONCISE INTRODUCTION TO CULTURAL ANTHROPOLOGY
Published by McGraw-Hill, a business unit of The McGraw-Hill Companies, Inc., 1221
Avenue of the Americas, New York, NY, 10020. Copyright © 2003, 1999, 1996, by The
McGraw-Hill Companies, Inc. All rights reserved. No part of this publication may be
reproduced or distributed in any form or by any means, or stored in a database or retrieval
system, without the prior written consent of The McGraw-Hill Companies, Inc., including,
but not limited to, in any network or other electronic storage or transmission, or broadcast
for distance learning.
Some ancillaries, including electronic and print components, may not be available to
customers outside the United States.

This book is printed on acid-free paper.

1 2 3 4 5 6 7 8 9 DOC/DOC 0 9 8 7 6 5 4 3 2

ISBN 0-07-241487-1

Editorial director: *Phillip A. Butcher*
Senior marketing manager: *Daniel M. Loch*
Media producer: *Shannon Rider*
Senior project manager: *Jean Hamilton*
Production supervisor: *Carol A. Bielski*
Photo research coordinator: *Judy Kausal*
Photo researcher: *Barbara Salz*
Lead supplement producer: *Marc Mattson*
Cover photo: *Bruno Barbey/Magnum Photos*
Cover design: *Mary E. Kazak*
Interior design: *Mary E. Kazak*
Type face: *10/12 New Aster*
Compositor: *GAC Indianapolis*
Printer: *R. R. Donnelley & Sons Company*

Library of Congress Cataloging-in-Publication Data

Kottak, Conrad Phillip.
    Mirror for humanity: a concise introduction to cultural anthropology/Conrad Phillip
Kottak.--3rd ed.
        p. cm.
    Includes bibliographical reference and index.
    ISBN 0-07-241487-1 (alk. paper)
    1. Ethnology. I. Title.

GN316 .K66 2003
306--dc21

                                                                        2002067872

www.mhhe.com

To My Daughter
Juliet Kottak Mavromatis

Ordinarily we are unaware of the special lens through which we look at life. It would hardly be fish who discovered the existence of water. Students who had not yet gone beyond the horizon of their own society could not be expected to perceive custom which was the stuff of their own thinking. Anthropology holds up a great mirror to man and lets him look at himself in this infinite variety.

(Kluckhohn 1944, p. 16—his emphasis)

Also available from McGraw-Hill by Conrad Kottak

Anthropology: The Exploration of Human Diversity, 9th ed. (2002)

Cultural Anthropology, 9th ed. (2002)

Assault on Paradise: Social Change in a Brazilian Village, 3rd ed. (1999)

The Teaching of Anthropology: Problems, Issues, and Decisions edited by Conrad Phillip Kottak, Jane White, Richard Furlow, and Patricia Rice (1997)

Brief Contents

Contents

Preface

OVERVIEW/APPROACH

Mirror for Humanity (MFH) is intended to provide a concise, relatively low-cost, introduction to cultural anthropology. The combination of shorter length and lower cost increases the instructor's options for assigning additional reading—case studies, readers, and other supplements—in a semester course. On the basis of experience with the first two editions, I can say MFH also works well in a quarter system, since traditional cultural anthropology texts may be too long for a one-quarter course.

I try to keep MFH up to date. Because anthropology, reflecting the world itself, seems to change at an increasing rate, **the introductory text should not restrict itself to subject matter defined decades ago, ignoring the pervasive changes affecting the peoples, places, and topics traditionally studied by anthropologists.** MFH thus includes discussions of ethnicity and nationalism in a global context and of diversity and multiculturalism in North America. Also highlighted are anthropology's increasingly transnational, multilocal, and longitudinal perspectives.

Rapid change notwithstanding, **anthropology has a core**. Even the briefest text must expose anthropology's nature, scope, and roles as a **science**, a **humanities** field, and a **mirror for humanity**. Anthropology is a *science*—a "systematic field of study or body of knowledge that aims, through experiment, observation, and deduction, to produce reliable explanations of phenomena, with reference to the material and physical world' (*Webster's New World Encyclopedia*, 1993, p. 937). Clyde Kluckhohn (1944, p. 9) called anthropology "the science of human similarities and differences," and his statement of the need for such a science still stands: "Anthropology provides a scientific basis for dealing with the crucial dilemma of the world today: how can peoples of different appearance, mutually unintelligible languages, and dissimilar ways of life get along peaceably together?" (Kluckhohn 1944, p. 9). Cultural anthropology has compiled an impressive body of knowledge, which this book attempts to encapsulate.

Anthropology has strong links to the humanities as well. In fact, cultural anthropology may well be the most humanistic of academic fields, because of its fundamental respect for human diversity. Anthropologists listen to, record, and represent voices from a multitude of nations and cultures. We strive to convince our students of the value of local knowledge, of diverse world views and perspectives. Cultural anthropology brings a comparative and nonelitist perspective to forms of creative expression, including art, narratives, music, and dance. Cultural anthropology is influenced by and influences the humanities. For example, adopting an anthropological view of creativity in its social and cultural context, recent approaches in the humanities have paid greater attention to mass and popular culture and to local creative expressions.

Anthropology's final basic role is as a *mirror for humanity*—a term derived from Clyde Kluckhohn's metaphor, expressed in his book *Mirror for Man* (1944), which suggested the title of this text. By looking at other cultures we can see ourselves more clearly:

> Ordinarily we are unaware of the special lens through which we look at life. It would hardly be fish who discovered the existence of water. Students who had not yet gone beyond the horizon of their own society could not be expected to perceive custom which was the stuff of their own thinking. *Anthropology holds up a great mirror to man and lets him look at himself in his infinite variety.* (Kluckhohn, 1944, p. 16—his emphasis)

This point reminds me of one of my teachers, Margaret Mead, who is remembered for her unparalleled success in demonstrating anthropology's value and relevance in allowing Americans to reflect on cultural variation and the plasticity of human nature. Mead conveyed the anthropological perspective to a broad public in a way no contemporary anthropologist does. She represented anthropology so effectively because she viewed it *as a humanistic science of unique value in understanding and improving the human condition.* This book is written in the belief that anthropologists should remember and emulate Margaret Mead's example.

CONTENT AND ORGANIZATION

No single or monolithic theoretical perspective orients this book. My e-mail, along with reviewers' comments, confirms that instructors with a wide range of views and approaches have been pleased with MFH as a teaching tool.

Mirror for Humanity, guided by very thoughtful reviewers, covers core and basics, as well as prominent current issues and approaches. MFH has five important chapters not consistently found in cultural anthropology texts: "Ethnicity and Race" (3), "Gender" (8), "The Modern World System"

(10), "Colonialism and Development" (11), and "Cultural Exchange and Survival" (12). These and other chapters explore the nature, role, and preservation of human diversity in the face of conquest and globalization. I recognize and try to show how linkages in the modern world system have both enlarged and erased old boundaries and distinctions as described in standard anthropology textbooks. People travel more than ever, but many migrants maintain their ties with home, so that they live multilocally. With so many people "in motion," the unit of anthropological study has expanded to include not only local communities, but also transnational diasporas.

I am pleased to have been one of the textbook authors chosen to participate in the **Gender in the Curriculum** Project of the American Anthropological Association. In that project I was paired with Yolanda Moses (a former President of the Association), who commented extensively on, and met with me to discuss, the treatment of gender (in writing and in the photo program) in my texts *Anthropology: The Exploration of Human Diversity and Cultural Anthropology.* I continue to draw on the lessons I learned. Gender issues are the focus of a separate chapter (8) here, but they are also considered throughout the text.

In considering ethnic, national, and transnational cultural identities, Chapter 3 examines multiculturalism in North America along with ethnic expression and conflict in eastern Europe, the former Soviet Union, and Central Asia. Chapter 12 focuses on issues of cultural exchange, creativity, and survival in a global culture driven by flows of people, technology, finance, images, information, and ideology. Indigenous peoples use various strategies to resist attacks on their autonomy, identity, and livelihood. New forms of political mobilization and cultural expression have emerged from the interplay of local, regional, national, and international cultural forces.

MFH concludes with four chapters especially relevant to anthropology's role in today's world: 'The Modern World System" (10), "Colonialism and Development" (11), "Cultural Exchange and Survival" (12), and "Applied Anthropology" (13).

WHAT'S NEW IN THE THIRD EDITION

Some chapters have been condensed, combined, or shortened for this new edition. By condensing I could add new topics (e.g., colonialism), without substantially increasing the length of the book. Throughout the book, charts, tables, and statistics have been updated with the most recent figures available for the United States and Canada.

What are the main differences between the second and third editions of MFH? Here are some of the most significant general changes:

- Two former chapters have been combined into one (Chapter 7) on political systems. As a result, this edition has one less chapter than the last edition.

- The last four chapters have been rearranged in this order, so as to form a more coherent unit:

    The Modern World System (10)

    Colonialism and Development (11)

    Cultural Exchange and Survival (12)

    Applied Anthropology (13)

- New sections have been added in many chapters (see below).

There are two new end-of-chapter study features:

- Numbered summaries.
- Case studies linking to *Culture Sketches*, 3rd ed., by Holly Peters-Golden.

Here are specific content changes, chapter by chapter:

In *Chapter 1* ("Exploring Cultural Diversity"):

- Applied anthropology is presented as a second dimension, rather than a fifth subfield, of anthropology.
- The section "Local, and the Ethnographer's, Beliefs and Perceptions" has been revised, with clearer illustrations of the emic/etic distinction.
- There is a new section on team research.
- The section "Survey Research and Complex Societies" has been condensed.

Chapter 2 ("Culture") contains:

- An expanded discussion of culture and nature.
- A new section on ethnocentrism, cultural relativism, and human rights.
- A new section on cultural change through globalization.

Chapter 3 ("Ethnicity and Race") features:

- Data from the U.S. Census 2000.
- A revised discussion of social statuses, with clearer graphic illustration.
- A new section on interracial, biracial, and multiracial identity.
- A new box on ethnic relations in the former Yugoslavia, including Bosnia and Kosovo.

Chapter 4 ("Language and Communication") has:

- A new section on nonverbal communication, including kinesics.
- A revised discussion of ebonics and Black English Vernacular.
- An expanded discussion of language and gender.
- An expanded discussion of language and thought, with new examples.
- A new table illustrating focal vocabulary (in sports).
- A new box: "Using Modern Technology to Preserve Linguistic and Cultural Diversity."

(To save space, the section on cyberspace communication has been moved to the book's Website.)

Chapter 5 ("Making a Living") contains:

- A new section on the implications of intensification for people and the environment.
- Expanded discussion of environmental context, influence, and effects.
- Additional ethnographic examples for pastoralism, redistribution, and negative reciprocity.

Chapter 6 ("Families, Kinship, and Marriage") features:

- An expanded discussion of extended families, including the Nayar exception.
- An updated discussion of trends in North American kinship, with Census 2000 data.
- Major new sections "Same-Sex Marriage," "Divorce," and "Marriage across Cultures."
- A new box "Love and Marriage," cross-culturally.

Chapter 7 ("Political Systems"):

- Former Chapters 7 ("Bands and Tribes") and 8 ("Chiefdoms and States") have been condensed and combined in a single chapter.
- The section "The Challenge to the State" has been moved to the book's Website.

Chapter 8 ("Gender") has:

- New sections "Sexualities and Gender" and "Patriarchy and Violence."
- Expanded discussions, with international scope, of the feminization of poverty and women's movements.
- Thorough updating of references and tables, including Census 2000 data.
- A new box: "Hidden Women, Public Men—Public Women, Hidden Men."

Chapter 9 ("Religion"):

- A new major section "Religion and Social Control" has a discussion of the Taliban.
- The section "Religion and Change" has new subsections: "Cargo Cults" and "A New Age" (on secularism and New Age religions).
- There is an expanded section "Secular Rituals."

Chapter 10 ("The Modern World System") has:

- New subsections "Malaysian Factory Women" and "Open and Closed Class Systems."
- A new box "Troubles in Swooshland" on Nike's labor problems in Asia.

Chapter 11 ("Colonialism and Development"):

- This chapter now precedes rather than follows the next chapter, for more logical flow of information.
- The completely new section on colonialism, which opens the chapter, has subsections "British Colonialism," "French Colonialism," and "Colonialism and Identity."

Chapter 12 ("Cultural Exchange and Survival") contains:

- A reorganized major section "Contact and Domination."
- A revised section "Cultural Imperialism."

Chapter 13 ("Applied Anthropology") has:

- A new subsection "Applied Anthropology and the Subdisciplines."
- A new section "Anthropology and Business."
- A new box: "Hot Asset in Corporate: Anthropology Degrees."

Note, too, that we have modified the design of MFH 3e, so as to make it more attractive and accessible and to reflect the mirror, reflection, water theme articulated so well in the Kluckhohn quote. We try to represent this theme by adding a color—blue—and express it in the new cover photo, too.

PEDAGOGY

The new edition incorporates suggestions made by users of my other texts as well as reviewers of the first two editions of MFH. The result, I hope, is a sound, well-organized, interesting, and "user-friendly" introduction to cultural anthropology.

MFH contains **boxes** at the end of each chapter, intended to give students a chance to consider anthropology's relevance to today's multicultural world and to their own lives. Some boxes examine current events or debates. Others are more personal accounts, which add human feeling to the presentation of cultural anthropology's subject matter. Many boxes illustrate a point with examples familiar to students from their enculturation or everyday experience.

A **glossary** defining key terms presented in each chapter is found at the end of the book, along with a **bibliography** of references cited.

Available for use with MFH 3e is the third edition of an **ethnographic case studies** book, *Culture Sketches,* by Holly Peters-Golden. This book profiles several of the societies discussed in MFH. New to this edition of MFH, at each chapter's end, is a link to a specific case study in the Peters-Golden book. Dr. Peters-Golden has taught introductory anthropology at the University of Michigan, using my textbook, for several years.

End-of-chapter summaries are now numbered, to make major points stand out.

SUPPLEMENTS

As a full-service publisher of quality educational products, McGraw-Hill does much more than just sell textbooks. They create and publish an extensive array of print, video, and digital supplements for students and instructors. This edition of MFH includes an exciting supplements package. Orders of new (versus used) textbooks help to defray the cost of developing such supplements, which is substantial. Please consult your local McGraw-Hill representative for more information on any of the supplements.

FOR THE STUDENT

Student's Online Learning Center—this free Web-based student supplement features the following helpful tools at www.mhhe.com/kottakmirror3:

- Chapter objectives, outlines, and overviews
- PowerPoint lecture notes
- Self-quizzes (multiple choice, true/false and short answer questions with feedback indicating why an answer is correct or incorrect)
- Essay questions
- Key terms
- Vocabulary flashcards
- Interactive maps
- Career opportunities
- Chapter-related readings
- Monthly updates
- Interactive exercises
- Internet exercises
- Web links

Culture Sketches: Case Studies in Anthropology, 3rd ed., by Holly Peters-Golden—this unique collection of mini-ethnographies is linked to MFH via the "Case Study" found at the end of every MFH chapter. The collection features coverage of 15 anthropologically significant cultures and provides real-world examples of everything from witchcraft to matriliny to economic development/change.

FOR THE INSTRUCTOR

Instructor's Manual/Test Bank—this indispensable instructor supplement features chapter outlines, lecture topics, film suggestions and a complete test bank.

Computerized Test Bank—this easy-to-use computerized testing program is available for both Windows and Macintosh computers and makes testing simple.

Instructor's Online Learning Center—password-protected access to important instructor support materials and downloadable supplements such as:
- The instructor's manual
- PowerPoint lecture slides
- Links to professional resources

PageOut—designed for the instructor just beginning to explore Web options, this technology supplement allows even novice computer users to create a course Website with a template provided by McGraw-Hill.

Videotapes—a wide variety of videotapes from the *Films for the Humanities and Social Sciences* series is available to adopters of the text.

ACKNOWLEDGMENTS

I'm grateful to many colleagues at McGraw-Hill. I thank Pam Gordon, freelance development editor, for her excellent ideas, suggestions, and guidance—involving four books, including MFH 3e. I continue to enjoy working with Phil Butcher, McGraw-Hill's editorial director for social sciences and humanities. I thank him for his unflagging support, as our association enters its second decade.

I thank Jean Hamilton for her work as project manager, guiding the manuscript through production and keeping everything moving on schedule. It's been a pleasure to work again with Barbara Salz, photo researcher, with whom I've worked for over a decade. I want to thank Chris Glew for his excellent work on the supplements for MFH, as well as for his hard and creative work on the last two editions of my longer texts. I also thank Peter deLissovoy, for his copyediting; Mary Kazak for conceiving and executing the design; and Dan Loch, a knowledgeable, creative, and enthusiastic marketing manager.

I'm very grateful to the following prepublication reviewers of MFH:

Diane Everett Barbolla—San Diego Mesa College

Jim Brady—California State University, Los Angeles

William L. Coleman—University of North Carolina, Greensboro

Les W. Field—University of New Mexico

Elizabeth Fortenbery—Pierce Community College

William Leons—University of Toledo

Daniel Maher—Westark College

Martin Oppenheimer—Kansas State University

Gerald F. Reid—Sacred Heart University

Eugene E. Ruyle—California State University, Long Beach

Betty A. Smith—Kennesaw State University

Mark Tromans—Broward Community College

I was delighted by the enthusiasm expressed in their comments, especially by those who have used MFH in their courses. My thanks also to several colleagues, especially Emiko Ohnuki-Tierney (University of Wisconsin–Madison), Norman Whitten (University of Illinois–Champaign-Urbana), Karla Valdes (Riverside Community College), and Michael McCrath (South Seattle Community College), for taking the time to e-mail me (some more than once) their helpful comments.

Students, too, regularly share their insights about MFH via e-mail. Particularly helpful comments have come from the College of William and Mary, Illinois Wesleyan University, Ohio University, Queens College (New York City), and Southern Oregon University. Anyone—student or instructor—with access to e-mail can reach me at the following address: **ckottak@umich.edu**

As usual, my family has offered me understanding, support, and inspiration during the preparation of MFH. This book is dedicated to my daughter, Juliet Kottak Mavromatis, who continues our family tradition of exploring human diversity and diagnosing and treating the human condition.

After 33 years of teaching, I have benefited from the knowledge, help, and advice of so many friends, colleagues, teaching assistants, and students that I can no longer fit their names into a short preface. I hope they know who they are and accept my thanks.

Annually since 1968 I've taught Anthropology 101 (Introduction to Anthropology), with the help of several teaching assistants each time. Feedback from students and teaching assistants keeps me up to date on the interests, needs, and views of the people for whom MFH is written. I continue to believe that effective textbooks are based in enthusiasm and in practice—in the enjoyment of teaching. I hope this product of my experience will continue to be helpful to others.

Conrad Phillip Kottak
Ann Arbor, Michigan
ckottak@umich.edu

About the Author

CONRAD PHILLIP KOTTAK (A.B. Columbia College, 1963; Ph.D. Columbia University, 1966) is Professor of Anthropology and Chair of the Department of Anthropology at the University of Michigan, where he has taught since 1968. In 1991 he was honored for his teaching by the University and the State of Michigan. In 1992 he received an excellence in teaching award from the College of Literature, Sciences, and the Arts of the University of Michigan. In 1999 the American Anthropological Association (AAA) awarded Professor Kottak the AAA/Mayfield Award for Excellence in the Undergraduate Teaching of Anthropology.

Professor Kottak has done ethnographic field work in Brazil (since 1962), in Madagascar (since 1966), and in the United States. His general interests are in the processes by which local cultures are incorporated—and resist incorporation—into larger systems. These interests link his earlier work on ecology and state formation in Africa and Madagascar to his more recent research on global change, national and international culture, and the mass media.

The third edition of Conrad Kottak's popular case study *Assault on Paradise: Social Change in a Brazilian Village*, based on his field work in Arembepe, Bahia, Brazil, was published in 1999 by McGraw-Hill. A research project during the 1980s blending ethnography and survey research in studying television's behavioral effects in Brazil was the basis of Professor Kottak's *Prime-Time Society: An Anthropological Analysis of Television and Culture* (Wadsworth 1990), a comparative study of the nature and impact of television in Brazil and the United States.

Conrad Kottak's other books include *The Past in the Present: History, Ecology and Cultural Variation in Highland Madagascar* (University of Michigan Press 1980), *Researching American Culture: A Guide for Student*

Anthropologists (University of Michigan Press 1982), and *Madagascar: Society and History* (Carolina Academic Press 1986).

The ninth editions of his texts *Anthropology: The Exploration of Human Diversity* and *Cultural Anthropology* were published by McGraw-Hill in 2002.

Conrad Kottak's articles have appeared in numerous academic journals, including *American Anthropologist, Journal of Anthropological Research, American Ethnologist, Ethnology, Human Organization,* and *Luso-Brazilian Review*. He has also written for more popular journals, including *Transaction/SOCIETY, Natural History, Psychology Today,* and *General Anthropology*.

In recent research projects, Professor Kottak and his colleagues have investigated the emergence of ecological awareness in Brazil, the social context of deforestation in Madagascar, and popular participation in economic development planning in northeastern Brazil. Since 1999 Professor Kottak has been active in the University of Michigan's Center for the Ethnography of Everyday Life, supported by the Alfred P. Sloan Foundation. In that capacity, for a research project entitled "Media, Family, and Work in a Middle-Class Midwestern Town," Professor Kottak is now investigating how middle-class families draw on various media in planning, managing, and evaluating their choices and solutions with respect to competing demands of work and family.

Conrad Kottak appreciates comments about his textbooks from professors and students. He can readily be reached by e-mail at the following Internet address: **ckottak@umich.edu**

List of Boxes

Chapter 1

Exploring Cultural Diversity

"That's just human nature." "People are pretty much the same all over the world." Such opinions, which we hear in conversations, in the mass media, and in a dozen scenes in daily life, promote the erroneous idea that people in other countries have the same desires, feelings, values, and aspirations that we do. Such statements proclaim that because people are essentially the same, they are eager to receive the ideas, beliefs, values, institutions, practices, and products of an expansive North American culture. Often this assumption turns out to be wrong.

Anthropology offers a broader view—a distinctive comparative, cross-cultural perspective. Most people think that anthropologists study nonindustrial societies, and they do. My research has taken me to remote villages in Brazil and Madagascar, a large island off the southeast coast of Africa. In Brazil I sailed with fishermen in simple sailboats on Atlantic waters. Among Madagascar's Betsileo people I worked in rice fields and took part in ceremonies in which I entered tombs to rewrap the corpses of decaying ancestors.

However, anthropology is much more than the study of nonindustrial peoples. It is a comparative science that examines all societies, ancient and modern, simple and complex. Most of the other social sciences tend to focus on a single society, usually an industrial nation such as the United States or Canada. Anthropology, however, offers a unique cross-cultural perspective, constantly comparing the customs of one society with those of others.

To become a cultural anthropologist, one normally does **ethnography** (the firsthand, personal study of local settings). Ethnographic fieldwork usually entails spending a year or more in another society, living with the local people and learning about their way of life. No matter how much the ethnographer discovers about the society, he or she remains an alien there. That experience of alienation has a profound impact. Having learned to respect other customs and beliefs, anthropologists can never forget that there is a wider world. There are normal ways of thinking and acting other than our own.

HUMAN DIVERSITY

Humans are the most adaptable animals in the world. In the Andes of South America, people awaken in villages 16,000 feet above sea level and then trek 1,500 feet higher to work in tin mines. Tribes in the Australian desert worship animals and discuss philosophy. People survive malaria in the tropics. Human beings have walked on the moon. The model of the *Starship Enterprise* in Washington's Smithsonian Institution symbolizes the desire to seek out new life and civilizations, to boldly go where no one has gone before. Wishes to know the unknown, control the uncontrollable, and bring order to chaos find expression among all peoples. Flexibility and adaptability are basic human attributes, and human diversity is the subject matter of anthropology.

Students are often surprised by the breadth of anthropology, which is a uniquely **holistic** science. It studies the whole of the human condition: past, present, and future; biology, society, language, and culture. People share **society**—organized life in groups—with other animals. Culture, however, is distinctly human. **Cultures** are traditions and customs, transmitted through learning that play a large role in determining the beliefs and behavior of the people exposed to them. Children *learn* these traditions by growing up in a particular society.

Cultural traditions include customs and opinions, developed over the generations, about proper and improper behavior. Cultural traditions answer such questions as: How should we do things? How do we interpret the world? How do we tell right from wrong? A common culture produces consistencies in behavior and thought in a given society.

The most critical element of cultural traditions is their transmission through learning rather than biological inheritance. Culture is not itself biological, but it rests on capacities that are based in hominid biology. (**Hominids** are members of the zoological family that includes fossil and living humans.) Human **adaptation** (the process by which organisms cope with environmental stresses) involves an interplay between culture and biology. For more than a million years, hominids have had at least some of the biological capacities on which culture depends. These abilities are to learn, to think symbolically, to use language, and to employ tools and other cultural features in organizing their lives and adapting to their environments.

Bound neither by time nor by space, anthropology attempts to answer major questions of human existence. By examining ancient bones and tools, anthropologists solve the mysteries of hominid origins. When did our own ancestors separate from those remote great-aunts and great-uncles whose descendants are the apes? Where and when did *Homo sapiens* originate? How has our species changed? What are we now and where are we going? How have changes in culture and society influenced and been influenced by biological change?

ANTHROPOLOGY

The academic discipline of anthropology, also known as **general anthropology,** includes four main subdisciplines or subfields: sociocultural, archaeological, biological, and linguistic anthropology. (From here on, I will use the shorter term *cultural anthropology* as a synonym for "sociocultural anthropology," the subject of this book.)

    Cultural anthropologists study human society and culture. They describe, interpret, and explain social and cultural similarities and differences. To study and interpret cultural diversity, cultural anthropologists engage in two kinds of activity: ethnography (based on field work) and ethnology (based on cross-cultural comparison). **Ethnography** provides an account of a particular community, society, or culture. During ethnographic field work the ethnographer gathers data, which he or she organizes, describes, analyzes, and interprets to build and present that account, which may be in the form of a book, article, or film. **Ethnology** examines, analyzes, and compares the results of ethnography—the data gathered in different societies. It uses such data to compare and contrast and to make generalizations about society and culture. Ethnologists look beyond the particular to the more general. They strive to explain cultural differences and similarities and to build theory to enhance our understanding of how social and cultural systems work. Ethnology gets its data for comparison not just from ethnography but also from the other subfields. For example, **archaeological anthropology** (more simply, archaeology) reconstructs, describes, and interprets human behavior and cultural patterns through material remains. Archaeologists are best known for studying prehistory (the period before the invention of writing, around 6,000 years ago), but they also study historical and even living cultures through their material remains.

    The subject matter of **biological,** or **physical, anthropology** is human biological diversity in time and space. Biological anthropologists study hominid evolution, human genetics, and human biological plasticity (the body's ability to cope with stresses, such as heat, cold, and altitude). Also part of biological anthropology is primatology—the study of the biology, evolution, behavior, and social life of monkeys, apes, and other nonhuman primates. Biological anthropologists collaborate with archaeologists in reconstructing cultural as well as biological aspects of human evolution. Often found with fossils are tools, which suggest the habits, customs, and lifestyles of the hominids that used them. Human biological and cultural

Through cross-cultural comparison, we
see that many differences between the
sexes arise from cultural learning and
expectations rather than from biology.
This female porter in Calcutta, India has
loaded heavy bricks on her head for
transport to a construction site.

evolution have been interrelated and complementary, and humans continue
to adapt both biologically and culturally.

We don't know (and probably never will know) when hominids began to
speak. However, well-developed, grammatically complex languages have existed for thousands of years. Like the other subfields, **linguistic anthropology** examines variation in time and space. Linguistic anthropologists study
languages of the present and make inferences about those of the past. Linguistic techniques are also useful to ethnographers because they permit
the rapid learning of unwritten languages. Linguistic and cultural anthropologists collaborate in studying links between language and other aspects
of culture.

Most American anthropologists, myself included, specialize in cultural
anthropology. However, most are also familiar with the basics of the other
subfields. Large departments of anthropology usually include members of
each subfield.

There are historical reasons for the inclusion of four subdisciplines in a
single field. American anthropology arose a century ago out of concern for
the history and cultures of the native populations of North America ("American Indians"). Interest in the origins and diversity of Native Americans

brought together studies of customs, social life, language, and physical traits. Such a unified anthropology did not develop in Europe, where the subdisciplines tend to exist separately.

The subdisciplines influence each other as anthropologists talk, read professional books and journals, and associate in professional organizations. General anthropology explores the basics of human biology, psychology, society, and culture and considers their interrelations. Anthropologists share certain key assumptions. One is that sound conclusions about "human nature" can't be drawn from a single cultural tradition.

We often hear "nature-nurture" and "genetics-environment" questions. For example, consider gender differences. Do male and female capacities, attitudes, and behavior reflect biological or cultural variation? Are there universal emotional and intellectual contrasts between the sexes? Are females less aggressive than males? Is male dominance a human universal? By examining diverse societies, anthropology shows that many contrasts between men and women arise from cultural learning rather than from biology.

Anthropology is not a science of the exotic carried on by quaint scholars in ivory towers. Rather, it is a holistic, comparative field with a lot to tell the public. Anthropology's foremost professional organization, the American Anthropological Association, has formally acknowledged a public service role by recognizing that anthropology has two dimensions: (1) theoretical/academic anthropology and (2) practicing or **applied anthropology.** The latter refers to the application of anthropological data, perspectives, theory, and methods to identify, assess, and solve contemporary social problems. More and more anthropologists from the four subfields now work in such "applied" areas as public health, family planning, and economic development.

RESEARCH METHODS

Cultural anthropology and sociology share an interest in social relations, organization, and behavior. However, important differences between these disciplines arose from the kinds of societies each traditionally studied. Initially sociologists focused on the industrial West; anthropologists, on nonindustrial societies. Different methods of data collection and analysis emerged to deal with those different kinds of societies. To study large-scale, complex nations, sociologists came to rely on questionnaires and other means of gathering masses of quantifiable data. For many years sampling and statistical techniques have been basic to sociology, whereas statistical training has been less common in anthropology (although this is changing as anthropologists increasingly work in modern nations).

Traditional ethnographers studied small, nonliterate (without writing) populations and relied on ethnographic methods appropriate to that context. "Ethnography is a research process in which the anthropologist closely observes, records, and engages in the daily life of another culture—an experience labeled as the fieldwork method—and then writes accounts of this culture, emphasizing descriptive detail" (Marcus and Fischer 1986, p. 18). One key method described in this quote is **participant observation**—taking part in the events one is observing, describing, and analyzing.

Anthropology started to separate from sociology around 1900. Early students of society, such as the French scholar . . . Émile Durkheim, were among the founders of both sociology and anthropology. Comparing the organization of simple and complex societies, Durkheim studied the religions of Native Australians (Durkheim 1912/1961), as well as mass phenomena (such as suicide rates) in modern nations (Durkheim 1897/1951). Eventually anthropology would specialize in the former, sociology in the latter.

ETHNOGRAPHY: ANTHROPOLOGY'S DISTINCTIVE STRATEGY

Anthropology developed into a separate field as early scholars worked on Indian (Native American) reservations and traveled to distant lands to study small groups of foragers (hunters and gatherers) and cultivators. Traditionally, the process of becoming a cultural anthropologist has required a field experience in another society. Early ethnographers lived in small-scale, relatively isolated societies, with simple technologies and economies.

Ethnography thus emerged as a research strategy in societies with greater cultural uniformity and less social differentiation than are found in large, modern, industrial nations. In such nonindustrial settings, ethnographers have needed to consider fewer paths of enculturation to understand social life. Traditionally, ethnographers have tried to understand the whole of a particular culture (or, more realistically, as much as they can, given limitations of time and perception). To pursue this holistic goal, ethnographers adopt a free-ranging strategy for gathering information. In a given society or community, the ethnographer moves from setting to setting, place to place, and subject to subject to discover the totality and interconnectedness of social life. Ethnography, by expanding our knowledge of the range of human diversity, provides a foundation for generalizations about human behavior and social life. Ethnographers draw on varied techniques to piece together a picture of otherwise alien lifestyles. Anthropologists usually employ several (but rarely all) of the techniques discussed here.

ETHNOGRAPHIC TECHNIQUES

The characteristic *field techniques* of the ethnographer include the following:

1. Direct, firsthand observation of daily behavior, including *participant observation.*
2. Conversation with varying degrees of formality, from the daily chitchat that helps maintain rapport and provides knowledge about what is going on, to prolonged *interviews,* which can be unstructured or structured.

3. The *genealogical method.*
4. Detailed work with *key consultants* about particular areas of community life.
5. In-depth interviewing, often leading to the collection of *life histories* of particular people (narrators).
6. Discovery of local (native) beliefs and perceptions, which may be compared with the ethnographer's own observations and conclusions.
7. Problem-oriented research of many sorts.
8. Longitudinal research—the continuous long-term study of an area or site.
9. Team research—coordinated research by multiple ethnographers.

Observation and Participant Observation

Ethnographers get to know their hosts and usually take an interest in the totality of their lives. Ethnographers must pay attention to hundreds of details of daily life, seasonal events, and unusual happenings. They should record what they see as they see it. Things will never seem quite as strange as they do during the first few weeks in the field. The ethnographer eventually gets used to, and accepts as normal, cultural patterns that were initially alien. Staying a bit more than a year in the field allows the ethnographer to repeat the season of his or her arrival, when certain events and processes may have been missed because of initial unfamiliarity and culture shock.

Many ethnographers record their impressions in a personal *diary*, which is kept separate from more formal *field notes*. Later, this record of early impressions will help point out some of the most basic aspects of cultural diversity. Such aspects include distinctive smells, noises people make, how they cover their mouths when they eat, and how they gaze at others. These patterns, which are so basic as to seem almost trivial, are part of what Bronislaw Malinowski called "the imponderabilia of native life and of typical behavior" (Malinowski 1922/1961, p. 20). These features of culture are so fundamental that natives take them for granted. They are too basic even to talk about, but the unaccustomed eye of the fledgling ethnographer picks them up. Thereafter, becoming familiar, they fade to the edge of consciousness. Initial impressions are valuable and should be recorded. First and foremost, ethnographers should be accurate observers, recorders, and reporters of what they see in the field.

Ethnographers don't study animals in laboratory cages. The experiments that psychologists do with pigeons, chickens, and rats are very different from ethnographic procedure. Anthropologists don't systematically control subjects' exposure to certain stimuli. Our subjects are not speechless animals but human beings. It is not part of ethnographic procedure to manipulate people, control their environments, or experimentally induce in them certain behaviors.

Ethnographers strive to establish *rapport*, a good, friendly working relationship based on personal contact, with our hosts. One of ethnography's most characteristic procedures is participant observation, which means that

Bronislaw Malinowski (1884-1942), seated with villagers in the
Trobriand Islands. A Polish anthropologist who spent most of his
professional life in England, Malinowski is generally considered the
father of ethnography. Does this photo suggest anything about
Malinowski's relationship with the villagers?

we take part in community life as we study it. As human beings living
among others, we cannot be totally impartial and detached observers. We
must also take part in many events and processes we are observing and trying to comprehend. By participating, we may learn why natives find such
events meaningful, as we see how they are organized and conducted.

In Arembepe, Brazil, I learned about fishing by sailing on the Atlantic
with local fishermen. I gave Jeep rides into the capital to malnourished babies, to pregnant mothers, and once to a teenage girl possessed by a spirit.
All those people needed to consult specialists outside the village. I danced
on Arembepe's festive occasions, drank libations commemorating new
births, and became a godfather to a village girl. Most anthropologists have
similar field experiences. The common humanity of the student and the
studied, the ethnographer and the research community, makes participant
observation inevitable.

Conversation, Interviewing, and Interview Schedules

Participating in local life means that ethnographers constantly talk to people and ask questions. As their knowledge of the native language increases,
they understand more. There are several stages in learning a field language.
First is the naming phase—asking name after name of the objects around

us. Later we are able to pose more complex questions and understand the replies. We begin to understand simple conversations between two villagers. If our language expertise proceeds far enough, we eventually become able to comprehend rapid-fire public discussions and group conversations.

One data-gathering technique I have used in both Arembepe and Madagascar involves an ethnographic survey that includes an interview schedule. In 1964, my fellow field workers and I attempted to complete an interview schedule in each of Arembepe's 160 households. We entered almost every household (fewer than 5 percent refused to participate) to ask a set of questions on a printed form. Our results provided us with a census and basic information about the village. We wrote down the name, age, and gender of each household member. We gathered data on family type, political party, religion, present and previous jobs, income, expenditures, diet, possessions, and many other items on our eight-page form.

Although we were doing a survey, our approach differed from the survey research design routinely used by sociologists and other social scientists working in large, industrial nations. That survey research, discussed below, involves sampling (choosing a small, manageable study group from a larger population). We did not select a partial sample from the total population. Instead, we tried to interview in all households in the community we were studying (that is, to have a total sample). We used an interview schedule rather than a questionnaire. With the **interview schedule,** the ethnographer talks face to face with people, asks the questions, and writes down the answers. *Questionnaire* procedures tend to be more indirect and impersonal; the respondent often fills in the form.

Our goal of getting a total sample allowed us to meet almost everyone in the village and helped us establish rapport. Decades later, Arembepeiros still talk warmly about how we were interested enough in them to visit their homes and ask them questions. We stood in sharp contrast to the other outsiders the villagers had known, who considered them too poor and backward to be taken seriously.

Like other survey research, however, our interview schedule did gather comparable quantifiable information. It gave us a basis for assessing patterns and exceptions in village life. Our schedules included a core set of questions that were posed to everyone. However, some interesting side issues often came up during the interview, which we would pursue then or later.

We followed such leads into many dimensions of village life. One woman, for instance, a midwife, became the key cultural consultant we sought out later when we wanted detailed information about local childbirth. Another woman had done an internship in an Afro-Brazilian cult (*candomblé*) in the city. She still went there regularly to study, dance, and get possessed. She became our candomblé expert.

Thus, our interview schedule provided a structure that *directed but did not confine* us as researchers. It enabled our ethnography to be both quantitative and qualitative. The quantitative part consisted of the basic information we gathered and later analyzed statistically. The qualitative dimension came from our follow-up questions, open-ended discussions, pauses for gossip, and work with key consultants.

The Genealogical Method

As ordinary people, many of us learn about our own ancestry and relatives by tracing our genealogies. Various computer programs now allow us to trace our "family tree" and degrees of relationship. The **genealogical method** is a well-established ethnographic technique. Early ethnographers developed notation and symbols to deal with kinship, descent, and marriage. Genealogy is a prominent building block in the social organization of nonindustrial societies, where people live and work each day with their close kin. Anthropologists need to collect genealogical data to understand current social relations and to reconstruct history. In many nonindustrial societies, kin links are basic to social life. Anthropologists even call such cultures "kin-based societies." Everyone is related, and spends most of his or her time with relatives. Rules of behavior attached to particular kin relations are basic to everyday life. Marriage is also crucial in organizing nonindustrial societies because strategic marriages between villages, tribes, and clans create political alliances.

Key Cultural Consultants

Every community has people who by accident, experience, talent, or training can provide the most complete or useful information about particular aspects of life. These people are **key cultural consultants.** In Ivato, the Betsileo village in Madagascar where I spent most of my time, a man named Rakoto was particularly knowledgeable about village history. However, when I asked him to work with me on a genealogy of the fifty to sixty people buried in the village tomb, he called in his cousin Tuesdaysfather, who knew more about that subject. Tuesdaysfather had survived an epidemic of influenza that ravaged Madagascar, along with much of the world, around 1919. Immune to the disease himself, Tuesdaysfather had the grim job of burying his kin as they died. He kept track of everyone buried in the tomb. Tuesdaysfather helped me with the tomb genealogy. Rakoto joined him in telling me personal details about the deceased villagers.

Life Histories

In nonindustrial societies as in our own, individual personalities, interests, and abilities vary. Some villagers prove to be more interested in the ethnographer's work and are more helpful, interesting, and pleasant than others are. Anthropologists develop likes and dislikes in the field as we do at home. Often, when we find someone unusually interesting, we collect his or her **life history.** This recollection of a lifetime of experiences provides a more

A census taker in Paro, Bhutan, surrounded by villagers. How is census taking similar to, and different from, survey research, and from ethnograpy?

intimate and personal cultural portrait than would be possible otherwise. Life histories, which may be recorded or videotaped for later review and analysis, reveal how specific people perceive, react to, and contribute to changes that affect their lives. Such accounts can illustrate diversity, which exists within any community, since the focus is on how different people interpret and deal with some of the same problems.

Local, and the Ethnographer's, Beliefs and Perceptions

One goal of ethnography is to discover local (native) views, beliefs, and perceptions, which may be compared with the ethnographer's own observations and conclusions. In the field, ethnographers typically combine two research strategies, the emic (native-oriented) and the etic (scientist-oriented). These terms, derived from linguistics, have been applied to ethnography by various anthropologists. Marvin Harris (1968) has popularized the following meanings of the terms: An **emic** approach investigates how natives think. How do they perceive and categorize the world? What are their rules for behavior? What has meaning for them? How do they imagine and explain things? Operating emically, the ethnographer seeks the "native viewpoint" (see the box at the end of this chapter), relying on local people to explain things and to say whether something is significant or not. The term **cultural consultant** refers to individuals the ethnographer gets to know in the field, the people who teach him or her about their culture, who provide the emic perspective.

The **etic** (scientist-oriented) approach shifts the focus from native observations, categories, explanations, and interpretations to those of the anthropologist. The etic approach realizes that members of a culture are often too involved in what they are doing to interpret their cultures impartially. Operating etically, the ethnographer emphasizes what he or she (the observer) notices and considers important. As a trained scientist, the ethnographer should try to bring an objective and comprehensive viewpoint to the study of other cultures. Of course, the ethnographer, like any other scientist, is also a human being with cultural blinders that prevent complete objectivity. As in other sciences, proper training can reduce, but not totally eliminate, the observer's bias. But anthropologists do have special training to compare behavior between different societies.

What are some examples of emic versus etic perspectives? Consider our holidays. For North Americans, Thanksgiving Day has special significance. In our view (emically) it is a unique cultural celebration that commemorates particular historical themes. But a wider, etic, perspective sees Thanksgiving as just one more example of the post-harvest festivals held in many societies. Another example: natives (including many Americans) may believe that chills and drafts cause colds, which scientists know are caused by germs. In cultures that lack the germ theory of disease, illnesses are emically explained by various causes, ranging from spirits to ancestors to witches. *Illness* refers to a culture's (emic) perception and explanation of bad health, whereas *disease* refers to the scientific—etic—explanation of poor health, involving known pathogens.

Ethnographers typically combine emic and etic strategies in their field work. Native statements, perceptions, categories, and opinions help ethnographers understand how cultures work. Native beliefs are also interesting and valuable in themselves. However, natives often fail to admit, or even recognize, certain causes and consequences of their behavior. This is as true of North Americans as it is of people in other societies. To describe and interpret culture, ethnographers should recognize the biases that come from their own culture as well as those of the people being studied. More and more are doing so, as the box at the end of this chapter discusses.

Problem-Oriented Ethnography

Although anthropologists are interested in the whole context of human behavior, it is impossible to study everything. Most ethnographers now enter the field with a specific problem to investigate, and they collect data relevant to that problem (see Chiseri-Strater and Sunstein 2001, Kutsche 1998). And local people's answers to questions are not the only data source. Anthropologists also gather information on factors such as population density, environmental quality, climate, physical geography, diet, and land use. Sometimes this involves direct measurement—of rainfall, temperature, fields, yields, dietary quantities, or time allocation (Bailey 1990; Johnson 1978). Often it means that we consult government records or archives.

The information of interest to ethnographers is not limited to what local people can and do tell us. In an increasingly interconnected and complicated world, local people lack knowledge about many factors that affect their lives. Our local consultants may be as mystified as we are by the exercise of power from regional, national, and international centers.

Longitudinal Research

Geography limits anthropologists less now than in the past, when it could take months to reach a field site, and return visits were rare. New systems of transportation allow anthropologists to widen the area of their research and to return repeatedly. Ethnographic reports now routinely include data from two or more field stays. **Longitudinal research** is the long-term study of a community, region, society, culture, or other unit, usually based on repeated visits.

One example of such research is the longitudinal study of Gwembe District, Zambia. This study, planned in 1956 as a longitudinal project by Elizabeth Colson and Thayer Scudder, continues with Colson, Scudder, and their associates of various nationalities. Thus, as is often the case with longitudinal research, the Gwembe study also illustrates team research—coordinated research by multiple ethnographers. The Gwembe research project is both longitudinal (multi-time) and multi-site (considering several field sites) (Colson and Scudder 1975; Scudder and Colson 1980). Four villages, in different areas, have been followed for five decades. Periodic village censuses provide basic data on population, economy, kinship, and religious behavior. Censused people who have moved are traced and interviewed to see how their lives compare with those of people who have stayed in the villages.

A series of different research questions have emerged, while basic data on communities and individuals continue to be collected. The first focus of study was the impact of a large hydroelectric dam, which subjected the Gwembe people to forced resettlement. The dam also spurred road building and other activities that brought the people of Gwembe more closely in touch with the rest of Zambia. In subsequent research Scudder and Colson (1980) examined how education provided access to new opportunities as it also widened a social gap between people with different educational levels. A third study then examined a change in brewing and drinking patterns, including a rise in alcoholism, in relation to changing markets, transportation, and exposure to town values (Colson and Scudder 1988).

Team Research

As mentioned, longitudinal research is often team research. My own field site of Arembepe, Brazil, for example, first entered the world of anthropology as a field-team village in the 1960s. It was one of four sites for the now

Janet Dunn, one of many anthropologists who
have worked in Arembepe. Where is Arembepe,
and what kinds of research have been done there?

defunct Columbia-Cornell-Harvard-Illinois Summer Field Studies Program
in Anthropology. For at least three years, that program sent a total of about
twenty undergraduates annually, the author included, to do brief summer
research. We were stationed in rural communities in four countries: Brazil,
Ecuador, Mexico, and Peru. Since my wife, Isabel Wagley Kottak, and I began studying it in 1962, Arembepe has become a longitudinal field site.
Three generations of researchers have monitored various aspects of change
and development. The community has changed from a village into a town.
Its economy, religion, and social life have been transformed.

Brazilian and American researchers worked with us on team research
projects during the 1980s (on television's impact) and the 1990s (on ecological awareness and environmental risk perception.) Graduate students from
the University of Michigan have drawn on our baseline information from
the 1960s as they have studied various topics in Arembepe. In 1990 Doug
Jones, a Michigan student doing biocultural research, used Arembepe as a
field site to investigate standards of physical attractiveness. In 1996–97,
Janet Dunn studied family planning and changing female reproductive
strategies. Chris O'Leary, who first visited Arembepe in summer 1997, investigated a striking aspect of religious change in Arembepe—the arrival of
Protestantism; his dissertation (O'Leary 2002) research then examined
changing food habits and nutrition. Arembepe is thus a site where various
field workers have worked as members of a longitudinal team. The more recent researchers have built on prior contacts and findings to increase
knowledge about how local people meet and manage new circumstances.

SURVEY RESEARCH AND COMPLEX SOCIETIES

As anthropologists work increasingly in large-scale societies, they have developed innovative ways of blending ethnography and survey research (Fricke 1994). Before considering such combinations of field methods, I must describe survey research and the main differences between survey research and ethnography as traditionally practiced. Working mainly in large, populous nations, sociologists, political scientists, and economists have developed and refined the **survey research** design, which involves sampling, impersonal data collection, and statistical analysis. Survey research usually draws a **sample** (a manageable study group) from a much larger population. By studying a properly selected and representative sample, social scientists can make accurate inferences about the larger population.

In smaller-scale societies and local communities, ethnographers get to know most of the people. Given the greater size and complexity of nations, survey research cannot help being more impersonal. Survey researchers call the people they study *respondents*. These are people who respond to questions during a survey. Sometimes survey researchers personally interview them. Sometimes, after an initial meeting, they ask respondents to fill out a questionnaire. In other cases researchers mail printed questionnaires to randomly selected sample members or have paid assistants interview or telephone them. In a **random sample,** all members of the population have an equal statistical chance of being chosen for inclusion. A random sample is selected by randomizing procedures, such as tables of random numbers, which are found in many statistics textbooks.

Anyone who has grown up recently in the United States or Canada has heard of sampling. Probably the most familiar example is the polling used to predict political races. The media hire agencies to estimate outcomes and do exit polls to find out what kinds of people voted for which candidates. During sampling, researchers gather information about age, gender, religion, occupation, income, and political party preference. These characteristics (**variables**—attributes that vary among members of a sample or population) are known to influence political decisions.

Many more variables affect social identities, experiences, and activities in a modern nation than is the case in the small communities where ethnography grew up. In contemporary North America hundreds of factors influence our social behavior and attitudes. These social predictors include our religion; the region of the country we grew up in; whether we come from a town, suburb, or city; and our parents' professions, ethnic origins, and income levels.

Ethnography can be used to supplement and fine-tune survey research. Anthropologists can transfer the personal, firsthand, techniques of ethnography to virtually any setting that includes human beings. A combination of survey research and ethnography can provide new perspectives on life in **complex societies** (large and populous societies with social stratification and central governments). Preliminary ethnography can also help develop relevant and culturally appropriate questions for inclusion in national surveys.

In my own courses in Ann Arbor, Michigan, undergraduates have done ethnographic research on sororities, fraternities, teams, campus organizations, and the local homeless population. Other students have systematically observed behavior in public places such as racquetball courts, restaurants, bars, football stadiums, markets, malls, and classrooms. Other "modern anthropology" projects use anthropological techniques to interpret and analyze mass media. Anthropologists have been studying their own cultures for decades, and anthropological research in the United States and Canada is booming today. Wherever there is patterned human behavior, there is grist for the anthropological mill.

In any complex society, many predictor variables (*social indicators*) influence behavior and opinions. Because we must be able to detect, measure, and compare the influence of social indicators, many contemporary anthropological studies have a statistical foundation. Even in rural field work, more anthropologists now draw samples, gather quantitative data, and use statistics to interpret them (see Bernard 1994; Bernard, ed. 1998). Quantifiable information may permit a more precise assessment of similarities and differences between communities. Statistical analysis can support and round out an ethnographic account of local social life.

However, in the best studies, the hallmark of ethnography remains: Anthropologists enter the community and get to know the people. They participate in local activities, networks, and associations in the city, town, or countryside. They observe and experience social conditions and problems. They watch the effects of national policies and programs on local life. The ethnographic method and the emphasis on personal relationships in social research are valuable gifts that cultural anthropology brings to the study of a complex society.

S u m m a r y

1.   Anthropology is the holistic and comparative study of humanity. It is the systematic exploration of human biological and cultural diversity across time and space. The four subfields of general anthropology are sociocultural, archaeological, biological, and linguistic. All consider variation in time and space. Each also examines adaptation—the process by which organisms cope with environmental stresses.

2.   Cultural anthropology explores the cultural diversity of the present and the recent past. Ethnography is field work in a particular society. Ethnology involves cross-cultural comparison—the comparative study of ethnographic data, of society, and of culture.

3.   Archaeology uses material remains to reconstruct cultural patterns, often of prehistoric populations. Biological anthropology documents diversity involving fossils, genetics, growth and development, bodily responses, and nonhuman primates. Linguistic anthropology considers

diversity among languages. Anthropology has two dimensions: academic and applied. The latter uses anthropological knowledge and methods to identify and solve social problems.

4. Ethnographic methods include observation and participant observation, rapport building, interviewing, tracing genealogies, work with key consultants, collecting life histories, and problem-focused, longitudinal, and team research. Ethnographers do not systematically manipulate their subjects or conduct experiments. Rather, they work in actual communities and form personal relationships with local people as they study their lives.

5. An interview schedule is a form an ethnographer completes as he or she visits a series of households. The schedule organizes and guides each interview, ensuring that comparable information is collected from everyone. Key consultants teach us about particular areas of local life. Life histories dramatize the fact that culture bearers are individuals. Such case studies document personal experiences with culture and culture change. Genealogical information is particularly useful in societies in which principles of kinship and marriage organize social and political life. Emic approaches focus on native perceptions and explanations. Etic approaches give priority to the ethnographer's own observations and conclusions. Longitudinal research is the systematic study of an area or site over time.

6. Traditionally, anthropologists worked in small-scale societies; sociologists, in modern nations. Different techniques have developed to study such different kinds of societies. Social scientists working in complex societies use survey research to sample variation. Anthropologists do their fieldwork in communities and study the totality of social life. Sociologists study samples to make inferences about a larger population.

7. The diversity of social life in modern nations and cities requires social survey procedures. Anthropologists, however, add the intimacy and direct investigation characteristic of ethnography. Anthropologists may employ ethnographic procedures to study local life—in cities, towns, or rural areas.

Case Study
Trobriand Islands

The work of Bronislaw Malinowski has been highlighted in this chapter's discussion of ethnographic fieldwork, as well as in the box at the end of the chapter. Malinowski's first trip to New Guinea in 1914 helped establish the ethnographic tradition of living among and building rapport with local people, of fieldwork conducted in the local language and situated in a culture's own context. Some sixty years later, anthropologist Annette Weiner did her own fieldwork in the Trobriands. Her findings both added to Malinowski's earlier work and challenged some of its assumptions. In *Culture Sketches*, 3rd ed., by Holly Peters-Golden (New York: McGraw-Hill 2002), read the chapter on the Trobriand Islanders. Considering what you have just learned about fieldwork, how did Malinowski's and Weiner's approaches differ? What are some possible reasons for their different perspectives? What are some challenges that ethnographers face in the twenty-first century? How might modern technology change the way anthropologists do fieldwork?

The Evolution of Ethnography

The Polish anthropologist Bronislaw Malinowski (1884–1942), who spent most of his professional life in England, is generally considered the father of ethnography. Like most anthropologists of his time, Malinowski did *salvage ethnography*, in the belief that the ethnographer's job is to study and record cultural diversity threatened by Westernization. Early ethnographic accounts (*ethnographies*), such as Malinowski's classic *Argonauts of the Western Pacific* (1922/1961), were similar to earlier traveler and explorer accounts in describing the writer's discovery of unknown people and places. However, the *scientific* aims of ethnographies set them apart from books by explorers and amateurs.

The style that dominated "classic" ethnographies was *ethnographic realism*. The writer's goal was to present an accurate, objective, scientific account of a different way of life, written by someone who knew it firsthand. This knowledge came from an "ethnographic adventure" involving immersion in an alien language and culture. Ethnographers derived their authority—both as scientists and as voices of "the native" or "the other"—from this personal research experience.

Malinowski's ethnographies were guided by the assumption that aspects of culture are linked and intertwined. Beginning by describing a Trobriand sailing expedition, the ethnographer then follows the links between that entry point and other areas of the culture, such as magic, religion, myths, kinship, and trade. Compared with Malinowski's, today's ethnographies tend to be less inclusive and holistic, focusing on particular topics, such as kinship or religion.

According to Malinowski, a primary task of the ethnographer is "to grasp the native's point of view, his relation to life, to realize *his* vision of *his* world (1922/1961, p. 25—Malinowski's italics). This is a good statement of the need for the emic perspective, as was discussed earlier. Since the 1970s *interpretive anthropology* has considered the task of describing and interpreting that which is meaningful to natives. Interpretivists such as Clifford Geertz (1973) view cultures as meaningful texts which natives constantly "read" and which ethnographers must decipher. According to Geertz, anthropologists may choose anything in a culture that interests them, fill in details, and elaborate to inform their readers about meanings in that culture. Meanings are carried by public symbolic forms, including words, rituals, and customs.

A current trend in ethnographic writing is to question traditional goals, methods, and styles, including ethnographic realism and salvage ethnography (Marcus and Cushman 1982; Clifford 1982, 1988). Marcus and Fischer argue that experimentation in ethnographic writing is necessary because all peoples and cultures have already been "discovered" and must now be "*re*discovered . . . in changing historical circumstances" (1986, p. 24).

In general, experimental anthropologists see ethnographies as works of art as well as works of science. Ethnographic texts may be viewed as literary creations in which the ethnographer, as mediator, communicates information from the "natives" to readers. Some recent experimental ethnographies are "dialogic," presenting ethnography as a dialogue between the anthropologist and one or more native informants (e.g., Dwyer 1982, Behar 1993). These works draw attention to ways in which ethnographers, and by extension their readers, communicate with other cultures. However, some such ethnographies have been criticized for spending too much time talking about the anthropologist and too little time describing the natives and their culture.

The dialogic ethnography is one genre within a larger experimental category—that is, *reflexive ethnography*. Here the ethnographer-writer puts his or her personal feelings and reactions to the field situation right in the text. Experimental writing strategies are prominent in reflexive accounts. The ethnographer may adopt some of the conventions of the novel, including first-person narration, conversations, dialogues, and humor. Experimental ethnographies, using new ways of showing what it means to be a Samoan or a Brazilian, may convey to the reader a richer and more complex understanding of human experience.

Recent ethnographic writers have also attempted to correct the deficiency of *romanticized timelessness*, which is evident in many of the classics. Linked to salvage ethnography was the idea of the *ethnographic present*—the period before Westernization, when the "true" native culture flourished. This notion gives classic ethnographies an eternal, timeless quality. Providing the only jarring note in this idealized picture are occasional comments by the author about traders or missionaries, suggesting that in actuality the natives were already part of the world system.

Anthropologists now recognize that the ethnographic present is a rather unrealistic construct. Cultures have been in contact—and have been changing—throughout history. Most native cultures had at least one major foreign encounter before any anthropologist ever came their way. Most of them had already been incorporated in some fashion into nation-states or colonial systems.

Contemporary ethnographies usually recognize that cultures constantly change and that an ethnographic account applies to a particular moment. A current trend in ethnography is to focus on the ways in which cultural ideas serve political and economic interests. Another trend is to describe how various particular "natives" participate in broader historical, political, and economic processes (Shostak 1981).

Chapter 2

Culture

The concept of culture has long been basic to anthropology. More than a century ago, in his book *Primitive Culture*, the British anthropologist Edward Tylor proposed that cultures, systems of human behavior and thought, obey natural laws and therefore can be studied scientifically. Tylor's definition of culture still offers an overview of the subject matter of anthropology and is widely quoted.

"Culture . . . is that complex whole which includes knowledge, belief, arts, morals, law, custom, and any other capabilities and habits acquired by man as a member of society" (Tylor 1871/1958, p. 1). The crucial phrase here is "acquired by man as a member of society." Tylor's definition focuses on attributes that people acquire not through biological inheritance but by growing up in a particular society in which they are exposed to a specific cultural tradition. **Enculturation** is the process by which a child *learns* his or her culture.

WHAT IS CULTURE?

Culture Is Learned

The ease with which children absorb any cultural tradition rests on the uniquely elaborated human capacity to learn. Other animals may learn from experience, so that, for example, they avoid fire after discovering that it hurts. Social animals also learn from other members of their group. Wolves, for instance, learn hunting strategies from other pack members. Such social learning is particularly important among monkeys and apes, our closest biological relatives. But our own *cultural learning* depends on

Cultures have strikingly different standards of personal space, such as how far apart people should stand in normal encounters and interactions. Contrast the distance between the American businessmen with the closeness of the Israeli men on a stroll near the Western Wall of Jerusalem's Old City. Have you noticed such differences in your own interactions with others?

the uniquely developed human capacity to use **symbols,** signs that have no necessary or natural connection to the things they stand for or signify.

On the basis of cultural learning, people create, remember, and deal with ideas. They grasp and apply specific systems of symbolic meaning. Anthropologist Clifford Geertz defines culture as ideas based on cultural learning and symbols. Cultures have been characterized as sets of "control mechanisms—plans, recipes, rules, instructions, what computer engineers call programs for the governing of behavior" (Geertz 1973, p. 44). These programs are absorbed by people through enculturation in particular traditions. People gradually internalize a previously established system of meanings and symbols, which helps guide their behavior and perceptions throughout their lives.

Every person begins immediately, through a process of conscious and unconscious learning and interaction with others, to internalize, or incorporate, a cultural tradition through the process of enculturation. Sometimes culture is taught directly, as when parents tell their children to say "thank you" when someone gives them something or does them a favor.

Culture is also transmitted through observation. Children pay attention to the things that go on around them. They modify their behavior not just because other people tell them to but as a result of their own observations and growing awareness of what their culture considers right and wrong. Culture is also absorbed unconsciously. North Americans acquire their culture's notions about how far apart people should stand when they talk (see the box at the end of this chapter) not by being directly told to maintain a certain distance but through a gradual process of observation, experience, and conscious and unconscious behavior modification. No one tells Latins to stand closer together than North Americans do, but they learn to do so as part of their cultural tradition.

Culture Is Shared

Culture is an attribute not of individuals per se but of individuals as members of *groups*. Culture is transmitted in society. Don't we learn our culture by observing, listening, talking, and interacting with many other people? Shared beliefs, values, memories, and expectations link people who grow up in the same culture. Enculturation unifies people by providing us with common experiences.

People in the United States sometimes have trouble understanding the power of culture because of the value that American culture places on the idea of the individual. Americans are fond of saying that everyone is unique and special in some way. However, in American culture individualism itself is a distinctive shared value. Individualism is transmitted through hundreds of statements and settings in our daily lives. From TV's Mr. Rogers to parents, grandparents, and teachers, our enculturative agents insist that we are all "someone special."

Today's parents were yesterday's children. If they grew up in North America, they absorbed certain values and beliefs transmitted over the generations. People become agents in the enculturation of their children, just as their parents were for them. Although a culture constantly changes, certain fundamental beliefs, values, worldviews, and child-rearing practices endure. Consider a simple American example of enduring shared enculturation. As children, when we didn't finish a meal, our parents reminded us of starving children in some foreign country, just as our grandparents had done a generation earlier. The specific country changes (China, India, Bangladesh, Ethiopia, Somalia, Rwanda—what was it in your home?). Still, American culture goes on transmitting the idea that by eating all our brussels sprouts or broccoli, we can justify our own good fortune, compared to a hungry Third World child.

Culture Is Symbolic

Symbolic thought is unique and crucial to humans and to cultural learning. A symbol is something verbal or nonverbal, within a particular language or culture, that comes to stand for something else. Anthropologist Leslie White defined culture as

> dependent upon symbolling. . . . Culture consists of tools, implements, utensils, clothing, ornaments, customs, institutions, beliefs, rituals, games, works of art, language, etc. (White 1959, p. 3)

For White, culture originated when our ancestors acquired the ability to use symbols, that is, to originate and bestow meaning on a thing or event, and, correspondingly, to grasp and appreciate such meanings (White 1959, p. 3).

There need be no obvious, natural, or necessary connection between the symbol and what it symbolizes. The familiar pet that barks is no more naturally a *dog* than it is a *chien, Hund,* or *mbwa,* the words for "dog" in French, German, and Swahili, respectively. Language is one of the distinctive possessions of *Homo sapiens.* No other animal has developed anything approaching the complexity of language, with its multitude of symbols.

Symbols are often linguistic. There are also myriad nonverbal symbols, such as flags, which stand for the various countries, and arches symbolizing a particular hamburger chain. Holy water is a potent symbol in Roman Catholicism. As is true of all symbols, the association between a symbol (water) and what is symbolized (holiness) is arbitrary and conventional. Water is probably not intrinsically holier than milk, blood, or other natural liquids. Nor is holy water chemically different from ordinary water. Holy water is a symbol within Roman Catholicism, which is part of an international cultural system. A natural thing has been arbitrarily associated with a particular meaning for Catholics, who share common beliefs and experiences that are based on learning and that are transmitted across the generations.

For hundreds of thousands of years, humans have shared the abilities on which culture rests, the abilities to learn, to think symbolically, to manipulate language, and to use tools and other cultural products in organizing their lives and coping with their environments. Every contemporary human population has the ability to use symbols and thus to create and maintain culture. Our nearest relatives—chimpanzees and gorillas—have rudimentary cultural abilities. However, no other animal has elaborated cultural abilities—to learn, to communicate, and to store, process, and use information—to the extent that *Homo* has.

Culture and Nature

Culture takes the natural biological urges we share with other animals and teaches us how to express them in particular ways. People have to eat, but culture teaches us what, when, and how. In many cultures people have their main meal at noon, but most North Americans prefer a large dinner. English people eat fish for breakfast, but North Americans prefer hot cakes and cold cereals. Brazilians put hot milk into strong coffee, whereas many North Americans pour cold milk into a weaker brew. Midwesterners dine at five or six, Spaniards at ten.

Cultural habits, perceptions, and inventions mold "human nature" into many forms. People have to eliminate wastes from their bodies. But some cultures teach people to defecate standing, while others tell them to do it sitting down. Frenchmen aren't embarrassed to urinate in public, stepping into barely shielded outdoor *pissoirs*. Peasant women in the Andean highlands squat in the streets and urinate, getting all the privacy they need from their massive skirts. All these habits are parts of cultural traditions that have converted natural acts into cultural customs.

Our culture—and cultural changes—affect how we perceive nature, human nature, and "the natural." Through science, invention, and discovery, cultural advances have overcome many "natural" limitations. We prevent and cure diseases such as polio and smallpox, which felled our ancestors. We use Viagra to enhance or restore sexual potency. Through cloning, scientists have challenged the way we think about biological identity and the meaning of life itself. Culture, of course, does not always protect us from natural threats. Hurricanes, floods, earthquakes and other natural forces regularly overthrow our wishes to modify the environment through building, development, and expansion. Can you think of other ways in which nature strikes back at culture?

Culture Is All-Encompassing

For anthropologists, culture includes much more than refinement, good taste, sophistication, education, and appreciation of the fine arts. Not only college graduates but all people are "cultured." The most interesting and significant cultural forces are those that affect people every day of their lives, particularly those that influence children during enculturation. *Culture*, as defined anthropologically, encompasses features that are sometimes regarded as trivial or unworthy of serious study, such as those of "popular" culture. To understand contemporary North American culture, we must consider television, fast-food restaurants, sports, and games. As a cultural manifestation, a rock star may be as interesting as a symphony conductor (or vice versa); a comic book may be as significant as a book-award winner.

Culture Is Integrated

Cultures are not haphazard collections of customs and beliefs. Cultures are integrated, patterned systems. If one part of the system (the overall economy, for instance) changes, other parts change as well. For example, during the 1950s most American women planned domestic careers as homemakers and mothers. Most of today's college women, by contrast, expect to get paying jobs when they graduate.

What are some of the social repercussions of this particular economic change? Attitudes and behavior regarding marriage, family, and children have changed. Late marriage, "living together," and divorce have become more common. The average age at first marriage for American women rose from 20 in 1955 to 25 in 2000 (Saluter 1996, Fields 2001). The comparable figures for men were 23 and 27 (Fields 2001). The number of currently

Cultures are integrated systems: When one custom, belief, or value changes, others change, too. During the 1950s, most American women expected to have domestic careers. Today, most women plan to balance cash employment and family responsibilities. Contrast the "fifties Mom" with modern career women, such as Florida's House Women's Caucus, photographed on May 4, 2001.

divorced Americans quadrupled from 4 million in 1970 to more than 19 million in 1998 (Lugaila 1999). Work competes with marriage and family responsibilities and reduces the time available to invest in child care.

Cultures are integrated not simply by their dominant economic activities and related social patterns but also by sets of values, ideas, symbols, and judgments. Cultures train their individual members to share certain personality traits. A set of characteristic **core values** (key, basic, central values) integrates each culture and helps distinguish it from others. For instance, the work ethic and individualism are core values that have integrated American culture for generations. Different sets of dominant values influence the patterns of other cultures.

People Use Culture Actively

Although cultural rules tell us what to do and how to do it, people don't always do what the rules say they should. People use their culture actively and creatively, rather than blindly following its dictates (see Archer 1996). We are not passive beings who are doomed to follow our cultural traditions like programmed robots. Instead, people can learn, interpret, and manipulate the same rule in different ways. Also, culture is contested. That is, different groups in society often struggle with one another over whose ideas, values, and beliefs will prevail (see Lindholm 2001). Even common symbols may have radically different *meanings* to different people and groups in the same culture. Golden arches may cause one person to salivate while another plots a vegetarian protest. The flag is a national symbol for the United States, but its meaning varies radically among Americans.

Even if they agree about what should and shouldn't be done, people don't always do as their culture directs or as other people expect. Many rules are violated, some very often (for example, automobile speed limits). Some anthropologists find it useful to distinguish between ideal and real culture. The *ideal culture* consists of what people say they should do and of what they say they do. *Real culture* refers to their actual behavior as observed by the anthropologist. This contrast is similar to the emic-etic distinction discussed in Chapter 1.

Culture is public yet private, both in the world and in people's minds. Anthropologists are interested not only in collective or outward behavior but also in how individuals think, feel, and personally act. The individual and culture are linked through the human social process in which *individuals* internalize the meanings of *public* cultural messages. Then, alone and in groups, people in turn influence culture by converting their private understandings into public expressions (D'Andrade 1984, Lindholm 2001).

Culture Can Be Adaptive and Maladaptive

Humans have both biological and cultural ways of coping with environmental stresses. Besides our biological means of adaptation, we also use "cultural adaptive kits," which contain customary activities and tools that aid us. Although humans continue to adapt biologically, reliance on social and cultural means of adaptation has increased during human evolution and plays a crucial role.

Sometimes, adaptive behavior that offers short-term benefits to particular subgroups or individuals may harm the environment and threaten the group's long-term survival. Economic growth may benefit some people

while it depletes resources needed for society at large or for future generations (Bennett 1969, p. 19). Thus, cultural traits, patterns, and inventions
can also be *maladaptive*, threatening the group's continued existence (survival and reproduction). Air conditioners help us deal with heat, as fires and
furnaces protect us against the cold. Automobiles permit us to make a living
by getting us from home to workplace. But the by-products of such "beneficial" technology often create new problems. Chemical emissions increase
air pollution, deplete the ozone layer, and contribute to global warming.
Many cultural patterns such as overconsumption and pollution appear to be
maladaptive in the long run. Can you think of others?

Levels of Culture

We distinguish between different levels of culture: national, international,
and subcultural. In today's world these distinctions are increasingly important. **National culture** embodies the beliefs, learned behavior patterns, values, and institutions shared by citizens of the same nation. **International
culture** extends beyond and across national boundaries. Because culture is
transmitted through learning rather than genetically, cultural traits can
spread through borrowing or *diffusion* from one group to another.

   Through diffusion or migration, sometimes via multinational organizations, or because of a common history or focus of interest, many cultural
traits and patterns acquire international scope. The contemporary United
States, Canada, Great Britain, and Australia share cultural traits they have
inherited from their common linguistic and cultural ancestors in Great
Britain. Roman Catholics in many different countries share beliefs, symbols, experiences, and values transmitted by their church. The World Cup
has become an international cultural event, as people in many countries
know the rules of, play, and follow soccer.

   Cultures can also be smaller than nations. Although people who live in
the same country share a national cultural tradition, all cultures also contain diversity. Individuals, families, communities, regions, classes, and other
groups within a culture have different learning experiences as well as shared
ones. **Subcultures** are different symbol-based patterns and traditions associated with particular groups in the same complex society. In large or diverse nations such as the United States or Canada, a variety of subcultures
originate in region, ethnicity, language, class, and religion. The religious
backgrounds of Jews, Baptists, and Roman Catholics create subcultural differences between them. While sharing a common national culture, U.S.
northerners and southerners also differ in their beliefs, values, and customary behavior as a result of national and regional history. French-speaking
Canadians sometimes pointedly contrast with English-speaking people in
the same country. Italian Americans have ethnic traditions different from
those of Irish, Polish, and African Americans.

   Nowadays, many anthropologists are reluctant to use the term *subcul-
ture*. They feel that the prefix "sub-" is offensive because it means "below."
"Subcultures" may thus be perceived as "less than" or somehow inferior to

Illustrating the international level of culture, Roman Catholics in different nations share knowledge, symbols, beliefs, and values transmitted by their church. Here we see a prayer vigil in Seoul, Korea. In addition to religious conversion, what other forces work to spread international culture?

a dominant, elite, or national culture. In this discussion of levels of culture, I intend no such implication. My point is simply that nations may contain many different culturally defined groups. As mentioned earlier, culture is contested. Various groups may strive to promote the correctness and value of their own practices, values, and beliefs in comparison with those of other groups or the nation as a whole.

Ethnocentrism, Cultural Relativism, and Human Rights

Ethnocentrism is the tendency to view one's own culture as superior and to apply one's own cultural values in judging the behavior and beliefs of people raised in other cultures. Ethnocentrism contributes to social solidarity, a sense of value and community, among people who share a cultural tradition. People everywhere think that the familiar explanations, opinions, and customs are true, right, proper, and moral. They regard different behavior as strange, immoral, or savage. Often other societies are not considered fully human. Their members may be castigated as cannibals, thieves, or people who do not bury their dead.

Among several tribes in the Trans-Fly region of Papua New Guinea homosexuality is valued over heterosexuality (see the chapter in this book on gender). Men who grow up in the Etoro tribe (Kelly 1976) favor oral sex between men, while their neighbors the Marind-anim encourage men to engage in anal sex. (In both groups heterosexual coitus is stigmatized and allowed only for reproduction.) Etoro men consider Marind-anim anal sex to be disgusting, while seeing nothing abnormal about their own oral homosexual practices.

Opposing ethnocentrism is **cultural relativism,** the viewpoint that behavior in one culture should not be judged by the standards of another culture. This position while once in vogue can also present problems. At its most extreme, cultural relativism argues that there is no superior, international, or universal morality, that the moral and ethical rules of all cultures deserve equal respect. In the extreme relativist view, Nazi Germany would be evaluated as nonjudgmentally as Athenian Greece.

In today's world, human rights advocates challenge many of the tenets of cultural relativism. For example, several societies in Africa and the Middle East have traditions of female genital modification. *Clitoridectomy* is the removal of a girl's clitoris. *Infibulation* involves sewing the lips (labia) of the vagina, so as to constrict the vaginal opening. Both procedures reduce female sexual pleasure, and, it is believed in some cultures, the likelihood of adultery. Such practices, characterized as female genital mutilation, have been opposed by human rights advocates, especially women's rights groups. The idea is that the tradition infringes on a basic human right—disposition over one's body and one's sexuality. Some African countries have banned or otherwise discouraged the procedures, as have Western nations that receive immigration from such cultures. Similar issues arise with circumcision and other male genital operations. Is it right for a baby boy to be circumcised without his knowledge and permission, as has been routinely done in the United States? Is it proper to require adolescent boys to undergo collective circumcision to fulfill cultural tradition, as is done traditionally in parts of Africa and Australia?

The idea of **human rights** challenges cultural relativism by invoking a realm of justice and morality beyond and superior to the laws and customs of particular countries, cultures, and religions (see R. Wilson, ed. 1996). Human rights include the right to speak freely, to hold religious beliefs without persecution, and to not be murdered, injured, or enslaved or imprisoned without charge. Such rights are seen as *inalienable* (nations cannot abridge or terminate them) and international (larger than and superior to individual nations and cultures). Four United Nations documents describe nearly all the human rights that have been internationally recognized. Those documents are the UN Charter; the Universal Declaration of Human Rights; the Covenant on Economic, Social and Cultural Rights; and the Covenant on Civil and Political Rights.

Alongside the human rights movement has arisen an awareness of the need to preserve cultural rights. Unlike human rights, **cultural rights** are vested not in individuals but in *groups,* such as religious and ethnic minorities and indigenous societies. Cultural rights include a group's ability to

preserve its culture, to raise its children in the ways of its forebears, to continue its language, and not to be deprived of its economic base by the nation
in which it is located (Greaves 1995). The related notion of indigenous
intellectual property rights (IPR) has arisen in an attempt to conserve
each society's cultural base—its core beliefs, knowledge, and practices.
Much traditional cultural knowledge has commercial value. Examples
include ethnomedicine (traditional medical knowledge and techniques),
cosmetics, cultivated plants, foods, folklore, arts, crafts, songs, dances, costumes, and rituals. According to the IPR concept, a particular group may
determine how indigenous knowledge and its products may be used and
distributed and the level of compensation required.

The notion of cultural rights is related to the idea of cultural relativism,
and the problem discussed previously arises again. What does one do about
cultural rights that interfere with human rights? I believe that anthropology's main job is to present accurate accounts and explanations of cultural
phenomena. The anthropologist doesn't have to approve infanticide, canni-
balism, or torture to record their existence and determine their causes.
However, each anthropologist has a choice about where he or she will do
field work. Some anthropologists choose not to study a particular culture
because they discover in advance or early in field work that behavior they
consider morally repugnant is practiced there. Anthropologists respect human diversity. Most ethnographers try to be objective, accurate, and sensi-
tive in their accounts of other cultures. However, objectivity, sensitivity, and
a cross-cultural perspective don't mean that anthropologists have to ignore
international standards of justice and morality. What do you think?

UNIVERSALITY, PARTICULARITY, AND GENERALITY

Anthropologists agree that cultural learning is uniquely elaborated among
humans and that all humans have culture. Anthropologists also accept a
doctrine termed in the nineteenth century "the psychic unity of man." This
means that although *individuals* differ in their emotional and intellectual
tendencies and capacities, all human *populations* have equivalent capacities
for culture. Regardless of their genes or their physical appearance, people
can learn *any* cultural tradition.

To understand this point, consider that contemporary Americans and
Canadians are the genetically mixed descendants of people from all over the
world. Our ancestors were biologically varied, lived in different countries
and continents, and participated in hundreds of cultural traditions. However, early colonists, later immigrants, and their descendants have all become active participants in American and Canadian life. All now share a
common national culture.

To recognize biopsychological equality is not to deny differences among
populations. In studying human diversity in time and space, anthropologists
distinguish among the universal, the generalized, and the particular. Certain

biological, psychological, social, and cultural features are **universal,** found in every culture. Others are merely **generalities,** common to several but not all human groups. Still other traits are **particularities,** unique to certain cultural traditions.

Biologically based universals include a long period of infant dependency, year-round (rather than seasonal) sexuality, and a complex brain that enables us to use symbols, languages, and tools. Among the social universals is life in groups and in some kind of family (see Brown 1991). Generalities occur in certain times and places but not in all cultures. They may be widespread, but they are not universal. One cultural generality that is present in many but not all societies is the *nuclear family*, a kinship group consisting of parents and children. Although many middle-class Americans ethnocentrically view the nuclear family as a proper and "natural" group, it is not universal. It is absent, for example, among the Nayars, who live on the Malabar Coast of India. The Nayars live in female-headed households, and husbands and wives do not live together. And in many other societies, the nuclear family is submerged in larger kin groups, such as extended families, lineages, and clans.

At the opposite extreme from universality stand uniqueness and particularity. Cultures are integrated and patterned differently and display tremendous variation and diversity. Many cultures ritually observe such universal life-cycle events as birth, puberty, marriage, parenthood, and death. But cultures vary in just which event merits special celebration. Americans regard expensive weddings as more socially appropriate than lavish funerals. However, the Betsileo of Madagascar take the opposite view. The marriage ceremony is a minor event that brings together just the couple and a few close relatives. However, a funeral is a measure of the deceased person's social position and lifetime achievement, and it may attract a thousand people. Why use money on a house, the Betsileo say, when one can use it on the tomb where one will spend eternity in the company of dead relatives? How different from contemporary Americans' growing preference for quick and inexpensive funerals and cremation, which would horrify the Betsileo, whose ancestral bones and relics are important ritual objects. By focusing on and trying to explain alternative customs, anthropology forces us to reappraise our familiar ways of thinking. In a world full of cultural diversity, contemporary American culture is just one cultural variant, more powerful perhaps, but no more natural, than the others.

MECHANISMS OF CULTURAL CHANGE

Why and how do cultures change? One way is **diffusion** or borrowing of traits between cultures. Such exchange of information and products has gone on throughout human history because cultures have never been truly isolated. Contact between neighboring groups has always existed and has extended over vast areas (Boas 1940/1966). Diffusion is *direct* when two cultures trade with, intermarry among, or wage war on one another. Diffusion is *forced* when one culture subjugates another and imposes its customs on the dominated group. Diffusion is *indirect* when items or traits move from group A to group C via group B without any firsthand contact between A and C. In this case, group B might consist of traders or merchants who take products from a variety of places to new markets. Or group B might be geographically situated between A and C, so that what it gets from A eventually winds up in C, and vice versa. In today's world, much international diffusion is indirect—culture spread by the mass media and advanced information technology.

Acculturation, a second mechanism of cultural change, is the exchange of cultural features that results when groups have continuous firsthand contact. The cultures of either or both groups may be changed by this contact (Redfield, Linton, and Herskovits 1936). With acculturation, parts of the cultures change, but each group remains distinct. One example of acculturation is a *pidgin*, a mixed language that develops to ease communication between members of different cultures in contact. This usually happens in situations of trade or colonialism. Pidgin English, for example, is a simplified form of English. It blends English grammar with the grammar of a native language. Pidgin English was first used for commerce in Chinese ports. Similar pidgins developed later in Papua New Guinea and West Africa. In situations of continuous contact, cultures have also exchanged and blended foods, recipes, music, dances, clothing, tools, and technologies.

Independent invention—the process by which humans innovate, creatively finding solutions to problems—is a third mechanism of cultural change. Faced with comparable problems and challenges, people in different societies have innovated and changed in similar ways, which is one reason cultural generalities exist. One example is the independent invention of agriculture in the Middle East and Mexico. Over the course of human history, major innovations have spread at the expense of earlier ones. Often a major invention, such as agriculture, triggers a series of subsequent interrelated changes. These economic revolutions have social and cultural repercussions. Thus in both Mexico and the Middle East, agriculture led to many social, political, and legal changes, including notions of property and distinctions in wealth, class, and power (see Naylor 1996).

GLOBALIZATION

The term **globalization** encompasses a series of processes, including diffusion and acculturation, working to promote change in a world in which nations and people are increasingly interlinked and mutually dependent. Promoting such linkages are economic and political forces, along with modern systems of transportation and communication. The forces of globalization include international commerce, travel and tourism, transnational migration, the media, and various high-tech information flows (see Scholte 2000). During the Cold War, which ended with the fall of the Soviet Union, the basis of international alliance was political, ideological, and military. Now, international pacts tend to focus on trade and economic issues. Multinational mergers are in the news daily. New economic unions have been created through NAFTA (the North American Free Trade Agreement), GATT (the General Agreement on Tariffs and Trade), and EEC (the European Economic Community).

Long-distance communication is easier, faster, and cheaper than ever, and extends to remote areas. The mass media help propel a globally spreading culture of consumption, stimulating participation in the world cash economy. Within nations and across their borders, the media spread information about products, services, rights, institutions, and lifestyles. Emigrants transmit information and resources transnationally, as they maintain their ties with home (phoning, faxing, e-mailing, making visits, sending money). In a sense such people live multilocally—in different places and cultures at once. They learn to play various social roles and to change behavior and identity depending on the situation.

Local people must increasingly cope with forces generated by progressively larger systems—region, nation, and world. An army of alien actors and agents now intrudes on people everywhere. Tourism has become the world's number one industry. Economic development agents and the media promote the idea that work should be for cash rather than mainly for subsistence. Indigenous peoples and traditional societies have devised various strategies to deal with threats to their autonomy, identity, and livelihood. New forms of political mobilization and cultural expression, including the rights movements discussed previously, are emerging from the interplay of local, regional, national, and international cultural forces.

S u m m a r y

1. Culture refers to customary behavior and beliefs that are passed on through enculturation. Culture rests on the human capacity for cultural learning. Culture encompasses shared rules for conduct that are internalized in human beings. Such rules lead people to think and act in characteristic ways.

2. Other animals learn, but only humans have cultural learning, dependent on symbols. Humans think symbolically—arbitrarily bestowing meaning on things and events. By convention, a symbol stands for something with which it has no necessary or natural relation. Symbols have special meaning for people who share memories, values, and beliefs because of common enculturation. People absorb cultural lessons consciously and unconsciously.

3. Cultural traditions mold biologically based desires and needs in particular directions. Everyone is cultured, not just people with elite educations. Cultures may be integrated and patterned through

economic and social forces, key symbols, and core values. Cultural rules don't rigidly dictate our behavior. There is room for creativity, flexibility, diversity, and disagreement within societies. Cultural means of adaptation have been crucial in human evolution. Aspects of culture can also be maladaptive.

4. There are levels of culture, which can be larger or smaller than a nation. Diffusion and migration carry cultural traits and patterns to different areas. Such traits are shared across national boundaries. Nations also include cultural differences associated with ethnicity, region, and social class.

5. Using a comparative perspective, anthropology examines biological, psychological, social, and cultural universals and generalities. There are also unique and distinctive aspects of the human condition. North American cultural traditions are no more natural than any others. Mechanisms of cultural change include diffusion, acculturation, and independent invention. Globalization describes a series of processes that promote change in our world in which nations and people are increasingly interlinked and mutually dependent.

Case Study
Aztec

Most people regard the Aztecs as part of a civilization that was lost long ago. However, in Mexico today there are indigenous social movements that seek to link the present directly with an Aztec past. In *Culture Sketches* by Holly Peters-Golden read the chapter on the Aztec: Ancient Legacy, Modern Pride. Think about the uses and meanings of culture you've read about in your textbook. What might motivate contemporary Nahua peoples and others in Mexico to embrace Aztec culture? What is the significance of the ways in which they have chosen to recognize the Aztec heritage? Is this phenomenon something you recognize as happening among other groups, in other nations?

Touching, Affection, Love, and Sex

Comparing the United States to Brazil—or virtually any Latin nation—we can see a striking cultural contrast between a culture that discourages physical contact and demonstrations of affection and one in which the contrary is true.

"Don't touch me." "Take your hands off me." Such statements are not uncommon in North America, but they are virtually never heard in Brazil, the Western Hemisphere's second most populous country. Brazilians like to be touched (and kissed) more than North Americans do. The world's cultures have strikingly different notions about displays of affection and about matters of personal space. When North Americans talk, walk, and dance, they maintain a certain distance from others—their personal space. Brazilians, who maintain less physical distance, interpret this as a sign of coldness. When conversing with a North American, the Brazilian characteristically moves in as the North American "instinctively" retreats. In these body movements, neither Brazilian nor North American is trying consciously to be especially friendly or unfriendly. Each is merely executing a program written on the self by years of exposure to a particular cultural tradition. Because of different ideas about proper social space, cocktail parties in international meeting places such as the United Nations can resemble an elaborate insect mating ritual as diplomats from different cultures advance, withdraw, and sidestep.

One easily evident cultural difference between Brazil and the United States involves kissing, hugging, and touching. Middle-class Brazilians teach their kids—both boys and girls—to kiss (on the cheek, two or three times, coming and going) every adult relative they ever see. Given the size of Brazilian extended families, this can mean hundreds of people. Females continue kissing throughout their lives. They kiss male and female kin, friends, relatives of friends, friends of relatives, friends of friends, and, when it seems appropriate, more casual acquaintances. Males go on kissing their female relatives and friends. Until they are adolescents, boys also kiss adult male relatives. Brazilian

men, brothers, cousins, nephews and uncles, and friends, typically greet each other with hearty handshakes and a traditional male hug *(abraço)*. The closer the relationship, the tighter and longer-lasting the embrace. Many Brazilian men keep on kissing their fathers and uncles throughout their lives. Could it be that homophobia (fear of homosexuality) prevents American men from engaging in such displays of affection with other men? Are American women more likely to show affection toward each other than American men are?

Like other North Americans who spend time in a Latin culture, I miss the numerous kisses and handshakes when I get back to the United States. After several months in Brazil, I find North Americans rather cold and impersonal. Many Brazilians share this opinion. I have heard similar feelings expressed by Italian Americans as they compare themselves with North Americans of different ethnic backgrounds.

According to clinical psychologist David E. Klimek, who has written about intimacy and marriage in the United States, "in American society, if we go much beyond simple touching, our behavior takes on a minor sexual twist" (Slade 1984). North Americans define demonstrations of affection between males and females with reference to marriage. Love and affection are supposed to unite the married pair, and they blend into sex. When a wife asks her husband for "a little affection," she may mean, or he may think she means, sex.

A certain lack of clarity in North American definitions of love, affection, and sex is evident on Valentine's Day, which used to be just for lovers. Valentines used to be sent to wives, husbands, girlfriends, and boyfriends. Now, after years of promotion by the greeting card industry, they also go to mothers, fathers, sons, daughters, aunts, and uncles. There is a blurring of sexual and nonsexual affection. In Brazil, Lovers' Day retains its autonomy. Mother, father, and children each have their own separate days of recognition.

It's true, of course, that in a good marriage love and affection exist alongside sex. Nevertheless, affection does not necessarily imply sex. The Brazilian culture shows that there can be rampant kissing, hugging, and touching without sex—or fears of improper sexuality. In Brazilian culture, physical demonstrations help cement many kinds of close personal relationships that have no sexual component.

Ethnicity and Race

We know from the last chapter that culture is learned, shared, symbolic, integrated, and all-encompassing. Now we consider the relation between culture and ethnicity. Ethnicity is based on cultural similarities and differences in a society or nation. The similarities are with members of the same ethnic group; the differences are between that group and others.

ETHNIC GROUPS AND ETHNICITY

As with any culture, members of an **ethnic group** *share* certain beliefs, values, habits, customs, and norms because of their common background. They define themselves as different and special because of cultural features. This distinction may arise from language, religion, historical experience, geographic isolation, kinship, or "race." Markers of an ethnic group may include a collective name, belief in common descent, a sense of solidarity, and an association with a specific territory, which the group may or may not hold (Ryan 1990, pp. xiii, xiv).

   Ethnicity means identification with, and feeling part of, an ethnic group and exclusion from certain other groups because of this affiliation. Ethnic feelings and associated behavior vary in intensity within ethnic groups and countries and over time. A change in the degree of importance attached to an ethnic identity may reflect political changes (Soviet rule ends

—ethnic feeling rises) or individual life-cycle changes (young people relinquish, or old people reclaim, an ethnic background).

We saw in the last chapter that people participate in various levels of
culture. Groups within a culture (including ethnic groups in a nation) have
different learning experiences as well as shared ones. Subcultures originate
in ethnicity, class, region, and religion. Individuals often have more than
one group identity. People may be loyal (depending on circumstances) to
their neighborhood, school, town, state or province, region, nation, continent, religion, ethnic group, or interest group (Ryan 1990, p. xxii). In a
complex society such as the United States or Canada, people constantly negotiate their social identities. All of us "wear different hats," presenting ourselves sometimes as one thing, sometimes as another.

The term **status** can be used to refer to such a "hat"—to any position
that determines where someone fits in society (Light, Keller, and Calhoun
1994). Social statuses include parent, professor, student, factory worker, De-
mocrat, shoe salesperson, labor leader, ethnic group member, and thousands of others. People always occupy multiple statuses (e.g., Hispanic,
Catholic, infant, brother). Among the statuses we occupy, particular ones
dominate in particular settings, such as son or daughter at home and student in the classroom.

Some statuses are **ascribed:** People have little or no choice about occupying them. Age is an ascribed status; people can't choose not to age. Race
and ethnicity are usually ascribed; people are born members of a certain
group and remain so all their lives. **Achieved** statuses, by contrast, aren't
automatic but come through traits, talents, actions, efforts, activities, and
accomplishments. (See Figure 3-1.)

Status Shifting

Sometimes statuses, particularly ascribed ones, are mutually exclusive. It's
hard to bridge the gap between black and white, or male and female. Sometimes, taking a status or joining a group requires a conversion experience,
acquiring a new and overwhelming primary identity, such as becoming a
"born again" Christian.

Some statuses aren't mutually exclusive, but contextual. People can be
both black and Hispanic, or both a mother and a senator. One identity is
used in certain settings, another in different ones. We call this the *situational negotiation of social identity*. When ethnic identity is flexible and situational (Moerman 1965), it can become an achieved status.

Hispanics, for example, may move through levels of culture (shifting
ethnic affiliations) as they negotiate their identities. "Hispanic" is an ethnic
category based mainly on language. It includes whites, blacks, and "racially"
mixed Spanish speakers and their ethnically conscious descendants. (There
are also "Native American," and even "Asian," Hispanics.) "Hispanic" lumps
together millions of people of diverse geographic origin—Puerto Rico,
Mexico, Cuba, El Salvador, Guatemala, the Dominican Republic, and other

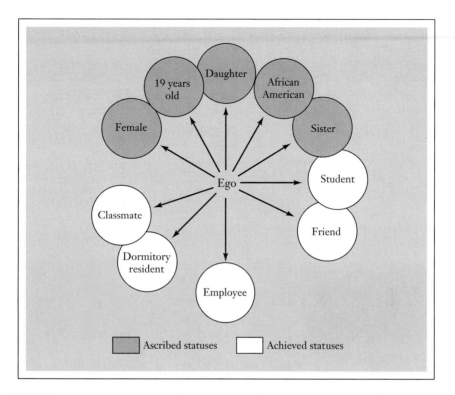

FIGURE 3-1 Social statuses. The person in this figure—"ego," or "I"—
occupies many social statuses. The gray circles indicate ascribed statuses; the
white circles represent achieved statuses.

Spanish-speaking countries of Central and South America and the Caribbean. "Latino" is a broader category, which can also include Brazilians (who
speak Portuguese). The number of Mexican Americans increased by 53 percent and the number of Hispanic Americans rose by 13 million between
1990 and 2000. The national origins of American Hispanics/Latinos in 2000
were as shown in Table 3-1.

Mexican Americans (Chicanos), Cuban Americans, and Puerto Ricans may
mobilize to promote general Hispanic issues (e.g., opposition to "English-
only" laws) but act as three separate interest groups in other contexts.
Cuban Americans are richer on average than Chicanos and Puerto Ricans
are, and their class interests and voting patterns differ. Cubans often vote
Republican, but Puerto Ricans and Chicanos generally favor Democrats.
Some Mexican Americans whose families have lived in the United States for
generations have little in common with new Hispanic immigrants, such as
those from Central America. Many Americans (especially those fluent in
English) claim Hispanic ethnicity in some contexts but shift to a general
"American" identity in others.

TABLE 3-1	American Hispanics, Latinos, 2000
National Origin	**Millions of People**
Mexican American	20.6
Puerto Rican	3.4
Cuban	1.2
Central American	1.7
South American	1.4
Dominican	0.8
Other Hispanic/Latino origin	6.1
Total	35.3

Source: http://www.census.gov/Press-Release/www/2001/cb01-81.html.

The ethnic label "Hispanic" lumps together millions of people of diverse "racial" types and countries of origin. Hispanics of diverse national backgrounds, like these Cuban-Americans in the "Little Havana" neighborhood of Miami, may mobilize to promote general Hispanic issues (such as opposition to "English-only" laws), but act as separate interest groups in other contexts.

In many societies an ascribed status is associated with a position in the social-political hierarchy. Certain groups, called **minority groups,** are subordinate. They have inferior power and less secure access to resources than do **majority groups** (which are superordinate, dominant, or controlling). Minorities need not have fewer members than the majority group does. Women in the United States and blacks in South Africa have been numerical majorities but minorities in terms of income, authority, and power. Often ethnic groups are minorities. When an ethnic group is assumed to have a biological basis (shared "blood" or genes), it is called a **race.** Discrimination against such a group is called **racism** (Cohen 1998, Montagu 1997, Shanklin 1995).

RACE

Race, like ethnicity in general, is a cultural category rather than a biological reality. That is, ethnic groups, including "races," derive from contrasts perceived and perpetuated in particular societies, rather than from scientific classifications based on common genes.

It is not possible to define races biologically. Only cultural constructions of race are possible—even though the average person conceptualizes "race" in biological terms. The belief that races exist and are important is much more common among the public than it is among scientists. Most Americans, for example, believe that their population includes biologically based "races" to which various labels have been applied. These labels include "white," "black," "yellow," "red," "Caucasoid," "Negroid," "Mongoloid," "Amerindian," "Euro-American," "African American," "Asian American," and "Native American."

We hear the words *ethnicity* and *race* frequently, but American culture doesn't draw a very clear line between them. As illustration, consider two articles in the *New York Times* of May 29, 1992. One, discussing the changing ethnic composition of the United States, states (correctly) that Hispanics "can be of any race" (Barringer 1992, p. A12). In other words, "Hispanic" is an ethnic category that cross-cuts "racial" contrasts such as that between "black" and "white." The other article reports that during the Los Angeles riots of spring 1992, "hundreds of Hispanic residents were interrogated about their immigration status on the basis of their *race* alone [emphasis added]" (Mydans 1992*a*, p. A8). Use of "race" here seems inappropriate because "Hispanic" is usually perceived as referring to a linguistically based (Spanish-speaking) ethnic group, rather than a biologically based race. Since these Los Angeles residents were being interrogated because they were Hispanic, the article is actually reporting on ethnic, not racial, discrimination. However, given the lack of a precise distinction between race and ethnicity, it is probably better to use the term "ethnic group" instead of "race" to describe *any* such social group, for example, African Americans, Asian Americans, Irish Americans, Anglo-Americans, or Hispanics.

SOCIAL RACE

Races are ethnic groups assumed (by members of a particular culture) to have a biological basis, but actually race is socially constructed. The "races" we hear about every day are cultural, or social, rather than biological categories. In Charles Wagley's terms (Wagley 1959/1968), they are **social races** (groups assumed to have a biological basis but actually defined in a culturally arbitrary, rather than a scientific, manner). Many Americans mistakenly assume that "whites" and "blacks," for example, are biologically distinct and that these terms stand for discrete races. But these labels, like racial terms used in other societies, really designate culturally perceived rather than biologically based groups.

Hypodescent: Race in the United States

How is race culturally constructed in the United States? In American culture, one acquires his or her racial identity at birth, as an ascribed status, but race isn't based on biology or on simple ancestry. Take the case of the child of a "racially mixed" marriage involving one black and one white parent. We know that 50 percent of the child's genes come from one parent and 50 percent from the other. Still, American culture overlooks heredity and classifies this child as black. This rule is arbitrary. From genotype (genetic composition), it would be just as logical to classify the child as white.

American rules for assigning racial status can be even more arbitrary. In some states, anyone known to have any black ancestor, no matter how remote, is classified as a member of the black race. This is a rule of **descent** (it assigns social identity on the basis of ancestry), but of a sort that is rare outside the contemporary United States. It is called **hypodescent** (Harris and Kottak 1963) (*hypo* means "lower") because it automatically places the children of a union or mating between members of different groups in the minority group. Hypodescent divides American society into groups that have been unequal in their access to wealth, power, and prestige.

The following case from Louisiana is an excellent illustration of the arbitrariness of the hypodescent rule and of the role that governments (federal or, in this case, state) play in legalizing, inventing, or eradicating "race" and ethnicity (B. Williams 1989). Susie Guillory Phipps, a light-skinned woman with "Caucasian" features and straight black hair, discovered as an adult that she was "black." When Phipps ordered a copy of her birth certificate, she found her race listed as "colored." Since she had been "brought up white and married white twice," Phipps challenged a 1970 Louisiana law declaring anyone with at least one-thirty-second "Negro blood" to be legally black. Although the state's lawyer admitted that Phipps "looks like a white person," the state of Louisiana insisted that her racial classification was proper (Yetman, et. 1991, pp. 3–4).

Cases like Phipps's are rare because "racial" identity is usually ascribed at birth and doesn't change. The rule of hypodescent affects blacks, Asians, Native Americans, and Hispanics differently. It's easier to negotiate Indian or Hispanic identity than black identity. The ascription rule isn't as definite, and the assumption of a biological basis isn't as strong.

To be considered "Native American," one ancestor out of eight (great-grandparents) or four (grandparents) may suffice. This depends on whether the assignment is by federal or state law or by an Indian tribal council. The child of a Hispanic may (or may not, depending on context) claim Hispanic identity. Many Americans with an Indian or Latino grandparent consider themselves "white" and lay no claim to minority group status.

The U.S. Census Bureau has gathered data by race since 1790. Initially this was done because the Constitution specified that a slave counted as three-fifths of a white person, and because Indians were not taxed. The racial categories included in the 1990 census were "White," "Black or Negro," "Indian (American)," "Eskimo," "Aleut or Pacific islander," and "Other." A separate question was asked about Spanish-Hispanic heritage. Check out Figure 3-2 for the racial categories in the 2000 census. What changes do you notice?

An attempt by social scientists and interested citizens to add a "multiracial" census category has been opposed by the National Association for the Advancement of Colored People (NAACP) and the National Council of La Raza (a Hispanic advocacy group). Racial classification is a political issue, involving access to resources, including jobs, voting districts, and federal funding of programs aimed at minorities. The hypodescent rule results in all the population growth being attributed to the minority category. Minorities fear their political clout will decline if their numbers go down.

But things are changing. Choice of "some other race" in the U.S. Census more than doubled from 1980 (6.8 million) to 2000 (over 15 million)—suggesting imprecision in and dissatisfaction with the existing categories

→ NOTE: Please answer BOTH Questions 5 and 6.

5. **Is this person Spanish/Hispanic/Latino?** *Mark* ⊠ *the* *"No" box if not Spanish/Hispanic/Latino.*

  ☐ **No,** not Spanish/Hispanic/Latino   ☐ Yes, Puerto Rican
  ☐ Yes, Mexican, Mexican Am., Chicano   ☐ Yes, Cuban
  ☐ Yes, other Spanish/Hispanic/Latino —Print group. ↗

6. **What is this person's race?** *Mark* ⊠ *one or more races to* *indicate what this person considers himself/herself to be.*

  ☐ White
  ☐ Black, African Am., or Negro
  ☐ American Indian or Alaska Native —*Print name of enrolled or principal tribe.* ↗

  ☐ Asian Indian ☐ Japanese   ☐ Native Hawaiian
  ☐ Chinese   ☐ Korean   ☐ Guamanian or Chamorro
  ☐ Filipino   ☐ Vietnamese   ☐ Samoan
  ☐ Other Asian —*Print race.* ↗ ☐ Other Pacific Islander —*Print race.* ↗

  ☐ Some other race —*Print race.* ↗

FIGURE 3-2 Reproduction of Questions on Race and Hispanic Origin from Census 2000
Source: U.S. Census Bureau, Census 2000 questionnaire.

TABLE 3-2	Americans Reporting They Belonged to Just One Race	
White		75.1%
Black or African American		12.3%
American Indian and Alaska Native		0.9%
Asian		3.6%
Native Hawaiian and Other Pacific Islander		0.1%
Some other race		5.5%

Source: http://www.census.gov/Press-Release/www/2001/cb01cn61.html.

(Mar 1997). In the year 2000, 274.6 million Americans (out of 281.4 million censused) reported they belonged to just one race, as shown in Table 3-2.

Hispanics totaled 35.3 million, or about 13 percent, of the total U.S. population. Nearly 48 percent of Hispanics identified as White alone, and about 42 percent as "some other race" alone. In the 2000 census, 2.4 percent of Americans, or 6.8 million people, chose a first-ever option of identifying themselves as belonging to more than one race. About 6 percent of Hispanics reported two or more races, compared with less than 2 percent of non-Hispanics (http://www.census.gov/Press-Release/www/2001/cb01cn61.html).

The number of interracial marriages and children is increasing, with implications for the traditional system of American racial classification. "Interracial," "biracial," or "multiracial" children who group up with both parents undoubtedly identify with particular qualities of either parent. It is troubling for many of them to have so important an identify as race dictated by the arbitrary rule of hypodescent. It may be especially discordant when racial identity doesn't parallel gender identity, for instance, a boy with a white father and a black mother, or a girl with a white mother and a black father.

Not Us: Race in Japan

American culture ignores considerable diversity in biology, language, and geographic origin as it socially constructs race in the United States. North Americans also overlook diversity by seeing Japan as a nation that is homogeneous in race, ethnicity, language, and culture—an image the Japanese themselves cultivate. Thus in 1986 former Prime Minister Nakasone created an international furor by contrasting his country's supposed homogeneity (responsible, he suggested, for Japan's success at that time in international business) with the ethnically mixed United States.

Japan is hardly the uniform entity Nakasone described. Scholars estimate that 10 percent of Japan's national population are minorities of various sorts. These include aboriginal Ainu, annexed Okinawans, outcast *burakumin,* children of mixed marriages, and immigrant nationalities, especially Koreans, who number more than 700,000 (De Vos et al. 1983).

To describe racial attitudes in Japan, Jennifer Robertson (1992) uses Kwame Anthony Appiah's (1990) term "intrinsic racism"—the belief that a (perceived) racial difference is a sufficient reason to value one person less than another. In Japan the valued group is majority ("pure") Japanese, who are believed to share "the same blood." Thus, the caption to a printed photo of a Japanese-American model reads: "She was born in Japan but raised in Hawaii. Her nationality is American but no foreign blood flows in her veins" (Robertson 1992, p. 5). Something like hypodescent also operates in Japan, but less precisely than in the United States, where mixed offspring automatically become members of the minority group. The children of mixed marriages between majority Japanese and others (including Euro-Americans) may not get the same "racial" label as their minority parent, but they are still stigmatized for their non-Japanese ancestry (De Vos and Wagatsuma 1966).

How is race culturally constructed in Japan? The (majority) Japanese define themselves by opposition to others, whether minority groups in their own nation or outsiders—anyone who is "not us." The "not us" should stay that way; assimilation is generally discouraged. Cultural mechanisms, especially residential segregation and taboos on "interracial" marriage, work to keep minorities "in their place."

In its construction of race, Japanese culture regards certain ethnic groups as having a biological basis, when there is no evidence that they do. The best example is the *burakumin,* a stigmatized group of at least 4 million outcasts, sometimes compared to India's untouchables. The burakumin are physically and genetically indistinguishable from other Japanese. Many of them "pass" as (and marry) majority Japanese, but a deceptive marriage can end in divorce if burakumin identity is discovered (Aoki and Dardess, eds. 1981).

Burakumin are perceived as standing apart from the majority Japanese lineage. Through ancestry, descent (and thus, it is assumed, "blood," or genetics) burakumin are "not us." Majority Japanese try to keep their lineage pure by discouraging mixing. The burakumin are residentially segregated in neighborhoods (rural or urban) called *buraku,* from which the racial label is derived. Compared with majority Japanese, the burakumin are less likely to attend high school and college. When burakumin attend the same schools as majority Japanese, they face discrimination. Majority children and teachers may refuse to eat with them because burakumin are considered unclean.

In applying for university admission or a job and in dealing with the government, Japanese must list their address, which becomes part of a household or family registry. This list makes residence in a buraku, and likely burakumin social status, evident. Schools and companies use this information to discriminate. (The best way to pass is to move so often that the *buraku* address eventually disappears from the registry.) Majority Japanese also limit "race" mixture by hiring marriage mediators to check out the family histories of prospective spouses. They are especially careful to check for burakumin ancestry (De Vos et al. 1983).

The origin of the burakumin lies in a historical tiered system of stratification (from the Tokugawa period—1603–1868). The top four ranked categories were warrior-administrators (*samurai*), farmers, artisans, and merchants. The ancestors of the burakumin were below this hierarchy, an outcast group who did unclean jobs such as animal slaughter and disposal of the dead. Burakumin still do similar jobs, including work with leather and other animal products. The burakumin are more likely than majority Japanese to do manual labor (including farm work) and to belong to the national lower class. Burakumin and other Japanese minorities are also more likely to have careers in crime, prostitution, entertainment, and sports (De Vos et al. 1983).

Like blacks in the United States, the burakumin are class-stratified. Because certain jobs are reserved for the burakumin, people who are successful in those occupations (e.g., shoe factory owners) can be wealthy. Burakumin have also found jobs as government bureaucrats. Financially successful burakumin can temporarily escape their stigmatized status by travel, including foreign travel.

Discrimination against the burakumin is strikingly like the discrimination that blacks have experienced in the United States. The burakumin often live in villages and neighborhoods with poor housing and sanitation. They

Japan's stigmatized burakumin are physically and genetically indistinguishable from other Japanese. In response to burakumin political mobilization, Japan has dismantled the legal structure of discrimination against burakumin. This Sports Day for burakumin children is one kind of mobilization.

have limited access to education, jobs, amenities, and health facilities. In response to burakumin political mobilization, Japan has dismantled the legal structure of discrimination against burakumin and has worked to improve conditions in the buraku. Still, Japan has yet to institute American-style affirmative action programs for education and jobs. Discrimination against nonmajority Japanese is still the rule in companies. Some employers say that hiring burakumin would give their company an unclean image and thus create a disadvantage in competing with other businesses (De Vos et al. 1983).

Phenotype and Fluidity: Race in Brazil

There are more flexible, less exclusionary ways of constructing social race than those used in the United States and Japan. Along with the rest of Latin America, Brazil has less exclusionary categories, which permit individuals to change their racial classification. Brazil shares a history of slavery with the United States, but it lacks the hypodescent rule. Nor does Brazil have racial aversion of the sort found in Japan.

Brazilians use many more racial labels—over 500 have been reported (Harris 1970)—than Americans or Japanese do. In northeastern Brazil I found forty different racial terms in use in Arembepe, a village of only 750 people (Kottak 1999). Through their classification system Brazilians recognize and attempt to describe the physical variation that exists in their population. The system used in the United States, by recognizing only three or four races, blinds Americans to an equivalent range of evident physical contrasts. The system Brazilians use to construct social race has other special features. In the United States one's race is an ascribed status; it is assigned automatically by hypodescent and doesn't usually change. In Brazil racial identity is more flexible, more of an achieved status. Brazilian racial classification pays attention to phenotype. **Phenotype** refers to an organism's evident traits, its "manifest biology"—physiology and anatomy, including skin color, hair form, facial features, and eye color. A Brazilian's phenotype and racial label may change because of environmental factors, such as the tanning rays of the sun or the effects of humidity on the hair.

As physical characteristics change (sunlight alters skin color, humidity affects hair form), so do racial terms. Furthermore, racial differences may be so insignificant in structuring community life that people may forget the terms they have applied to others. Sometimes they even forget the ones they've used for themselves. In Arembepe, I made it a habit to ask the same person on different days to tell me the races of others in the village (and my own). In the United States I am always "white" or "Euro-American," but in Arembepe I got lots of terms besides *branco* ("white"). I could be *claro* ("light"), *louro* ("blond"), *sarará* ("light-skinned redhead"), *mulato claro* ("light mulatto"), or *mulato* ("mulatto"). The racial term used to describe me or anyone else varied from person to person, week to week, even day to day. My best informant, a man with very dark skin color, changed the term he used for himself all the time—from *escuro* ("dark") to *preto* ("black") to *moreno escuro* ("dark brunet").

The American and Japanese racial systems are creations of particular cultures, rather than scientific—or even accurate—descriptions of human biological differences. Brazilian racial classification is also a cultural construction, but Brazilians have developed a way of describing human biological diversity that is more detailed, fluid, and flexible than the systems used in most cultures. Brazil lacks Japan's racial aversion, and it also lacks a rule of descent like that which ascribes racial status in the United States (Harris 1964; Degler 1970).

For centuries the United States and Brazil have had mixed populations, with ancestors from Native America, Europe, Africa, and Asia. Although "races" have mixed in both countries, Brazilian and American cultures have constructed the results differently. The historical reasons for this contrast lie mainly in the different characteristics of the settlers of the two countries. The mainly English early settlers of the United States came as women, men, and families, but Brazil's Portuguese colonizers were mainly men—merchants and adventurers. Many of these Portuguese men married Native American women and recognized their "racially mixed" children as their heirs. Like their North American counterparts, Brazilian plantation owners had sexual relations with their slaves. But the Brazilian landlords more often freed the children that resulted—for demographic and economic reasons. (Sometimes these were their only children.) Freed offspring of master and slave became plantation overseers and foremen and filled many intermediate positions in the emerging Brazilian economy. They were not classed with the slaves, but were allowed to join a new intermediate category. No hypodescent rule ever developed in Brazil to ensure that whites and blacks remained separate (see Harris 1964; Degler 1970).

STRATIFICATION AND "INTELLIGENCE"

Over the centuries groups with power have used racial ideology to justify, explain, and preserve their privileged social positions. Dominant groups have declared minorities to be *innately,* that is biologically, inferior. Racial ideas are used to suggest that social inferiority and presumed shortcomings (in intelligence, ability, character, or attractiveness) are immutable and passed across the generations. This ideology defends stratification as inevitable, enduring, and "natural"—based in biology rather than society. Thus the Nazis argued for the superiority of the "Aryan race," and European colonialists asserted the "white man's burden." South Africa institutionalized *apartheid.* Again and again, to justify exploitation of minorities and native peoples, those in control have proclaimed the innate inferiority of the oppressed. In the United States the supposed superiority of whites was once standard segregationist doctrine. Belief in the biologically based inferiority of National Americans has been an argument for their slaughter, confinement, and neglect.

However, anthropologists know that most of the behavioral variation among contemporary human groups rests on culture rather than biology. The cultural similarities revealed through thousands of ethnographic studies leave no doubt that capacities for cultural evolution are equal in all human populations. There is also excellent evidence that within any **stratified** (class-based) society, differences in performance between economic, social, and ethnic groups reflect different experiences and opportunities rather than genetic makeup. (Stratified societies are those with marked differences in wealth, prestige, and power between social classes.)

Stratification, political domination, prejudice, and ignorance continue to exist. They propagate the mistaken belief that misfortune and poverty result from lack of ability. Occasionally doctrines of innate superiority are even set forth by scientists, who, after all, tend to come from the favored stratum of society. Among recent examples, one of the best known is Jensenism, named for the educational psychologist Arthur Jensen (Jensen 1969; Herrnstein 1971), its leading proponent. Jensenism is a highly questionable interpretation of the observation that African Americans, on average, perform less well on intelligence tests than Euro-Americans do. Jensenism asserts that blacks are hereditarily incapable of performing as well as whites do. Richard Herrnstein, writing with Charles Murray, makes a similar argument in the 1994 book *The Bell Curve,* to which the following critique also applies.

Environmental explanations for test scores are much more convincing than are the genetic tenets of Jensen, Herrnstein, and Murray. An environmental explanation does not deny that some people may be smarter than others. In any society, for many reasons, genetic and environmental, the talents of individuals vary. An environmental explanation does deny, however, that these differences can be generalized to whole groups. Even when talking about individual intelligence, however, we have to decide which of several abilities is an accurate measure of intelligence.

Most tests are written by educated people in Europe and North America. They reflect the experiences of the people who devise them. It is not surprising that middle- and upper-class children do better since they are more likely to share the test makers' educational background and standards. Numerous studies have shown that performance on Scholastic Achievement Tests (SATs) can be improved by coaching and preparation. Parents who can afford $500 or more for an SAT preparation course enhance their kids' chances of getting high scores. Standardized college entrance exams are similar to IQ tests in that they purportedly measure intellectual aptitude. They may do this, but they also measure type and quality of high school education, linguistic and cultural background, and parental wealth. No test is free of class, ethnic, and cultural biases.

Tests invariably measure particular learning histories, not the potential for learning. They use middle-class performance as a standard for determining what should be known at a given chronological age. Furthermore, tests are usually administered by middle-class white people who give instructions in a dialect or languages that may not be totally familiar to the child being tested. Test performance improves when the subcultural, socioeconomic, and linguistic backgrounds of subjects and test personnel are similar (Watson 1972).

Examples of cultural biases in intelligence testing abound. Biases affect performance by people in other cultures and by different groups within the same culture, such as Native Americans in the United States. Many Native Americans have grown up on reservations or under conditions of urban or rural poverty. They have suffered social, economic, political, and cultural discrimination. In one study, Native Americans had the lowest IQ test scores (a mean of 81, compared with a standard of 100) of any minority group in the United States (Klineberg 1951). But when the environment offers opportunities similar to those available to middle-class Americans, test performance tends to equalize. Consider the Osage Indians, on whose reservation oil was discovered. Profiting from oil sales, the Osage did not experience the stresses of poverty. They developed a good school system, and their average IQ was 104. Here the relationship between test performance and environment is particularly clear. The Osage did not settle on the reservation because they knew that oil was there. There is no reason to believe that these people were innately more intelligent than were Indians on different reservations. They were just luckier.

Similar relationships between social, economic, and educational environment and test performance show up in comparisons of American blacks and whites. At the beginning of World War I, intelligence tests were given to approximately 1 million American army recruits. Blacks from some northern states had higher average scores than did whites from some southern states. This was caused by the fact that at that time northern blacks got a better public education than did many southern whites. Thus, their superior performance is not surprising. On the other hand, southern whites did better than southern blacks. This is also expectable, given the unequal school systems then open to whites and blacks in the South.

Some people tried to get around the environmental explanation for the superior performance of northern blacks over southern whites by suggesting selective migration—smarter blacks had moved north. However, it was possible to test this hypothesis, which turned out to be false. If smarter blacks had moved north, their superior intelligence should have been obvious in their school records while they were still living in the South. It was not. Furthermore, studies in New York, Washington, and Philadelphia showed that as length of residence increased, test scores also rose.

Studies of identical twins raised apart also illustrate the impact of environment on identical heredity. In a study of nineteen pairs of twins, IQ scores varied directly with years in school. The average difference in IQ was only 1.5 points for the eight twin pairs with the same amount of schooling. It was 10 points for the eleven pairs with an average of five years' difference. One subject, with fourteen years more education than his twin, scored 24 points higher (Bronfenbrenner 1975).

These and similar studies provide overwhelming evidence that test performance measures education and social, economic, and cultural background rather than genetically determined intelligence. During the past 500 years Europeans and their descendants extended their political and economic control over most of the world. They colonized and occupied environments that they reached in their ships and conquered with their weapons. Most people in the most powerful contemporary nations—located in North America, Europe, and Asia—have light skin color. Some people in these currently powerful countries may incorrectly assert and believe that their world position has resulted from innate biological superiority. However, all contemporary human populations seem to have comparable learning abilities.

We are living in and interpreting the world at a particular time. In the past there were far different associations between centers of power and human physical characteristics. When Europeans were barbarians, advanced civilizations thrived in the Middle East. When Europe was in the Dark Ages, there were civilizations in West Africa, on the East African coast, in Mexico, and in Asia. Before the Industrial Revolution, the ancestors of many white Europeans and Americans were living much more like precolonial Africans than like current members of the American middle class. Their average performance on twentieth-century IQ tests would have been abominable.

ETHNIC GROUPS, NATIONS, AND NATIONALITIES

The term **nation** was once synonymous with "tribe" or "ethnic group." All three of these terms referred to a single culture sharing a single language, religion, history, territory, ancestry, and kinship. Thus one could speak interchangeably of the Seneca (American Indian) nation, tribe, or ethnic group. Now *nation* has come to mean **state**—an independent, centrally organized political unit, or a government. *Nation* and *state* have become synonymous. Combined in **nation-state** they refer to an autonomous political entity, a "country—like the United States, "one nation, indivisible" (see Gellner 1997, Hastings 1997).

Because of migration, conquest, and colonialism (see below), most nation-states are not ethnically homogeneous. Of 132 nation-states existing in 1971, Connor (1972) found just 12 (9 percent) to be ethnically homogeneous. In another 25 (19 percent) a single ethnic group accounted for more than 90 percent of the population. Forty percent of the countries contained more than five significant ethnic groups. In a later study, Nielsson (1985) classified only 45 of 164 states as "single nation-group" (i.e., ethnic-group) states (with one ethnic group accounting for more than 95 percent of the population).

Nationalities and Imagined Communities

Ethnic groups that once had, or wish to have or regain, autonomous political status (their own country) are called **nationalities.** In the words of Benedict Anderson (1991), they are "imagined communities." Even when they become nation-states, they remain imagined communities, because most of their members, though feeling comradeship, will never meet (Anderson 1991, pp. 6–10). They can only imagine they all participate in the same unit.

Anderson traces Western European nationalism, which arose in imperial powers such as England, France, and Spain, back to the eighteenth century. He stresses that language and print played a crucial role in the growth of European national consciousness. The novel and the newspaper were "two forms of imagining" communities (consisting of all the people who read the same sources and thus witnessed the same events) that flowered in the eighteenth century (Anderson 1991, pp. 24–25).

Over time, political upheavals, wars, and migration have divided many imagined national communities that arose in the eighteenth and nineteenth centuries. The German and Korean homelands were artificially divided after wars, and according to communist and capitalist ideologies. World War I split the Kurds, who remain an imagined community, forming a majority in no state. Kurds are a minority group in Turkey, Iran, Iraq, and Syria.

In creating multitribal and multiethnic states, colonialism often erected boundaries that corresponded poorly with preexisting cultural divisions. But colonial institutions also helped created new "imagined communities" beyond nations. A good example is the idea of **négritude** ("Black identity") developed by African intellectuals in Francophone (French-speaking) West Africa. *Négritude* can be traced to the association and common experience of youths from Guinea, Mali, the Ivory Coast, and Senegal at the William Ponty school in Dakar, Senegal (Anderson 1991, pp. 123–124).

ETHNIC TOLERANCE AND ACCOMMODATION

Ethnic diversity may be associated with positive group interaction and co-existence or with conflict (discussed below). There are nation-states in which multiple cultural groups live together in reasonable harmony, including some less developed countries.

Assimilation

Assimilation describes the process of change that a minority ethnic group may experience when it moves to a country where another culture dominates. By assimilating, the minority adopts the patterns and norms of its host culture. It is incorporated into the dominant culture to the point that it no longer exists as a separate cultural unit. Some countries, such as Brazil, are more assimilationist than others. Germans, Italians, Japanese, Middle Easterners, and East Europeans started migrating to Brazil late in the nineteenth century. These immigrants have assimilated to a common Brazilian culture, which has Portuguese, African, and Native American roots. The descendants of these immigrants speak the national language (Portuguese) and participate in the national culture. (During World War II, Brazil, which was on the Allied side, forced assimilation by banning instruction in any language other an Portuguese—especially in German.)

The Plural Society

Assimilation isn't inevitable, and there can be ethnic harmony without it. Ethnic distinctions can persist despite generations of interethnic contact. Through a study of three ethnic groups in Swat, Pakistan, Fredrik Barth (1958/1968) challenged an old idea that interaction always leads to assimilation. He showed that ethnic groups can be in contact for generations without assimilating and can live in peaceful coexistence.

Barth (1958/1968, p. 324) defines **plural society** (an idea he extends from Pakistan to the entire Middle East) as a society combining ethnic contrasts, ecological specialization (i.e., use of different environmental resources by each ethnic group), and the economic interdependence of those groups. Consider his description of the Middle East (in the 1950s): "The 'environment' of any one ethnic group is not only defined by natural conditions, but also by the presence and activities of the other ethnic groups on which it depends. Each group exploits only part of the total environment, and leaves large parts of it open for other groups to exploit." The ecological interdependence (or, at least, the lack of competition) between ethnic groups may be based on different activities in the same region or on long-term occupation of different regions in the same nation-state.

In Barth's view, ethnic boundaries are most stable and enduring when the groups occupy different ecological niches. That is, they make their living in different ways and don't compete. Ideally, they should depend on each other's activities and exchange with one another. When different ethnic groups exploit the *same* ecological niche, the militarily more powerful group will normally replace the weaker one. If they exploit more or less the same niche, but the weaker group is better able to use marginal environments, they may also coexist (Barth 1958/1968, p. 331). Given niche specialization, ethnic boundaries, distinctions, and interdependence can be maintained, although the specific cultural features of each group may change. By shifting the analytic focus from individual cultures or ethnic groups to *relationships* between cultures or ethnic groups, Barth (1958/ 1968 and 1969) has made important contributions to ethnic studies.

Multiculturalism and Ethnic Identity

The view of cultural diversity in a country as something good and desirable is called **multiculturalism.** The multicultural model is the opposite of the assimilationist model, in which minorities are expected to abandon their cultural traditions and values, replacing them with those of the majority population. The multicultural view encourages the practice of cultural-ethnic traditions. A multicultural society socializes individuals not only into the dominant (national) culture but also into an ethnic culture. Thus in

In the United States and Canada, multiculturalism is of growing
importance. Especially in large cities such as Toronto (shown
here), people of diverse backgrounds attend ethnic fairs and
festivals and feast on ethnic foods. What are some other
expressions of multiculturalism in your society?

the United States millions of people speak both English and another language, eat both "American" (apple pie, steak, hamburgers) and "ethnic"
foods, and celebrate both national (July 4, Thanksgiving) and ethnic-
religious holidays.

In the United States and Canada multiculturalism is of growing importance. This reflects an awareness that the number and size of ethnic groups
have grown dramatically in recent years. If this trend continues, the ethnic
composition of the United States will change dramatically (see Figure 3-3).

Because of immigration and differential population growth, whites are
now outnumbered by minorities in many urban areas. For example, of the
8,008,278 people living in New York City in 2000, 27 percent were black, 27
percent Hispanic, 10 percent Asian, and 36 percent other—including non-
Hispanic whites. The comparable figures for Los Angeles (3,694,820 people)
were 11 percent black, 47 percent Hispanic, 9 percent Asian, and 33 percent
other—including non-Hispanic whites (Census 2000, www.census.gov).

One response to ethnic diversification and awareness has been for many
whites to reclaim ethnic identities (Italian, Albanian, Serbian, Lithuanian,
etc.) and to joint ethnic associations (clubs, gangs). Some such groups are
new. Others have existed for decades, although they lost members during
the assimilationist years of the 1920s through the 1950s.

Multiculturalism seeks ways for people to understand and interact that
don't depend on sameness but rather on respect for differences. Multiculturalism stresses the interaction of ethnic groups and their contribution to

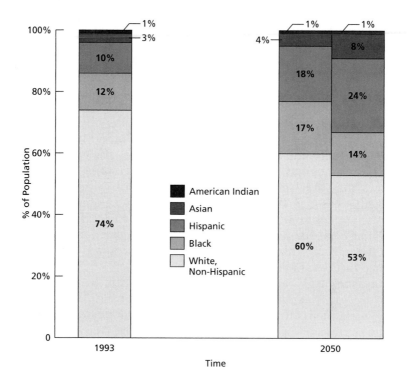

FIGURE 3-3 Ethnic composition of the United States. The proportion of the American population that is white and non-Hispanic is declining. Consider two projections of the ethnic composition of the United States in A.D. 2050. The first assumes an annual immigration rate of zero; the second assumes continuation of the current level of immigration—about 880,000 immigrants per year. With either projection, the non-Hispanic white proportion of the population declines dramatically.

the country. It assumes that each group has something to offer and learn from the others.

Several forces have propelled North America away from the assimilationist model toward multiculturalism. First, multiculturalism reflects the fact of recent large-scale migration, particularly from the "less developed countries" to the "developed" nations of North America and Western Europe. The global scale of modern migration introduces unparalleled ethnic variety to host nations. Multiculturalism is related to globalization: People use modern means of transportation to migrate to nations whose lifestyles they learn about through the media and from tourists who increasingly visit their own countries.

Migration is also fueled by rapid population growth, coupled with insufficient jobs (both for educated and uneducated people), in the less developed countries. As traditional rural economies decline or mechanize, displaced farmers move to cities, where they and their children are often unable to find jobs. As people in the less developed countries get better educations, they seek more skilled employment. They hope to partake in an international culture of consumption that includes such modern amenities as refrigerators, televisions, and automobiles.

In a world with growing rural-urban and transnational migration, ethnic identities are used increasingly to form self-help organizations focused mainly on enhancing the group's economic competitiveness (Williams 1989). People claim and express ethnic identities for political and economic reasons. Michel Laguerre's (1984) study of Haitian immigrants in New York City shows that they mobilize to deal with the discriminatory structure (racist in this case, since Haitians tend to be black) of American society. Ethnicity (their common Haitian creole language and cultural background) is an evident basis for their mobilization. Haitian ethnicity then helps distinguish them from African Americans and other ethnic groups who may be competing for the same resources and recognition.

In the face of globalization, much of the world, including the entire "democratic West," is experiencing an "ethnic revival." The new assertiveness of long-resident ethnic groups extends to the Basques and Catalans in Spain, the Bretons and Corsicans in France, and the Welsh and Scots in the United Kingdom. The United States and Canada are becoming increasingly multicultural, focusing on their internal diversity. "Melting pots" no longer, they are better described as ethnic "salads" (each ingredient remains distinct, although in the same bowl, with the same dressing). In 1992, then New York mayor David Dinkins called his city a "gorgeous mosaic."

ROOTS OF ETHNIC CONFLICT

Ethnicity, based on perceived cultural similarities and differences in a society or nation, can be expressed in peaceful multiculturalism or in discrimination or violent interethnic confrontation. Culture can be both adaptive and maladaptive. The perception of cultural differences can have disastrous effects on social interaction.

The roots of ethnic differentiation—and therefore, potentially, of ethnic conflict—can be political, economic, religious, linguistic, cultural, or "racial." Why do ethnic differences often lead to conflict and violence? The causes include a sense of injustice because of resource distribution, economic and/or political competition, and reaction to discrimination, prejudice, and other expressions of threatened or devalued identity (Ryan 1990, p. xxvii).

Prejudice and Discrimination

Ethnic conflict often arises in reaction to prejudice (attitudes and judgments) or discrimination (action). **Prejudice** means devaluing (looking down on) a group because of its assumed behavior, values, capabilities, or attributes. People are prejudiced when they hold stereotypes about groups and apply them to individuals. (**Stereotypes** are fixed ideas—often unfavorable—about what the members of a group are like.) Prejudiced people assume that members of the group will act as they are "supposed to act" (according to the stereotype) and interpret a wide range of individual behaviors as evidence of the stereotype. They use this behavior to confirm their stereotype (and low opinion) of the group.

Discrimination refers to policies and practices that harm a group and its members. Discrimination may be *de facto* (practiced, but not legally sanctioned) or *de jure* (part of the law). An example of de facto discrimination is the harsher treatment that American minorities (compared with other Americans) tend to get from the police and the judicial system. This unequal treatment isn't legal, but it happens anyway. Segregation in the southern United States and *apartheid* in South Africa provide two examples of de jure discrimination, which are no longer in existence. In both systems, by law, blacks and whites had different rights and privileges. Their social interaction ("mixing) was legally curtailed.

Chips in the Mosaic

Although the multicultural model is increasingly prominent in North America, ethnic competition and conflict are just as evident. There is conflict between new arrivals, for instance, Central Americans and Koreans, and long-established ethnic groups, such as African Americans. Ethnic antagonism flared in South-Central Los Angeles in spring 1992 in rioting that followed the acquittal of four white police officers who were tried for the videotaped beating of Rodney King (see Abelmann and Lie 1995).

Angry blacks attacked whites, Koreans, and Latinos. This violence expressed frustration by African Americans about their prospects in an increasingly multicultural society. A *New York Times* CBS News Poll conducted May 8, 1992, just after the Los Angeles riots, found that blacks had a bleaker outlook than whites about the effects of immigration on their lives. Only 23 percent of the blacks felt they had more opportunities than recent immigrants, compared with twice that many whites (Toner 1992).

Korean stores were hard hit during the 1992 riots, and more than a third of the businesses destroyed were Latino-owned. A third of those who died in the riots were Latinos. These mainly recent migrants lacked deep roots to the neighborhood and, as Spanish speakers, faced language barriers (Newman 1992). Many Koreans also had trouble with English.

Koreans interviewed on ABC's *Nightline* on May 6, 1992, recognized that blacks resented them and considered them unfriendly. One man explained, "It's not part of our culture to smile." African Americans interviewed on the same program did complain about Korean unfriendliness. "They come into our neighborhoods and treat us like dirt." These comments suggest a shortcoming of the multicultural perspective: Ethnic groups (blacks here) expect other ethnic groups in the same nation-state to assimilate to some extent to a shared (national) culture. The African Americans' comments invoked a general American value system that includes friendliness, openness, mutual respect, community participation, and "fair play." Los Angeles blacks wanted their Korean neighbors to act more like generalized Americans— and good neighbors.

Aftermaths of Oppression

Fueling ethnic conflict are such forms of discrimination as forced assimilation, ethnocide, and cultural colonialism. A dominant group may try to destroy the cultures of certain ethnic groups (**ethnocide**) or force them to adopt the dominant culture (**forced assimilation**). Many countries have penalized or banned the language and customs of an ethnic group (including its religious observances). One example of forced assimilation is the anti-Basque campaign that the dictator Francisco Franco (who ruled between 1939 and 1975) waged in Spain. Franco banned Basque books, journals, newspapers, signs, sermons, and tombstones and imposed fines for using the Basque language in schools. His policies led to the formation of a Basque terrorist group and spurred strong nationalist sentiment in the Basque region (Ryan 1990).

A policy of **ethnic expulsion** aims at removing groups who are culturally different from a country. There are many examples, including Bosnia-Herzegovina in the 1990s. Uganda expelled 74,000 Asians in 1972. The neofascist parties of contemporary Western Europe advocate repatriation (expulsion) of immigrant workers (West Indians in England, Algerians in France, and Turks in Germany) (Ryan 1990, p. 9).

A policy of expulsion may create **refugees**—people who have been forced (involuntary refugees) or who have chosen (voluntary refugees) to flee a country, to escape persecution or war.

Colonialism, another form of oppression, refers to the political, social, economic, and cultural domination of a territory and its people by a foreign power for an extended time (Bell 1981). The British and French colonial empires are familiar examples of colonialism, but we can extend the term to the former Soviet empire, formerly known as the "Second World."

Using the labels "First World," "Second World," and "Third World" is a common, although clearly ethnocentric, way of categorizing nations. The **First World** refers to the "democratic West"—traditionally conceived in opposition to a "Second World" ruled by "communism." The First World includes Canada, the United States, Western Europe, Japan, Australia, and New Zealand. The **Second World** refers to the Warsaw Pact nations, including the former Soviet Union and the Socialist and once-Socialist countries of Eastern Europe and Asia. Proceeding with this classification, the "less developed countries" or "developing nations" make up the **Third World.**

The frontiers imposed by colonialism weren't usually based on, and often didn't reflect, preexisting cultural units. In many countries, colonial nation-building left ethnic strife in its wake. Thus, over a million Hindus and Muslims were killed in the violence that accompanied the division of the Indian subcontinent into India and Pakistan. Problems between Arabs and Jews in Palestine began during the British mandate period.

Multiculturalism may be growing in the United States and Canada, but the opposite is happening in the disintegrating Second World, where ethnic groups (nationalities) want their own nation-states. The flowering of ethnic feeling and conflict as the Soviet empire disintegrated illustrates that years of political repression and ideology provide insufficient common ground for lasting unity.

Cultural colonialism refers to internal domination—by one group and its culture/ideology over others. One example is the domination over the former Soviet empire by Russian people, language, and culture, and by communist ideology. The dominant culture makes itself the official culture. This is reflected in schools, the media, and public interaction. Under Soviet rule ethnic minorities had very limited self-rule in republics and regions controlled by Moscow. All the republics and their peoples were to be united by the oneness of "socialist internationalism." One common technique in cultural colonialism is to flood ethnic areas with members of the dominant ethnic group. Thus, in the former Soviet Union, ethnic Russian colonists were sent to many areas, to diminish the cohesion and clout of the local people.

"The Commonwealth of Independent States" is all that remains of the Soviet Union. In this group of new nations, ethnic groups (nationalities) are seeking to establish separate and viable nation-states based on cultural boundaries. This celebration of ethnic autonomy is part of an ethnic florescence that—as surely as globalization and transnationalism—is a trend of the late twentieth and early twenty-first centuries.

S u m m a r y

1. An "ethnic group" refers to a particular culture in a nation or region that contains others. Ethnicity is based on cultural similarities (among members of the same ethnic group) and differences (between that group and others). Ethnic distinctions can be based on language, religion, history, geography, kinship, or "race." A race is an ethnic group assumed to have a biological basis. Usually race and ethnicity are ascribed statuses; people are born members of a group and remain so all their lives.

2. Race is a cultural category, not a biological reality. "Races" derive from contrasts perceived in particular societies, rather than from scientific classifications based on common genes. In the United States "racial" labels such as "white" and "black" designate social races—categories defined by American culture. American racial classification, governed by the rule of hypodescent, is based neither on phenotype nor genes. Children of mixed unions, no matter what their appearance, are classified with the minority group parent.

3. Racial attitudes in Japan illustrate "intrinsic racism"—the belief that a perceived racial difference is a sufficient reason to value one person less than another. The valued group is majority ("pure") Japanese, who are believed to share "the same blood." Majority Japanese define themselves by opposition to others. These may be minority groups in Japan or outsiders—anyone who is "not us." Residential segregation and taboos on "interracial" marriage work against minorities. The burakumin are physically and genetically indistinguishable from other Japanese, but they still face discrimination as a social race.

4. Such exclusionary racial systems are not inevitable. Although Brazil shares a history of slavery with the United States, it lacks the hypodescent rule. Brazilian racial identity is more of an achieved status. It can change during someone's lifetime, reflecting phenotypical changes. Given the correlation between poverty and dark skin, the class structure affects Brazilian racial classification. Someone with light skin who is poor will be classified as darker than a comparably colored person who is rich.

5. Some people assert genetic differences in the learning abilities of "races," classes, and ethnic groups. But environmental variables (particularly educational, economic, and social background) provide better explanations for performance on intelligence tests by such groups. Intelligence tests reflect the life experiences of those who develop and administer them. All tests are to some extent culture-bound. Equalized environmental opportunities show up in test scores.

6. The term *nation* was once synonymous with "ethnic group." Now nation has come to mean a state—a centrally organized political unit. Because of migration, conquest, and colonialism, most nation-states are not ethnically homogeneous. Ethnic groups that seek autonomous political status (their own country) are nationalities. Political upheavals, wars, and migrations have divided many imagined national communities.

7. Assimilation describes the process of change an ethnic group may experience when it moves to a country where another culture dominates. By assimilating, the minority adopts the patterns and norms of its host culture. Assimilation isn't inevitable, and there can be ethnic harmony without it. A plural society combines ethnic contrasts and economic interdependence between ethnic groups. The view of cultural diversity in a nation-state as good and desirable is multiculturalism. A multicultural society socializes individuals not only into the dominant (national) culture but also into an ethnic one.

8. Ethnicity can be expressed in peaceful multiculturalism, or in discrimination or violent confrontation. Ethnic conflict often arises in reaction to prejudice (attitudes and judgments) or discrimination

(action). The most extreme form of ethnic discrimination is genocide, the deliberate elimination of a group through mass murder. A dominant group may try to destroy certain ethnic practices (ethnocide), or to force ethnic group members to adopt the dominant culture (forced assimilation). A policy of ethnic expulsion may create refugees. Colonialism is the political, social, economic, and cultural domination of a territory and its people by a foreign power for an extended time. Cultural colonialism refers to internal domination— by one group and its culture and/or ideology over others.

Case Study
Hmong

This chapter has discussed ethnic pride, along with ethnic discrimination and violence. The Hmong are a tribal people who traditionally have lived in remote mountain villages throughout China, Laos, Thailand, and Vietnam. Their history is one of struggle, rebellion, and perseverance. For centuries, Hmong have suffered persecution by many groups, while fiercely defending their ethnic heritage. Despite war and resettlement, they continue to strive to maintain their traditions. In *Culture Sketches* by Holly Peters-Golden, read the chapter on the Hmong: Struggle and Perseverance. Hmong in the United States have been criticized as unwilling to assimilate. Why might they be viewed this way? How might their long history of ethnic discrimination influence the way they think about themselves and their cultural heritage? How might you account for the clashes described in their adjustment to life in the United States?

Ethnic Nationalism Runs Wild

The Socialist Federal Republic of Yugoslavia was a nonaligned country outside the former Soviet Union (U.S.S.R.). Like the U.S.S.R., Yugoslavia fell apart, mainly along ethnic and religious lines, in the early 1990s. Among Yugoslavia's ethnic groups were Roman Catholic Croats, Eastern Orthodox Serbs, Muslim Slavs, and ethnic Albanians. Citing ethnic and religious differences, several republics broke away from Yugoslavia in 1991–92. These included Slovenia, Croatia, and Bosnia-Herzegovina (see Figure 3-4). Serbia and Montenegro are the two remaining republics within Yugoslavia. In Kosovo, which is a province in Serbia, but whose population is 90 percent ethnic Albanian, there has been a strong movement for independence, led by the Kosovo Liberation Army.

FIGURE 3-4 Former Yugoslavia, with Province and Republics. The former Yugoslavia, although a socialist nation, was a nonaligned country outside the former Soviet Union. Like the U.S.S.R., Yugoslavia disintegrated in the early 1990s. The breakaway portions included Slovenia, Croatia, and Bosnia-Herzegovina.

Much of the ethnic differentiation in Yugoslavia has been based on religion, culture, political and military history, and some differences involving language. Serbo-Croatian is a Slavic language spoken, with dialect variation, by Serbs, Croats, and Muslim Slavs alike. (Albanian is a separate language.) Croats and Serbs use different alphabets. The Croats have adopted our Roman alphabet, but the Serbs use the Cyrillic alphabet, which they share with Russia and Bulgaria. The two alphabets help promote ethnic differentiation and nationalism. Serbs and Croats, who share speech, are divided by writing—by literature, newsprint, and political manifestos.

The Yugoslav Serbs reacted violently—with military intervention—after a 1992 vote for the independence of Muslim-led Bosnia-Herzegovina, whose population is one-third Serbian. In Bosnia, the Serbs initiated a policy of forced expulsion—"ethnic purification" —against Croats, but mainly against Muslim Slavs. Serbs in Yugoslavia, who controlled the National Army, lent their support to the Bosnian Serbs in their "ethnic-cleansing" campaign.

Backed by the Yugoslav army, Bosnian Serb militias rounded up Bosnian Muslims, killed groups of them, and burned and looted their homes. Thousands of Slavs fled. Hundreds of thousands of Muslims became involuntary refugees in tent camps, school gyms, and parks.

The Serbs had no use for the ethnic coexistence that the previous Yugoslav socialist government had encouraged. The Serbs also wished to avenge historic affronts by Muslims and Croats. In the fifteenth century, Muslim Turks had overthrown a Serbian ruler, persecuted the Serbs, and—eventually—converted many local people to Islam during their

In 1999 thousands of refugees returned to a ravaged Kosovo. On June 22, 1999, this ethnic Albanian inspects the remains of her kitchen as she returns to her house, reportedly destroyed by Serbs.

centuries of rule in this area. Bosnian Serbs still resent Muslims—including the descendants of the converts—for the Turkish conquest.

Bosnian Serbs claimed to be fighting to resist the Muslim-dominated government of Bosnia-Herzegovina. They feared that a policy of Islamic fundamentalism might arise and threaten the Serbian Orthodox Church and other expressions of Serbian identity. The Serbs' goal was to carve up Bosnia along ethnic lines, and they wanted two-thirds of it for themselves. A stated aim of Bosnia's ethnic purification was to ensure that the Serbs would never again be dominated by another ethnic group (Burns 1992*a*).

Although the Croats and the Muslim Slavs also carried out forced deportations in other parts of the former Yugoslavia, the Serbian campaign in Bosnia was the widest and the most systematic. More than 200,000 people were killed during the Bosnian conflict (Cohen 1995). With Bosnia's capital, the multiethnic city of Sarajevo, under siege, the conflict was suspended following a December 1995 peace settlement signed in Dayton, Ohio.

In spring 1999 NATO began a 78-day bombing campaign against Yugoslavia in retaliation for Serbian atrocities against ethnic Albanians in the separatist province of Kosovo. In May 1999 then Yugoslav President Slobodan Milosevic was indicted for abuses against the Kosovar Albanian population by the war crimes tribunal in The Hague, Netherlands. By June 1999, accords ending 78 days of NATO bombing placed Kosovo under international control, enforced by NATO peacekeepers, who remain there as of this writing (July 2001). In the year 2000 Yugoslavia itself took several steps toward democracy. In September 2000, Milosevic was voted out of office and replaced by a new president, Vajislav Kostinica. Parliamentary elections in December 2000 removed the last vestiges of power that Milosevic had built up during the previous decade. On June 28, 2001, Milosevic was transferred from a

Belgrade jail to a prison cell in The Hague, Netherlands, for eventual trial by the United Nations war crimes tribunal there.

How can we explain Yugoslavia's ethnic conflict? According to Fredrik Barth (1968) ethnic differences are most secure and enduring where the groups occupy different ecological niches: They make their living in different ways or places, don't compete, and are mutually dependent. In Bosnia, the Serbs, the Croats, and the Muslim Slavs were more mixed than in any other former Yugoslav republic (Burns 1992b). Is it possible that the boundaries among the three groups were not sharp enough to keep them together by keeping them apart?

Chapter 4

Language and Communication

Depending on where we live, North Americans have certain stereotypes about how people in other regions talk. Some stereotypes, spread by the mass media, are more generalized than others. Most Americans think they can imitate a "Southern accent." We also have nationwide stereotypes about speech in New York City (the pronunciation of *coffee,* for example) and Boston ("I pahked the kah in Hahvahd Yahd").

Regional patterns influence the way all Americans speak. In whichever state, college students from out of state easily recognize that their in-state classmates speak differently. In-state students, however, have difficulty hearing their own speech peculiarities, because they are accustomed to them and view them as normal.

It is sometimes thought that Midwesterners don't have accents. This belief stems from the fact that Midwestern dialects don't have many stigmatized linguistic variants—speech patterns that people in other regions recognize and look down on, such as *r*lessness and *dem, dese,* and *dere* (instead of *them, these,* and *there*).

Far from having no accents, Midwesterners, even in the same high school, exhibit linguistic diversity (see Eckert 1989, 2000). Dialect differences are immediately obvious to people, like me, who come from other parts of the country. One of the best examples of variable Midwestern speech, involving vowels, is pronunciation of the *e* sound (called the /e/ phoneme), in such words as *ten, rent, French, section, lecture, effect, best,* and *test.* In southeastern Michigan, where I live and teach, there are four different ways of pronouncing this *e* sound. Speakers of Black English and immigrants from Appalachia often pronounce *ten* as *tin*, just as Southerners habitually do. Some Michiganders say *ten*, the correct pronunciation in Standard English. However, two other pronunciations are more common. Instead of *ten*, many Michiganders say *tan*, or *tun* (as though they were using the word *ton*, a unit of weight).

My students often astound me with their pronunciation. One day I met one of my Michigan-raised teaching assistants in the hall. She was deliriously happy. When I asked why, she replied, "I've just had the best suction."

"What?" I said.

She finally spoke more precisely. "I've just had the best saction." She considered this a clearer pronunciation of the word *section*.

Another TA complimented me, "You luctured to great effuct today." After an exam a student lamented that she had not done her "bust on the tust."

The truth is, regional patterns affect the way we all speak.

LANGUAGE

Linguistic anthropology illustrates anthropology's characteristic interests in diversity, comparison, and change–but here the focus is on language. Language, spoken (*speech*) and written (*writing*—which has existed for about 6,000 years), is our primary means of communication. Like culture in general, of which language is a part, language is transmitted through learning, as part of enculturation. Language is based on arbitrary, learned associations between words and the things they stand for. Unlike the communication systems of other animals, language allows us to discuss the past and future, share our experiences with others, and benefit from their experiences.

Anthropologists study language in its social and cultural context. Some linguistic anthropologists reconstruct ancient languages by comparing their contemporary descendants and in so doing make discoveries about history. Others study linguistic differences to discover the varied world views and patterns of thought in a multitude of cultures. Sociolinguists examine dialects and styles in a single language to show how speech reflects social differences, as in the previous discussion of regional speech contrasts. Linguistic anthropologists also explore the role of language in colonization and in the expansion of the world economy (Geis 1987, Thomas 1999).

NONVERBAL COMMUNICATION

Language is our principal means of communicating, but it isn't the only one we use. We communicate whenever we transmit information about ourselves to others and receive such information from them. Our facial expressions, bodily stances, gestures, and movements, even if unconscious, convey information and are part of our communication styles. Deborah Tannen (1990, 1993) discusses differences in the communication styles of American men and women, and her comments go beyond language. She notes that girls and women tend to look directly at each other when they talk, whereas boys and men do not. Males are more likely to look straight ahead rather than to turn and make eye contact with someone, especially another man, seated beside them. Also, in conversational groups, men tend to relax and sprawl out. Women may adopt a similar relaxed posture in all-female groups, but when they are with men they tend to draw in their limbs and adopt a tighter stance.

Kinesics is the study of communication through body movements, stances, gestures, and facial expressions. Related to kinesics is Chapter 2's examination of cultural differences in personal space and displays of affection. Linguists pay attention not only to what is said but to how it is said, and to features besides language itself that convey meaning. We use gestures, such as a jab of the hand, for emphasis. A speaker's enthusiasm is conveyed not only through words, but also through facial expressions, gestures, and other signs of animation. We use verbal and nonverbal ways of communicating our moods—enthusiasm, sadness, joy, regret. We vary our intonation and the pitch or loudness of our voices. We communicate through strategic pauses and even by being silent. Culture teaches us that certain manners and styles should accompany certain kinds of speech. Our demeanor, verbal and nonverbal, when our favorite team is winning would be out of place at a funeral, or when a somber subject is being discussed.

Some of our facial expressions reflect our primate heritage. We can see them in monkeys and especially in the apes. How "natural" and universal are the meanings conveyed by facial expressions? Throughout the world smiles, laughs, frowns, and tears tend to have similar meanings, but culture does intervene. In some cultures, people smile less than in others. In a given culture, men may smile less than women; and adults less than children. A lifetime of smiling and frowning marks the face, so that smile lines and frown furrows develop. In North America, smile lines may be more marked in women than men.

As we saw in Chapter 2, culture always plays a role in shaping the "natural." Animals communicate through odors, using scent to mark territories, a chemical means of communication. Among modern North Americans, the perfume, mouthwash, and deodorant industries are based on the idea that the sense of smell plays a role in communication and social interaction. But other cultures are more tolerant of "natural" odors than ours is.

Cross-culturally, nodding does not always mean affirmative, nor does head shaking from side to side always mean negative. Brazilians wag a finger to mean no. Americans say "uh huh" to affirm, whereas in Madagascar a similar sound is made to deny. Americans point with their fingers; the people of Madagascar point with their lips. Patterns of "lounging around" vary, too. Outside, when resting, some people may sit or lie on the ground; others squat; others lean against a tree.

Body movements communicate social differences. Lower-class Brazilians, especially women, offer limp handshakes to their social superiors. In Japan bowing is a regular part of social interaction, but different bows are used depending on the social status of the people who are interacting. In Madagascar and Polynesia, people of lower status should not hold their heads above those of people of higher status. When one approaches someone older or of higher status, one bends one's knees and lowers one's head as a sign of respect. In Madagascar, one always does this, for politeness, when passing between two people. Although our gestures, facial expressions, and body stances have roots in our primate heritage, and can been seen in the monkeys and the apes, they have not escaped the cultural shaping described in previous chapters. Language, which is so highly dependent on the use of symbols, is the domain of communication in which culture plays the strongest role.

THE STRUCTURE OF LANGUAGE

The scientific study of a spoken language (*descriptive linguistics*) involves several interrelated areas of analysis: phonology, morphology, lexicon, and syntax. **Phonology,** the study of speech sounds, considers which sounds are present and significant in a given language. **Morphology** studies the forms in which sounds combine to form *morphemes*—words and their meaningful parts. Thus, the word *cats* would be analyzed as containing two morphemes—*cat,* the name for a kind of animal, and *-s,* a morpheme indicating plurality. A language's **lexicon** is a dictionary containing all its morphemes and their meanings. **Syntax** refers to the arrangement and order of words in phrases and sentences. For example, do nouns usually come before or after verbs? Do adjectives normally precede or follow the nouns they modify?

Speech Sounds

From the movies and TV, and from actually meeting foreigners, we know something about foreign accents and mispronunciations. We know that someone with a marked French accent doesn't pronounce *r* like an American does. But at least someone from France can distinguish between "craw" and "claw," which someone from Japan may not be able to do. The difference between *r* and *l* makes a difference in English and in French, but it doesn't in Japanese. In linguistics we say that the difference between *r* and *l* is *phonemic* in English and French but not in Japanese. In English and French *r* and *l* are phonemes but not in Japanese. A **phoneme** is a sound contrast that makes a difference, that differentiates meaning.

We find the phonemes in a given language by comparing *minimal pairs*, words that resemble each other in all but one sound. The words have totally different meanings, but they differ in just one sound. The contrasting sounds are therefore phonemes in that language. An example in English is the minimal pair *pit/bit*. These two words are distinguished by a single sound contrast between /p/ and /b/ (we enclose phonemes in slashes). Thus /p/ and /b/ are phonemes in English. Another example is the different vowel sound of *bit* and *beat* (Figure 4-1). This contrast serves to distinguish these two words and the two vowel phonemes written /I/ and /i/ in English.

Standard (American) English (SE), the "region-free" dialect of TV network newscasters, has about thirty-five phonemes—at least eleven vowels and twenty-four consonants. The number of phonemes varies from language to language—from fifteen to sixty, averaging between thirty and forty. The number of phonemes also varies between dialects of a given language. In North American English, for example, vowel phonemes vary noticeably from dialect to dialect. Readers should pronounce the words in Figure 4-1, paying attention to (or asking someone else) whether they distinguish each of the vowel sounds. Most North Americans don't pronounce them all.

Phonetics is the study of speech sounds in general, what people actually say in various languages, like the differences in vowel pronunciation described in the discussion of Midwestern speech at the beginning of the

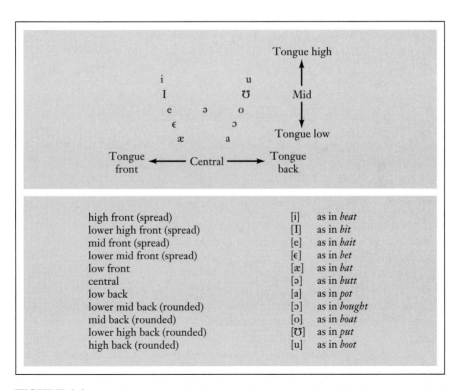

FIGURE 4-1 Vowel phonemes in Standard American English shown according to height of tongue and tongue position at front, center, or back of mouth. Phonetic symbols are identified by English words that include them; note that most are minimal pairs.
Source: Bolinger 1975.

chapter. **Phonemics** studies only the *significant* sound contrasts (phonemes) of a given language. In English, like /r/ and /l/ (remember *craw* and *claw*), /b/ and /v/ are also phonemes, occurring in minimal pairs like *bat* and *vat*. In Spanish, however, the contrast between [b] and [v] doesn't distinguish meaning, and they are therefore not phonemes (we enclose sounds that are not phonemic in brackets). Spanish speakers normally use the [b] sound to pronounce words spelled with either *b* or *v*.

In any language a given phoneme extends over a phonetic range. In English the phoneme /p/ ignores the phonetic contrast between the [pʰ] in *pin* and the [p] in *spin*. Most English speakers don't even notice that there is a phonetic difference. [pʰ] is aspirated, so that a puff of air follows the [p]. The [p] in *spin* is not. (To see the difference, light a match, hold it in front of your mouth, and watch the flame as you pronounce the two words.) The contrast between [pʰ] and [p] is phonemic in some languages, such as Hindi (spoken in India). That is, there are words whose meaning is distinguished only by the contrast between an aspirated and an unaspirated [p].

Native speakers vary in their pronunciation of certain phonemes, such as the /e/ phoneme in the Midwestern United States. This variation is important in the evolution of language. With no shifts in pronunciation, there can be no linguistic change. The section on sociolinguistics below considers phonetic variation and its relationship to social divisions and the evolution of language.

LANGUAGE, THOUGHT, AND CULTURE

The well-known linguist Noam Chomsky (1955) has argued that the human brain contains a limited set of rules for organizing language, so that all languages have a common structural basis. (Chomsky calls this set of rules *universal grammar*.) That people can learn foreign languages and that words and ideas translate from one language to another supports Chomsky's position that all humans have similar linguistic abilities and thought processes. Another line of support comes from creole languages. Such languages develop from pidgins, languages that form in situations of acculturation, when different societies come into contact and must devise a system of communication. Pidgins based on English and native languages developed through trade and colonialism in China, Papua New Guinea, and West Africa. Eventually, after generations of being spoken, pidgins may develop into *creole languages*. These are more mature languages, with developed grammatical rules and native speakers (that is, people who learn the language as their primary means of communication during enculturation).

Creoles are spoken in several Caribbean societies. Gullah, which is spoken by African Americans on coastal islands in South Carolina and Georgia, is a creole language. Supporting the idea that creoles are based on universal grammar is the fact that such languages all share certain features. Syntactically, all use particles (e.g., will, was) to form future and past tenses and multiple negation to deny or negate (e.g., he don't got none). Also, all form questions by changing inflection rather than by changing word order. For example, "You're going home for the holidays?" (with a rising tone at the end) rather than "Are you going home for the holidays?"

The Sapir-Whorf Hypothesis

Other linguists and anthropologists take a different approach to the relation between language and thought. Rather than seeking universal linguistic structures and processes, they believe that different languages produce different ways of thinking. This position is sometimes known as the **Sapir-Whorf hypothesis** after Edward Sapir (1931) and his student Benjamin Lee Whorf (1956), its prominent early advocates. Sapir and Whorf argued that the grammatical categories of particular languages lead their speakers to think about things in different ways. For example, English divides time into past, present, and future. Hopi, a language of the Pueblo region of the Native American Southwest, does not. Rather, Hopi distinguishes between events that exist or have existed (what we use present and past to discuss) and those which don't or don't yet (our future events, along with imaginary and hypothetical events). Whorf argued that this difference leads Hopi speakers to think about time and reality in different ways than English speakers do.

A similar example comes from Portuguese, which employs a future subjunctive verb form, introducing a degree of uncertainty into discussions of

Shown here in 1995, is Leigh Jenkins, who was or is Director of Cultural Preservation for the Hopi tribal council. Would the Hopi language have to distinguish between *was* and *is* in that sentence?

the future. In English we routinely use the future tense to talk about something we think will happen. We don't feel the need to qualify "The sun'll
come out tomorrow," by adding "if it doesn't go supernova." We don't hesi-
tate to proclaim "I'll see you next year," even when we can't be absolutely
sure we will. The Portuguese future subjunctive qualifies the future event,
recognizing that the future can't be certain. Our way of expressing the future as certain is so ingrained that we don't even think about it, just as the
Hopi don't see the need to distinguish between present and past, both of
which are real, while the future remains hypothetical. It seems, however,
that language does not tightly restrict thought, because cultural changes can
produce changes in thought and in language, as we'll see in the next section
(see also Gumperz and Levinson 1996)

Focal Vocabulary

A lexicon (or vocabulary) is a language's dictionary, its set of names for
things, events, and ideas. Lexicon influences perception. Thus, Eskimos (or
Inuit) have several distinct words for different types of snow that in English
are all called *snow*. Most English speakers never notice the differences between these types of snow and might have trouble seeing them even if someone pointed them out. Eskimos recognize and think about differences in
snow that English speakers don't see because our language gives us just
one word.

Similarly, the Nuer of Sudan have an elaborate vocabulary to describe
cattle. Eskimos have several words for snow and Nuer have dozens for cattle because of their particular histories, economies, and environments
(Eastman 1975; Brown 1958). When the need arises, English speakers can
also elaborate their snow and cattle vocabularies. For example, skiers name
varieties of snow with words that are missing from the lexicons of Florida
retirees. Similarly, the cattle vocabulary of a Texas rancher is much more
ample than that of a salesperson in a New York City department store. Such
specialized sets of terms and distinctions that are particularly important to
certain groups (those with particular *foci* of experience or activity) are
known as **focal vocabulary.**

Vocabulary is the area of language that changes most readily. New
words and distinctions, when needed, appear and spread. For example, who
would have "faxed" anything a generation ago? Names for items get simpler
as they become common and important. A television has become a *TV,* an
automobile a *car,* and a videocassette recorder a *VCR.*

Language, culture, and thought are interrelated. Opposing the Sapir-
Whorf hypothesis, however, it would be more accurate to say that changes
in culture produce changes in language and thought than to say the reverse.
Consider differences between female and male Americans regarding the
color terms they use (Lakoff 1975). Distinctions implied by such terms as
salmon, rust, peach, beige, teal, mauve, cranberry, and *dusky orange* aren't in
the vocabularies of most American men. However, many of them weren't

Germany tries to score against Belarus in a preliminary game played May 2, 2001, in the race for the Men's Ice Hockey World Championship. How would a hockey insider use focal vocabulary to describe this situation?

even in American women's lexicons fifty years ago. These changes reflect changes in American economy, society, and culture. Color terms and distinctions have increased with the growth of the fashion and cosmetic industries. A similar contrast (and growth) in Americans' lexicons shows up in football, basketball, and hockey vocabularies. Sports fans, more often males than females, use more terms concerning, and make more elaborate distinctions between, the games they watch, such as hockey (see Table 4-1). Thus, cultural contrasts and changes affect lexical distinctions (for instance, *peach* versus *salmon*) within semantic domains (for instance, color terminology). **Semantics** refers to a language's meaning system.

The ways in which people divide up the world—the lexical contrasts they perceive as meaningful or significant—reflect their experiences. Anthropologists have discovered that certain sets of vocabulary items evolve in a determined order. For example, after studying more than 100 languages, Berlin and Kay (1969/1992) discovered ten basic color terms: *white, black, red, yellow, blue, green, brown, pink, orange,* and *purple* (they evolved in more or less that order). The number of terms varied with cultural complexity. Representing one extreme were Papua New Guinea cultivators and Australian hunters and gatherers, who used only two basic terms, which translate as

TABLE 4-1	Focal vocabulary for hockey. Insiders have special terms for the major elements of the game.

Elements of Hockey	Insiders' Term
puck	biscuit
goal/net	pipes
penalty box	sin bin
hockey stick	twig
helmet	bucket
space between a goalie's leg pads	five hole

black and *white* or *dark* and *light*. At the other end of the continuum were European and Asian languages with all the color terms. Color terminology was most developed in areas with a history of using dyes and artificial coloring.

SOCIOLINGUISTICS

No language is a uniform system in which everyone talks just like everyone else. The field of **sociolinguistics** investigates relationships between social and linguistic variation. How do different speakers use a given language? How do linguistic features correlate with social stratification, including class, ethnic, and gender differences (Tannen 1990; Tannen, ed. 1993)? How is language used to express, reinforce, or resist power (Geis 1987)?

Sociolinguists focus on features that vary systematically with social position and situation. To study variation, sociolinguists must do field work. They must observe, define, and measure variable use of language in real world situations. To show that linguistic features correlate with social, economic, and political differences, the social attributes of speakers must also be measured and related to speech (Fasold 1990; Labov 1972a).

Variation within a language at a given time is historical change in progress. The same forces that, working gradually, have produced large-scale linguistic change over the centuries are still at work today. Linguistic change doesn't occur in a vacuum but in society. When new ways of speaking are associated with social factors, they are imitated, and they spread. In this way, a language changes.

Linguistic Diversity within Nations

As an illustration of the linguistic variation encountered in all nations, consider the contemporary United States. Ethnic diversity is revealed by the fact that millions of Americans learn first languages other than English. Spanish is the most common. Most of those people eventually become bilinguals, adding English as a second language. In many multilingual (including

Ethnic and linguistic diversity characterizes many nations, especially in big cities, as is illustrated by this multilingual advertising on New York's Lower East Side.

colonized) nations, people use two languages on different occasions—one in the home, for example, and the other on the job or in public.

Whether bilingual or not, we all vary our speech in different contexts; we engage in **style shifts.** In certain parts of Europe, people regularly switch dialects. This phenomenon, known as **diglossia,** applies to "high" and "low" variants of the same language, for example, in German and Flemish (spoken in Belgium). People employ the "high" variant at universities and in writing, professions, and the mass media. They use the "low" variant for ordinary conversation with family members and friends.

Just as social situations influence our speech, so do geographical, cultural, and socioeconomic differences. Many dialects coexist in the United States with Standard (American) English (SE). SE itself is a dialect that differs, say, from "BBC English," which is the preferred dialect in Great Britain. Different dialects are equally effective as systems of communication, which is language's main job. Our tendency to think of particular dialects as cruder or more sophisticated than others is a social rather than a linguistic judgment. We rank certain speech patterns as better or worse because we recognize that they are used by groups that we also rank. People who say *dese, dem,* and *dere* instead of *these, them,* and *there* communicate perfectly well with anyone who recognizes that the *d* sound systematically replaces the *th* sound in their speech. However, this form of speech has become an indicator of low social rank. We call it, like the use of *ain't,* "uneducated speech." The use of *dem, dese,* and *dere* is one of many phonological differences that Americans recognize and look down on.

Gender Speech Contrasts

Comparing men and women, there are differences in phonology, grammar, and vocabulary, and in the body stances and movements that accompany speech (Tannen 1990). In phonology, American women tend to pronounce their vowels more peripherally ("rant," "rint" when saying the word "rent"), whereas men tend to pronounce theirs more centrally ("runt"). In public contexts, Japanese women tend to adopt an artificially high voice, for the sake of politeness, according to their traditional culture. Women tend to be more careful about "uneducated speech." This trend shows up in both the United States and England. Men may adopt working-class speech because they associate it with masculinity. Perhaps women pay more attention to the media, in which standard dialects are employed.

According to Robin Lakoff (1975), the use of certain types of words and expressions has been associated with women's traditional lesser power in American society (see also Coates 1986; Romaine 1999; Tannen 1990, 1993). For example, *Oh dear, Oh fudge,* and *Goodness!* are less forceful than *Hell* and *Damn.* Men's customary use of "forceful" words reflects their traditional public power and presence. Watch the lips of a disgruntled athlete in a televised competition, such as a football game. What's the likelihood he's saying "Phooey on you"? Women, by contrast, are more likely to use such adjectives as *adorable, charming, sweet, cute, lovely,* and *divine* than men are.

Let's return to sports and color terminology for additional illustration of differences in lexical (vocabulary) distinctions that men and women make. Men typically know more terms related to sports, make more distinctions among them (e.g., runs versus points), and try to use the terms more precisely than women do. Correspondingly, influenced more by the fashion and cosmetics industries than men are, women use more color terms and attempt to use them more specifically than men do. Thus, when I lecture on sociolinguistics, and to make this point, I bring an off-purple shirt to class. Holding it up, I first ask women to say aloud what color the shirt is. The women rarely answer with a uniform voice, as they try to distinguish the actual shade (mauve, lavender, wisteria, or some other purplish hue). Then I ask the men, who consistently answer as one, "PURPLE." Rare is the man who on the spur of the moment can imagine the difference between *fuchsia* and *magenta.*

Differences in the linguistic strategies and behavior of men and women are examined in several books by the well-known sociolinguist Deborah Tannen (1990, 1993). Tannen uses the terms "rapport" and "report" to contrast women's and men's overall linguistic styles. Women, says Tannen, typically use language and the body movements that accompany it to build rapport, social connections with others. Men, on the other hand, tend to make reports, reciting information that serves to establish a place for themselves in a hierarchy, as they also attempt to determine the relative ranks of their conversation mates.

Stratification and Symbolic Domination

We use and evaluate speech in the context of *extralinguistic* forces—social, political, and economic. Mainstream Americans evaluate the speech of low-status groups negatively, calling it "uneducated." This is not because these ways of speaking are bad in themselves but because they have come to symbolize low status. Consider variation in the pronunciation of *r.* In some parts of the United States *r* is regularly pronounced, and in other (*r*less) areas it is not. Originally, American *r*less speech was modeled on the fashionable speech of England. Because of its prestige, *r*lessness was adopted in many areas and continues as the norm around Boston and in the South.

New Yorkers sought prestige by dropping their *r*'s in the nineteenth century, after having pronounced them in the eighteenth. However, contemporary New Yorkers are going back to the eighteenth-century pattern of pronouncing *r*'s. What matters, and what governs linguistic change, is not the reverberation of a strong Midwestern *r* but *social* evaluation, whether *r*'s happen to be "in" or "out."

Studies of *r* pronunciation in New York City have clarified the mechanisms of phonological change. William Labov (1972*b*) focused on whether *r* was pronounced after vowels in such words as *car, floor, card,* and *fourth.* To get data on how this linguistic variation correlated with social class, he used a series of rapid encounters with employees in three New York City department stores, each of whose prices and locations attracted a different socioeconomic group. Saks Fifth Avenue (68 encounters) catered to the upper middle class, Macy's (125) attracted middle-class shoppers, and S. Klein's (71) had predominantly lower-middle-class and working-class customers. The class origins of store personnel reflected those of their customers.

Having already determined that a certain department was on the fourth floor, Labov approached ground-floor salespeople and asked where that department was. After the salesperson had answered, "Fourth floor," Labov repeated his "Where?" in order to get a second response. The second reply was more formal and emphatic, the salesperson presumably thinking that Labov hadn't heard or understood the first answer. For each salesperson, therefore, Labov had two samples of /r/ pronunciation in two words.

Labov calculated the percentages of workers who pronounced /r/ at least once during the interview. These were 62 percent at Saks, 51 percent at Macy's, but only 20 percent at S. Klein's. He also found that personnel on upper floors, where he asked "What floor is this?" (and where more expensive items were sold), pronounced *r* more often than ground floor salespeople did.

In Labov's study, *r* pronunciation was clearly associated with prestige. Certainly the job interviewers who had hired the salespeople never counted *r*'s before offering employment. However, they did use speech evaluations to make judgments about how effective certain people would be in selling particular kinds of merchandise. In other words, they practiced sociolinguistic discrimination, using linguistic features in deciding who got certain jobs.

Our speech habits help determine our access to employment and other material resources. Because of this, "proper language" itself becomes a strategic resource—and a path to wealth, prestige, and power (Gal 1989). Illustrating this, many ethnographers have described the importance of verbal skill and oratory in politics (Beeman 1986; Bloch, ed. 1975; Brenneis 1988; Geis 1987, Lakoff 2000). Ronald Reagan, known as a "great communicator," dominated American society in the 1980s as a two-term President. Another twice-elected president, Bill Clinton, despite his Southern accent, was known for his verbal skills in certain contexts (e.g., televised debates and town-hall meetings). Communications flaws may have helped doom the presidencies of Gerald Ford, Jimmy Carter, and George Bush the elder ("couldn't do that"; "wouldn't be prudent"). Does his use of language affect your perception of the current president of the United States?

The French anthropologist Pierre Bourdieu views linguistic practices as *symbolic capital* which properly trained people may convert into economic and social capital. The value of a dialect—its standing in a "linguistic market"—depends on the extent to which it provides access to desired positions in the labor market. In turn, this reflects its legitimation by formal institutions—educational institutions, state, church, and prestige media. Even people who don't use the prestige dialect accept its authority and correctness, its "symbolic domination" (Bourdieu 1982, 1984). Thus, linguistic

Whether it's fair or not, people judge you by the way you speak. "Proper language" becomes a strategic resource, correlated with wealth, prestige, and power. Linguistic stratification can reflect both class and ethnic contrasts. In Guatemala a Spanish-speaking elite couple enjoy a garden breakfast served by an Indian maid. Can you think of ways in which speech habits help determine access to employment?

forms, which lack power in themselves, take on the power of the groups they symbolize. The education system, however (defending its own worth), denies this. It misrepresents prestige speech as being inherently better. The linguistic insecurity often felt by lower-class and minority speakers is a result of this symbolic domination.

Black English Vernacular (BEV), a.k.a. "Ebonics"

No one makes a strong social judgment when someone says "runt" instead of "rent." But some nonstandard speech carries more of a stigma. Sometimes stigmatized speech is linked to region, class, or educational background; sometimes it is associated with ethnicity or "race."

A national debate involving language, race, and education was triggered by a vote on December 18, 1996, by the Oakland, California, school board. The Board unanimously declared that many black students did not speak standard English but instead spoke a distinct language called "ebonics" (from "ebony" and "phonics"), with roots in West African languages. Soon disputing this claim were the poet Maya Angelou, the Reverend Jesse Jackson, and the Clinton administration. Indeed, professional linguists do regard ebonics as a dialect of English rather than a separate language. Linguists call ebonics BEV (Black English Vernacular) or AAEV (African American English Vernacular.)

Some saw the Oakland resolution as a ploy designed to permit the school district to increase its access to federal funds available for bilingual programs for Hispanic and Asian students. According to Federal law, Black English is not a separate language eligible for Title 7 funds. Funds for bilingual education (itself a controversial issue, especially in California politics) have been available to support the educations of immigrant students (Golden 1997). Some educators have argued that similar support should be available to blacks. If ebonics were accepted as a foreign language, teachers could receive merit pay for studying Black English and for using their knowledge of it in their lessons (Applebome 1996).

Early in 1997, responding to the widespread negative reaction to its original resolution, the Oakland educational task force proposed a new resolution. This one required only the recognition of language differences among black students, in order to improve their proficiency in English. School officials emphasized that they had never intended to teach black students in ebonics. They just sought to employ some of the same tools used with students brought up speaking a foreign language to help black students improve their English-language skills. The Oakland school board planned to expand its 10-year-old pilot program for black students, which taught the phonetic and grammatical differences between standard English and what the students spoke outside the classroom (Golden 1997).

While recognizing ebonics as a dialect of American English rather than as a separate language, most linguists see nothing wrong with the Oakland schools' goal of understanding the speech patterns of black students and respecting that speech while teaching standard English. Indeed, this is policy and teaching strategy in many American school districts. The Linguistic Society of America (LSA) considers ebonics or Black English Vernacular (BEV) to be "systematic and rule-governed" (Applebome 1997).

BEV isn't an ungrammatical hodgepodge but a complex linguistic system with its own rules, which linguists have described. The phonology and syntax of BEV are similar to those of southern dialects. This reflects generations of contact between southern whites and blacks, with mutual influence on each other's speech patterns. Many features that distinguish BEV from SE (Standard English) also show up in southern white speech, but less often than in BEV.

Linguists disagree about exactly how BEV originated (Rickford 1999). Smitherman (1986) calls it an Africanized form of English reflecting both an African heritage and the conditions of servitude in America. She notes certain structural similarities between West African languages and BEV. Their African linguistic backgrounds no doubt influenced how early African Americans learned English. Did they restructure English to fit African linguistic patterns? Or did they quickly learn English from whites, with little continuing influence from the African linguistic heritage? Another possibility is that English was fused with African languages to form a pidgin or creole in Africa or the Caribbean. This creole might then have been brought to the American colonies by the many slaves who were imported from the Caribbean during the seventeenth and eighteenth centuries (Rickford 1999, Rickford and Rickford 2000).

Origins aside, there are phonological and grammatical differences between ebonics and SE. One phonological difference is that BEV speakers are less likely to pronounce *r* than SE speakers are. Actually, many SE speakers don't pronounce *r*'s that come right before a consonant (ca*r*d) or at the end of a word (ca*r*). But SE speakers do usually pronounce an *r* that comes right before a vowel, either at the end of a word (fou*r* o'clock) or within a word (Ca*r*ol). BEV speakers, by contrast, are much more likely to omit such intervocalic (between vowels) *r*'s. The result is that speakers of the two dialects have different *homonyms* (words that sound the same but have different meanings). BEV speakers who don't pronounce intervocalic *r*'s have the following homonyms: Carol/Cal; Paris/pass. BEV's phonological rules also dictate that certain word-final consonants, such as *t*'s, *d*'s and the *s* in *he's*, be dropped.

Observing these phonological rules, BEV speakers pronounce certain words differently than SE speakers do. Particularly in the elementary school context, where the furor over ebonics has raged, the homonyms of BEV-speaking students typically differ from those of their SE-speaking teachers. To evaluate reading accuracy, teachers should determine whether students are recognizing the different meanings of such BEV homonyms as *passed*, *past*, and *pass*. Teachers need to make sure students understand what they are reading, which is probably more important than whether they are pronouncing words correctly according to the SE norm.

Phonological rules may lead BEV speakers to omit *-ed* as a past-tense marker and *-s* as a marker of plurality. However, other speech contexts demonstrate that BEV speakers do understand the difference between past and present verbs and between singular and plural nouns. Confirming this are irregular verbs (e.g., *tell*, *told*) and irregular plurals (e.g., *child*, *children*), in which BEV works the same as SE.

SE is not superior to BEV as a linguistic system, but it does happen to be the prestige dialect—the one used in the mass media, in writing, and in most public and professional contexts. SE is the dialect that has the most "symbolic capital." In areas of Germany where there is diglossia, speakers of Plattdeusch (Low German) learn the High German dialect to communicate appropriately in the national context. Similarly, upwardly mobile BEV-speaking students learn SE.

HISTORICAL LINGUISTICS

Sociolinguists study contemporary variation in speech—language change in progress. **Historical linguistics** deals with longer-term change. Historical linguists can reconstruct many features of past languages by studying contemporary **daughter languages.** These are languages that descend from the same parent language and that have been changing separately for hundreds or even thousands of years. We call the original language from which they diverge the **protolanguage.** Romance languages such as French and Spanish, for example, are daughter languages of Latin, their common protolanguage. German, English, Dutch, and the Scandinavian languages are daughter languages of proto-Germanic. The Romance languages and the Germanic languages all belong to the Indo-European language family. Their common protolanguage is called PIE, Proto-IndoEuropean. Historical linguists classify languages according to their degree of relationship (see Figure 4-2—PIE family tree).

Language changes over time. It evolves—varies, spreads, divides into **subgroups** (languages within a taxonomy of related languages that are most closely related). Dialects of a single parent language become distinct daughter languages, especially if they are isolated from one another. Some of them split, and new "granddaughter" languages develop. If people remain in the ancestral homeland, their speech patterns also change. The evolving speech in the ancestral homeland should be considered a daughter language like the others.

A close relationship between languages doesn't necessarily mean that their speakers are closely related biologically or culturally, because people can adopt new languages. In the equatorial forests of Africa, "pygmy" hunters have discarded their ancestral languages and now speak those of the cultivators who have migrated to the area. Immigrants to the United States spoke many different languages on arrival, but their descendants now speak fluent English.

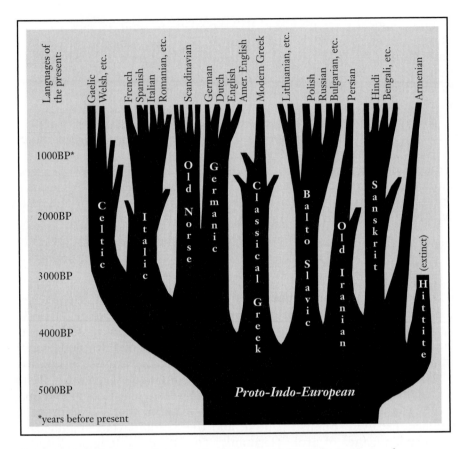

FIGURE 4-2 Main languages and subgroups of the Indo-European language stock, showing approximate time of their divergence.

Knowledge of linguistic relationships is often valuable to anthropologists interested in history, particularly events during the past 5,000 years. Cultural features may (or may not) correlate with the distribution of language families. Groups that speak related languages may (or may not) be more culturally similar to each other than they are to groups whose speech derives from different linguistic ancestors. Of course, cultural similarities aren't limited to speakers of related languages. Even groups whose members speak unrelated languages have contact through trade, intermarriage, and warfare. Ideas and inventions diffuse widely among human groups. Many items of vocabulary in contemporary English come from French. Even without written documentation of France's influence after the Norman Conquest of England in 1066, linguistic evidence in contemporary English would reveal a long period of important firsthand contact with France. Similarly, linguistic evidence may confirm cultural contact and borrowing when written history is lacking. By considering which words have been borrowed, we can also make inferences about the nature of the contact.

Summary

1. Humans use nonverbal communication, such as facial expressions, gestures, and body stances and movements. But language is the main system humans use to communicate.

2. No language uses all the sounds the human vocal tract can make. Phonology—the study of speech sounds—focuses on sound contrasts (phonemes) that distinguish meaning. The grammars and lexicons of particular languages can lead their speakers to perceive and think in certain ways.

3. Linguistic anthropologists share anthropology's general interest in diversity in time and space. Sociolinguistics investigates relationships between social and linguistic variation by focusing on the actual use of language. Only when features of speech acquire social meaning are they imitated. If they are valued, they will spread. People vary their speech, shifting styles, dialects, and languages.

4. As linguistic systems, all languages and dialects are equally complex, rule-governed, and effective for communication. However, speech is used, is evaluated, and changes in the context of political, economic, and social forces. Often the linguistic traits of a low-status group are negatively evaluated. This devaluation is not because of linguistic features per se. Rather, it reflects the association of such features with low social status. One dialect, supported by the dominant institutions of the state, exercises symbolic domination over the others.

5. Historical linguistics is useful for anthropologists interested in historical relationships among populations. Cultural similarities and differences often correlate with linguistic ones. Linguistic clues can suggest past contacts between cultures. Related languages—members of the same language family—descend from an original protolanguage. Relationships between languages don't necessarily mean there are biological ties between their speakers, because people can learn new languages.

Using Modern Technology to Preserve Linguistic and Cultural Diversity

Jesús Salinas Pedraza, a rural school-teacher in the Mexican state of Hidalgo, sat down to a word processor a few years back and produced a monumental book, a 250,000-word description of his own Indian culture written in the Nähñu language. Nothing seems to be left out: folktales and traditional religious beliefs, the practical uses of plants and minerals and the daily flow of life in field and village.

Mr. Salinas is neither a professional anthropologist nor a literary stylist. He is, though, the first person to write a book in Nähñu (NYAW-hnyu), the native tongue of several hundred thousand Indians but a previously unwritten language.

Such a use of microcomputers and desktop publishing for languages with no literary tradition is now being encouraged by anthropologists for recording ethnographies from an insider's perspective. They see this as a means of preserving cultural diversity and a wealth of human knowledge. With even greater urgency, linguists are promoting the techniques as a way of saving some of the world's languages from imminent extinction.

Half of the world's 6,000 languages are considered by linguists to be endangered. These are the languages spoken by small societies that are dwindling with the encroachment of larger, more dynamic cultures. Young people feel economic pressure to learn only the language of the dominant culture, and as the older people die, the nonwritten language vanishes, unlike languages with a history of writing, such as Latin.

Dr. H. Russell Bernard, the anthropologist at the University of Florida at Gainesville who taught Mr. Salinas to read and write his native language, said: "Languages have always come and gone. . . . But languages seem to be disappearing faster than ever before."

Dr. Michael E. Krauss, the director of the Alaska Native Language Center at the University of Alaska in Fairbanks, estimates that 300 of the 900 indigenous languages in the Americas are moribund. That is, they are no longer being spoken by children, and so could disappear in a generation or two. Only two of the 20 native languages in Alaska are still being learned by children.

In an effort to preserve language diversity in Mexico, Dr. Bernard and Mr. Salinas decided in 1987 on a plan to teach the Indian people to read and write their own language using microcomputers. They established a native literacy center in Oaxaca, Mexico, where others could follow in the footsteps of Mr. Salinas and write books in other Indian languages.

The Oaxaca center goes beyond most bilingual education programs, which concentrate on teaching people to speak and read their native languages. Instead, it operates on the premise that, as Dr. Bernard decided, what most native languages lack is native authors who write books in their own languages.

The Oaxaca project's influence is spreading. Impressed by the work of Mr. Salinas and others, Dr. Norman Whitten, an anthropologist at the University of Illinois, arranged for schoolteachers from Ecuador to visit Oaxaca and learn the techniques.

Now Ecuadorian Indians have begun writing about their cultures in the Quechua and Shwara languages. Others from Bolivia and Peru are learning to use the computers to write their languages, including Quecha, the tongue of the ancient Incas, still spoken by about 12 million Andean Indians.

Dr. Bernard emphasizes that these native literacy programs are not intended to discourage people from learning the dominant language of their country as well. "I see nothing useful or charming about remaining monolingual in any Indian language if that results in being shut out of the national economy," he said.

Source: excerpted from John Noble Wilford, "In a Publishing Coup, Books in 'Unwritten' Languages," *The New York Times,* December 31, 1991, pp. B5,6.

Chapter 5

Making a Living

In today's world, societies and communities are being incorporated, at an accelerating rate, into larger systems. The origin (around 10,000 years ago) and spread of food production (plant cultivation and animal domestication) led to the formation of larger and more powerful social and political systems. Food production led to major changes in human life. The pace of cultural transformation increased enormously. This chapter provides a framework for understanding a variety of human adaptive strategies and economic systems.

ADAPTIVE STRATEGIES

The anthropologist Yehudi Cohen (1974) used the term *adaptive strategy* to describe a society's system of economic production. Cohen argued that the most important reason for similarities between two (or more) unrelated societies is their possession of a similar adaptive strategy. In other words, similar economic causes have similar sociocultural effects. For example, there are clear similarities among societies that have a foraging (hunting and gathering) strategy. Cohen developed a typology of societies based on correlations between their economies and their social features. His typology includes these five adaptive strategies: foraging, horticulture, agriculture, pastoralism, and industrialism. Industrialism is discussed in Chapter 10, "The Modern World System." The present chapter focuses on the first four adaptive strategies.

Foraging

Until 10,000 years ago people everywhere were foragers. However, environmental differences did create contrasts among the world's foragers. Some, like the people who lived in Europe during the ice ages, were big game hunters. Today, hunters in the Arctic still focus on large animals and herd animals; they have much less vegetation and variety in their diets than do tropical foragers. Moving from colder to hotter areas, the number of species increases. The tropics contain tremendous biodiversity, and tropical foragers typically hunt and gather a wide range of plant and animal species. The same may be true in temperate areas. For example, on the North Pacific Coast of North America, foragers could draw on varied sea, river, and land species, such as salmon and other fish, sea mammals, berries, and mountain goats. Despite differences caused by such environmental variation, all foraging economies have shared one essential feature: People rely on nature to make their living.

Animal domestication (initially of sheep and goats) and plant cultivation (of wheat and barley) began 10,000 to 12,000 years ago in the Middle East. Cultivation based on different crops, such as corn (maize), manioc (cassava), and potatoes, arose independently some 3,000 to 4,000 years later in the Americas. In both hemispheres the new economy spread rapidly. Most foragers eventually turned to food production. Today most foragers have at least some dependence on food production or on food producers (Kent 1992).

The foraging way of life held on in certain environments, including certain islands, forests, deserts, and very cold areas—places where food production was not practicable with simple technology (see Lee and Daly 1999). In many areas, foragers were exposed to the "idea" of food production but never adopted it because their own economies provided a perfectly adequate and nutritious diet—with a lot less work. In some places, people reverted to foraging after trying food production and abandoning it. In most areas where hunter-gatherers did survive, foraging should be described as "recent" rather than "contemporary." All modern foragers live in nation-states and depend to some extent on government assistance. They are in contact with food-producing neighbors and also missionaries and other outsiders. We should not view contemporary foragers as isolated or pristine survivors of the Stone Age. Modern foragers are influenced by regional forces (e.g., trade and war), national and international policies, and political and economic events in the world system. (See the box in Chapter 7, "Political Systems.")

Although foraging is disappearing as a way of life, the outlines of Africa's two broad belts of recent foraging remain evident. One is the Kalahari Desert of southern Africa. This is the home of the San ("Bushmen"), who include the Ju/'hoansi (see Lee 1993, Kent 1996). The other main African foraging area is the equatorial forest of central and eastern Africa, home of the Mbuti, Efe, and other "pygmies" (Turnbull 1965; Bailey et al. 1989).

People still do subsistence foraging in certain remote forests in Madagascar, Southeast Asia, Malaysia, the Philippines, and on certain islands off the Indian coast. Some of the best-known recent foragers are the aborigines of Australia. Those Native Australians lived on their island continent for more than 40,000 years without developing food production.

The western hemisphere also had recent foragers. The Eskimos, or Inuit, of Alaska and Canada are well-known hunters. These (and other) northern foragers now use modern technology, including rifles and snowmobiles, in their subsistence activities (Pelto 1973). The native populations of California, Oregon, Washington, and British Columbia were all foragers, as were those of inland subarctic Canada and the Great Lakes. For many Native Americans fishing, hunting, and gathering remain important subsistence (and sometimes commercial) activities.

Coastal foragers also lived near the southern tip of South America, in Patagonia. On the grassy plains of Argentina, southern Brazil, Uruguay, and Paraguay, there were other hunter-gatherers. The contemporary Aché of Paraguay are usually called "hunter-gatherers" although they get just a third of their livelihood from foraging. The Aché also grow crops, have domesticated animals, and live in or near mission posts, where they receive food from missionaries (Hawkes et al. 1982; Hill et al. 1987).

Throughout the world, foraging survived mainly in environments that posed major obstacles to food production. (Some foragers took refuge in such areas after the rise of food production, the state, colonialism, or the modern world system.) The difficulties of cultivating at the North Pole are obvious. In southern Africa the Dobe Ju/'hoansi San area studied by Richard Lee and others is surrounded by a waterless belt 70 to 200 kilometers in breadth (Solway and Lee 1990).

Environmental obstacles to food production aren't the only reason foragers survived. Their niches have one thing in common—their marginality. Their environments haven't been of immediate interest to farmers, herders, or colonialists. The foraging way of life did persist in a few areas that could be cultivated, even after contact with farmers. Those tenacious foragers, like the indigenous peoples of what is now California and the Pacific Northwest, did not turn to food production, because they were supporting themselves adequately by hunting and gathering. As the modern world system spreads, the number of foragers continues to decline. See Figure 5-1 for distribution of recent hunter-gatherers.

Correlates of Foraging

Typologies, such as Cohen's adaptive strategies, are useful because they suggest **correlations**—that is, association or covariation between two or more variables. (Correlated variables are factors that are linked and interrelated, such as food intake and body weight, such that when one increases or

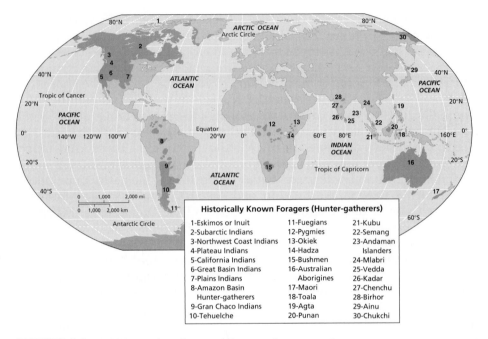

FIGURE 5-1 Worldwise distribution of recent hunter-gatherers.
Source: Gäran Burenhult, ed., *People of the Stone Age: Hunters and Gatherers and Early Farmers* (San Francisco: HarperCollins, 1993).

decreases, the other changes, too.) Ethnographic studies in hundreds of so-cieties have revealed many correlations between the economy and social life. Associated (correlated) with each adaptive strategy is a bundle of par-ticular sociocultural features. Correlations, however, are rarely perfect. Some foragers lack cultural features usually associated with foraging, and some of those features are found in groups with other adaptive strategies.

What, then, are the usual correlates of foraging? People who subsist by hunting and gathering often, but not always (see the section on potlatch-ing), live in band-organized societies. Their basic social unit, the **band,** is a small group of fewer than a hundred people, all related by kinship or mar-riage. Band size varies between societies and often from one season to the next in a given society. Among some foragers, band size stays about the same year-round. In others, the band splits up for part of the year. Families leave to gather resources that are better exploited by just a few people. Later, they regroup for cooperative work and ceremonies.

One typical characteristic of the foraging life is mobility. In many San groups, as among the Mbuti of Congo, people shift band membership sev-eral times in a lifetime. One may be born, for example, in a band in which one's mother has kin. Later, one's family may move to a band in which the father has relatives. Because bands are exogamous (people marry outside their own band) one's parents come from two different bands, and one's grandparents may come from four. People may join any band to which they have kin or marital links. A couple may live in, or shift between, the husband's and the wife's band.

All human societies have some kind of division of labor based on gender. Among foragers, men typically hunt and fish while women gather and collect, but the specific nature of the work varies among cultures. Sometimes women's work contributes most to the diet. Sometimes male hunting and fishing predominate. Among foragers in tropical and semitropical areas, gathering tends to contribute more to the diet than hunting and fishing do.

All foragers make social distinctions based on age. Often old people receive great respect as guardians of myths, legends, stories, and traditions. Younger people value the elders' special knowledge of ritual and practical matters. Most foraging societies are *egalitarian*. This means that contrasts in prestige are minor and are based on age and gender.

When considering issues of "human nature," we should remember that the egalitarian band was a basic form of human social life for most of our history. Food production has existed less than 1 percent of the time *Homo* has spent on earth. However, it has produced huge social differences. We now consider the main economic features of food-producing strategies.

CULTIVATION

In Cohen's typology, the three adaptive strategies based on food production in nonindustrial societies are horticulture, agriculture, and pastoralism. In nonindustrial societies, just as they do in the United States and Canada, people carry out a variety of economic activities. Each adaptive strategy refers to the main economic activity. Pastoralists (herders), for example, consume milk, butter, blood, and meat from their animals as mainstays of their diet. However, they also add grain to the diet by doing some cultivating or by trading with neighbors.

Horticulture

Horticulture and agriculture are two types of cultivation found in nonindustrial societies. Both differ from the farming systems of industrial nations like the United States and Canada, which use large land areas, machinery, and petrochemicals. According to Cohen, **horticulture** is cultivation that makes intensive use of *none* of the factors of production: land, labor, capital, and machinery. Horticulturalists use simple tools such as hoes and digging sticks to grow their crops. Their fields are not permanent property and lie fallow for varying lengths of time.

Horticulture often involves *slash-and-burn* techniques. Here, horticulturalists clear land by cutting down (slashing) and burning forest or bush or by setting fire to the grass covering the plot. The vegetation is broken down, pests are killed, and the ashes remain to fertilize the soil. Crops are then sown, tended, and harvested. Use of the plot is not continuous. Often it is cultivated for only a year or two.

When horticulturalists abandon a plot because of soil exhaustion or a thick weed cover, they clear another piece of land, and the original plot reverts to forest. After several years of fallowing, the cultivator returns to farm the original plot again. Because the relationship between people and land is not permanent, horticulture is also called *shifting cultivation.* Shifting cultivation does not mean that whole villages must move when plots are abandoned. Among the Kuikuru of the South American tropical forest, one village of 150 people remained in the same place for ninety years (Carneiro

In slash-and-burn horticulture, the land is cleared by cutting down (slashing) and burning trees and bush, using simple technology. After such clearing, this woman uses a digging stick to plant mountain rice in Madagascar. What might be the environmental effects of slash-and-burn cultivation?

1956). Kuikuru houses are large and well made. Because the work involved in building them is great, the Kuikuru would rather walk farther to their fields than construct a new village. They shift their plots rather than their settlements. On the other hand, horticulturalists in the montaña (Andean foothills) of Peru live in small villages of about thirty people (Carneiro 1961/1968). Their houses are small and simple. After a few years in one place, these people build new villages near virgin land. Because their houses are so simple, they prefer rebuilding to walking even a half mile to their fields.

Agriculture

Agriculture is cultivation that requires more labor than horticulture does, because it uses land intensively and continuously. The greater labor demands associated with agriculture reflect its use of domesticated animals, irrigation, and/or terracing.

Domesticated Animals   Many agriculturists use animals as means of production—for transport, as cultivating machines, and for their manure. Asian farmers typically incorporate cattle and/or water buffalo into agricultural economies based on rice production. Rice farmers may use cattle to trample pre-tilled flooded fields, thus mixing soil and water, before transplanting. Many agriculturists attach animals to plows and harrows for field preparation before planting or transplanting. Also, agriculturists typically collect manure from their animals, using it to fertilize their plots, thus increasing yields. Animals are attached to carts for transport and also to implements of cultivation.

Irrigation   While horticulturalists must await the rainy season, agriculturists can schedule their planting in advance, because they control water. Like other irrigation experts in the Philippines, the Ifugao irrigate their fields with canals from rivers, streams, springs, and ponds. Irrigation makes it possible to cultivate a plot year after year. Irrigation enriches the soil because the irrigated field is a unique ecosystem with several species of plants and animals, many of them minute organisms, whose wastes fertilize the land.

An irrigated field is a capital investment that usually increases in value. It takes time for a field to start yielding; it reaches full productivity only after several years of cultivation. The Ifugao, like other irrigators, have farmed the same fields for generations. In some agricultural areas, including the Middle East, however, salts carried in the irrigation water can make fields unusable after fifty or sixty years.

Terracing   Terracing is another agricultural technique the Ifugao have mastered. Their homeland has small valleys separated by steep hillsides. Because the population is dense, people need to farm the hills. However, if

Agriculture requires more labor than horticulture does and uses land intensively and continuously. Labor demands associated with agriculture reflect its use of domesticated animals, irrigation, and terracing. Shown here, rice terraces in southern China.

they simply planted on the steep hillsides, fertile soil and crops would be washed away during the rainy season. To prevent this, the Ifugao cut into the hillside and build stage after stage of terraced fields rising above the valley floor. Springs located above the terraces supply their irrigation water. The labor necessary to build and maintain a system of terraces is great. Terrace walls crumble each year and must be partially rebuilt. The canals that bring water down through the terraces also demand attention.

Costs and Benefits of Agriculture   Agriculture requires human labor to build and maintain irrigation systems, terraces, and other works. People must feed, water, and care for their animals. But agricultural land can yield one or two crops annually for years, or even generations. An agricultural field does not necessarily produce a higher single-year yield than does a horticultural plot. The first crop grown by horticulturalists on long-idle land may be larger than that from an agricultural plot of the same size. Furthermore, because agriculturists work harder than horticulturalists do, agriculture's yield relative to labor is also lower. Agriculture's main advantage is that the long-term yield per area is far greater and more dependable. Because a single field sustains its owners year after year, there is no need to maintain a reserve of uncultivated land as horticulturalists do. This is why agricultural societies tend to be more densely populated than horticultural ones are.

Agricultural Intensification: People and the Environment

The range of environments available for food production has widened as people have increased their control over nature. For example, in arid areas of California, where Native Americans once foraged, modern irrigation technology now sustains rich agricultural estates. Agriculturalists live in many areas that are too arid for nonirrigators or too hilly for nonterracers. Increasing labor intensity and permanent land use have major demographic, social, political, and environmental consequences.

Thus, because of their permanent fields, agriculturists are sedentary. People live in larger and more permanent communities located closer to other settlements. Growth in population size and density increases contact between individuals and groups. There is more need to regulate interpersonal relations, including conflicts of interest. Economies that support more people usually require more coordination in the use of land, labor, and other resources.

Intensive agriculture has significant environmental effects. Irrigation ditches and paddies (fields with irrigated rice) become repositories for organic wastes, chemicals (such as salts), and disease microorganisms. Intensive agriculture typically spreads at the expense of trees and forests, which are cut down to be replaced by fields. Accompanying such deforestation is loss of environmental diversity. Agricultural economies grow increasingly specialized. They focus on one or a few caloric staples, such as rice, and on the animals that are raised and tended to aid the agricultural economy. Because tropical horticulturalists typically cultivate dozens of plant species simultaneously, a horticultural plot mirrors the botanical diversity that is found in a tropical forest. Agricultural plots, by contrast, reduce ecological diversity by cutting down trees and concentrating on just a few staple foods. Such crop specialization is true of agriculturists both in the tropics (e.g., Indonesian paddy farmers) and outside the tropics (e.g., Middle-Eastern irrigation farmers).

Agriculturists attempt to reduce risk in production by favoring stability in the form of a reliable annual harvest and long-term production. Tropical foragers and horticulturalists, by contrast, attempt to reduce risk by relying on multiple species and benefiting from ecological diversity. The agricultural strategy is to put all one's eggs in one big and very dependable basket. The strategy of tropical foragers and horticulturalists is to have several smaller baskets, a few of which may fail without endangering subsistence. The agricultural strategy makes sense when there are lots of children to raise and adults to be fed. Foraging and horticulture, of course, are associated with smaller, sparser, and more mobile populations.

Agricultural economies also pose a series of regulatory problems—which central governments have often arisen to solve. How is water to be managed? How are disputes about access to and distribution of water to be resolved? With more people living closer together on more valuable land, agriculturists are more likely to come into conflict than foragers and horticulturalists are. The social and political implications of food production and intensification are examined more fully in Chapter 7, "Political Systems."

PASTORALISM

Pastoralists live in North Africa, the Middle East, Europe, Asia, and sub-Saharan Africa. These herders are people whose activities focus on such domesticated animals as cattle, sheep, goats, camels, and yak. East African pastoralists, like many others, live in symbiosis with their herds. (Symbiosis is an obligatory interaction between groups—here humans and animals—that is beneficial to each.) Herders attempt to protect their animals and to ensure their reproduction in return for food and other products, such as leather. Herds provide dairy products and meat. Animals are killed at ceremonies, which occur throughout the year, and so beef is available regularly.

People use livestock in various ways. Natives of North America's Great Plains, for example, didn't eat, but only rode, their horses. (Europeans reintroduced horses to the Western Hemisphere; the native American horse had become extinct thousands of years earlier.) For Plains Indians horses served as "tools of the trade," means of production used to hunt buffalo, a main target of their economies. So the Plains Indians were not true pastoralists but hunters who used horses—as many agriculturists use animals—as means of production.

Unlike the use of animals merely as productive machines, pastoralists typically make direct use of their herds for food. They consume their meat, blood, and milk, from which they make yogurt, butter, and cheese. Although some pastoralists rely on their herds more completely than others do, it is impossible to base subsistence solely on animals. Most pastoralists therefore supplement their diet by hunting, gathering, fishing, cultivating, or trading.

Unlike foraging and cultivation, which existed throughout the world before the Industrial Revolution, pastoralism was almost totally confined to the Old World. Before European conquest, the only pastoralists in the Americas lived in the Andean region of South America. They used their llamas and alpacas for food and wool and in agriculture and transport. Much more recently, Navajo of the southwestern United States developed a pastoral economy based on sheep, which were brought to North America by Europeans. The populous Navajo are now the major pastoral population in the western hemisphere.

Two patterns of movement occur with pastoralism: *nomadism* and *transhumance*. Both are based on the fact that herds must move to use pasture available in particular places in different seasons. In pastoral **nomadism,** the entire group—women, men, and children—moves with the animals throughout the year. The Middle East and North Africa provide numerous examples of pastoral nomads. In Iran, for example, the Basseri and the Qashqai ethnic groups traditionally followed a nomadic route more than 300 miles (480 kilometers) long.

With **transhumance,** part of the group moves with the herds, but most people stay in the home village. There are examples from Europe and Africa. In Europe's Alps it is just the shepherds and goatherds—not the whole village—who accompany the flocks to highland meadows in summer. Among the Turkana of Uganda, men and boys accompany the herds to distant pastures, while much of the village stays put and does some horticultural farming. Villages tend to be located in the best watered areas, which have the longest pasture season. This permits the village population to stay together during a large chunk of the year.

During their annual trek, pastoral nomads trade for crops and other products with more sedentary people. Transhumants don't have to trade for crops. Because only part of the population accompanies the herds, transhumants can maintain year-round villages and grow their own crops.

ECONOMIC SYSTEMS

An **economy** is a system of production, distribution, and consumption of resources; *economics* is the study of such systems. Economists focus on modern nations and capitalist systems. Anthropologists have broadened understanding of economic principles by gathering data on nonindustrial economies. Economic anthropology studies economics in a comparative perspective (see Plattner 1989, Wilk 1996, Gudeman, ed. 1999).

A **mode of production** is a way of organizing production—"a set of social relations through which labor is deployed to wrest energy from nature by means of tools, skills, organization, and knowledge" (Wolf 1982, p. 75). In the capitalist mode of production, money buys labor power, and there is a social gap between the people (bosses and workers) involved in the production process. By contrast, in nonindustrial societies, labor is not usually bought but is given as a social obligation. In such a *kin-based* mode of production, mutual aid in production is one among many expressions of a larger web of social relations.

Societies representing each of the adaptive strategies just discussed (e.g., foraging) tend to have a similar mode of production. Differences in the mode of production within a given strategy may reflect differences in environments, target resources, or cultural traditions. Thus a foraging mode of production may be based on individual hunters or teams, depending on whether the game is a solitary or a herd animal. Gathering is usually more individualistic than hunting, although collecting teams may assemble when

What kind of agricultural division of labor is suggested by this photo of women harvesting in Thailand? How does it compare with Madagascar, as discussed in the text?

abundant resources ripen and must be harvested quickly. Fishing may be done alone (as in ice or spear fishing) or in crews (as with open sea fishing and hunting of sea mammals).

Production in Nonindustrial Societies

Although some kind of division of economic labor related to age and gender is a cultural universal, the specific tasks assigned to each sex and to people of different ages vary. Many horticultural societies assign a major productive role to women, but some make men's work primary. Similarly, among pastoralists men generally tend large animals, but in some societies women do the milking. Jobs accomplished through teamwork in some cultivating societies are done in other societies by smaller groups or by individuals working over a longer period.

The Betsileo of Madagascar have two stages of teamwork in rice cultivation: transplanting and harvesting. Both feature a traditional division of labor by age and gender which is well known to all Betsileo and is repeated across the generations. The first job in transplanting is the trampling of a previously tilled flooded field by young men driving cattle, in order to mix earth and water. They bring cattle to trample the fields just before transplanting. The young men yell at and beat the cattle, striving to drive them into a frenzy so that they will trample the fields properly. Trampling breaks up clumps of earth and mixes irrigation water with soil to form a smooth mud into which women transplant seedlings. Once the tramplers leave the field, older men arrive. With their spades they break up the clumps that the cattle missed. Meanwhile, the owner and other adults uproot rice seedlings and bring them to the field. Women plant the seedlings.

At harvest time, four or five months later, young men cut the rice off the stalks. Young women carry it to the clearing above the field. Older women arrange and stack it. The oldest men and women then stand on the stack, stomping and compacting it. Three days later, young men thresh the rice, beating the stalks against a rock to remove the grain. Older men then attack the stalks with sticks to make sure all the grains have fallen off.

Means of Production

In nonindustrial societies there is a more intimate relationship between the worker and the means of production than there is in industrial nations. **Means, or factors, of production** include land (territory), labor, and technology.

Land   Among foragers, ties between people and land are less permanent than they are among food producers. Although many bands have territories, the boundaries are not usually marked, and there is no way they can be enforced. The hunter's stake in an animal is more important than where the animal finally dies. A person acquires the rights to use a band's territory by being born in the band or by joining it through a tie of kinship, marriage, or fictive kinship. In Botswana in southern Africa, Ju/'hoansi San women, whose work provides over half the food, habitually use specific tracts of berry-bearing trees. When a woman changes bands, she immediately acquires a new gathering area.

Among food producers, rights to the means of production also come through kinship and marriage. Descent groups (groups whose members claim common ancestry) are common among nonindustrial food producers, and those who descend from the founder share the group's territory and resources. If the adaptive strategy is horticulture, the estate includes garden and fallow land for shifting cultivation. As members of a descent group, pastoralists have access to animals to start their own herds, to grazing land, to garden land, and to other means of production.

Labor, Tools, and Specialization   Like land, labor is a means of production. In nonindustrial societies, access to both land and labor comes through social links such as kinship, marriage, and descent. Mutual aid in production is merely one aspect of ongoing social relations that are expressed on many other occasions.

Nonindustrial societies contrast with industrial nations regarding another means of production—technology. In bands and tribes manufacturing is often linked to age and gender. Women may weave and men may make pottery or vice versa. Most people of a particular age and gender share the technical knowledge associated with that age and gender. If married women customarily make baskets, most married women know how to make baskets. Neither technology nor technical knowledge is as specialized as it is in states.

Some tribal societies, however, do promote specialization. Among the Yanomami of Venezuela and Brazil, for instance, certain villages manufacture clay pots and others make hammocks. They don't specialize, as one might suppose, because certain raw materials happen to be available near particular villages. Clay suitable for pots is widely available. Everyone knows how to make pots, but not everybody does so. Craft specialization reflects the social and political environment rather than the natural environment. Such specialization promotes trade, which is the first step in creating an alliance with enemy villages (Chagnon 1997).

Alienation in Industrial Economies

There are some significant contrasts between industrial and nonindustrial economies. When factory workers produce for sale and for their employer's profit, they may be alienated from the items they make. Such alienation means they don't feel strong pride in or personal identification with their products. They see their product as belonging to someone else, not to the man or woman whose labor actually produced it. In nonindustrial societies, by contrast, people usually see their work through from start to finish and have a sense of accomplishment in the product.

In nonindustrial societies the economic relation between coworkers is just one aspect of a more general social relation. They aren't just coworkers but kin, in-laws, or celebrants in the same ritual. In industrial nations, people don't usually work with relatives and neighbors. If coworkers are friends, the personal relationship usually develops out of their common employment rather than being based on a previous association.

Thus, industrial workers have impersonal relations with their products, coworkers, and employers. People sell their labor for cash, and the economic domain stands apart from ordinary social life. In nonindustrial societies, however, the relations of production, distribution, and consumption are *social relations with economic aspects*. Economy is not a separate entity but is *embedded* in the society.

ECONOMIZING AND MAXIMIZATION

Economic anthropologists have been concerned with two main questions:

1.   How are production, distribution, and consumption organized in different societies? This question focuses on *systems* of human behavior and their organization.

2. What motivates people in different societies to produce, distribute or exchange, and consume? Here the focus is not on systems of behavior but on the *individuals* who participate in those systems.

Anthropologists view both economic systems and motivations in a cross-cultural perspective. Motivation is a concern of psychologists, but it has also been, implicitly or explicitly, a concern of economists and anthropologists. American economists assume that producers and distributors make decisions rationally, using the *profit motive,* as do consumers when they shop around for the best value. Although anthropologists know that the profit motive is not universal, the assumption that individuals try to maximize profits is basic to capitalism and to Western economic theory. In fact, the subject matter of economics is often defined as economizing, or the rational allocation of scarce means (or resources) to alternative ends (or uses).

What does that mean? Classical economic theory assumes that our wants are infinite and our means are limited. Since means are limited, people must make choices about how to use their scarce resources—their time, labor, money, and capital. (The box at the end of this chapter disputes the idea that people always make economic choices based on scarcity.) Western economists assume that when confronted with choices and decisions, people tend to make the one that maximizes profit. This is assumed to be the most rational choice.

The idea that individuals choose to maximize profits was a basic assumption of the classical economists of the nineteenth century and one held by many contemporary economists. However, certain economists now recognize that individuals in Western societies, as in others, may be motivated by many other goals. Depending on the society and the situation, people may try to maximize profit, wealth, prestige, pleasure, comfort, or social harmony. Individuals may want to realize their personal or family ambitions or those of another group to which they belong.

Alternative Ends

To what uses do people in various societies put their scarce resources? Throughout the world, people devote some of their time and energy to building up a *subsistence fund* (Wolf 1966). In other words, they have to work to eat, to replace the calories they use in their daily activity. People must also invest in a *replacement fund*. They must maintain their technology and other items essential to production. If a hoe or plow breaks, they must repair or replace it. They must also obtain and replace items that are essential not to production but to everyday life, such as clothing and shelter.

People everywhere also have to invest in a *social fund*. They have to help their friends, relatives, in-laws, and neighbors. It is useful to distinguish between a social fund and a *ceremonial fund*. The latter term refers to expenditures on ceremonies or rituals. To prepare a festival honoring one's ancestors, for example, requires time and the outlay of wealth.

Citizens of nonindustrial states must also allocate scarce resources to a *rent fund*. We think of rent as payment for the use of property. Rent fund, however, has a wider meaning. It refers to resources that people must render to an individual or agency that is superior politically or economically. Tenant farmers and sharecroppers, for example, either pay rent or give some of their produce to their landlords, as peasants did under feudalism.

Peasants are small-scale agriculturists who live in nonindustrial states and have rent fund obligations (see Kearney 1996). They produce to feed themselves, to sell their produce, and to pay rent. All peasants have two things in common:

1. They live in state-organized societies.
2. They produce food without the elaborate technology—chemical fertilizers, tractors, airplanes to spray crops, and so on—of modern farming or agribusiness.

Besides paying rent to landlords, peasants must satisfy government obligations, paying taxes in the form of money, produce, or labor. The rent fund is not simply an *additional* obligation for peasants. Often it becomes their foremost and unavoidable duty. Sometimes, to meet the obligation to pay rent, their own diets suffer. The demands of social superiors may divert resources from subsistence, replacement, social, and ceremonial funds.

Motivations vary from society to society, and people often lack freedom of choice in allocating their resources. Because of obligations to pay rent, peasants may allocate their scarce means toward ends that are not their own but those of government officials. Thus, even in societies in which there is a profit motive, people are often prevented from rationally maximizing self-interest by factors beyond their control.

DISTRIBUTION, EXCHANGE

The economist Karl Polanyi (1968) stimulated the comparative study of exchange, and several anthropologists followed his lead. To study exchange cross-culturally, Polanyi defined three principles orienting exchanges: the market principle, redistribution, and reciprocity. These principles can all be present in the same society, but in that case they govern different kinds of transactions. In any society, one of them usually dominates. The principle of exchange that dominates in a given society is the one that allocates the means of production.

The Market Principle

In today's world capitalist economy, the **market principle** dominates. It governs the distribution of the means of production—land, labor, natural resources, technology, and capital. With market exchange, items are bought and sold, using money, with an eye to maximizing profit, and value is determined by the *law of supply and demand* (things cost more the scarcer they are and the more people want them). Bargaining is characteristic of market-principle exchanges. The buyer and seller strive to maximize—to get their "money's worth." Bargaining doesn't require that the buyer and seller meet. Consumers bargain whenever they shop around or use advertisements in their decision making.

Redistribution

Redistribution operates when goods, services, or their equivalent move from the local level to a center. The center may be a capital, a regional collection point, or a storehouse near a chief's residence. Products often move through a hierarchy of officials for storage at the center. Along the way officials and their dependents may consume some of them, but the exchange principle here is *re*distribution. The flow of goods eventually reverses direction—out from the center, down through the hierarchy, and back to the common people.

One example of a redistributive system comes from the Cherokee, the original owners of the Tennessee Valley. Productive farmers who subsisted on maize, beans, and squash, supplemented by hunting and fishing, the Cherokee had chiefs. Each of their main villages had a central plaza, where meetings of the chief's council took place and where redistributive feasts were held. According to Cherokee custom, each family farm had an area where the family, if they wished, could set aside part of their annual harvest for the chief. This supply of corn was used to feed the needy, as well as travelers and warriors journeying through friendly territory. This store of food was available to all who needed it, with the understanding that it "belonged" to the chief and was dispersed through his generosity. The chief also hosted the redistributive feasts held in the main settlements (Harris 1978).

Reciprocity

Reciprocity is exchange between social equals, who are normally related by kinship, marriage, or another close personal tie. Because it occurs between social equals, it is dominant in the more egalitarian societies—among foragers, cultivators, and pastoralists. There are three degrees of reciprocity: *generalized, balanced,* and *negative* (Sahlins 1968, 1972; Service 1966). These may be imagined as areas of a continuum defined by these questions:

1. How closely related are the parties to the exchange?
2. How quickly and unselfishly are gifts reciprocated?

Generalized reciprocity, the purest form of reciprocity, is characteristic of exchanges between closely related people. In balanced reciprocity, social distance increases, as does the need to reciprocate. In negative reciprocity, social distance is greatest and reciprocation is most calculated.

With **generalized reciprocity,** someone gives to another person and expects nothing concrete or immediate in return. Such exchanges are not primarily economic transactions but expressions of personal relationships. Most parents don't keep accounts of every penny they spend on their children. They merely hope that the children will respect their culture's customs involving love, honor, loyalty, and other obligations to parents.

Among foragers, generalized reciprocity tends to govern exchanges. People routinely share with other band members (Bird-David 1992; Kent 1992). So strong is the ethic of reciprocal sharing that most foragers lack an expression for "thank you." To offer thanks would be impolite because it would imply that a particular act of sharing, which is the keystone of egalitarian society, was unusual. Among the Semai, foragers of central Malaysia (Dentan 1979), to express gratitude would suggest surprise at the hunter's generosity or success (Harris 1974).

Balanced reciprocity applies to exchanges between people who are more distantly related than are members of the same band or household. In a horticultural society, for example, a man presents a gift to someone in another village. The recipient may be a cousin, a trading partner, or a brother's fictive kinsman. The giver expects something in return. This may not come immediately, but the social relationship will be strained if there is no reciprocation.

Exchanges in nonindustrial societies may also illustrate **negative reciprocity,** mainly in dealing with people outside or on the fringes of their social systems. To people who live in a world of close personal relations, exchanges with outsiders are full of ambiguity and distrust. Exchange is one way of establishing friendly relations with outsiders, but especially when trade begins, the relationship is still tentative. Often the initial exchange is close to being purely economic; people want to get something back immediately. Just as in market economies, but without using money, they try to get the best possible immediate return for their investment.

Generalized reciprocity and balanced reciprocity are based on trust and a social tie. Negative reciprocity involves the attempt to get something for as little as possible, even if it means being cagey or deceitful or cheating. Among the most extreme and "negative" examples of negative reciprocity was nineteenth century horse thievery by North American Plains Indians. Men would sneak into camps and villages of neighboring tribes to steal horses. A similar pattern of livestock (cattle) raiding continues today in East Africa, among tribes such as the Kuria (Fleisher 2000). In these cases, the party that starts the raiding can expect reciprocity—a raid on their own village—or worse. The Kuria hunt down cattle thieves and kill them. It's still reciprocity, governed by "Do unto others as they have done unto you."

One way of reducing the tension in situations of potential negative reciprocity is to engage in "silent trade." One example is the silent trade of the Mbuti "pygmy" foragers of the African equatorial forest and their neighboring horticultural villagers. There is no personal contact during their exchanges. A Mbuti hunter leaves game, honey, or another forest product at a customary site. Villagers collect it and leave crops in exchange. Often the parties bargain silently. If one feels the return is insufficient, he or she simply leaves it at the trading site. If the other party wants to continue trade, it will be increased.

Coexistence of Exchange Principles

In today's North America, the market principle governs most exchanges, from the sale of the means of production to the sale of consumer goods. We also have redistribution. Some of our tax money goes to support the government, but some of it also comes back to us in the form of social services, education, health care, and road building. We also have reciprocal exchanges. Generalized reciprocity characterizes the relationship between parents and children. However, even here the dominant market mentality surfaces in comments about the high cost of raising children and in the stereotypical statement of the disappointed parent: "We gave you everything money could buy."

Exchanges of gifts, cards, and invitations exemplify reciprocity, usually balanced. Everyone has heard remarks like "They invited us to their daughter's wedding, so when ours gets married, we'll have to invite them" and "They've been here for dinner three times and haven't invited us yet. I don't think we should ask them back until they do." Such precise balancing of reciprocity would be out of place in a foraging band, where resources are communal (common to all) and daily sharing based on generalized reciprocity is an essential ingredient of social life and survival.

POTLATCHING

One of the most famous cultural practices studied by ethnographers is the **potlatch.** This is a festive event within a regional exchange system among tribes of the North Pacific Coast of North America, including the Salish and Kwakiutl of Washington and British Columbia. Some tribes still practice the potlatch, sometimes as a memorial to the dead (Kan 1986, 1989). At each such event, assisted by members of their communities, potlatch sponsors traditionally gave away food, blankets, pieces of copper, or other items. In return for this, they got prestige. To give a potlatch enhanced one's reputation. Prestige increased with the lavishness of the potlatch, the value of the goods given away in it.

The potlatching tribes were foragers, but atypical ones for relatively recent times. They were sedentary and had chiefs. And unlike the environments of most other recent foragers, theirs wasn't marginal. They had access to a wide variety of land and sea resources. Among their most important foods were salmon, herring, candlefish, berries, mountain goats, seals, and porpoises (Piddocke 1969).

This historic photo shows Tlingit clan members attending a
potlatch at Sitka, Alaska in 1904. Such ancestral headdresses have
been repatriated recently from museums back to Tlingit clans. Have
you ever partaken in anything like a potlatch?

If the profit motive is universal, with the goal of maximizing material
benefits, how does one explain the potlatch, in which wealth is given away?
Many scholars once cited the potlatch as a classic case of economically
wasteful behavior. In this view, potlatching was based on an economically ir-
rational drive for prestige. This interpretation stressed the lavishness and
supposed wastefulness, especially of the Kwakiutl displays, to support the
contention that in some societies people strive to maximize prestige at the
expense of their material well-being. This interpretation has been challenged.

Ecological anthropology, also known as *cultural ecology*, is a theoretical
school that attempts to interpret cultural practices, such as the potlatch, in
terms of their long-term role in helping humans adapt to their environments. A different interpretation of the potlatch has been offered by
the ecological anthropologists Wayne Suttles (1960) and Andrew Vayda
(1961/1968). These scholars see potlatching not in terms of its immediate
wastefulness, but in terms of its long-term role as a cultural adaptive mechanism. This view not only helps us understand potlatching, it also has comparative value because it helps us understand similar patterns of lavish
feasting throughout the world. Here is the ecological interpretation: Customs such as the potlatch are cultural adaptations to alternating periods of
local abundance and shortage.

How does this work? The overall natural environment of the North Pacific Coast is favorable, but resources fluctuate from year to year and place
to place. Salmon and herring aren't equally abundant every year in a given
locality. One village can have a good year while another is experiencing a

bad one. Later their fortunes reverse. In this context, the potlatch cycle of the Kwakiutl and Salish had adaptive value, and the potlatch was not a competitive display that brought no material benefit.

A village enjoying an especially good year had a surplus of subsistence items, which it could trade for more durable wealth items, blankets, canoes, or pieces of copper. Wealth, in turn, by being distributed, could be converted into prestige. Members of several villages were invited to any potlatch and got to take home the resources that were given away. In this way, potlatching linked villages together in a regional economy—an exchange system that distributed food and wealth from wealthy to needy communities. In return, the potlatch sponsors and their villages got prestige. The decision to potlatch was determined by the health of the local economy. If there had been subsistence surpluses, and thus a buildup of wealth over several good years, a village could afford a potlatch to convert its food and wealth into prestige.

The long-term adaptive value of intercommunity feasting becomes clear when we consider what happened when a formerly prosperous village had a run of bad luck. Its people started accepting invitations to potlatches in villages that were doing better. The tables were turned as the temporarily rich became temporarily poor and vice versa. The newly needy accepted food and wealth items. They were willing to receive rather than bestow gifts and thus to relinquish some of their stored-up prestige. They hoped their luck would eventually improve so that resources could be recouped and prestige regained.

The potlatch linked local groups along the North Pacific Coast into a regional alliance and exchange network. Potlatching and intervillage exchange had adaptive functions, regardless of the motivations of the individual participants. The anthropologists who stressed rivalry for prestige were not wrong. They were merely emphasizing motivations at the expense of an analysis of economic and ecological systems.

The use of feasts to enhance individual and community reputations and to redistribute wealth is not peculiar to populations of the North Pacific Coast. Competitive feasting is widely characteristic of nonindustrial food producers. But among most surviving foragers, who live, remember, in marginal areas, resources are too meager to support feasting on such a level. In such societies, sharing rather than competition prevails.

Like many other cultural practices that have attracted considerable anthropological attention, the potlatch does not, and did not, exist apart from larger world events. For example, within the spreading world capitalist economy of the nineteenth century, the potlatching tribes, particularly the Kwakiutl, began to trade with Europeans (fur for blankets, for example). Their wealth increased as a result. Simultaneously, a huge proportion of the Kwakiutl population died from previously unknown diseases brought by the Europeans. As a result, the increased wealth from trade flowed into a drastically reduced population. With many of the traditional sponsors dead (such as chiefs and their families), the Kwakiutl extended the right to give a potlatch to the entire population. This stimulated very intense competition for prestige. Given trade, increased wealth, and a decreased population, the

Kwakiutl also started converting wealth into prestige by destroying wealth items such as blankets, pieces of copper, and houses (Vayda 1961/1968). Blankets and houses could be burned, and coppers could be buried at sea. Here, with dramatically increased wealth and a drastically reduced population, Kwakiutl potlatching changed its nature. It became much more destructive than it had been previously and than potlatching continued to be among tribes that were less affected by trade and disease.

In any case, note that potlatching also served to prevent the development of socioeconomic stratification, a system of social classes. Wealth relinquished or destroyed was converted into a nonmaterial item—prestige. Under capitalism we reinvest our profits (rather than burning our cash), with the hope of making an additional profit. However, the potlatching tribes were content to relinquish their surpluses rather than use them to widen the social distance between themselves and their fellow tribe members.

Summary

1. Cohen's adaptive strategies include foraging (hunting and gathering), horticulture, agriculture, pastoralism, and industrialism. Foraging was the only human adaptive strategy until the advent of food production (farming and herding) 10,000 years ago. Food production eventually replaced foraging in most places. Almost all modern foragers have some dependence on food production or food producers.

2. Horticulture doesn't use land or labor intensively. Horticulturalists cultivate a plot for one or two years (sometimes longer) and then abandon it. There is always a fallow period. Agriculturalists farm the same plot of land continuously and use labor intensively. They use one or more of the following: irrigation, terracing, domesticated animals as means of production, and manuring.

3. The pastoral strategy is mixed. Nomadic pastoralists trade with cultivators. Part of a transhumant pastoral population cultivates while another part takes the herds to pasture. Except for some Peruvians and the Navajo, who are recent herders, the New World lacks native pastoralists.

4. Economic anthropology is the cross-cultural study of systems of production, distribution, and consumption. In nonindustrial societies, a kin-based mode of production prevails. One acquires rights to resources and labor through membership in social groups, not impersonally through purchase and sale. Work is just one aspect of social relations expressed in varied contexts.

5. Economics has been defined as the science of allocating scarce means to alternative ends. Western economists assume the notion of scarcity is universal—which it isn't—and that in making choices, people strive

to maximize personal profit. In nonindustrial societies, indeed as in our own, people often maximize values other than individual profit. Furthermore, people may lack free choice in allocating their resources.

6. In nonindustrial societies, people invest in subsistence, replacement, social, and ceremonial funds. States add a rent fund: People must share their output with their social superiors. In states, the obligation to pay rent often becomes primary.

7. Besides studying production, economic anthropologists study and compare exchange systems. The three principles of exchange are the market principle, redistribution, and reciprocity, which may coexist in a given society. The primary exchange mode is the one that allocates the means of production.

8. Patterns of feasting and exchanges of wealth among villages are common among nonindustrial food producers, as among the potlatching societies of North America's North Pacific Coast. Such systems help even out the availability of resources over time.

Case Study
Basseri

This chapter has examined systems of production, distribution, and consumption among societies with various adaptive strategies. In *Culture Sketches* by Holly Peters-Golden read the chapter on the Basseri: Pastoral Nomads on the il-Rah. What are some ways in which the Basseri's adaptive strategy, pastoral nomadism, influences their other social institutions and relationships? How might Basseri life change with increasing sedentism?

Scarcity and the Betsileo

From October 1966 through December 1967 my wife and I lived among the Betsileo people of Madagascar, studying their economy and social life (Kottak 1980). Soon after our arrival we met two well-educated schoolteachers who were interested in our research. The woman's father was a congressman who became a cabinet minister during our stay. Our schoolteacher friends told us that their family came from a historically impor-

tant and typical Betsileo village called Ivato, which they invited us to visit with them.

We had traveled to many other villages, where we were often displeased with our reception. As we drove up, children would run away screaming. Women would hurry inside. Men would retreat to doorways, where they lurked bashfully. Eventually someone would summon the courage to ask what we wanted. This behavior expressed the Betsileo's great fear of the *mpakafo*. Believed to cut out and devour his victim's heart and liver, the *mpakafo* is the Malagasy vampire. These cannibals are said to have fair skin and to be very tall. Because I have light skin and stand six feet four inches tall, I was a natural suspect. The fact that such creatures were not known to travel with their wives helped convince the Betsileo that I wasn't really a *mpakafo*.

When we visited Ivato, we found that its people were different. They were friendly and hospitable. Our very first day there we did a brief census and found out who lived in which households. We learned people's names and their relationships to our schoolteacher friends and to each other. We met an excellent informant who knew all about the local history. In a few afternoons I learned much more than I had in the other villages in several sessions.

Ivatans were willing to talk because I had powerful sponsors, village natives who had made it in the outside world, people the Ivatans knew would protect them. The schoolteachers vouched for us, but even more significant was the cabinet minister, who was like a grandfather and benefactor to everyone in town. The Ivatans had no reason to fear me because their more influential native son had asked them to answer my questions.

Once we moved to Ivato, the elders established a pattern of visiting us every evening. They came to talk, attracted by the inquisitive foreigners but also by the wine, cigarettes, and food we offered. I asked questions about their customs and beliefs. I eventually developed interview schedules about various subjects, including rice production. I mimeographed these forms to use in Ivato and in two other villages I was studying less intensively. Never have I interviewed as easily

as I did in Ivato. So enthusiastic were the Ivatans about my questions that even people from neighboring villages came to join the study. Since these people knew nothing about the social scientist's techniques, I couldn't discourage them by saying that they weren't in my sample. Instead, I agreed to visit each village, where I filled out the interview schedule in just one house. Then I told the other villagers that the household head had done such a good job of teaching me about their village I wouldn't need to ask questions in the other households.

As our stay drew to an end, the elders of Ivato began to lament, saying, "We'll miss you. When you leave, there won't be any more cigarettes, any more wine, or any more questions." They wondered what it would be like for us back in the United States. They knew that I had an automobile and that I regularly purchased things, including the wine, cigarettes, and food I shared with them. I could afford to buy products they would never have. They commented, "When you go back to your country, you'll need a lot of money for things like cars, clothes, and food. We don't need to buy those things. We make almost everything we use. We don't need as much money as you, because we produce for ourselves."

The Betsileo are not unusual among people whom anthropologists have studied. Strange as it may seem to an American consumer, some rice farmers actually believe that *they have all they need*. The lesson from the Betsileo is that scarcity, which economists view as universal, is variable. Although shortages do arise in nonindustrial societies, the concept of scarcity (insufficient means) is much less developed in stable subsistence-oriented societies than in the societies characterized by industrialism, particularly as the reliance on consumer goods increases.

Chapter 6

Families, Kinship, and Marriage

The kinds of societies that anthropologists traditionally have studied have stimulated a strong interest in families, along with larger systems of kinship and marriage. The web of kinship—as vitally important in daily life in nonindustrial societies as work outside the home is in our own—has become an essential part of anthropology because of its importance to the people we study. We are ready to take a closer look at the systems of kinship and marriage that have organized human life for much of our history.

Ethnographers quickly recognize social divisions, groups, within any society they study. In the field, the anthropologist learns about significant groups by observing their activities and composition. People often live in the same village or neighborhood or work, pray, or celebrate together because they are related in some way. For example, the most significant local groups may consist of descendants of the same grandfather. These people may live in neighboring houses, farm adjoining fields, and help each other in daily tasks. Other sorts of groups, based on other kin links, get together less often.

The nuclear family is one kind of kin group that is widespread in human societies. Other kin groups include extended families (families consisting of three or more generations) and descent groups—lineages and clans. Descent groups, which are composed of people claiming common ancestry, are basic units in the social organization of nonindustrial food producers.

FAMILIES

Nuclear and Extended Families

A nuclear family lasts only as long as the parents and children remain together. Most people belong to at least two nuclear families at different times in their lives. They are born into a family consisting of their parents and siblings. When they reach adulthood, they may marry and establish a nuclear family that includes the spouse and eventually the children. Since most societies permit divorce, some people establish more than one family through marriage.

Anthropologists distinguish between the **family of orientation** (the family in which one is born and grows up) and the **family of procreation** (formed when one marries and has children). From the individual's point of view, the critical relationships are with parents and siblings in the family of orientation and with spouse and children in the family of procreation.

Nuclear family organization is widespread but not universal. In certain societies, the nuclear family is rare or nonexistent. In others, the nuclear family has no special role in social life. Other social units—most notably extended families and descent groups—can assume most or all of the functions otherwise associated with the nuclear family. In other words, there are many alternatives to nuclear family organization.

Consider an example from the former Yugoslavia. Traditionally, among the Muslims of western Bosnia (Lockwood 1975), nuclear families lacked autonomy. Several such families lived in an extended-family household called a *zadruga*. The zadruga was headed by a male household head and his wife, the senior woman. It included married sons and their wives and children, and unmarried sons and daughters. Each nuclear family had a sleeping room, decorated and partly furnished from the bride's trousseau. However, possessions—even clothing and trousseau items—were shared by zadruga members. Such a residential unit is known as a *patrilocal* extended family, because each couple resides in the husband's father's household after marriage.

The zadruga took precedence over its component units. Social interaction was more usual among the women, the men, or the children of the zadruga than between spouses or between parents and children. There were three successive meal settings—for men, women, and children respectively. Traditionally, all children over the age of 12 slept together in boys' or girls' rooms. When a woman wished to visit another village, she sought the permission of the male zadruga head. Although men usually felt closer to their own children than to those of their brothers, they were obliged to treat them equally. Children were disciplined by any adult in the household. When a nuclear family broke up, children under age 7 went with the mother. Older children could choose between their parents. Children were considered part of the household where they were born even if their mother left. One widow

Among herders living in the steppe region of the Mongolian People's Republic, patrilocal extended families often span four generations. Is the family here more like a zadruga or a tarawad?

who remarried had to leave her five children, all over the age of 7, in their father's zadruga, now headed by his brother.

Another example of an alternative to the nuclear family is provided by the Nayars (or Nair), a large and powerful caste on the Malabar Coast of southern India (Gough 1959, Shivaram 1996). Their traditional kinship system was matrilineal (descent traced only through females). Nayar lived in matrilineal extended family compounds called *tarawads*. The tarawad was a residential complex with several buildings, its own temple, granary, water well, orchards, gardens, and land holdings. Headed by a senior woman, assisted by her brother, the tarawad housed her siblings, sisters' children, and other matrikin—matrilineal relatives.

Traditional Nayar marriage seems to have been hardly more than a formality—a kind of coming of age ritual. A young woman would go through a marriage ceremony with a man, after which they might spend a few days together at her tarawad. Then the man would return to his own tarawad, where he lived with his sisters, aunts, and other matrikin. Nayar men belonged to a warrior class, who left home regularly for military expeditions, returning permanently to their tarawad on retirement. Nayar women could have multiple sexual partners. Children became members of the mother's tarawad; they were not considered to be relatives of their biological father. Indeed, many Nayar children didn't even know who their biological father (genitor) was. Child care was the responsibility of the tarawad. Nayar society therefore reproduced itself biologically without the nuclear family.

Industrialism and Family Organization

For many Americans and Canadians, the nuclear family is the only well-defined kin group. Family isolation arises from geographic mobility, which is associated with industrialism, so that a nuclear family focus is characteristic of many modern nations. Born into a family of orientation, North Americans leave home for college or work, and the break with parents is under way. Selling our labor on the market, we often move to places where jobs are available. Eventually most North Americans marry and start a family of procreation.

Many married couples live hundreds of miles from their parents. Their jobs have determined where they live. Such a postmarital residence pattern is **neolocality:** Married couples are expected to establish a new place of residence—a "home of their own." Among middle-class North Americans, neolocal residence is both a cultural preference and a statistical norm. Most middle-class Americans eventually establish households and nuclear families of their own.

There are significant differences between middle-class and poorer North Americans. For example, in the lower class the incidence of *expanded family households* (those that include nonnuclear relatives) is greater than it is in the middle class. When an expanded family household includes three or more generations, it is an **extended family.** Another type of expanded family is the *collateral household*, which includes siblings and their spouses and children.

The higher proportion of expanded family households among poorer Americans has been explained as an adaptation to poverty (Stack 1975). Unable to survive economically as nuclear family units, relatives band together in an expanded household and pool their resources. Adaptation to poverty causes kinship values and attitudes to diverge from middle-class norms. Thus, when North Americans raised in poverty achieve financial success, they often feel obligated to provide financial help to a wide circle of less fortunate relatives.

Changes in North American Kinship

Although the nuclear family remains a cultural ideal for many Americans, Table 6-1 and Figure 6-1 show that nuclear families accounted for just 24 percent of American households in 2000. Other domestic arrangements now outnumber the "traditional" American household more than three to one. There are several reasons for the changing household composition documented in Table 6-1 and Figure 6-1. Women are increasingly joining men in the cash workforce. This often removes them from their family of orientation while making it economically feasible to delay marriage. Furthermore, job demands compete with romantic attachments. The median age at first marriage for American women jumped from 20 years in 1955 to over 25 in 2000 (Saluter 1996, Fields 2001). The comparable ages for men were 23 and 27 (*World Almanac 1992*, p. 943; Fields 2001).

TABLE 6-1	Changes in Family and Household Organization in the United States: 1970 vs. 2000
1970	**2000**
Married couples with children made up 40 percent of households	Married couples with children made up 24 percent of households
3.1 people per household	2.6 people per household
81 percent of households were family households	69 percent of households were family households
21 percent of households had five or more people	10 percent of households had five or more people
People living alone made up 17 percent of households	People living alone made up 26 percent of households
3 million single-mother families	12 million single-mother families
393,000 single-father families	2 million single-father families
45 percent of households included own children under 18	33 percent of households included own children under 18

Source: Fields 2001.

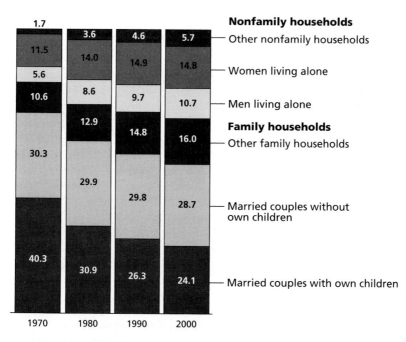

FIGURE 6-1 Households by Type: Selected Years, 1970 to 2000 (percent distribution)
Source: U.S. Census Bureau, Current Population Survey, March Supplements: 1970 to 2000.

Also, the U.S. divorce rate has risen, with the number of divorced Americans more than quadrupling from 4.3 million in 1970 to over 19 million in 2000 (Lugaila 1999). Single-parent families increased from fewer than 4 million in 1970 to 12 million in 2000. Kids in fatherless households tripled from 8 percent in 1960 to 26 percent in 2000. The percentage in motherless households increased from 1 percent in 1960 to 5 percent in 2000. Only 56 percent of American men were currently married in 2000, compared with 65 percent in 1970. The comparable figures for women were 52 percent in 2000 versus 60 percent in 1970 (Fields 2001).

Table 6-2 documents comparable changes in family and household size in the United States and Canada between 1975 and 2000. Those figures confirm a general trend toward smaller families and living units in North America (see also Hansen and Garey, eds. 1998). This trend is also detectable in western Europe and other industrial nations.

The entire range of kin attachments is narrower for North Americans, particularly those in the middle class, than it is for nonindustrial peoples. Although we recognize ties to our grandparents, uncles, aunts, and cousins, we have less contact with, and depend less on, those relatives than people in other cultures do. We see this when we answer a few questions: Do we know exactly how we are related to all our cousins? How much do we know about our ancestors, such as their full names and where they lived? How many of the people with whom we associate regularly are our relatives?

In contemporary North America, single-parent families have increased at a rapid rate. In 1960, 88 percent of American children lived with both parents, compared with 68 percent today. This divorced mom, Valerie Jones, enjoys a candlelight dinner with her kids. What do you see as the main differences between nuclear families and single-parent families?

TABLE 6-2	Household and Family Size in the United States and Canada, 1975 vs. 2000.		
		1975	2000
Average family size:			
United States		3.4	3.2
Canada		3.5	3.1
Average household size:			
United States		2.9	2.6
Canada		2.9	2.6

Sources: Fields 2001; U.S. Census Bureau, *Statistical Abstract of the United States, 2000;* and *Statistics Canada,* Catalogue no. 91-213, http://www.StatCan.CA/english/Pgdb/People/Famili.htm#fam.

Immigrants are often shocked by what they perceive as weak kinship bonds and lack of proper respect for family in contemporary North America. In fact, most of the people whom middle-class North Americans see every day are either nonrelatives or members of the nuclear family. On the other hand, Stack's (1975) study of welfare-dependent families in a ghetto area of a Midwestern city shows that regular sharing with nonnuclear relatives is an important strategy that the urban poor use to adapt to poverty.

The Family among Foragers

Foraging societies are far removed from industrial nations in terms of social complexity. Here again, however, the nuclear family is often the most significant kin group, although in no foraging society is it the only group based on kinship. The two basic social units of traditional foraging societies are the nuclear family and the band.

Unlike middle-class couples in industrial nations, foragers don't usually reside neolocally. Instead, they join a band in which either the husband or the wife has relatives. However, couples and families may move from one band to another several times. Although nuclear families are ultimately as impermanent among foragers as they are in any other society, they are usually more stable than bands are.

Many foraging societies lacked year-round band organization. The Native American Shoshone of Utah and Nevada provide an example. The resources available to the Shoshone were so meager that for most of the year families traveled alone through the countryside hunting and gathering. In certain seasons families assembled to hunt cooperatively as a band, but after just a few months together they dispersed.

Industrial and foraging economies do have something in common. In neither type are people tied permanently to the land. The mobility and the emphasis on small, economically self-sufficient family units promote the nuclear family as a basic kin group in both types of societies.

DESCENT

We've seen that the nuclear family is important in industrial nations and among foragers. The analogous group among nonindustrial food producers is the descent group. A **descent group** is a permanent social unit whose members claim common ancestry. Descent group members believe they all descend from those common ancestors. The group endures even though its membership changes, as members are born and die, move in and move out. Often, descent-group membership is determined at birth and is lifelong. In this case, it is an ascribed status (see Chapter 3).

Descent Groups

Descent groups frequently are exogamous (members seek their mates from other descent groups). Two common rules serve to admit certain people as descent-group members while excluding others. With a rule of **patrilineal descent,** people automatically have lifetime membership in their father's group. The children of the group's men join the group, but the children of the group's women are excluded. With **matrilineal descent,** people join the mother's group automatically at birth and stay members throughout life. Matrilineal descent groups therefore include only the children of the group's women. (In Figures 6-2 and 6-3, which show patrilineal and matrilineal descent groups respectively, the triangles stand for males and the circles for females.) Matrilineal and patrilineal descent are types of **unilineal descent.** This means the descent rule uses one line only, either the male or the female line. Patrilineal descent is much more common than matrilineal descent is. In a sample of 564 societies (Murdock 1957), about three times as many were found to be patrilineal (247 to 84).

Descent groups may be **lineages** or **clans.** Common to both is the belief that members descend from the same *apical ancestor,* the person who stands at the apex, or top, of the common genealogy. For example, Adam and Eve are the apical ancestors of the Biblical Jews, and, according to the Bible, of all humanity. Since Eve is said to have come from Adam's rib, Adam stands as the original apical ancestor for the patrilineal genealogy laid out in the Bible.

How do lineages and clans differ? A lineage uses *demonstrated descent.* Members can recite the names of their forebears in each generation from the apical ancestor through the present. (This doesn't mean their recitations are accurate, only that lineage members think they are.) In the Bible the litany of men who "begat" other men is a demonstration of genealogical descent for a large patrilineage that ultimately includes Jews and Arabs (who share Abraham as their last common apical ancestor).

Unlike lineages, clans use *stipulated descent.* Clan members merely say they descend from the apical ancestor, without trying to trace the actual genealogical links. The Betsileo of Madagascar have both clans and lineages.

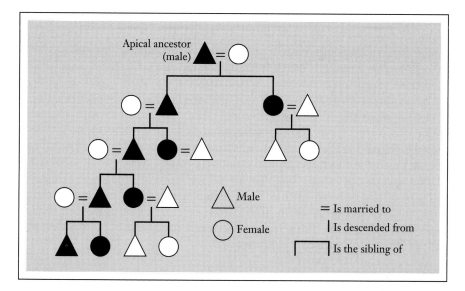

FIGURE 6-2 A patrilineage five generations deep. Lineages are based on demonstrated descent from an apical ancestor. With patrilineal descent, children of the group's men (black) are included as descent-group members. Children of the group's women are excluded; they belong to *their* father's patrilineage. Also, notice lineage exogamy.

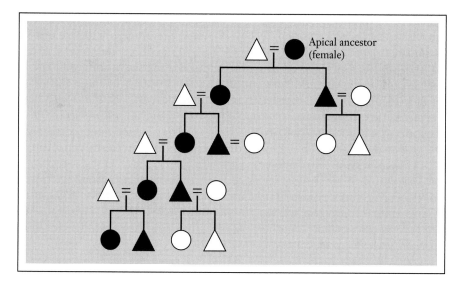

FIGURE 6-3 A matrilineage five generations deep. Matrilineages are based on demonstrated descent from a female ancestor. Only the children of the group's women (black) belong to the matrilineage. The children of the group's men are excluded; they belong to *their* mother's matrilineage.

Descent may be demonstrated for the most recent 8–10 generations, then stipulated for the more remote past—sometimes with mermaids and vaguely defined foreign royalty mentioned among the founders (Kottak 1980). Like the Betsileo, many societies have both lineages and clans. In such a case, clans have more members and cover a larger geographical area than lineages do. Sometimes a clan's apical ancestor is not a human at all but an animal or plant (called a *totem*).

The economic types that usually have descent group organization are horticulture, pastoralism, and agriculture, as discussed in the last chapter. Such societies tend to have several descent groups. Any one of them may be confined to a single village, but they usually span more than one village. Any branch of a descent group that lives in one place is a *local descent group*. Two or more local branches of different descent groups may live in the same village. Descent groups in the same village or different villages may establish alliances through frequent intermarriage.

Lineages, Clans, and Residence Rules

As we've seen, descent groups, unlike families, are permanent and enduring units, with new members added in every generation. Members have access to the lineage estate, where some of them must live, in order to benefit from and manage that estate across the generations. An easy way to keep members at home is to have a rule about who belongs to the descent group and where they should live after they get married. Patrilineal and matrilineal descent, and the post-marital residence rules that usually accompany them, ensure that about half the people born in each generation will live out their lives on the ancestral estate.

Patrilocality is the rule that when a couple marries, it moves to the husband's community, so that their children will grow up in their father's village. Patrilocality is associated with patrilineal descent. This makes sense. If the group's male members are expected to exercise their rights in the ancestral estate, it's a good idea to raise them on that estate and to keep them there after they marry. This can be done by having wives move to the husband's village, rather than vice versa.

A less common postmarital residence rule, often associated with matrilineal descent, is **matrilocality:** Married couples live in the wife's community, and their children grow up in their mother's village. This rule keeps related women together. Together, patrilocality and matrilocality are known as *unilocal* rules of postmarital residence.

MARRIAGE

No definition of marriage is broad enough to apply easily to all societies and situations. A commonly quoted definition comes from *Notes and Queries in Anthropology:*

> Marriage is a union between a man and a woman such that the children born to the woman are recognized as legitimate offspring of both partners. (Royal Anthropological Institute 1951, p. 111)

This definition isn't universally valid for several reasons. One is that marriages may unite more than two spouses. Here we speak of *plural marriages,* as when a woman weds a group of brothers—an arrangement called *fraternal polyandry* that is characteristic of certain Himalayan cultures. Also, some societies, including the modern nations of Belgium and the Netherlands, recognize same-sex marriages. Traditionally in Africa's Sudan a Nuer woman could marry another woman if her father had only daughters but no male heirs, who are necessary if his patrilineage is to survive. He might ask his daughter to stand as a son in order to take a bride. This was a symbolic and social relationship rather than a sexual one. This woman's "wife" had sex with a man or men (whom her female "husband" had to approve) until she got pregnant. The children born to the wife were accepted as the offspring of both husband and wife. Although the female husband was not the actual **genitor,** the biological father of the children, she was their **pater,** or socially recognized father. Kinship is socially constructed. The bride's children were considered the legitimate offspring of her "husband," who was biologically a woman but socially a man, and the descent line continued.

The British anthropologist Edmund Leach (1955) despaired of ever arriving at a universal definition of marriage. Instead, he suggested that depending on the society, several different kinds of rights are transmitted by institutions classified as marriage. These rights vary from one culture to another, and no single one is widespread enough to provide a basis for defining marriage.

According to Leach, marriage can accomplish the following:

1. Establish the legal father of a woman's children and the legal mother of a man's.
2. Give either or both spouses a monopoly in the sexuality of the other.
3. Give either or both spouses rights to the labor of the other.
4. Give either or both spouses rights over the other's property.
5. Establish a joint fund of property—a partnership—for the benefit of the children.
6. Establish a socially significant "relationship of affinity" between spouses and their relatives.

Same-Sex Marriage

Increasingly we hear discussions of same-sex marriage. Gay men and lesbians are the strongest supporters of the idea, while religious conservatives are its strongest opponents. This section on same-sex marriage will serve to illustrate the six rights just listed, by seeing what happens in their absence.

What if same-sex marriages, which are generally illegal in the United States, were legal? Could a same-sex marriage establish legal parentage of

Marriage conveys certain rights, obligations, and benefits. Here we see one of several same-sex couples who were "married" in 1993 at a demonstration in front of the Internal Revenue Service. This Saturday event, at which clergy officiated, was part of a giant 1993 march on Washington for lesbian and gay civil rights, including equal treatment by the IRS.

children born to one or both partners? In the case of a different-sex marriage, children born to the wife after the marriage takes place are legally her husband's regardless of whether or not he is the genitor. Nowadays, of course, DNA testing makes it possible to establish paternity, just as modern reproductive technology makes it possible for a lesbian couple to have one or both partners inseminated. If same-sex marriages were legal, the social construction of kinship could easily make both partners parents. If a Nuer woman married to a woman can be the pater of a child she did not father, why can't two lesbians be the **maters** (socially recognized mothers) of a child one of them did not father. And if a married different-sex couple can adopt a child and have it be theirs through the social and legal construction of kinship, the same logic could be applied to a gay male or lesbian couple.

Continuing with Leach's list of the rights transmitted by marriage, same-sex marriage could certainly give each spouse rights to the sexuality of the other. Unable to marry legally, gay men and lesbians use various devices, such as the mock wedding shown in the photo, to declare their commitment and desire for a monogamous sexual relationship. Same-sex marriages, as forms of monogamous commitment, have been endorsed by representatives of many religions, including Unitarians, Quakers (the Society of Friends), and reform Jewish synagogues (Eskridge 1996).

Same-sex marriages could easily give each spouse rights to the other spouse's labor and its products. Some societies do allow marriage between members of the same biological sex. Several Native American groups had figures known as *berdaches*. These were biological men who assumed many of the mannerisms and activities of women. Sometimes berdaches married men, who shared the products of their labor from hunting and other traditional male roles, as the berdache fulfilled the wifely role. Also, in some Native American cultures, a marriage of a "manly hearted woman" to another woman brought the traditional male-female division of labor to their household. The manly woman hunted and did other male tasks, while the wife played the traditional female role.

There's no logical reason why same-sex marriage could not give spouses rights over the other's property. But in the United States, the inheritance rights that apply to male-female couples do not apply to same-sex couples. For instance, even in the absence of a will, property can pass to a widow or a widower without going through probate. The wife or husband pays no inheritance tax. This benefit is not available to gay men and lesbians. When a same-sex partner is in a nursing home, prison, or hospital, the other partner typically lacks the visiting rights that a husband, wife, or biological relative would have (Weston 1991).

What about Leach's fifth right—to establish a joint fund of property—to benefit the children? Here again gay and lesbian couples are at a disadvantage. If there are children, property is separately, rather than jointly, transmitted. Some organizations do make staff benefits, such as health and dental insurance, available to same-sex domestic partners.

Finally, there is the matter of establishing a socially significant "relationship of affinity" between spouses and their relatives. In many societies one of the main roles of marriage is to establish an alliance between groups, in addition to the individual bond. Affinals are relatives through marriage, such as a brother-in-law or mother-in-law. For same sex-couples in contemporary North America, affinal relations are problematic. In an unofficial union, terms such as "daughter-in-law" and "mother-in-law" may sound strange. Many parents are suspect of their children's sexuality and life style choices and may not recognize a relationship of affinity with a child's partner of the same sex.

This discussion of same-sex marriage has been intended to illustrate the different kinds of rights that typically accompany marriage, by seeing what may happen when there is a permanent pair bond without legal sanction. In 2000 Vermont passed a law making that state the first to offer gay couples virtually all the legal rights and benefits of marriage. At present, no other state legally condones same-sex marriage. As we have seen, same-sex marriages have been recognized in different historical and cultural settings. In situations in which women, such as prominent market women in West Africa, are able to amass property and other forms of wealth, they may take a wife. Such marriage allows the prominent woman to strengthen her social status and the economic importance of her household (Amadiume 1987, Murray and Roscoe, eds. 1998).

Exogamy and the Incest Taboo

In nonindustrial societies, a person's social world includes two main categories—friends and strangers. Strangers are potential or actual enemies. Marriage is one of the primary ways of converting strangers into friends, of creating and maintaining personal and political alliances, relationships of affinity. **Exogamy,** the practice of seeking a mate outside one's own group, has adaptive value because it links people into a wider social network that nurtures, helps, and protects them in times of need.

Incest refers to sexual relations with a close relative. All cultures have taboos against it. However, although the taboo is a cultural universal, cultures define their kin, and thus incest, differently. When unilineal descent is very strongly developed, the parent who does not belong to one's own descent group isn't considered a relative. Thus, with strict patrilineality, the mother is not a relative but a kind of in-law who has married a member of one's own group—one's father. With strict matrilineality, the father isn't a relative, because he belongs to a different descent group.

The Lakher of Southeast Asia are strictly patrilineal (Leach 1961). Using the male ego (the reference point, the person in question) in Figure 6-4, let's suppose that ego's father and mother get divorced. Each remarries and has a daughter by a second marriage. A Lakher always belongs to his or her father's group, all the members of which (one's *agnates*, or patrikin) are considered too closely related to marry because they are members of the same patrilineal descent group. Therefore, ego can't marry his father's daughter by the second marriage, just as in contemporary North America it's illegal for half-siblings to marry.

However, in contrast to our society, where all half-siblings are tabooed in marriage, the Lakher would permit ego to marry his mother's daughter by a different father. She is not ego's relative because she belongs to her own father's descent group rather than ego's. The Lakher illustrate very well that definitions of relatives, and therefore of incest, vary from culture to culture.

Endogamy

The practice of exogamy pushes social organization outward, establishing and preserving alliances among groups. In contrast, rules of **endogamy** dictate mating or marriage within a group to which one belongs. Endogamic rules are less common but are still familiar to anthropologists. Indeed, most cultures *are* endogamous units, although they usually do not need a formal rule requiring people to marry someone from their own society. In our own society, classes and ethnic groups are quasi-endogamous groups. Members of an ethnic or religious group often want their children to marry within that group, although many of them do not do so. The

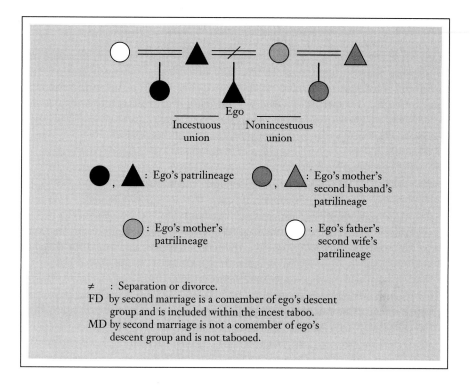

FIGURE 6-4 Patrilineal descent-group identity and incest among the Lakher.

outmarriage rate varies among such groups, with some more committed to endogamy than others.

Caste   An extreme example of endogamy is India's caste system, which was formally abolished in 1949, although its structure and effects linger. Castes are stratified groups in which membership is ascribed at birth and is lifelong. Indian castes are grouped into five major categories, or *varna*. Each is ranked relative to the other four, and these categories extend throughout India. Each varna includes a large number of castes (*jati*), each of which includes people within a region who may intermarry. All the jati in a single varna in a given region are ranked, just as the varna themselves are ranked.

Occupational specialization often sets off one caste from another. A community may include castes of agricultural workers, merchants, artisans, priests, and sweepers. The untouchable varna, found throughout India, includes castes whose ancestry, ritual status, and occupations are considered so impure that higher-caste people consider even casual contact with untouchables to be defiling.

The belief that intercaste sexual unions lead to ritual impurity for the higher-caste partner has been important in maintaining endogamy. A man who has sex with a lower-caste woman can restore his purity with a bath and a prayer. However, a woman who has intercourse with a man of a lower caste has no such recourse. Her defilement cannot be undone. Because the women have the babies, these differences protect the purity of the caste line, ensuring the pure ancestry of high-caste children. Although Indian castes are endogamous groups, many of them are internally subdivided into exogamous lineages. Traditionally this meant that Indians had to marry a member of another descent group from the same caste. This shows that rules of exogamy and endogamy can coexist in the same society.

MARRIAGE ACROSS CULTURES

Outside industrial societies, marriage is often more a relationship between groups than one between individuals. We think of marriage as an individual matter. Although the bride and groom usually seek their parents' approval, the final choice (to live together, to marry, to divorce) lies with the couple. The idea of romantic love symbolizes this individual relationship.

In nonindustrial societies, although there can be romantic love, as we see in the box at the end of the chapter, marriage is a group concern. People don't just take a spouse; they assume obligations to a group of in-laws. When residence is patrilocal, for example, a woman must leave the community where she was born. She faces the prospect of spending the rest of her life in her husband's village, with his relatives. She may even have to transfer her major allegiance from her own group to his.

Bridewealth and Dowry

In societies with descent groups, people enter marriage not alone but with the help of the descent group. Descent-group members often have to contribute to the **bridewealth,** a customary gift before, at, or after the marriage from the husband and his kin to the wife and her kin. Another word for bridewealth is *brideprice*, but this term is inaccurate because people with the custom don't usually think of marriage as a commercial relationship between a man and an object that can be bought and sold.

Bridewealth compensates the bride's group for the loss of her companionship and labor. More important, it makes the children born to the woman full members of her husband's descent group. For this reason, the institution is also called **progeny price.** Rather than the woman herself, it is her children who are permanently transferred to the husband's group. Whatever we call it, such a transfer of wealth at marriage is common in patrilineal groups. In matrilineal societies, children are members of the mother's group, and there is no reason to pay a progeny price.

Dowry is a marital exchange in which the wife's group provides substantial gifts to the husband's family. Dowry, best known from India but also practiced in Europe, correlates with low female status. Women are perceived as burdens. When husbands and their families take a wife, they expect to be compensated for the added responsibility.

Although India passed a law in 1961 against compulsory dowry, the practice continues. When her dowry is considered insufficient, the bride may be harassed and abused. Domestic violence can escalate to the point where the husband or his family burn the bride, often by pouring kerosene on her and lighting it, usually killing her. In 1990, 4,835 Indian women were reported to have been killed in such incidents. (http://metalab.unc.edu/ucis/pubs/Carolina_Papers/Abuse/figure1.html).

Bridewealth exists in many more cultures than dowry does, but the nature and quantity of transferred items differ. In many African societies, cattle constitute bridewealth, but the number of cattle given varies from society to society. As the value of bridewealth increases, *marriages become more stable.* Bridewealth is insurance against divorce.

Imagine a patrilineal society in which a marriage requires the transfer of about twenty-five cattle from the groom's descent group to the bride's. Michael, a member of descent group A, marries Sarah from group B. His relatives help him assemble the bridewealth. He gets the most help from his close agnates—his older brother, father, father's brother, and closest patrilineal cousins.

The distribution of the cattle once they reach Sarah's group mirrors the manner in which they were assembled. Sarah's father, or her oldest brother if the father is dead, receives her bridewealth. He keeps most of the cattle to use as bridewealth for his sons' marriages. However, a share also goes to everyone who will be expected to help when Sarah's brothers marry.

When Sarah's brother David gets married, many of the cattle go to a third group—C, which is David's wife's group. Thereafter, they may serve as bridewealth to still other groups. Men constantly use their sisters' bridewealth cattle to acquire their own wives. In a decade, the cattle given when Michael married Sarah will have been exchanged widely.

In such societies marriage entails an agreement between descent groups. If Sarah and Michael try to make their marriage succeed but fail to do so, both groups may conclude that the marriage can't last. Here it becomes especially obvious that marriages are relationships between groups as well as between individuals. If Sarah has a younger sister or niece (her older brother's daughter, for example), the concerned parties may agree to Sarah's replacement by a kinswoman.

However, incompatibility isn't the main problem that threatens marriage in societies with bridewealth. Infertility is a more important concern. If Sarah has no children, she and her group have not fulfilled their part of the marriage agreement. If the relationship is to endure, Sarah's group must furnish another woman, perhaps her younger sister, who can have children. If this happens, Sarah may choose to stay in her husband's village. Perhaps she will someday have a child. If she does stay on, her husband will have established a plural marriage.

Most nonindustrial food-producing societies, unlike most industrial nations, allow **plural marriages,** or *polygamy*. There are two varieties, one is
common and the other is very rare. The more common variant is **polygyny,**
in which a man has more than one wife. The rare variant is **polyandry,** in
which a woman has more than one husband. If the infertile wife remains
married to her husband after he has taken a substitute wife provided by her
descent group, this is polygyny.

Durable Alliances

It is possible to exemplify the group-alliance nature of marriage by examining still another common practice—continuation of marital alliances when
one spouse dies.

Sororate   What happens if Sarah dies young? Michael's group will ask
Sarah's group for a substitute, often her sister. This custom is known as the
sororate (Figure 6-5). If Sarah has no sister or if all her sisters are already
married, another woman from her group may be available. Michael marries
her, there is no need to return the bridewealth, and the alliance continues.
The sororate exists in both matrilineal and patrilineal societies. In a
matrilineal society with matrilocal postmarital residence, a widower may
remain with his wife's group by marrying her sister or another female
member of her matrilineage (Figure 6-5).

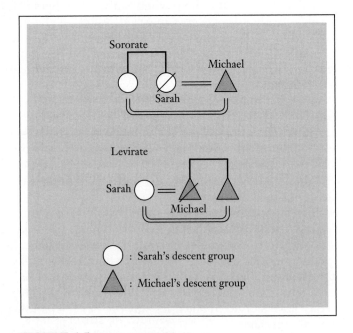

FIGURE 6-5 Sororate and levirate.

Levirate   What happens if the husband dies? In many societies, the widow may marry his brother. This custom is known as the **levirate** (Figure 6-5). Like the sororate, it is a continuation marriage that maintains the alliance between descent groups, in this case by replacing the husband with another member of his group. The implications of the levirate vary with age. A recent study found that in African societies the levirate, although widely permitted, rarely involves cohabitation of the widow and her new husband. Furthermore, widows don't automatically marry the husband's brother just because they are allowed to. Often they prefer to make other arrangements (Potash 1986).

DIVORCE

In some societies marriages may seem to go on forever, but in our own they are fairly brittle. Ease of divorce varies across cultures. What factors work for and against divorce? As we've seen, marriages that are political alliances between groups are more difficult to dissolve than are marriages that are more individual affairs, of concern mainly to the married couple and their children. Substantial bridewealth may decrease the divorce rate for individuals; replacement marriages (levirate and sororate) also work to preserve group alliances. Divorce tends to be more common in matrilineal than in patrilineal societies. When residence is matrilocal (in the wife's home village), the wife may simply send off a man with whom she's incompatible. Divorce is harder in a patrilineal society, especially when substantial bridewealth would have to be reassembled and repaid if the marriage failed. A woman residing patrilocally (in her husband's village) might be reluctant to leave him. Their children, after all, would need to stay with their father, as members of his patrilineage.

Among foragers, different factors favor or oppose divorce. What factors work against durable marriages? Since foragers tend to lack descent groups, the political alliance functions of marriage are less important to them than they are to food producers. Foragers also tend to have minimal material possessions. The process of dissolving a joint fund of property is less complicated when spouses do not hold substantial resources in common. What factors work in opposition to divorce among foragers? In societies in which the family is an important year-round unit with a gender-based division of labor, ties between spouses tend to be durable. Also, sparse populations mean few alternative spouses if a marriage doesn't work out.

In contemporary Western societies, we have the idea that romantic love is necessary for a good marriage (see the box at the end of the chapter). When romance fails, so may the marriage. Or it may not fail, if the other rights associated with marriage, as discussed previously in this chapter, are compelling. Economic ties and obligations to children, along with other factors, such as concern about public opinion, or simple inertia, may keep marriages intact after sex, romance, and/or companionship fade. Also, even in modern societies, royalty, leaders, and other elites may have political marriages similar to arranged marriages.

Divorce is more common now than it was a century ago or even a generation ago. Cherlin (1992) has done a study of changing patterns of American marriage, divorce, and remarriage, using four generations of American women, the first born in 1908–12, the last born in 1970. Although there was little change in the first marriage rate across the generations, the likelihood of divorce changed strikingly. Likelihood for the first generation was 22 percent, versus its double, 44 percent, for women born in 1970. The chance of remarriage and redivorce also increased across the generations. The likelihood of a second divorce was 2 percent for the oldest generation, versus 16 percent for women born in 1970 (see also Simpson 1998).

PLURAL MARRIAGES

In contemporary North America, where divorce is fairly easy and common, polygamy (marriage to more than one spouse at the same time) is against the law. Marriage in industrial nations joins individuals, and relationships between individuals can be severed more easily than can those between groups. As divorce grows more common, North Americans practice *serial monogamy*: Individuals have more than one spouse but never, legally, more than one at the same time. As stated earlier, the two forms of polygamy are polygyny and polyandry. Polyandry is practiced in only a few societies, notably among certain groups in Tibet, Nepal, and India. Polygyny is much more common.

Polygyny

We must distinguish between the social approval of plural marriage and its actual frequency in a particular society. Many cultures approve of a man's having more than one wife. However, even when polygyny is encouraged, most people are monogamous, and polygyny characterizes only a fraction of the marriages. Why?

One reason is equal sex ratios. In the United States, about 105 males are born for every 100 females. In adulthood the ratio of men to women equalizes, and eventually it reverses. The average North American woman outlives the average man. In many nonindustrial societies as well, the male-biased sex ratio among children reverses in adulthood.

The custom of men marrying later than women also promotes polygyny. Among Nigeria's Kanuri people (Cohen 1967), men get married between the ages of eighteen and thirty; women, between twelve and fourteen. The age difference between spouses means there are more widows than widowers. Most of the widows remarry, some in polygynous unions. Among the Kanuri and in other polygynous societies, such as the Tiwi of northern Australia, widows make up a large number of the women involved in plural marriages (Hart, Pilling, and Goodale 1988).

In certain societies, the first wife requests a second wife to help with household chores. The second wife's status is lower than that of the first; they are senior and junior wives. The senior wife sometimes chooses the junior one from among her close kinswomen. Among the Betsileo of Madagascar, the different wives always lived in different villages. A man's first and senior wife, called "Big Wife," lived in the village where he cultivated his best rice field and spent most of his time. High-status men with several rice fields and multiple wives had households near each field. They spent most of their time with the senior wife but visited the others throughout the year.

Plural wives can play important political roles in nonindustrial states. The king of the Merina, a society with more than 1 million people in the highlands of Madagascar, had palaces for each of his twelve wives in different provinces. He stayed with them when he traveled through the kingdom. They were his local agents, overseeing and reporting on provincial matters. The king of Buganda, the major precolonial state of Uganda, took hundreds of wives, representing all the clans in his nation. Everyone in the kingdom became the king's in-law, and all the clans had a chance to provide the next ruler. This was a way of giving the common people a stake in the government.

These examples show there is no single explanation for polygyny. Its context and function vary from society to society and even within the same society. Some men are polygynous because they have inherited a widow from a brother. Others have plural wives because they seek prestige or want to increase household productivity. Men and women with political and economic ambitions cultivate marital alliances that serve their aims. In many societies, including the Betsileo of Madagascar and the Igbo of Nigeria, women arrange the marriages.

Polyandry

Polyandry is rare and is practiced under very specific conditions. Most of the world's polyandrous peoples live in South Asia—Tibet, Nepal, India, and Sri Lanka. In some of these areas, polyandry seems to be a cultural adaptation to mobility associated with customary male travel for trade, commerce, and military operations. Polyandry ensures there will be at least one man at home to accomplish male activities within a gender-based division of labor. Fraternal polyandry is also an effective strategy when resources are scarce. Brothers with limited resources (in land) pool their resources in expanded (polyandrous) households. They take just one wife. Polyandry restricts the number of wives and heirs. Less competition among heirs means that land can be transmitted with minimal fragmentation.

Polyandry in northwest Nepal. The seated young woman is Terribal, age 15. She holds her youngest husband, age 5. Left of Terribal is another husband, age 12. Standing directly behind her is her third husband, age 9. The two older standing men are brothers who are married to the same woman, standing to the right. These are Terribal's "fathers" and mother.

S u m m a r y

1. Kinship and marriage organize social and political life in nonindustrial societies. One widespread kin group is the nuclear family, consisting of a married couple and their children. Other groups, such as extended families and descent groups, may assume functions usually associated with the nuclear family. Nuclear families tend to be especially important in foraging and industrial societies.

2. In contemporary North America, the nuclear family is the characteristic kin group for the middle class. Expanded households and sharing with extended family kin occur more frequently among the poor, who may pool their resources in dealing with poverty. Today, however, even in the American middle class, nuclear family households are declining as single-person households and other domestic arrangements increase.

3. The descent group is a basic kin group among nonindustrial food producers (farmers and herders). Unlike families, descent groups have perpetuity, lasting for generations. Descent-group members share and manage an estate. Lineages are based on demonstrated descent; clans, on stipulated descent. Unilineal (patrilineal and matrilineal) descent is

associated with unilocal (respectively, patrilocal and matrilocal) postmarital residence.

4. Marriage, usually a form of domestic partnership, is hard to define. The discussion of same-sex marriage, which, by and large, is illegal in contemporary North America, illustrates the various rights that go along with different-sex marriages. Marriage establishes the legal parents of children. It gives spouses rights to the sexuality, labor, and property of the other. And it establishes a socially significant "relationship of affinity" between spouses and each other's relatives.

5. All societies have an incest taboo. Because kinship is socially constructed, the taboo applies to different relatives in different societies. Exogamy extends social and political ties outward; endogamy does the reverse. Endogamic rules are common in stratified societies. One extreme example is India, where castes are the endogamous units.

6. In societies with descent groups, marriages are relationships between groups as well as between spouses. With bridewealth, the groom and his relatives transfer wealth to the bride and her relatives. As the bridewealth's value increases, the divorce rate declines. Bridewealth customs show that marriages among nonindustrial food producers create and maintain group alliances. So do the sororate, by which a man marries the sister of his deceased wife, and the levirate, by which a woman marries the brother of her deceased husband.

7. The ease and frequency of divorce vary across cultures. When marriage is a matter of intergroup alliance, as is typically true in societies with descent groups, divorce is less common. A large fund of joint property also complicates divorce.

8. Many societies permit plural marriages. The two kinds of polygamy are polygyny and polyandry. The former involves multiple wives; the latter, multiple husbands. Polygyny is much more common than is polyandry.

Case Study
Tiwi

A tradition, no longer practiced, that all Tiwi females had to be married led to the betrothal of baby girls and the mandatory remarriage of all widows. This practice served several social ends. In *Culture Sketches* by Holly Peters-Golden read the chapter on the Tiwi: Tradition in Australia. How do Tiwi marriage customs illustrate the social functions of marriage, as discussed in this chapter? How do Tiwi customs compare with the rules and functions of marriage in your own society? Have those changed, over time? If so, what might be the reason?

Love and Marriage

Love and marriage, the song says, go together like a horse and carriage. But the link between love and marriage, like the horse-carriage combination, isn't a cultural universal. The following news item describes a cross-cultural survey, published in the anthropological journal *Ethnology*, which found romantic ardor to be widespread, perhaps universal. Previously anthropologists had tended to ignore evidence for romantic love in other cultures, probably because arranged marriages were so common. Today, diffusion, mainly via the mass media, of Western ideas about the importance of love for marriage appears to be influencing marital decisions in other cultures.

Some influential Western social historians have argued that romance was a product of European medieval culture that spread only recently to other cultures. They dismissed romantic tales from other cultures as representing the behavior of just the elites. Under the sway of this view, Western anthropologists did not even look for romantic love among the peoples they studied. But they are now beginning to think that romantic love is universal.

"For decades anthropologists and other scholars have assumed romantic love was unique to the modern West," said Dr. Leonard Plotnicov, an anthropologist at the University of Pittsburgh and editor of the journal *Ethnology*. "Anthropologists came across it in their field work, but they rarely mentioned it because it wasn't supposed to happen."

"Why has something so central to our culture been so ignored by anthropology?" asked Dr. William Jankowiak, an anthropologist at the University of Nevada.

The reason, in the view of Dr. Jankowiak and others, is a scholarly bias throughout the social sciences that viewed romantic love as a luxury in human life, one that could be indulged only by people in Westernized cultures or among the educated elites of other societies. For example it was assumed in societies where life is hard that romantic love has less chance to blossom, because higher economic standards and more leisure time create more opportunity for dalliance. That also contributed to the belief that romance was for the ruling class, not the peasants.

But, said Dr. Jankowiak, "There is romantic love in cultures around the world." Last year Dr. Jankowiak, with Dr. Edward Fischer, an anthropologist at Tulane University, published in *Ethnology* the first cross-cultural study, systematically comparing romantic love in many cultures.

In the survey of ethnographies from 166 cultures, they found what they considered clear evidence that romantic love was known in 147 of them—89 percent. And in the other 19 cultures, Dr. Jankowiak said, the absence of conclusive evidence seemed due more to anthropologists' oversight than to a lack of romance.

Some of the evidence came from tales about lovers, or folklore that offered love potions or other advice on making someone fall in love.

Another source was accounts by informants to anthropologists. For example, Nisa, a !Kung woman among the Bushmen of the Kalahari, made a clear distinction between the affection she felt for her husband and that which she felt for her lovers, which was "passionate and exciting," though fleeting. Of these extramarital affairs, she said: "When two people come together their hearts are on fire and their passion is very great. After a while the fire cools and that's how it stays."

While finding that romantic love appears to be a human universal, Dr. Jankowiak allows that it is still an alien idea in many cultures that such infatuation has anything to do with the choice of a spouse.

"What's new in many cultures is the idea that romantic love should be the reason to marry someone," said Dr. Jankowiak. "Some cultures see being in love as a state to be pitied. One tribe in the mountains of Iran ridicules people who marry for love."

Of course, even in arranged marriages, partners may grow to feel romantic love for each other. For example, among villagers in the Kangra valley of northern India, "people's romantic longings and yearnings ideally would become focused on the person they're matched with by their families," said Dr. Kirin Narayan, an anthropologist at the University of Wisconsin.

But that has begun to change, Dr. Narayan is finding, under the influence of popular songs and movies. "In these villages the elders are worried that the younger men and women are getting a different idea of romantic love, one where you choose a partner yourself," said Dr. Narayan. "There are starting to be elopements, which are absolutely scandalous."

The same trend toward love matches, rather than arranged marriages, is being noted by anthropologists in many other cultures. Among aborigines in Australia's Outback, for example, marriages had for centuries been arranged when children were very young.

That pattern was disrupted earlier in this century by missionaries, who urged that marriage not occur until children reached adolescence. Dr. Victoria Burbank, an anthropologist at the University of California at Davis, said that in premissionary days the average age of a girl at marriage was always before menarche, sometimes as young as 9 years. Today the average age at marriage is 17; girls are more independent by the time their parents try to arrange a marriage for them.

"More and more adolescent girls are breaking away from arranged marriages," said Dr. Burbank. "They prefer to go off into the bush for a 'date' with someone they like, get pregnant, and use that pregnancy to get parental approval for the match."

Even so, parents sometimes are adamant that the young people should not get married. They prefer, instead, that the girls follow the traditional pattern of having their mothers choose a husband for them.

"Traditionally among these people, you can't choose just any son-in-law," said Dr. Burbank. "Ideally, the mother wants to find a boy who is her maternal grandmother's brother's son, a pattern that insures partners are in the proper kin group."

Dr. Burbank added: "These groups have critical ritual functions. A marriage based on romantic love, which ignores what's a proper partner, undermines the system of kinship, ritual, and obligation."

Nevertheless, the rules for marriage are weakening. "In the grandmothers' generation, all marriages were arranged. Romantic love had no place, though there were a few stories of a young man and woman in love running off together. But in the group I studied, in only one recent case did the girl marry the man selected for her. All the rest are love matches."

Source: Daniel Goleman, "Anthropology Goes Looking in All the Old Places," *New York Times,* November 24, 1992, p. B1.

Political Systems

Anthropologists and political scientists share an interest in political systems and organization, but the anthropological approach is global and comparative. Anthropological data reveal substantial variations in power, authority, and legal systems in different societies. (Power is the ability to exercise one's will over others; authority is the socially approved use of power.) (See Cheater, ed. 1999, Kurtz 2001, Wolf with Silverman 2001).

Decades ago the anthropologist Elman Service (1962) listed four types, or levels, of political organization: band, tribe, chiefdom, and state. Bands, as we have seen, are small *kin-based* groups (all members of the group are related to each other by kinship or marriage ties) found among foragers. **Tribes** are associated with nonintensive food production (horticulture and pastoralism). They have villages and/or descent groups, but they lack a formal government and social classes (socioeconomic stratification). In a tribe, there is no reliable means of enforcing political decisions. The **chiefdom** is a form of sociopolitical organization that is intermediate between the tribe and the state. In chiefdoms, social relations are mainly based on kinship, marriage, descent, age, generation, and gender—just as they are in bands and tribes. Although chiefdoms are kin-based, they feature differential access to resources (some people have more wealth, prestige, and power than others do) and a permanent political structure. The **state** is a form of sociopolitical organization based on a formal government structure and socioeconomic stratification.

Many anthropologists have criticized Service's typology for being too neat and simple, because it condenses a wide range of political complexity into just four categories. Nevertheless, Service's typology does offer a handy set of labels for highlighting some major contrasts in political organization.

For example, in bands and tribes, unlike states, the political order, or *polity*, is not a separate entity that stands out from the total social order. In bands and tribes, it is difficult to characterize an act or event as political rather than merely social.

Recognizing that political organization is sometimes just an aspect of social organization, Morton Fried offered this definition:

> Political organization comprises those portions of social organization that specifically relate to the individuals or groups that manage the affairs of *public policy* or seek to control the appointment or activities of those individuals or groups. (Fried 1967, pp. 20–21, emphasis added)

This definition certainly fits contemporary North America. Under "individuals or groups that manage the affairs of public policy" come federal, state (provincial), and local (municipal) governments. Those who seek to control the activities of the groups that manage public policy include such interest groups as political parties, unions, corporations, consumers, activists, action committees, and religious groups.

Fried's definition is much less applicable to bands and tribes, where it is often difficult to detect any "public policy." Consequently, I prefer to speak of *socio*political organization in discussing the regulation or management of interrelations among groups and their representatives. In a general sense *regulation* is the process that ensures that variables stay within their normal ranges, corrects deviations from the norm, and thus maintains a system's

Citizens often use collective action to influence public policy. Politicians are well aware that the elderly are the most reliable of all voters. Shown here, a 1995 Washington, D.C., protest against Medicare cuts. Have your actions ever influenced public policy?

integrity. For *political* regulation, this includes such things as decision making and conflict resolution. The study of political regulation points out those
who make decisions and resolve conflicts (are there formal leaders?).

TYPES AND TRENDS

Ethnographic and archaeological studies in hundreds of places have revealed many correlations between economy and social and political organization. Band, tribe, chiefdom, and state are categories or types in a system
of **sociopolitical typology**. These types are correlated with the adaptive
strategies (*economic typology*) discussed in Chapter 5, "Making a Living."
Thus, foragers (an economic type) tend to have band organization (a sociopolitical type). Similarly, many horticulturalists and pastoralists live in
tribal societies (or, more simply, tribes). The economies of chiefdoms tend
to be based on intensive horticulture or agriculture, but some pastoralists
also participate in chiefdoms. Nonindustrial states usually have an agricultural base.

Food producers tend to have larger, denser populations and more complex economies than foragers do. These features create new regulatory
problems, which lead to more complex relations and linkages. Many
sociopolitical trends reflect the increased regulatory demands associated
with food production. Archaeologists have studied these trends through
time, and cultural anthropologists have observed them among contemporary groups.

This chapter examines a series of societies with different political systems. A common set of questions will be addressed for each. What kinds of
social groups does the society have? How do people affiliate with those
groups? How do the groups link with larger ones? How do the groups represent themselves to each other? How are their internal and external relations regulated? To answer these questions we begin with bands and tribes,
then move on to chiefdoms and states.

FORAGING BANDS

In most foraging societies only two kinds of groups are significant: the nuclear family and the band. Unlike sedentary villages (which appear in tribal
societies), bands are impermanent. They form seasonally as component nuclear families come together. The particular combination of families in a
band may vary from year to year. In such settings the main social building
blocks are the personal relationships of individuals. For example, marriage
and kinship create ties between members of different bands. Because one's
parents and grandparents come from different bands, a person has relatives
in several of these groups. Trade and visiting also link local groups. Inuit

men, for example, traditionally had trade partners, whom they treated almost like brothers, in different bands.

Foraging bands are fairly egalitarian in terms of power and authority, although particular talents do lead to special respect. For example, someone can sing or dance well, is an especially good storyteller, or can go into a trance and communicate with spirits. Band leaders are leaders in name only. They are first among equals. Sometimes they give advice or make decisions, but they have no way to enforce their decisions.

Foragers lack formal **law** in the sense of a legal code that includes trial and enforcement. But they do have methods of social control and dispute settlement. The absence of law doesn't mean total anarchy. The aboriginal Inuit (Hoebel 1954, 1968) provide a good example of methods of settling disputes in stateless societies. As described by E. A. Hoebel (1954) in a study of Inuit conflict resolution, a sparse population of some 20,000 Inuit spanned 9,500 kilometers (6,000 miles) of the Arctic region. The most significant social groups were the nuclear family and the band. Personal relationships linked the families and bands. Some bands had headmen. There were also shamans (part-time religious specialists). However, these positions conferred little power on those who occupied them.

Unlike tropical foragers, among whom gathering—usually a female task—is more important, hunting and fishing by men were the primary Inuit subsistence activities. The diverse and abundant plant foods available in warmer areas were absent in the Arctic. Traveling on land and sea in a bitter environment, Inuit men faced more dangers than women did. The traditional male role took its toll in lives. Adult women would have outnumbered men substantially without occasional female *infanticide* (killing of a baby), which Inuit culture permitted.

Despite this crude (and to us unthinkable) means of population regulation, there were still more adult women than men. This permitted some men to have two or three wives. The ability to support more than one wife conferred a certain amount of prestige, but it also encouraged envy. (**Prestige** is esteem, respect, or approval for culturally valued acts or qualities.) If a man seemed to be taking additional wives just to enhance his reputation, a rival was likely to steal one of them. Most disputes were between men and originated over women, caused by wife stealing or adultery. If a man discovered that his wife had been having sexual relations without his permission, he considered himself wronged.

Although public opinion would not let the husband ignore the matter, he had several options. He could try to kill the wife stealer. However, if he succeeded, one of his rival's kinsmen would surely try to kill him in retaliation. One dispute could escalate into several deaths as relatives avenged a succession of murders. No government existed to intervene and stop such a *blood feud* (a murderous feud between families). However, one could also challenge a rival to a song battle. In a public setting, contestants made up insulting songs about each other. At the end of the match, the audience judged one of them the winner. However, if a man whose wife had been stolen won, there was no guarantee she would return. Often she would decide to stay with her abductor.

Several acts of killing that are crimes in contemporary North America were not considered criminal by the Inuit. Infanticide has already been mentioned. Furthermore, people who felt that, because of age or infirmity, they were no longer useful might kill themselves or ask others to kill them. Old people or invalids who wished to die would ask a close relative, such as a son, to end their lives. It was necessary to ask a close relative to ensure that the kin of the deceased did not take revenge on the killer.

Thefts are common in societies with marked property differentials, like our own, but thefts are uncommon among foragers. Each Inuit had access to the resources needed to sustain life. Every man could hunt, fish, and make the tools necessary for subsistence. Every woman could obtain the materials needed to make clothing, prepare food, and do domestic work. Inuit men could even hunt and fish in territories of other local groups. There was no notion of private ownership of territory or animals.

TRIBAL SOCIETIES

Tribes usually have a horticultural or pastoral economy and are organized by village life and/or descent-group membership. Socioeconomic stratification (i.e., a class structure) and a formal government are absent. Many tribes have small-scale warfare, often as intervillage raiding (see Kelly 2000). Tribes have more effective regulatory mechanisms than foragers do, but tribal societies have no sure means of enforcing political decisions. The main regulatory officials are village heads, "big men," descent-group leaders, village councils, and leaders of pantribal associations. All these figures and groups have limited authority.

Like foragers, horticulturalists tend to be egalitarian, although some have marked *gender stratification*—an unequal distribution of resources, power, prestige, and personal freedom between men and women. Horticultural villages are usually small, with low population density and open access to strategic resources. Age, gender, and personal traits determine how much respect people receive and how much support they get from others. Egalitarianism diminishes, however, as village size and population density increase. Horticultural villages usually have headmen—rarely, if ever, headwomen.

The Village Head

The Yanomami (Chagnon 1997) are Native Americans who live in southern Venezuela and adjacent Brazil. Their tribal society has about 20,000 people living in 200 to 250 widely scattered villages, each with a population between 40 and 250. The Yanomami are horticulturalists who also hunt and gather. Their staple crops are bananas and plantains (a banana-like crop).

There are more significant social groups among the Yanomami than exist in a foraging society. The Yanomami have nuclear families, villages, and descent groups. Their descent groups are patrilineal and exogamous. They span more than one village. However, local branches of two different descent groups may live in the same village and intermarry.

As in many village-based tribal societies, the only leadership position among the Yanomami is that of **village head** (always a man). His authority, like that of the foraging band leader, is severely limited. If a headman wants something done, he must lead by example and persuasion. The headman lacks the right to issue orders. He can only persuade, harangue, and try to influence public opinion. For example, if he wants people to clean up the central plaza in preparation for a feast, he must start sweeping it himself, hoping that his covillagers will take the hint and relieve him.

When conflict erupts, the headman may be called on as a mediator who listens to both sides. He will give an opinion and advice. If a disputant is unsatisfied, the headman can do nothing. He has no power to back up his decisions and no way to impose punishments. Like the band leader, he is first among equals.

A Yanomami village headman must also lead in generosity. Because he must be more generous than any other villager, he cultivates more land. His garden provides much of the food consumed when his village holds a feast for another village. The headman represents the village in its dealings with outsiders. Sometimes he visits other villages to invite people to a feast.

The way a person acts as headman depends on his personal traits and the number of supporters he can muster. One village headman, Kaobawa, intervened in a dispute between a husband and wife and kept him from killing her (Chagnon 1997). He also guaranteed safety to a delegation from a village with which a covillager of his wanted to start a war. Kaobawa was a particularly effective headman. He had demonstrated his fierceness in battle, but he also knew how to use diplomacy to avoid offending other villagers. No one in the village had a better personality for the headmanship. Nor (because Kaobawa had many brothers) did anyone have more supporters. Among the Yanomami, when a group is dissatisfied with a village headman, its members can leave and found a new village; this is done from time to time.

Yanomami society, with its many villages and descent groups, is more complex than a band-organized society. The Yanomami also face more regulatory problems. A headman can sometimes prevent a specific violent act, but there is no government to maintain order. In fact, intervillage raiding in which men are killed and women are captured has been a feature of some areas of Yanomami territory, particularly those studied by Chagnon (1997).

We must also stress that the Yanomami are not isolated from outside events (although there are still uncontacted villages). The Yanomami live in two nation-states, Venezuela and Brazil, and external warfare waged by Brazilian ranchers and miners has increasingly threatened them (*Cultural Survival Quarterly* 1989, Ferguson 1995, Chagnon 1997). During a Brazilian gold rush between 1987 and 1991, one Yanomami died each day, on average, from external attacks. Some 40,000 Brazilian miners had penetrated the Yanomami homeland. Some Indians were killed outright. The miners also waged biological warfare by introducing new diseases, and the swollen population ensured that old diseases became epidemic. By 1991 Brazilian Yanomami were dying at a rate of 10 percent annually, and their fertility rate had dropped to zero. Since then, both the Brazilian and the Venezuelan governments have intervened to protect the Yanomami. The Brazilian president declared a huge Yanomami territory off-limits to outsiders. Unfortunately, local politicians, miners, and ranchers have managed to evade the ban. External attacks pose a much more serious threat to Yanomami survival that does traditional intervillage raiding. The future of the Yanomami remains uncertain.

The "Big Man"

In many areas of the South Pacific, particularly the Melanesian Islands and Papua New Guinea, several native societies have a kind of political leader that we call the big man. The **big man** (usually a male) is an elaborate version of the village head, but there is one very significant difference. The village head's leadership is within one village; the big man has supporters in several villages. He is therefore a regulator of regional political organization. Here we see the trend toward expansion in the scale of a sociopolitical regulation—from village to region.

The Kapauku Papuans live in Irian Jaya, Indonesia (which is on the island of New Guinea). Anthropologist Leopold Pospisil (1963) studied the Kapauku (45,000 people), who grow crops (with the sweet potato as their staple) and raise pigs. Their economy is too complex to be described as simple horticulture. Beyond the household, the only political figure among the Kapauku is the big man, known as a *tonowi*. A tonowi achieves his status through hard work, amassing wealth in pigs and other native riches. Characteristics that can distinguish a big man from his fellows include wealth, generosity, eloquence, physical fitness, bravery, and supernatural powers. Big men are what they are because they have certain personalities. They amass their resources during their lifetimes, rather than inheriting their wealth or position.

Any man who is determined enough can become a big man, because people create their own wealth through hard work and good judgment. Wealth depends on successful pig breeding and trading. As a man's pig herd and prestige grow, he attracts supporters. He sponsors ceremonial pig feasts in which pigs are slaughtered and their meat is distributed to guests.

The big man has some advantages that the Yanomami village head lacks. His wealth exceeds that of his fellows. His primary supporters, in recognition of past favors and anticipation of future rewards, recognize him as a leader and accept his decisions as binding. He is an important regulator of regional events in Kapauku life. He helps determine the dates for feasts and markets. He persuades people to sponsor feasts, which distribute

The "big man" persuades people to organize feasts, which distribute pork and wealth. Shown here is such a regional event, drawing on several villages, in Papua New Guinea. Big men owe their status to their individual personalities rather than to inherited wealth or position. Does our society have equivalents of big men?

pork and wealth. He initiates economic projects that require the cooperation of a regional community.

The Kapauku big man again exemplifies a generalization about leadership in tribal societies: If people achieve wealth and widespread respect and support, they must be generous. The big man works hard not to hoard wealth but to be able to give away the fruits of his labor, to convert wealth into prestige and gratitude. If a big man is stingy, he loses his supporters, and his reputation plummets. The Kapauku take even more extreme measures against big men who hoard. Selfish and greedy rich men may be murdered by their fellows.

Political figures such as the big man emerge as regulators both of demographic growth and of economic complexity. Kapauku cultivation uses varied techniques for specific kinds of land. Labor-intensive cultivation in valleys involves mutual aid in turning the soil before planting. The digging of long drainage ditches is even more complex. Kapauku plant cultivation supports a larger and denser population than does the simpler horticulture of the Yanomami. Kapauku society could not survive in its present form without collective cultivation and political regulation of the more complex economic tasks.

Pantribal Sodalities and Age Grades

We've just seen that events initiated by big men temporarily unite people from different villages. Other sociopolitical mechanisms also serve to link local groups within a region. Often kinship and descent provide such sociopolitical linkages in tribal societies. Clans, for example, often span several villages.

Principles other than kinship also may link local groups. In a modern nation, a labor union, national sorority or fraternity, political party, or religious denomination may provide such a nonkin-based link. In tribes, nonkin groups called associations or *sodalities* may serve the same linking function. Often sodalities are based on common age or gender, with all-male sodalities more common than all-female ones.

Pantribal sodalities (those which extend across the whole tribe, spanning several villages) tend to be found in areas where two or more different societies come into regular contact. They are especially likely to develop when there is warfare between tribes (as opposed to raiding between villages of the same tribe, as practiced by the Yanomami). Sodalities help organize the warfare that men wage against neighboring societies. Since sodalities draw their members from different villages of the same tribe, they can mobilize men in many local groups for attack or retaliation against another tribe. Pantribal sodalities have military value because they facilitate temporary regional mobilization. In particular, pantribal sodalities are common among pastoralists. One society's sodality may organize raids to steal cattle or horses from another.

In the cross-cultural study of nonkin groups, we must distinguish between those which are confined to a single village and those which span several local groups. Only the latter, the pantribal groups, are important in general military mobilization and regional political organization. Localized men's houses and clubs, limited to particular villages, are found in many horticultural societies in tropical South America, Melanesia, and Papua New Guinea. These groups may organize village activities and even intervillage raiding. However, their leaders are similar to village heads and their political scope is mainly local. The following discussion, which continues our examination of the growth in scale of regional sociopolitical organization, concerns pantribal groups.

The best examples of pantribal sodalities come from the Central Plains of North America and from tropical Africa. During the eighteenth and nineteenth centuries, Native American societies of the Great Plains of the United

States and Canada experienced a rapid growth of pantribal sodalities. This development reflected an economic change that followed the spread of horses, which had been reintroduced to the Americas by the Spanish, to the states between the Rocky Mountains and the Mississippi River. Many Plains Indian societies changed their adaptive strategies because of the horse. At first they had been foragers who hunted bison (buffalo) on foot. Later they adopted a mixed economy based on hunting, gathering, and horticulture. Finally they changed to a much more specialized economy based on horseback hunting of bison (eventually with rifles).

As the Plains tribes were undergoing these changes, other Indians also adopted horseback hunting and moved into the Plains. Attempting to occupy the same area, groups came into conflict. A pattern of warfare developed in which the members of one tribe raided another, usually for horses. The new economy demanded that people follow the movement of the bison herds. During the winter, when the bison dispersed, a tribe fragmented into small bands and families. In the summer, as huge herds assembled on the Plains, members of the tribe reunited. They camped together for social, political, and religious activities, but mainly for communal bison hunting.

Only two activities in the new adaptive strategy demanded strong leadership: organizing and carrying out raids on enemy camps (to capture horses) and managing the summer bison hunt. All the Plains societies developed pantribal sodalities, and leadership roles within them, to police the summer hunt. Leaders coordinated hunting efforts, making sure that people did not cause a stampede with an early shot or an ill-advised action. Leaders imposed severe penalties, including seizure of a culprit's wealth, for disobedience.

Some Plains sodalities were **age sets** of increasing rank. Each set included all the men—from that tribe's component bands—born during a certain time span. Each set had its distinctive dance, songs, possessions, and privileges. Members of each set had to pool their wealth to buy admission to the next higher level as they moved up the age hierarchy. Most Plains societies had pantribal warrior associations whose rituals celebrated militarism. As noted previously, the leaders of these associations organized bison hunting and raiding. They also arbitrated disputes during the summer, when many people came together.

Many tribes that adopted this Plains strategy of adaptation had once been foragers for whom hunting and gathering had been individual or small-group affairs. They had never come together previously as a single social unit. *Age and gender were available* as social principles that could quickly and efficiently forge unrelated people into pantribal groups.

Raiding of one tribe by another, this time for cattle rather than horses, was also common in eastern and southeastern Africa, where pantribal sodalities, including age sets, also developed. Among the pastoral Masai of Kenya, men born during the same four-year period were circumcised together and belonged to the same named group, an age set, throughout their lives. The sets moved through grades, the most important of which was the warrior grade. Members of the set who wished to enter the warrior grade were at first discouraged by its current occupants, who eventually vacated the warrior grade and married. Members of a set felt a strong allegiance to one another and eventually had sexual rights to each other's wives. Masai women lacked comparable set organization, but they also passed through culturally recognized age grades: the initiate, the married woman, and the postmenopausal woman.

To understand the difference between an age set and an age grade, think of a college class, the Class of 2004, for example, and its progress through the university. The age set would be the group of people constituting the Class of 2004, while the first ("freshman"), sophomore, junior, and senior years would represent the age grades.

Not all societies with age grades also have age sets. When there are no sets, men can enter or leave a particular grade individually or collectively, often by going through a predetermined ritual. The grades most commonly recognized in Africa are these:

1. Recently initiated youths.
2. Warriors.
3. One or more grades of mature men who play important roles in pan-tribal government.
4. Elders, who may have special ritual responsibilities.

Among the Masai of Kenya, men born during the same four-year period were circumcised together. They belonged to the same named group, an age set, throughout their lives. The sets moved through grades, of which the most important was the warrior grade. Here we see the warrior (*ilmurran*) age grade dancing with a group of girls of a lower age grade (*intoyie*). Do we have any equivalents of age sets or grades in our own society?

In certain parts of West Africa and Central Africa, the pantribal sodalities are *secret societies*, made up exclusively of men or women. Like our college fraternities and sororities, these associations have secret initiation ceremonies. Among the Mende of Sierra Leone, men's and women's secret societies are very influential. The men's group, the Poro, trains boys in social conduct, ethics, and religion and supervises political and economic activities. Leadership roles in the Poro often overshadow village headship and play an important part in social control, dispute management, and tribal political regulation. Like descent, then, age, gender, and ritual can link members of different local groups into a single social collectivity in tribal society and thus create a sense of ethnic identity, of belonging to the same cultural tradition.

Nomadic Politics

Although many pastoralists, such as the Masai, live in tribes, a range of demographic and sociopolitical diversity occurs with pastoralism. A comparison of pastoralists shows that as regulatory problems increase, political hierarchies become more complex. Political organization becomes less personal, more formal, and less kinship-oriented. The pastoral strategy of adaptation does not dictate any particular political organization. Unlike the Masai and other tribal herders, some pastoralists have chiefs and live in nation-states.

The scope of political authority among pastoralists expands considerably as regulatory problems increase in densely populated regions. Consider two Iranian pastoral nomadic tribes—the Basseri and the Qashqai (Salzman 1974). Starting each year from a plateau near the coast, these groups took their animals to grazing land 5,400 meters (17,000 feet) above sea level. The Basseri and the Qashqai shared this route with one another and with several other ethnic groups.

Use of the same pasture land at different times was carefully scheduled. Ethnic-group movements were tightly coordinated. Expressing this schedule is *il-rah*, a concept common to all Iranian nomads. A group's il-rah is its customary path in time and space. It is the schedule, different for each group, of when specific areas can be used in the annual trek.

Each tribe had its own leader, known as the *khan* or *il-khan*. The Basseri khan, because he dealt with a smaller population, faced fewer problems in coordinating its movements than did the leaders of the Qashqai. Correspondingly, his rights, privileges, duties, and authority were weaker. Nevertheless, his authority exceeded that of any political figure we have discussed so far. However, the khan's authority still came from his personal traits rather than from his office. That is, the Basseri followed a particular khan not because of a political position he happened to fill but because of their personal allegiance and loyalty to him as a man. The khan relied on the support of the heads of the descent groups into which Basseri society was divided.

In Qashqai society, however, allegiance shifts from the person to the office. The Qashqai had multiple levels of authority and more powerful chiefs or khans. Managing 400,000 people required a complex hierarchy. Heading it was the il-khan, helped by a deputy, under whom were the heads of constituent tribes, under each of whom were descent-group heads.

A case illustrates just how developed the Qashqai authority structure was. A hailstorm prevented some nomads from joining the annual migration at the appointed time. Although everyone recognized that they were not responsible for their delay, the il-khan assigned them less favorable grazing land, for that year only, in place of their usual pasture. The tardy herders and other Qashqai considered the judgment fair and didn't question it. Thus, Qashqai authorities regulated the annual migration. They also adjudicated disputes between people, tribes, and descent groups.

These Iranian cases illustrate the fact that pastoralism is often just one among many specialized economic activities within complex nation-states and regional systems. As part of a larger whole, pastoral tribes are constantly pitted against other ethnic groups. In these nations, the state becomes a final authority, a higher-level regulator that attempts to limit conflict between ethnic groups. State organization arose not just to manage agricultural economies but also to regulate the activities of ethnic groups within expanding social and economic systems.

CHIEFDOMS

Having looked at bands and tribes, we turn to more complex forms of sociopolitical organization—chiefdoms and states. The first states emerged in the Old World about 5,500 years ago. The first chiefdoms developed perhaps a thousand years earlier, but few survive today. The chiefdom was a transitional form of organization that emerged during the evolution of tribes into states. State formation began in Mesopotamia (currently Iran and Iraq). It next occurred in Egypt, the Indus Valley of Pakistan and India, and northern China. A few thousand years later states also arose in two parts of the western hemisphere—Mesoamerica (Mexico, Guatemala, Belize) and the central Andes (Peru and Bolivia). Early states are known as *archaic states*, or nonindustrial states, in contrast to modern industrial nation-states. Robert Carneiro defines the state as "an autonomous political unit encompassing many communities within its territory, having a centralized government with the power to collect taxes, draft men for work or war, and decree and enforce laws" (Carneiro 1970, p. 733).

The chiefdom and the state, like many categories used by social scientists, are *ideal types*. That is, they are labels that make social contrasts seem sharper than they really are. In reality there is a continuum from tribe to chiefdom to state. Some societies have many attributes of chiefdoms but retain tribal features. Some advanced chiefdoms have many attributes of archaic states and thus are difficult to assign to either category. Recognizing this "continuous change" (Johnson and Earle 2000), some anthropologists speak of "complex chiefdoms" (Earle 1987, 1997), which are almost states.

Political and Economic Systems in Chiefdoms

Chiefdoms developed in several parts of the world, including the circum-Caribbean (e.g., Caribbean islands, Panama, Colombia), lowland Amazonia, what is now the southeastern United States, and Polynesia. Between the emergence and spread of food production and the expansion of the Roman empire, much of Europe was organized at the chiefdom level. Europe reverted to this level for centuries after the fall of Rome in the fifth century A.D. Chiefdoms created the megalithic cultures of Europe, such as the one that built Stonehenge.

Much of our ethnographic knowledge about chiefdoms comes from Polynesia, where they were common at the time of European exploration. In chiefdoms, social relations are mainly based on kinship, marriage, descent, age, generation, and gender—just as they are in bands and tribes. This is a fundamental difference between chiefdoms and states. States bring nonrelatives together and oblige them all to pledge allegiance to a government.

Unlike bands and tribes, however, chiefdoms are characterized by *permanent political regulation* of the territory they administer. They have a clear-cut and enduring regional political system. Chiefdoms may include thousands of people living in many villages and/or hamlets. Regulation is carried out by the chief and his or her assistants, who occupy political offices. An **office** is a permanent position, which must be refilled when it is vacated by death or retirement. Because offices are systematically refilled, the structure of a chiefdom endures across the generations, ensuring permanent political regulation.

In the Polynesian chiefdoms, the chiefs were full-time political specialists in charge of regulating the economy—production, distribution, and consumption. Polynesian chiefs relied on religion to buttress their authority. They regulated production by commanding or prohibiting (using religious taboos) the cultivation of certain lands and crops. Chiefs also regulated distribution and consumption. At certain seasons—often on a ritual occasion such as a first-fruit ceremony—people would offer part of their harvest to the chief through his or her representatives. Products moved up the hierarchy, eventually reaching the chief. Conversely, illustrating obligatory sharing with kin, chiefs sponsored feasts at which they gave back much of what they had received.

Such a flow of resources to and then from a central office is known as *chiefly redistribution*. Redistribution offers economic advantages. If the different areas specialized in particular crops, goods, or services, chiefly redistribution made those products available to the whole society. Chiefly redistribution also played a role in risk management. It stimulated production beyond the immediate subsistence level and provided a central storehouse for goods that might become scarce at times of famine (Earle 1987, 1997). Chiefdoms and archaic states had similar economies, often based on intensive cultivation, and both administered systems of regional trade or exchange.

Social Status in Chiefdoms

Social status in chiefdoms was based on seniority of descent. Because rank, power, prestige, and resources came through kinship and descent, Polynesian chiefs kept extremely long genealogies. Some chiefs (without writing) managed to trace their ancestry back fifty generations. All the people in the chiefdom were thought to be related to each other. Presumably, all were descended from a group of founding ancestors.

The chief (usually a man) had to demonstrate seniority in descent. Degrees of seniority were calculated so intricately on some islands that there were as many ranks as people. For example, the third son would rank below the second, who in turn would rank below the first. The children of an eldest brother, however, would all rank above the children of the next brother, whose children would in turn outrank those of younger brothers. However, even the lowest-ranking person in a chiefdom was still the chief's relative. In

Social status in chiefdoms is based on seniority of descent. In the modern world system, seniority may still confer prestige, but the differences in wealth and power between chiefs and their juniors are often minor. Shown here is a contemporary chief (center) in the Marquesas Islands, Polynesia. How does the status of chief compare with the status of king or queen in today's world?

such a kin-based context, everyone, even a chief, had to share with his or her relatives.

Because everyone had a slightly different status, it was difficult to draw a line between elites and common people. Other chiefdoms calculated seniority differently and had shorter genealogies than did those in Polynesia. Still, the concern for seniority and the lack of sharp gaps between elites and commoners are features of all chiefdoms.

Status Systems in Chiefdoms and States

The status systems of chiefdoms and states are similar in that both are based on **differential access** to resources. This means that some men and women had privileged access to power, prestige, and wealth. They controlled strategic resources such as land, water, and other means of production. Earle characterizes chiefs as "an incipient aristocracy with advantages in wealth and lifestyle" (1987, p. 290). Nevertheless, differential access in chiefdoms was still very much tied to kinship. The people with privileged access were generally chiefs and their nearest relatives and assistants.

Compared with chiefdoms, archaic states drew a much firmer line between elites and masses, distinguishing at least between nobles and commoners. Kinship ties did not extend from the nobles to the commoners because of *stratum endogamy*—marriage within one's own group. Commoners married commoners; elites married elites.

Such a division of society into socioeconomic strata contrasts strongly with bands and tribes, whose status systems are based on prestige, rather than on differential access to resources. The prestige differentials that do exist in bands reflect special qualities and abilities. Good hunters get respect from their fellows if they are generous. So does a skilled curer, dancer, storyteller—or anyone else with a talent or skill that others appreciate.

In tribes, some prestige goes to descent-group leaders, to village heads, and especially to the big man, a regional figure who commands the loyalty and labor of others. All these figures must be generous, however. If they accumulate more resources—i.e., property or food—than others in the village, they must share them with the others. Since strategic resources are available to everyone, social classes based on the possession of unequal amounts of resources can never exist.

In many tribes, particularly those with patrilineal descent, men have much greater prestige and power than women do. The gender contrast in rights may diminish in chiefdoms, where prestige and access to resources are based on seniority of descent, so that some women are senior to some men. Unlike big men, chiefs are exempt from ordinary work and have rights and privileges that are unavailable to the masses. Like big men, however, they still return much of the wealth they take in.

The status system in chiefdoms, although based on differential access, differed from the status system in states because the privileged few were always relatives and assistants of the chief. However, this type of status

This employee of the Chirping Chicken fast food store, shown with her coworkers, just won $22,500,000 in the New York State lottery. Wealth and prestige are not always correlated. Do you imagine the winner's eating habits will change? Will her prestige rise?

system didn't last very long. Chiefs would start acting like kings and try to erode the kinship basis of the chiefdom. In Madagascar they would do this by demoting their more distant relatives to commoner status and banning marriage between nobles and commoners (Kottak 1980). Such moves, if accepted by the society, created separate social strata—*unrelated* groups that differ in their access to wealth, prestige, and power. (A *stratum* is one of two or more groups that contrast in social status and access to strategic resources. Each stratum includes people of both sexes and all ages.) The creation of separate social strata is called **stratification,** and its emergence signified the transition from chiefdom to state. *The presence of stratification is one of the key distinguishing features of a state.*

The influential sociologist Max Weber (1962/1922) defined three related dimensions of social stratification: (1) Economic status, or **wealth,** encompasses all a person's material assets, including income, land, and other types of property (Schaefer and Lamm 1992). (2) **Power,** the ability to exercise one's will over others—to do what one wants—is the basis of political status. (3) **Prestige**—the basis of social status—refers to esteem, respect, or approval for acts, deeds, or qualities considered exemplary. Prestige, or "cultural capital" (Bourdieu 1984), gives people a sense of worth and respect, which they may often convert into economic advantage (Table 7-1).

TABLE 7-1	Max Weber's Three Dimensions of Stratification
wealth $\longrightarrow$	economic status
power $\longrightarrow$	political status
prestige $\longrightarrow$	social status

These Weberian dimensions of stratification are present to varying degrees in chiefdoms. However, chiefdoms lack the sharp division into classes that characterized states. Wealth, power, and prestige in chiefdoms are all tied to kinship factors.

In archaic states—for the first time in human evolution—there were contrasts in wealth, power, and prestige between entire groups (social strata) of men and women. Each stratum included people of both sexes and all ages. The **superordinate** (the higher or elite) stratum had privileged access to wealth, power, and other valued resources. Access to resources by members of the **subordinate** (lower or underprivileged) stratum was limited by the privileged group.

Socioeconomic stratification continues as a defining feature of all states, archaic or industrial. The elites control a significant part of the means of production, for example, land, herds, water, capital, farms, or factories. Those born at the bottom of the hierarchy have reduced chances of social mobility. Because of elite ownership rights, ordinary people lack free access to resources. Only in states do the elites get to keep their differential wealth. Unlike big men and chiefs, they don't have to give it back to the people whose labor has built and increased it.

STATES

Table 7-2 summarizes the information presented so far on bands, tribes, chiefdoms, and states. States, remember, are autonomous political units with social classes and a formal government, based on law. States tend to be large and populous, as compared to bands, tribes, and chiefdoms. Certain statuses, systems, and subsystems with specialized functions are found in all states. They include the following:

1. *Population control:* fixing of boundaries, establishment of citizenship categories, and the taking of a census.
2. *Judiciary:* laws, legal procedure, and judges.
3. *Enforcement:* permanent military and police forces.
4. *Fiscal:* taxation.

In archaic states, these subsystems were integrated by a ruling system or government composed of civil, military, and religious officials (Fried 1960).

TABLE 7-2	Economic Basis of and Political Regulation in Bands, Tribes, Chiefdoms, and States		
Sociopolitical Type	Economic Type	Examples	Type of Regulation
Band	Foraging	Inuit, San	Local
Tribe	Horticulture, pastoralism	Yanomami, Masai, Kapauku	Local, temporary, regional
Chiefdom	Intensive horticulture, pastoral nomadism, agriculture	Qashqai, Polynesia, Cherokee	Permanent, regional
State	Agriculture, industrialism	Ancient Mesopotamia, contemporary U.S., and Canada	Permanent, regional

Population Control

To know whom they govern, all states conduct censuses. States demarcate boundaries that separate them from other societies. Customs agents, immigration officers, navies, and coast guards patrol frontiers. Even nonindustrial states have boundary-maintenance forces. In Buganda, an archaic state on the shores of Lake Victoria in Uganda, the king rewarded military officers with estates in outlying provinces. They became his guardians against foreign intrusion.

States also control population through administrative subdivision: provinces, districts, "states," counties, subcounties, and parishes. Lower-level officials manage the populations and territories of the subdivisions.

In nonstates, people work and relax with their relatives, in-laws, fictive kin, and age mates—people with whom they have a personal relationship. Such a personal social life existed throughout most of human history, but food production spelled its eventual decline. After millions of years of human evolution, it took a mere 4,000 years for the population increase and regulatory problems spawned by food production to lead from tribe to chiefdom to state. With state organization, kinship's pervasive role diminished. Descent groups may continue as kin groups within archaic states, but their importance in political organization declines.

States foster geographic mobility and resettlement, severing long-standing ties among people, land, and kin. Population displacements have increased in the modern world. War, famine, and job seeking across national boundaries churn up migratory currents. People in states come to identify themselves by new statuses, both ascribed and achieved. These include ethnicity, residence, occupation, party, religion, and team or club affiliation, rather than only as members of a descent group or extended family.

States also manage their populations by granting different rights and obligations to citizens and noncitizens. Status distinctions among citizens are also common. Many archaic states granted different rights to nobles, commoners, and slaves. Unequal rights within state-organized societies persist in today's world. In recent American history, before the Emancipation Proclamation, there were different laws for slaves and free people. In European colonies, separate courts judged cases involving only natives and cases involving Europeans. In contemporary America, a military code of justice and court system continue to coexist alongside the civil judiciary.

Judiciary

States have *laws* based on precedent and legislative proclamations. Without writing, laws may be preserved in oral tradition, with justices, elders, and other specialists responsible for remembering them. Oral traditions as repositories of legal wisdom have continued in some nations with writing, such as Great Britain. Laws regulate relations between individuals and groups.

Crimes are violations of the legal code, with specified types of punishment. However, a given act, such as killing someone, may be legally defined in different ways (e.g., as manslaughter, justifiable homicide, or first-degree murder). Furthermore, even in contemporary North America, where justice is supposed to be "blind" to social distinctions, the poor are prosecuted more often and more severely than are the rich.

To handle disputes and crimes, all states have courts and judges. Precolonial African states had subcounty, county, and district courts, plus a high court formed by the king or queen and his or her advisers. Most states allow appeals to higher courts, although people are encouraged to solve problems locally.

A striking contrast between states and nonstates is intervention in family affairs. In states, aspects of parenting and marriage enter the domain of public law. Governments step in to halt blood feuds and regulate previously private disputes. States attempt to curb *internal* conflict, but they aren't always successful. About 85 percent of the world's armed conflicts since 1945 have begun within states—in efforts to overthrow a ruling regime or as disputes over tribal, religious, and ethnic minority issues. Only 15 percent have been fights across national borders (Barnaby, ed. 1984). Rebellion, resistance, repression, terrorism, and warfare continue. Indeed, recent states have perpetrated some of history's bloodiest deeds.

Enforcement

All states have agents to enforce judicial decisions. Confinement requires jailers. If there is a death penalty, it requires executioners. Agents of the state have the power to collect fines and confiscate property.

As a relatively new form of sociopolitical organization, states have competed successfully with nonstates throughout the world. A government suppresses internal disorder (with police) and guards the nation against external threats (with the military). Military organization helps states subdue neighboring nonstates, but this is not the only reason for the spread of state organization. Although states impose hardships, they also offer advantages. They provide protection from outsiders and preserve internal order. By promoting internal peace, states enhance production. Their economies support massive, dense populations, which supply armies and colonists to promote expansion. A major concern of government is to defend hierarchy, property, and the power of the law.

Fiscal Systems

A financial or **fiscal** system is needed in states to support rulers, nobles, officials, judges, military personnel, and thousands of other specialists. As in the chiefdom, the state intervenes in production, distribution, and consumption. The state may decree that a certain area will produce certain things or forbid certain activities in particular places. Although, like chiefdoms, states also have redistribution (through taxation), generosity and sharing are played down. Less of what comes in flows back to the people.

In nonstates, people customarily share with relatives, but residents of states face added obligations to bureaucrats and officials. Citizens must turn over a substantial portion of what they produce to the state. Of the resources that the state collects, it reallocates part for the general good and uses another part (often larger) for the elite.

The state does not bring more freedom or leisure to the common people, who usually work harder than do the people in nonstates. They may be called on to build monumental public works. Some of these projects, such as dams and irrigation systems, may be economically necessary. People also build temples, palaces, and tombs for the elites.

Monument building began in chiefdoms, where "ceremonies of place" were associated with the creation of a "sacred landscape" through constructions such as (stone) henges of Europe, the mounds of the southeastern United States, and the temples of Hawaii (Earle 1987, 1997). Like chiefs, state officials may use religion to buttress their authority. Archaeology shows that temples abounded in early states. Even in mature states, rulers may link themselves to godhood through divine right or claim to be deities or their earthly representatives. Rulers convoked peons or slaves to build magnificent castles or tombs, cementing the ruler's place in history or status in the afterlife. Monumental architecture survives as an enduring reminder of the exalted prestige of priests and kings.

Markets and trade are usually under at least some state control, with officials overseeing distribution and exchange, standardizing weights and measures, and collecting taxes on goods passing into or through the state. Taxes support government and the ruling class, which is clearly separated from the common people in regard to activities, privileges, rights, and obligations. Taxes also support the many specialists—administrators, tax collectors, judges, lawmakers, generals, scholars, and priests. As the state matures, the segment of the population freed from direct concern with subsistence grows.

The elites of archaic states reveled in the consumption of *sumptuary goods*—jewelry, exotic food and drink, and stylish clothing reserved for, or affordable only by, the rich. Peasants' diets suffered as they struggled to meet government demands. Commoners perished in territorial wars that had little relevance to their own needs.

S u m m a r y

1. Many anthropologists use a sociopolitical typology that classifies societies as bands, tribes, chiefdoms, or states. Foragers tend to live in egalitarian, band-organized, societies. Personal networks link individuals, families, and bands. Band leaders are first among equals, with no sure way to enforce decisions. Disputes rarely arise over strategic resources, which are open to all.

2. Political authority and power tend to increase along with population and the scale of regulatory problems. More people mean more relations among individuals and groups to regulate. Increasingly complex economies pose further regulatory problems.

3. Heads of horticultural villages are local leaders with limited authority. They lead by example and persuasion. Big men have support and authority beyond a single village. They are regional regulators, but temporary ones. In organizing a feast, they mobilize labor from several villages. Sponsoring such events leaves them with little wealth but with prestige and a reputation for generosity.

4. Age and gender can also be used for regional political integration. Among North America's Plains Indians, men's associations (pantribal sodalities) organized raiding and buffalo hunting. Such men's associations tend to emphasize the warrior grade. They serve for offense and defense when there is intertribal raiding for animals. Among pastoralists, the degree of authority and political organization reflects population size and density, interethnic relations, and pressure on resources.

5. The state is an autonomous political unit that encompasses many communities. Its government collects taxes, drafts people for work and war, and decrees and enforces laws. The state is a form of sociopolitical organization based on central government and social stratification—a division of society into classes. Early states are known as archaic, or nonindustrial, states, in contrast to modern industrial nation-states.

6. Unlike tribes, but like states, chiefdoms have permanent regional regulation and differential access to resources. But chiefdoms lack stratification. Unlike states, but like bands and tribes, chiefdoms are organized by kinship, descent, and marriage. Chiefdoms emerged in several areas, including the circum-Caribbean, lowland Amazonia, the southeastern United States, and Polynesia.

7. Weber's three dimensions of stratification are wealth, power, and prestige. In early states—for the first time in human history—contrasts in wealth, power, and prestige between entire groups of men and women came into being. A socioeconomic stratum includes people of both sexes and all ages. The superordinate—higher or elite—stratum enjoys privileged access to resources.

8. Certain systems are found in all states: population control, judiciary, enforcement, and fiscal. These are integrated by a ruling system or government composed of civil, military, and religious officials. States conduct censuses and demarcate boundaries. Laws are based on precedent and legislative proclamations. Courts and judges handle disputes and crimes. A police force maintains internal order, as a military defends against external threats. A financial or fiscal system supports rulers, officials, judges, and other specialists.

Case Study
Kapauku

This chapter has discussed the formal and informal leadership roles found in various societies, among them that of the "big man." In *Culture Sketches* by Holly Peters-Golden read the chapter on the Kapauku: New Guinea "Capitalists." An important role in Kapauku society is the *tonowi*, a "big man." How is this leadership role related to the other key features of Kapauku society, such as individualism and economics?

The Great Forager Debate

How representative are modern hunter-gatherers of Stone Age peoples, all of whom were foragers? G. P. Murdock (1934) described living hunter-gatherers as "our primitive contemporaries." This label gave an image of foragers as living fossils—frozen, primitive, unchanging social forms that had managed to hang on in remote areas.

Later, many anthropologists followed the prolific ethnographer Richard Lee (1984) in using the San ("Bushmen") of the Kalahari Desert of southern Africa to represent the hunting-gathering way of life. But critics increasingly wonder about how much modern foragers can tell us about the economic and social relations that characterized humanity before food production. Modern foragers, after all, live mainly in marginal environments, as well as in nation-states and an increasingly interlinked world.

For generations, the pygmies of Congo have traded with their neighbors who are cultivators. They exchange forest products (e.g., honey and meat) for crops (e.g., bananas and manioc). The San speakers of southern Africa have been influenced by Bantu speakers (farmers and herders) for 2,000 years and by Europeans for centuries. All foragers now trade with food producers, and most rely on governments and on missionaries for at least part of what they consume. The Aché of Paraguay get food from missionaries, grow crops, and have domesticated animals (Hawkes et al. 1982; Hill et al. 1987). They spend only a third of their subsistence time foraging.

There is a debate in hunter-gatherer studies between "traditionalists" (e.g., Richard Lee) and "revisionists" (e.g., Edwin Wilmsen). Reconsideration of the status of contemporary foragers is related to the reaction against the ethnographic present discussed in the box in Chapter 1. Anthropologists have rejected the old tendency to depict societies as uniform and frozen in time and space. Attempts to capture the ethnographic present often ignored internal variation, change, and the influence of the world system.

The debate over foragers has focused on the San, whom the traditionalists view as autonomous foragers with a cultural identity different from that of their neighbors who are herders and cultivators (Lee 1979; Silberbauer 1981; Tanaka 1980). These scholars depict most San as egalitarian band-organized people who until recently were nomadic or seminomadic. Traditionalists recognize contact between the San and food producers, but they don't think this contact has destroyed San culture.

The revisionists claim the San tell us little about the ancient world in which all humans were foragers. They argue that the San have been linked to food producers for generations, and that this contact has changed the basis of their culture. For Edwin Wilmsen (1989) the San are far from being isolated survivors of a pristine era. They are a rural underclass in a larger political and economic system dominated by Europeans and Bantu food producers. Many San now tend cattle for wealthier Bantu, rather than foraging independently. Wilmsen also argues that many San descend from herders who were pushed into the desert by poverty or oppression.

The isolation and autonomy of foragers have also been questioned for African pygmies (Bailey et al. 1989) and for foragers in the Philippines (Headland and Reid 1989). The Mikea of southwest Madagascar may have moved into their remote forest habitat to escape a nearby state. Eventually the Mikea became an economically specialized group of hunter-gatherers on the fringes of that state. The Tasaday of the Philippines maintain ties with food producers and probably descend from cultivating ancestors. This is true despite the initial "Lost Tribe" media accounts. The reports that followed the "discovery" of the Tasaday portrayed them as survivors of the Stone Age, hermetically sealed in a pristine world all their own. Many scholars now question the authenticity of the Tasaday as a separate cultural group (Headland, ed. 1992).

The debate about foragers raises a larger question: Why do the ethnographic accounts and interpretations vary? The reasons include variation in space and time in the society, and different assumptions by ethnographers. Susan Kent (1992, 1996) notes a tendency to stereotype foragers, to treat them as all alike. Foragers used to be stereotyped as isolated, primitive survivors of the Stone Age. A new stereotype sees them as culturally deprived people forced by states, colonialism, or world events into marginal environments. This view is probably more accurate, although often exaggerated. Ethnographic studies have inevitably focused on foragers living in marginal environments—that is, on those hunter-gatherers who managed to survive (or to take refuge from) the spread of food production and the world system. All contemporary foragers have links with external systems, including food producers and nation-states. Because of this they differ substantially from Stone Age hunter-gatherers.

Another reason contemporary foragers shouldn't be seen as emblematic of ancient foragers is the likelihood that foraging peoples have always chosen, when they could choose, to live in rich, rather than marginal, environments. This may well have been true during the long period of human history in which foraging was the only way in which people got food. The foragers of the Pacific Northwest and California (whose potlatch was examined in Chapter 5) are the last foragers in relatively recent times to inhabit rich habitats. Les W. Field (personal communication) suggests that those Pacific foragers may be more representative of hunter-gatherer life ways in general than are the foragers of polar, desert, and other marginal regions.

Kent (1996) stresses variation among foragers. For example, San economic adaptations range from hunting and gathering to fishing, farming, herding, and wage work. The nature of San life has changed appreciably since the 1950s and 1960s, when a series of anthropologists from Harvard University, including Richard Lee, embarked on a systematic study of life in the Kalahari. Lee and others have documented many of the changes in various publications. Such longitudinal research monitors variation in time, while field work in many San areas has revealed variation in space. One of the most important contrasts is between settled (sedentary) and nomadic groups (Kent and Vierich 1989). Sedentism is increasing, but some San groups (along rivers) have been sedentary, or have traded with outsiders, for generations. Others, including Lee's Dobe Ju/'hoansi San and Kent's Kutse San, have been more cut off and have retained more of the hunter-gatherer life style.

Modern foragers are not Stone Age relics, living fossils, lost tribes, or noble savages. Still, to the extent that foraging is the basis of subsistence, modern hunter-gatherers can illustrate links between a foraging economy and other aspects of culture. For example, San groups that are still mobile, or that were so until recently, emphasize social, political, and gender equality. Social relations that stress kinship, reciprocity, and sharing work well in an economy with limited resources and few people. The nomadic pursuit of wild plants and animals tends to discourage permanent settlements, accumulation of wealth, and status distinctions. People have to share meat when they get it; otherwise it rots. Kent (1996) suggests that by studying diversity among the San, we can better understand foraging and how it is influenced by sedentism and other factors. Such study will enhance our knowledge of past, present, and future small-scale societies.

Chapter 8

Gender

Because anthropologists study biology, society, and culture, they are in a unique position to comment on nature (biological predispositions) and nurture (environment) as determinants of human behavior. Human attitudes, values, and behavior are limited not only by our genetic predispositions—which are often difficult to identify—but also by our experiences during enculturation. Our attributes as adults are determined both by our genes and by our environment during growth and development.

Debate about the effects of nature and nurture proceeds today in scientific and public arenas. **Biological determinists** assume that some—they differ about how much—of human behavior and social organization is biologically determined. **Cultural determinists** find most attempts to link behavior to genes unconvincing. They assume that human evolutionary success rests on flexibility, or the ability to adapt in various ways. Because human adaptation relies so strongly on cultural learning, we can change our behavior more readily than members of other species can.

The nature-nurture debate emerges in the discussion of human sex-gender roles and sexuality. Men and women differ genetically. Women have two X chromosomes, and men have an X and a Y. The father determines a baby's sex because only he has the Y chromosome to transmit. The mother always provides an X chromosome.

The chromosomal difference is expressed in hormonal and physiological contrasts. Humans are sexually dimorphic. **Sexual dimorphism** refers to marked differences in male and female biology besides the contrasts in breasts and genitals. Men and women differ not just in primary (genitalia and reproductive organs) and secondary (breasts, voice, hair distribution) sexual characteristics but in average weight, height, and strength.

Just how far, however, do such genetically and physiologically determined differences go? What effect do they have on the way men and women act and are treated in different societies? On the cultural determinist side, anthropologists have discovered substantial variability in the roles of men and women in different societies. The anthropological position on sex-gender roles and biology has been stated as follows:

> The biological nature of men and women [should be seen] not as a narrow enclosure limiting the human organism, but rather as a broad base upon which a variety of structures can be built. (Friedl 1975, p. 6)

Sex differences are biological, but *gender* encompasses all the traits that a culture assigns to and inculcates in males and females. "Gender," in other words, refers to the cultural construction of male and female characteristics (Rosaldo 1980*b*). Given the "rich and various constructions of gender" within the realm of cultural diversity, Susan Bourque and Kay Warren (1987) note that the same images of masculinity and femininity do not always apply. Margaret Mead did an early ethnographic study of variation in gender roles. Her book *Sex and Temperament in Three Primitive Societies* (1935/1950) was based on field work in three societies in Papua New Guinea: Arapesh, Mundugumor, and Tchambuli. The extent of personality variation in men and women in these three societies on the same island amazed Mead. She found that Arapesh men and women both acted as Americans have traditionally expected women to act—in a mild, parental, responsive way. Mundugumor men and women both, in contrast, acted as she believed we expect men to act—fiercely and aggressively. Tchambuli men were "catty," wore curls, and went shopping, but Tchambuli women were energetic and managerial and placed less emphasis on personal adornment than did the men. Drawing on their recent case study of the Tchambuli, whom they call the Chambri, Errington and Gewertz (1987), while recognizing gender malleability, have disputed the specifics of Mead's account.

There is a well-established field of feminist scholarship within anthropology (di Leonardo, ed. 1991; Miller 1993; Nash and Safa 1986; Rosaldo 1980*b*; Strathern 1988). Anthropologists have gathered systematic ethnographic data about gender in many cultural settings (Bonvillain 2001; Kimmel and Messner, eds. 1995; Morgen, ed. 1989; Mukhopadhyay and Higgins 1988; Peplau, ed. 1999; Ward 1999). We can see that the gender roles vary with environment, economy, adaptive strategy, and type of political system. Before we examine the cross-cultural data, some definitions are in order.

Gender roles are the tasks and activities that a culture assigns to the sexes. Related to gender roles are **gender stereotypes,** which are oversimplified but strongly held ideas about the characteristics of males and females. **Gender stratification** describes an unequal distribution of rewards (socially valued resources, power, prestige, and personal freedom) between men and women, reflecting their different positions in a social hierarchy (Light, Keller, and Calhoun 1997).

The realm of cultural diversity contains richly different social constructions and expressions of gender, as is illustrated by these Bororo male dancers. For what reasons do men decorate their bodies in your society?

In stateless societies, gender stratification is often more obvious in regard to prestige than it is in regard to wealth. In her study of the Ilongots of northern Luzon in the Philippines, Michelle Rosaldo (1980*a*) described gender differences related to the positive cultural value placed on adventure, travel, and knowledge of the external world. More often than women, Ilongot men, as headhunters, visited distant places. They acquired knowledge of the external world, amassed experiences there, and returned to express their knowledge, adventures, and feelings in public oratory. They received acclaim as a result. Ilongot women had inferior prestige because they lacked external experiences on which to base knowledge and dramatic expression. On the basis of Rosaldo's study and findings in other stateless societies, Ong (1989) argues that we must distinguish between prestige systems and actual power in a given society. High male prestige may not entail economic or political power held by men over their families.

GENDER AMONG FORAGERS

Several studies have shown that economic roles affect gender stratification. In one cross-cultural study Peggy Sanday (1974) found that gender stratification decreased when men and women made roughly equal contributions to subsistence. She found that gender stratification was *greatest* when the women contributed either *much more* or *much less* than the men did.

This finding applied mainly to food producers, not to foragers. In foraging societies gender stratification was most marked when men contributed much *more* to the diet than women did. This was true among the Inuit and other northern hunters and fishers. Among tropical and semitropical foragers, by contrast, gathering usually supplies more food than hunting and fishing do. Gathering is generally women's work. Men usually hunt and fish, but women also do some fishing and may hunt small animals. When gathering is prominent, gender status tends to be more equal than it is when hunting and fishing are the main subsistence activities.

Gender status is also more equal when the domestic and public spheres aren't sharply separated. (*Domestic* means within or pertaining to the home.) Strong differentiation between the home and the outside world is called the **domestic-public dichotomy** or the *private-public contrast*. The outside world can include politics, trade, warfare, or work. Often when domestic and public spheres are clearly separated, public activities have greater prestige than domestic ones do. This can promote gender stratification, because men are more likely to be active in the public domain than women are. Cross-culturally, women's activities tend to be closer to home than men's are. Thus, another reason hunter-gatherers have less gender stratification than food producers do is that the domestic-public dichotomy is more developed among food producers.

A division of labor linked to gender has been found in all societies. However, the particular tasks assigned to men and women don't always reflect differences in strength and endurance. Food producers often assign the arduous tasks of carrying water and firewood and of pounding grain to women. In 1967 in the former Soviet Union women filled 47 percent of the factory positions, including many unmechanized jobs requiring hard physical labor. Most Soviet sanitation workers, physicians, and nurses were women (Martin and Voorhies 1975). Many jobs that men do in some societies are done by women in others, and vice versa.

Certain roles are more sex-linked than others. Men are the usual hunters and warriors. Given such weapons as spears, knives, and bows, men make better fighters because they are bigger and stronger on average than are women in the same population (Divale and Harris 1976). The male hunter-fighter role also reflects a tendency toward greater male mobility.

In foraging societies, women are either pregnant or lactating during most of their childbearing period. Late in pregnancy and after childbirth, carrying a baby limits a woman's movements, even her gathering. However, among the Agta of the Philippines (Griffin and Estioko-Griffin, eds. 1985), women not only gather, they also hunt with dogs while carrying their babies with them. Still, given the effects of pregnancy and lactation on mobility, it is rarely feasible for women to be the primary hunters (Friedl 1975). Warfare, which also requires mobility, is not found in most foraging societies, nor is interregional trade well developed. Warfare and trade are two public arenas that contribute to status inequality of males and females among food producers.

The Ju/'hoansi San illustrate the extent to which the activities and spheres of influence of men and women may overlap among foragers (Draper 1975). Traditional Ju/'hoansi gender roles were interdependent. During gathering, women discovered information about game animals, which they passed on to the men. Men and women spent about the same amount of time away from the camp, but neither worked more than three days a week. The Ju/'hoansi saw nothing wrong in doing the work of the other gender. Men often gathered food and collected water. A general sharing ethos dictated that men distribute meat and that women share the fruits of gathering.

Patricia Draper's field work among the Ju/'hoansi is especially useful in showing the relationships between economy, gender roles, and stratification because she studied both foragers and a group of former foragers who had become sedentary. Draper studied sedentary Ju/'hoansi at Mahopa, a village where they herded, grew crops, worked for wages, and did a small amount of gathering. Their gender roles were becoming more rigidly defined. A domestic-public dichotomy was developing. With less gathering, women were confined more to the home. Boys could gain mobility through herding, but girls' movements were more limited. The equal and communal world of the bush was yielding to the social features of sedentary life. A differential ranking of men according to their herds, houses, and sons began to replace sharing. Males came to be seen as the more valuable producers.

If there is some degree of male dominance in every contemporary society, it may be because of changes such as those which have drawn the Ju/'hoansi into wage work, market sales, and thus the world capitalist economy. An interplay between local, national, and international forces influences systems of gender stratification (Ong 1989). In traditional foraging societies, however, egalitarianism extended to the relations between the sexes. The social spheres, activities, rights, and obligations of men and women overlapped. Foragers' kinship systems tend to be bilateral (calculated equally through males and females) rather than favoring either the mother's side or the father's side. Foragers may live with either the husband's or the wife's kin and often shift between one group and the other.

One last observation about foragers: It is among them that the public and private spheres are least separate, hierarchy is least marked, aggression and competition are most discouraged, and the rights, activities, and spheres of influence of men and women overlap the most. Our ancestors lived entirely by foraging until 10,000 years ago. Despite the popular stereotype of the club-wielding caveman dragging his mate by the hair, relative gender equality is a much more likely ancestral pattern.

GENDER AMONG HORTICULTURALISTS

Gender roles and stratification among cultivators vary widely, depending on specific features of the economy and social structure. Demonstrating this, Martin and Voorhies (1975) studied a sample of 515 horticultural societies, representing all parts of the world. They looked at several variables, including descent and postmarital residence, the percentage of the diet derived from cultivation, and the productivity of men and women.

Women were found to be the main producers in horticultural societies. In 50 percent of those societies, women did most of the cultivating. In 33 percent, contributions to cultivation by men and women were equal (see Table 8–1 on page 170). In only 17 percent did men do most of the work. Women tended to do a bit more cultivating in matrilineal compared with patrilineal societies. They dominated horticulture in 64 percent of the matrilineal societies versus 50 percent of the patrilineal ones.

Reduced Gender Stratification—Matrilineal, Matrilocal Societies

Cross-cultural variation in gender status is related to rules of descent and postmarital residence (Martin and Voorhies 1975; Friedl 1975). Among horticulturalists with matrilineal descent and *matrilocality* (residence after marriage with the wife's relatives), female status tends to be high. Matriliny and matrilocality disperse related males, rather than consolidating them. By contrast, patriliny and *patrilocality* (residence after marriage with the husband's kin) keep male relatives together, an advantage given warfare. Matrilineal-matrilocal systems tend to occur in societies where population pressure on strategic resources is minimal and warfare is infrequent.

Women tend to have high status in matrilineal, matrilocal societies for several reasons. Descent-group membership, succession to political positions, allocation of land, and overall social identity all come through female links. Among the matrilineal Malays of Negeri Sembilan, Malaysia (Peletz 1988), matriliny gave women sole inheritance of ancestral rice fields. Matrilocality created solidary clusters of female kin. These Malay women had considerable influence beyond the household (Swift 1963). In such matrilineal contexts, women are the basis of the entire social structure. Although public authority may be assigned to the men, much of the power and decision making may actually belong to the senior women.

Anthropologists have never discovered a **matriarchy,** a society ruled by women. Still, some matrilineal societies, including the Iroquois (Brown 1975), a confederation of tribes in aboriginal New York, show that women's political and ritual influence can rival that of the men.

We saw that among foragers gender status was most equal when there was no sharp separation of male and female activities and of public and domestic spheres. However, gender stratification can also be reduced by roles that remove men from the local community. We now refine our generalizations: It is the sharp contrast between male and female roles *within the local community* that promotes gender stratification. Gender stratification may be reduced when women play prominent local roles, while men pursue activities in a wider, regional system. Iroquois women, for example, played a major subsistence role, while men left home for long periods. As is usual in matrilineal societies, *internal* warfare was uncommon. Iroquois men waged war only on distant groups; this could keep them away for years.

Iroquois men hunted and fished, but women controlled the local economy. Women did some fishing and occasional hunting, but their major productive role was in horticulture. Women owned the land, which they inherited from matrilineal kinswomen. Women controlled the production and distribution of food.

Iroquois women lived with their husbands and children in the family compartments of a communal longhouse. Women born in a longhouse remained there for life. Senior women, or *matrons*, decided which men could join the longhouse as husbands, and they could evict incompatible men. Women therefore controlled alliances between descent groups, an important political job in tribal society.

Iroquois women thus managed production and distribution. Social identity, succession to office and titles, and property all came through the female line, and women were prominent in ritual and politics. Related tribes made up a confederacy, the League of the Iroquois, with chiefs and councils.

A council of male chiefs managed military operations, but chiefly succession was matrilineal. It went from brother to brother, or from a man to his sister's son. The matrons of each longhouse nominated a man as their representative. If the council rejected their first nominee, the women proposed others until one was accepted. Matrons constantly monitored the chiefs and could impeach them. Women could veto war declarations, withhold provisions for war, and initiate peace efforts. In religion, too, women shared power. Half the tribe's religious practitioners were women, and the matrons helped select the others.

Reduced Gender Stratification—Matrifocal Societies

Nancy Tanner (1974) also found that the combination of male travel and a prominent female economic role reduced gender stratification and promoted high female status. She based this finding on a survey of the **matrifocal** (mother-centered, often with no resident husband-father) organization of certain societies in Indonesia, West Africa, and the Caribbean. Matrifocal societies are not necessarily matrilineal. A few are even patrilineal.

For example, Tanner (1974) found matrifocality among the Igbo of eastern Nigeria, who are patrilineal, patrilocal, and polygynous. Each wife had her own house, where she lived with her children. Women planted crops next to their houses and traded surpluses. Women ran the local markets, while men did the long-distance trading.

In a case study of the Igbo, Ifi Amadiume (1987) noted that either sex could fill male gender roles. Before Christian influence, successful Igbo women and men used wealth to take titles and acquire wives. Wives freed husbands (male and female) from domestic work and helped them accumulate wealth. Female husbands were not considered masculine but preserved their femininity. Igbo women asserted themselves in women's groups, including those of lineage daughters, lineage wives, and a community-wide women's council led by titled women. The high status and influence of Igbo women rested on the separation of males from local subsistence and on a marketing system that allowed women to leave home and gain prominence in distribution and—through these accomplishments—in politics.

Increased Gender Stratification—Patrilineal-Patrilocal Societies

The Igbo are unusual among patrilineal-patrilocal societies, many of which have marked gender stratification. Martin and Voorhies (1975) link the decline of matriliny and the spread of the **patrilineal-patrilocal complex** (consisting of patrilineality, patrilocality, warfare, and male supremacy) to pressure on resources. Faced with scarce resources, patrilineal-patrilocal cultivators such as the Yanomami often wage warfare against other villages. This favors patrilocality and patriliny, customs that keep related men together in the same village, where they make strong allies in battle. Such societies tend to have a sharp domestic-public dichotomy, and men tend to dominate the prestige hierarchy. Men may use their public roles in warfare and trade and their greater prestige to symbolize and reinforce the devaluation or oppression of women.

The patrilineal-patrilocal complex characterizes many societies in highland Papua New Guinea. Women work hard growing and processing subsistence crops, raising and tending pigs (the main domesticated animal and a favorite food), and doing domestic cooking, but they are isolated from the public domain, which men control. Men grow and distribute prestige crops, prepare food for feasts, and arrange marriages. The men even get to trade the pigs and control their use in ritual.

In densely populated areas of the Papua New Guinea highlands, male-female avoidance is associated with strong pressure on resources (Lindenbaum 1972). Men fear all female contacts, including sex. They think that sexual contact with women will weaken them. Indeed, men see everything female as dangerous and polluting. They segregate themselves in men's houses and hide their precious ritual objects from women. They delay marriage, and some never marry.

By contrast, the sparsely populated areas of Papua New Guinea, such as recently settled areas, lack taboos on male-female contacts. The image of woman as polluter fades, heterosexual intercourse is valued, men and women live together, and reproductive rates are high.

Homosexual Behavior among the Etoro

One of the most extreme examples of male-female sexual antagonism in Papua New Guinea comes from the Etoro (Kelly 1976), a group of 400 people who subsist by hunting and horticulture in the Trans-Fly region. The

In some parts of Papua New Guinea, the patrilineal-patrilocal complex has extreme social repercussions. Regarding females as dangerous and polluting, men may segregate themselves in men's houses (such as this one, located near the Sepik River), where they hide their precious ritual objects from women. Are there places like this in your society?

Etoro also illustrate the power of culture in molding human sexuality. The following account applies only to Etoro males and their beliefs. Etoro cultural norms prevented the male anthropologist who studied them from gathering comparable information about female attitudes. Etoro opinions about sexuality are linked to their beliefs about the cycle of birth, physical growth, maturity, old age, and death.

Etoro men believe that semen is necessary to give life force to a fetus, which is said to be placed within a woman by an ancestral spirit. Because men are believed to have a limited supply of semen, sexuality saps male vitality. The birth of children, nurtured by semen, symbolizes a necessary (and unpleasant) sacrifice that will lead to the husband's eventual death. Heterosexual intercourse, which is required only for reproduction, is discouraged. Women who want too much sex are viewed as witches, hazardous to their husbands' health. Etoro culture permits heterosexual intercourse only about 100 days a year. The rest of the time it is tabooed. Seasonal birth clustering shows that the taboo is respected.

So objectionable is heterosexuality that it is removed from community life. It can occur neither in sleeping quarters nor in the fields. Coitus can happen only in the woods, where it is risky because poisonous snakes, the Etoro say, are attracted by the sounds and smells of sex.

Although coitus is discouraged, homosexual acts are viewed as essential. Etoro believe that boys cannot produce semen on their own. To grow into men and eventually give life force to their children, boys must acquire semen orally from older men. From the age of ten until adulthood, boys are inseminated by older men. No taboos are attached to this. Homosexual activity can go on in the sleeping area or garden. Every three years a group of boys around the age of twenty are formally initiated into manhood. They go to a secluded mountain lodge, where they are visited and inseminated by several older men.

Etoro homosexuality is governed by a code of propriety. Although homosexual relations between older and younger males are culturally essential, those between boys of the same age are discouraged. A boy who gets semen from other youths is believed to be sapping their life force and stunting their growth. When a boy develops very rapidly, this suggests that he is ingesting semen from other boys. Like a sex-hungry wife, he is shunned as a witch.

Etoro homosexuality rests not on hormones or genes but on cultural traditions. The Etoro share a cultural pattern, which Gilbert Herdt (1984) calls ritualized homosexuality, with some 50 other tribes in Papua New Guinea, especially in that country's Trans-Fly region. These societies illustrate one extreme of a male-female avoidance pattern that is widespread in Papua New Guinea and in patrilineal-patrilocal societies.

SEXUALITIES AND GENDER

Recently in the United States there has been a tendency to see sexual orientation as fixed and biologically based. There is not enough information at this time to say for sure that sexual orientation is based on biology. What we can say is that to some extent at least, all human activities and preferences, including erotic expression, are learned and malleable. **Sexual orientation** stands for a person's habitual sexual attraction to, and activities with persons of the opposite sex, *heterosexuality;* the same sex, *homosexuality;* or both sexes, *bisexuality. Asexuality*, indifference toward, or lack of attraction to either sex, is also a sexual orientation. All four of these forms are found in contemporary North America, and throughout the world. But each type of desire and experience holds different meanings for individuals and groups. For example, an asexual disposition may be acceptable in some places but may be perceived as a character flaw in others. Bisexuality may be a private orientation in Mexico, rather than socially sanctioned and encouraged as among the Sambia of Papua New Guinea (see also Blackwood and Wieringa, eds. 1999; Herdt 1981, Kottak and Kozaitis 1999; Lancaster and di Leonardo, eds. 1997).

In any culture, individuals will differ in the nature, range, and intensity of their sexual interests and urges. No one knows for sure why such individual sexual differences exist. Part of the answer may be biological, reflecting genes or hormones. Another part may have to do with experiences during growth and development. But whatever the reasons for individual variation, culture always plays a role in molding individual sexual urges toward a collective norm. And such sexual norms vary from culture to culture.

What do we know about variation in sexual norms from culture to culture, and over time? A classic cross-cultural study (Ford and Beach 1951) found wide variation in attitudes about masturbation, bestiality (sex with animals), and homosexuality. Even in a single culture, such as the United States, attitudes about sex differ with socioeconomic status, region, and rural versus urban residence. However, even in the 1950s, prior to the "age of sexual permissiveness" (the pre-HIV period from the mid-1960s through the 1970s), research showed that almost all American men (92 percent) and more than half of American women (54 percent) admitted to masturbation. In the famous Kinsey report (Kinsey, Pomeroy, and Martin 1948), 37 percent of the men surveyed admitted having had at least one sexual experience leading to orgasm with another male. In a later study of 1,200 unmarried women, 26 percent reported same-sex sexual activities.

Homosexual activities were absent, rare, or secret in only 37 percent of seventy-six societies for which data were available in the Ford and Beach study (1951). In the others, various forms of homosexuality were considered normal and acceptable. Sometimes sexual relations between people of the same sex involved transvestism on the part of one of the partners, like the *berdaches* discussed in Chapter 6. (See the box at the end of the chapter for other examples of transvestism and men who have sex with men.)

Transvestism did not characterize male-male sex among the Sudanese Azande, who valued the warrior role (Evans-Pritchard 1970). Prospective warriors—young men aged twelve to twenty—left their families and shared quarters with adult fighting men, who paid bridewealth for, and had sex with, them. During this apprenticeship, the young men did the domestic duties of women. Upon reaching warrior status, these young men took their own younger male brides. Later, retiring from the warrior role, Azande men married women. Flexible in their sexual expression, Azande males had no difficulty shifting from sex with older men (as male brides), to sex with younger men (as warriors), to sex with women (as husbands) (see Murray and Roscoe 1998).

Flexibility in human sexual expression seems to be an aspect of our primate heritage. Both masturbation and homosexual behavior exist among chimpanzees and other primates. Male bonobos (pygmy chimps) regularly engage in a form of mutual masturbation known as "penis fencing." Females get sexual pleasure from rubbing their genitals against those of other females (de Waal 1997). Our primate sexual potential is molded by culture, the environment, and reproductive necessity. Heterosexuality is practiced in all human societies—which, after all, must reproduce themselves—but alternatives are also widespread (Rathus, Nevid, and Fichner-Rathus 2000). The sexual component of human personality—just how we express our "natural" sexual urges—is a matter that culture and environment determine and limit.

GENDER AMONG AGRICULTURALISTS

As horticulture developed into agriculture, women lost their role as primary cultivators. Certain agricultural techniques, particularly plowing, were assigned to men because of their greater average size and strength (Martin and Voorhies 1975). Except when irrigation was used, plowing eliminated the need for constant weeding, an activity usually done by women.

Cross-cultural data illustrate these changes in productive roles. Women were the main workers in 50 percent of the horticultural societies surveyed but in only 15 percent of the agricultural groups. Male subsistence labor dominated 81 percent of the agricultural societies but only 17 percent of the horticultural ones (Martin and Voorhies 1975) (see Table 8-1).

With agriculture, women were cut off from production for the first time in human history. Belief systems started contrasting men's valuable extradomestic labor with women's domestic role, now viewed as inferior. (**Extradomestic** means outside the home; within or pertaining to the public domain.) Changes in kinship and postmarital residence patterns also hurt women. Descent groups and polygyny declined with agriculture, and the nuclear family became more common. Living with her husband and children,

TABLE 8-1	Male and Female Contributions to Production in Cultivating Societies	
	Horticulture (percentage of 104 societies)	Agriculture (percentage of 93 societies)
Women are primary cultivators	50%	15%
Men are primary cultivators	17	81
Equal contributions to cultivation	33	3

Source: Martin and Voorhies 1975, p. 283.

a woman was isolated from her kinswomen and cowives. Female sexuality is carefully supervised in agricultural economies; men have easier access to divorce and extramarital sex, reflecting a "double standard."

Still, female status in agricultural societies is not inevitably bleak. Gender stratification is associated with plow agriculture rather than with intensive cultivation per se. Studies of peasant gender roles and stratification in France and Spain (Harding 1975; Reiter 1975), which have plow agriculture, show that people think of the house as the female sphere and the fields as the male domain. However, such a dichotomy is not inevitable, as my own research among Betsileo agriculturalists in Madagascar shows.

Betsileo women play a prominent role in agriculture, contributing a third of the hours invested in rice production. They have their customary tasks in the division of labor, but their work is more seasonal than men's is. No one has much to do during the ceremonial season, between mid-June and mid-September. Men work in the rice fields almost daily the rest of the year. Women's cooperative work occurs during transplanting (mid-September through November) and harvesting (mid-March through early May). Along with other members of the household, women do daily weeding in December and January. After the harvest, all family members work together winnowing the rice and then transporting it to the granary.

Bilateral kinship systems, combined with subsistence economies in which the sexes have complementary roles in food production and distribution, have reduced gender stratification. Such features are common among Asian rice cultivators, such as the Ifugao of the Philippines (shown here).

If we consider the strenuous daily task of husking rice by pounding (a part of food preparation rather than production per se), women actually contribute slightly more than 50 percent of the labor devoted to producing and preparing rice before cooking.

Not just women's prominent economic role but traditional social organization enhances female status among the Betsileo. Although postmarital residence is mainly patrilocal, descent rules permit married women to keep membership in and a strong allegiance to their own descent groups. Kinship is broadly and bilaterally (on both sides—as in contemporary North America) calculated. The Betsileo exemplify Aihwa Ong's (1989) generalization that bilateral (and matrilineal) kinship systems, combined with subsistence economies in which the sexes have complementary roles in food production and distribution, are characterized by reduced gender stratification. Such societies are common among South Asian peasants (Ong 1989).

Traditionally, Betsileo men participate more in politics, but the women also hold political office. Women sell their produce and products in markets, invest in cattle, sponsor ceremonials, and are mentioned during offerings to ancestors. Arranging marriages, an important extradomestic activity, is more women's concern than men's. Sometimes Betsileo women seek their own kinswomen as wives for their sons, reinforcing their own prominence in village life and continuing kin-based female solidarity in the village.

The Betsileo illustrate the idea that intensive cultivation does not necessarily entail sharp gender stratification. We can see that gender roles and stratification reflect not just the type of adaptive strategy but also specific environmental variables and cultural attributes. Betsileo women continue to play a significant role in their society's major economic activity, rice production.

PATRIARCHY AND VIOLENCE

Patriarchy describes a political system ruled by men in which women have inferior social and political status, including basic human rights. Barbara Miller (1997), in a study of systematic neglect of females, describes women in rural northern India as "the endangered sex." Societies that feature a full-fledged patrilineal-patrilocal complex, replete with warfare and intervillage raiding, also typify patriarchy. Such practices as dowry murders, female infanticide, and clitoridectomy exemplify patriarchy, which extends from tribal societies such as the Yanomami to state societies such as India and Pakistan.

Although more prevalent in certain social settings than in others, family violence and domestic abuse of women are worldwide problems. Domestic violence certainly occurs in neolocal-nuclear family settings, such as Canada and the United States. In Canada, 62 percent of murdered women are killed by their husband or domestic partner, compared with 50 percent in Pakistan (Kantor 1996). Cities, with their impersonality and isolation from extended kin networks, are breeding groups for domestic violence.

We've seen that gender stratification is typically reduced in matrilineal, matrifocal, and bilateral societies in which women have prominent roles in the economy and social life. When a woman lives in her own village, she has kin nearby to look after and protect her interests. Even in patrilocal polygynous settings, women often count on the support of their cowives and sons in disputes with potentially abusive husbands. Such settings, which tend to provide a safe haven for women, are retracting rather than expanding in today's world, however. Isolated families and patrilineal social forms have spread at the expense of matrilineality. Many nations have declared polygyny illegal. More and more women, and men, find themselves cut off from extended kin and families of orientation.

With the spread of the women's rights movement and the human rights movement, attention to domestic violence and abuse of women has increased. Laws have been passed and mediating institutions established. Brazil's female-run police stations for battered women provide an example, as do shelters for victims of domestic abuse in the United States and Canada. But patriarchal institutions do persist in what should be a more enlightened world.

GENDER AND INDUSTRIALISM

The domestic-public dichotomy, which is developed most fully among patrilineal-patrilocal food producers and plow agriculturalists, has also affected gender stratification in industrial societies, including the United States and Canada. Recently, gender roles have been changing rapidly in North America. The "traditional" idea that "a woman's place is in the home" actually emerged in the United States as industrialism spread after 1900. Earlier, pioneer women in the Midwest and West had been recognized as fully productive workers in farming and home industry. Under industrialism, attitudes about gendered work came to vary with class and region. In early industrial Europe, men, women, and children had flocked to factories as wage laborers. American slaves of both sexes had done grueling work in cotton fields. With abolition, southern African American women continued working as field hands and domestics. Poor white women labored in the South's early cotton mills. In the 1890s more than 1 million American women held menial and repetitious unskilled factory positions (Margolis 1984; Martin and Voorhies 1975).

After 1900, European immigration produced a male labor force willing to work for wages lower than those of American-born men. Those immigrant men moved into factory jobs that previously had gone to women. As machine tools and mass production further reduced the need for female labor, the notion that women were biologically unfit for factory work began to gain ground (Martin and Voorhies 1975).

Maxine Margolis (1984, 2000) has shown how gendered work, attitudes, and beliefs have varied in response to American economic needs. For

During the world wars the notion that women were
biologically unfit for hard physical labor faded.
Shown here is World War II's famous Rosie the
Riveter. Is there a comparable poster women today?
What does her image say about modern gender roles?

example, wartime shortages of men have promoted the idea that work outside the home is women's patriotic duty. During the world wars the notion
that women are unfit for hard physical labor faded. Inflation and the culture
of consumption have also spurred female employment. When prices and/or
demand rise, multiple paychecks help maintain family living standards.

The steady increase in female paid employment since World War II also
reflects the baby boom and industrial expansion. American culture has traditionally defined clerical work, teaching, and nursing as female occupations. With rapid population growth and business expansion after World
War II, the demand for women to fill such jobs grew steadily. Employers
also found that they could increase their profits by paying women lower
wages than they would have to pay returning male war veterans.

TABLE 8-2	Cash Employment of American Mothers, Wives, and Husbands, 1960–2000*		
Year	Percentage of Married Women, Husband Present with Children under 6	Percentage of All Married Women[a]	Percentage of All Married Men[b]
1960	19%	32%	89%
1970	30	40	86
1980	45	50	81
1990	59	58	79
2000	63	61	77

*Civilian population sixteen years of age and older.
[a]Husband present.
[b]Wife present.
Source: Statistical Abstract of the United States, 2001, Table 577, p. 373; Table 575, p. 372.

Woman's role in the home has been stressed during periods of high unemployment, although when wages fall or inflation occurs simultaneously, female employment may still be accepted. Margolis (1984) contends that changes in the economy lead to changes in attitudes toward and about women. Economic changes paved the way for the contemporary woman's movement, which was also spurred by the publication of Betty Friedan's book *The Feminine Mystique* in 1963 and the founding of NOW, the National Organization of Women, in 1966. The movement in turn promoted expanded work opportunities for women, including equal pay for equal work. Between 1970 and 2000 the female percentage of the American workforce rose from 38 to 47 percent. In other words, almost half of all Americans who work outside the home are women. Some 66 million women now have paid jobs, compared with 75 million men. Women now fill more than half (54 percent) of all professional jobs (*Statistical Abstract of the United States, 2001,* pp. 367, 380). And it's not mainly single women working, as once was the case. Table 8-2 presents figures on the ever-increasing cash employment of American wives and mothers.

Note in Table 8-2 that the cash employment of American married men has been falling while that of American married women has been rising. There has been a dramatic change in behavior and attitudes since 1960, when 89 percent of all married men worked, compared with just 32 percent of married women. The comparable figures in 2000 were 77 percent and 61 percent. Ideas about the gender roles of males and females have changed. Compare your grandparents and your parents. Chances are you have a working mother, but that your grandmother was a stay-home mom. Your grandfather is more likely than your father to have worked in manufacturing and to have belonged to a union. Your father is more likely than your grandfather to have shared child care and domestic responsibilities. Age at

TABLE 8-3	Earnings in the United States (2000) by Gender and Job Type for Year-Round Full-Time Workers*			
		Median Annual Salary		*Ratio of Earnings Female/Male*
	Women	Men	2000	1989
Median earnings	$25,532	$33,592	76	68
By job type: Executive/administrative/ managerial	$35,672	$52,728	68	61
Professional	37,700	50,804	74	71
Sales	21,164	35,568	60	54
Service	16,432	21,528	76	62

*By occupation of longest job held.
Source: Based on data from the Statistical Abstract of the United States, 2001, Table 621, pp. 403.

marriage has been delayed for both men and women. College educations and professional degrees have increased. What other changes do you associate with the increase in female employment outside the home?

Table 8-3 details employment in the United States in 2000 by gender, income, and job type. Notice that the income gap between women and men was widest in sales, in which women averaged 60 percent of the male salary. Overall the ratio rose from 68 percent in 1989 to 76 percent in 2000.

Today's jobs aren't especially demanding in terms of physical labor. With machines to do the heavy work, the smaller average body size and lesser average strength of women are no longer impediments to blue-collar employment. The main reason we don't see more modern-day Rosies working alongside male riveters is that the U.S. workforce itself is abandoning heavy-goods manufacture. In the 1950s two-thirds of American jobs were blue-collar, compared with less than 16 percent today. The location of those jobs has shifted within the world capitalist economy. Third World countries with cheaper labor produce steel, automobiles, and other heavy goods less expensively than the United States can, but the United States excels at services. The American mass education system has many inadequacies, but it does train millions of people for service- and information-oriented jobs, from sales clerks to computer operators.

The Feminization of Poverty

Alongside the economic gains of many American women stands an opposite extreme: the feminization of poverty, or the increasing representation of women (and their children) among America's poorest people. Women head over half of U.S. households with incomes below the poverty line. In 1959

TABLE 8-4	Median Annual Income of U.S. Households, by Household Type, 1999		
	Number of Households (1000s)	Median Annual Income	Percentage of Median Earnings Compared with Married-Couple Households
All households	104,705	$40,816	72%
Family households	72,025	49,940	88
Married-couple households	55,311	56,827	100
Male earner, no wife	4,028	41,838	74
Female earner, no husband	12,687	26,164	46
Nonfamily households	32,680	24,566	43
Single male	14,641	30,753	54
Single female	18,039	19,919	35

Source: Based on data from the *Statistical Abstract of the United States, 2001*, Table 663, p. 434.

female-headed households accounted for just one-fourth of the American poor. Since then that figure has more than doubled.

Married couples are much more secure economically than single mothers are. The data in Table 8-4 demonstrate that the average income for married-couple families is more than twice that of families maintained by a woman. The average one-earner family maintained by a woman had an annual income of $26,164 in 1999. This was less than one-half the mean income ($56,827) of a married-couple household.

The feminization of poverty isn't just a North America trend. The percentage of female-headed households has been increasing worldwide. In Western Europe, for example, female-headed households rose from 24 percent in 1980 to 31 percent in 1990. The figure ranges from below 20 percent in certain South Asian and Southeast Asian countries to almost 50 percent in certain African countries and the Caribbean (Buvinic 1995).

Why must so many women be solo household heads? Where are the men going, and why are they leaving? Among the causes are male migration, civil strife (men off fighting), divorce, abandonment, widowhood, unwed adolescent parenthood, and, more generally, the idea that children are women's responsibility. Globally, households headed by women tend to be poorer than those headed by men. In one study, the percentage of single-parent families considered poor was 18 percent in Britain, 20 percent in Italy, 25 percent in Switzerland, 40 percent in Ireland, 52 percent in Canada, and 63 percent in the United States.

It is widely believed that one way to improve the situation of poor women is to encourage them to organize. New women's groups can in some cases revive or replace traditional forms of social organization that have been disrupted. Membership in a group can help women to mobilize resources, to rationalize production, and to reduce the risks and costs associated with credit. Organization also allows women to develop self-confidence and to decrease dependence on others. Through such organization, poor women throughout the world are working to determine their own needs and priorities and to change things so as to improve their social and economic situation (Buvinic 1995).

WHAT DETERMINES GENDER VARIATION?

We see that gender roles and stratification have varied widely across cultures and through history. Among many foragers and matrilineal cultivators, there is little gender stratification. Competition for resources leads to warfare and the intensification of production. These conditions favor patriliny and patrilocality. To the extent that women lose their productive roles in agricultural societies, the domestic-public dichotomy is accentuated and gender stratification is sharpened. With industrialism, attitudes about gender vary in the context of female extradomestic employment. Gender is flexible and varies with cultural, social, political, and economic factors. The variability of gender in time and space suggests that it will continue to change. The biology of the sexes is not a narrow enclosure limiting humans but a broad base upon which a variety of structures can be built (Friedl 1975).

S u m m a r y

1. Gender roles and gender stratification vary with environment, economy, adaptive strategy, level of social complexity, and degree of participation in the world economy. Gender roles are the tasks and activities a culture assigns to each sex. Gender stratification describes an unequal distribution of rewards by gender, reflecting different positions in a social hierarchy.

2. When gathering is prominent, gender status is more equal than when hunting or fishing dominates a foraging economy. Gender status is also more equal when the domestic and public spheres aren't sharply separated. Foragers lack two public arenas that contribute to higher male status among food producers: warfare and organized interregional trade.

3. Gender stratification is also linked to descent and residence. Women's status in matrilineal societies tends to be high because overall social identity comes through female links. Although there are no matriarchies, women in many societies wield power and make decisions. Scarcity of resources promotes intervillage warfare, patriliny, and patrilocality. The localization of related males is adaptive for military solidarity. Men may use their warrior role to symbolize and reinforce the social devaluation and oppression of women.

4. There has been a recent tendency to see sexual orientation as fixed and biologically based. But, to some extent at least, all human activities and preferences, including erotic expression, are influenced by culture. Sexual orientation stands for a person's habitual sexual attraction to, and activities with persons of the opposite sex, heterosexuality; the same sex, homosexuality; or both sexes, bisexuality. Sexual norms vary widely from culture to culture.

5. With the advent of plow agriculture, women were removed from production. The distinction between women's domestic work and men's "productive" labor reinforced the contrast between men as public and valuable and women as homebound and inferior. Patriarchy describes a political system ruled by men in which women have inferior social and political status, including basic human rights. Some expressions of patriarchy include female infanticide, dowry murders, domestic abuse, and forced genital operations.

6. Americans' attitudes toward gender roles vary with class and region. When the need for female labor declines, the idea that women are unfit for many jobs increases, and vice versa. Factors such as war, falling wages, and inflation help explain female cash employment and Americans' attitudes toward it. Countering the economic gains of many American women is the feminization of poverty. This has become a global phenomenon, as impoverished female-headed households have increased worldwide.

Case Study
Minangkabau

This chapter has discussed the influences of matrilineality and matrilocality on gender roles. In *Culture Sketches* by Holly Peters-Golden read the chapter on the Minangkabau: Merantau and Matriliny. What are some ways in which matrilineality influences, and is reflected in, other aspects of Minangkabau life?

Hidden Women, Public Men—Public Women, Hidden Men

For several years, one of Brazil's top sex symbols was Roberta Close, whom I first saw in a furniture commercial. Roberta, whose looks reminded me of those of the young Natalie Wood, ended her pitch with an admonition to prospective furni- ture buyers to accept no substitute for the advertised product. "Things," she warned, "are not always what they seem."

Nor was Roberta. This petite and in- credibly feminine creature was actually a man. Nevertheless, despite the fact that he—or she (speaking as Brazilians do)—is a man posing as a woman, Roberta has won a secure place in Brazilian mass culture. Her photos have decorated magazines. She has been a panelist on a TV variety show and has starred in a stage play in Rio with an actor known for his supermacho image. Roberta even inspired a well-known, and apparently heterosexual, pop singer to make a video honoring her. In it she pranced around Rio's Ipanema Beach in a bikini, showing off her ample hips and buttocks.

The video depicted the widespread male appreciation of Roberta's beauty. As confirmation, one heterosexual man told me that he had recently been on the same plane as Roberta and had been struck by her looks. Another man said he wanted to have sex with her. These comments, it seemed to me, illustrated striking cultural contrasts about gender and sexuality. In Brazil, a Latin American country noted for its machismo, heterosexual men don't feel that attraction toward a transvestite blemishes their masculine identities.

Roberta Close exists in relation to a gender-identity scale that jumps from extreme femininity to extreme masculinity, with little in between. Masculinity is stereotyped as active and public, femininity as passive and domestic. The male-female contrast in rights and behavior is much stronger in Brazil than it is in North America. Brazilians confront a more rigidly defined masculine role than North Americans do.

The active-passive dichotomy also provides a stereotypical model for male-male sexual relations. One man is supposed to be the active, masculine (inserting) partner, whereas the other is the passive, effeminate one. The latter man is derided as a *bicha* (intestinal worm), but little stigma attaches to the inserter. Indeed, many "active" (and married) Brazilian men like to have sex with transvestite prostitutes, who are biological males.

If a Brazilian man is unhappy pursuing either active masculinity or passive effeminacy, there is one other choice—active femininity. For Roberta Close and others like her, the cultural demand of ultramasculinity has yielded to a performance of ultrafemininity. These men-women form a third gender in relation to Brazil's polarized male-female identity scale.

Transvestites such as Roberta are particularly prominent in Rio de Janeiro's annual Carnaval, when an ambience of inversion rules the city. In the culturally accurate words of the American popular novelist Gregory McDonald, who sets one of his books in Brazil at Carnaval time:

> Everything goes topsy-turvy. . . . Men become women; women become men; grown-ups become children; rich people pretend they're poor; poor people, rich; sober people become drunkards; thieves become generous. Very topsy-turvy. (McDonald 1984, p. 154)

Most notably in this costumed inversion (DaMatta 1991), men dress as women. Carnaval expresses and revels in normally hidden tensions and conflicts as social life is turned upside down. Reality is illuminated through a dramatic presentation of its opposite.

This is the final key to Roberta's cultural meaning. She emerged in a setting in which male-female inversion is part of the year's most popular festival. Transvestites are the pièces de résistance at Rio's Carnaval balls, where they dress as scantily as the real women do. They wear postage-stamp bikinis, sometimes with no tops. Photos of real women and transformed ones vie for space in the magazines. It is often impossible to tell the born women from the hidden men. Roberta Close became a permanent incarnation of Carnaval—a year-round reminder of the spirit of Carnavals past, present, and yet to come.

Roberta emerged from a Latin culture whose gender roles contrast strongly with those of the United States. From small village to massive city, Brazilian males are public and Brazilian females are private creatures. Streets, beaches, and bars belong to the men. Although bikinis adorn Rio's beaches on weekends and holidays, there are many more men than women there on weekdays. The men revel in ostentatious sexual displays as they sun themselves, flex muscles, and play soccer and volleyball.

Brazilian men must work hard at this public image, constantly acting out their culture's definition of masculine behavior. Public life is a play whose strong roles go to men. Roberta Close, of course, is a public figure. Given that Brazilian culture defines the public world as male, we can perhaps better understand now why the nation's number one sex symbol has been a man who excels at performing in public as a woman.

Chapter 9

Religion

EXPRESSIONS OF RELIGION
  Animism • Mana and Taboo • Magic and Religion • Uncertainty, Anxiety, Solace • Rituals •
  Rites of Passage • Totemism
SOCIAL CONTROL
KINDS OF RELIGION
RELIGION AND CHANGE
  Revitalization Movements • Cargo Cults • A New Age
SECULAR RITUALS
Box: Sacred Cattle in India

The anthropologist Anthony F. C. Wallace has defined **religion** as "belief and ritual concerned with supernatural beings, powers, and forces" (1966, p. 5). Like ethnicity or language, religion may be associated with social divisions within and between societies and nations. Religious behavior and beliefs both unite and divide. Participation in common rites may affirm, and thus maintain, the social solidarity of a religion's adherents. On the other hand, religious differences may be associated with bitter enmity.

In studying religion cross-culturally, anthropologists pay attention not only to the social roles of religion but also to the content and nature of religious acts, events, processes, settings, practitioners, and organizations. We also consider such verbal manifestations of religious beliefs as prayers, chants, myths, texts, and statements about ethics and morality (see Child and Child 1993; Hicks, ed. 1999; Klass and Weisgrau, eds. 1999; Lehmann and Meyers, eds. 2000).

The supernatural is the extraordinary realm outside (but believed to impinge on) the observable world. It is nonempirical, mysterious, and inexplicable in ordinary terms. It must be accepted "on faith." Supernatural beings—gods and goddesses, ghosts, and souls—are not of the material world. Nor are supernatural forces, some of which are wielded by beings. Other sacred forces are impersonal; they simply exist. In many societies, however, people believe they can benefit from, become imbued with, or manipulate supernatural forces.

Religion, as defined here, exists in all human societies. It is a cultural universal. However, we'll see that it isn't always easy to distinguish the supernatural from the natural and that different cultures conceptualize supernatural entities very differently.

EXPRESSIONS OF RELIGION

When did religion begin? No one knows for sure. There are suggestions of religion in Neandertal burials and on European cave walls, where painted stick figures may represent shamans, early religious specialists. Nevertheless, any statement about when, where, why, and how religion arose, or any description of its original nature, can be only speculative. Although such speculations are inconclusive, however, many have revealed important functions and effects of religious behavior. Several theories will be examined now.

Animism

The founder of the anthropology of religion was the Englishman Sir Edward Burnett Tylor (1871/1958). Religion was born, Tylor thought, as people tried to understand conditions and events they could not explain by reference to daily experience. Tylor believed that our ancestors—and contemporary nonindustrial peoples—were particularly intrigued with death, dreaming, and trance. In dreams and trances, people see images they may remember when they wake up or come out of the trance state.

Tylor concluded that attempts to explain dreams and trances led early humans to believe that two entities inhabit the body, one active during the day and the other—a double or soul—active during sleep and trance states. Although they never meet, they are vital to each other. When the double permanently leaves the body, the person dies. Death is departure of the soul. From the Latin for soul, *anima*, Tylor named this belief animism. The soul was one sort of spiritual entity; people remembered various images from their dreams and trances—other spirits. For Tylor, **animism**, the earliest form of religion, was a belief in spiritual beings.

Tylor proposed that religion evolved through stages, beginning with animism. *Polytheism* (the belief in multiple gods) and then *monotheism* (the belief in a single, all-powerful deity) developed later. Because religion originated to explain things people didn't understand, Tylor thought it would decline as science offered better explanations. To an extent, he was right. We now have scientific explanations for many things that religion once elucidated. Nevertheless, because religion persists, it must do something more than explain the mysterious. It must, and does, have other functions and meanings.

Mana and Taboo

Besides animism—and sometimes coexisting with it in the same society—is a view of the supernatural as a domain of impersonal power, or *force*, which people can control under certain conditions. (You'd be right to think of *Star Wars*.) Such a conception of the supernatural is particularly prominent in Melanesia, the area of the South Pacific that includes Papua New Guinea and adjacent islands. Melanesians believed in **mana,** a sacred impersonal force existing in the universe. Mana can reside in people, animals, plants, and objects.

Melanesian mana was similar to our notion of efficacy or luck. Melanesians attributed success to mana, which people could acquire or manipulate in different ways, such as through magic. Objects with mana could change someone's luck. For example, a charm or amulet belonging to a successful hunter might transmit the hunter's mana to the next person who held or wore it. A woman might put a rock in her garden, see her yields improve dramatically, and attribute the change to the force contained in the rock.

Beliefs in manalike forces are widespread, although the specifics of the religious doctrines vary. Consider the contrast between mana in Melanesia and Polynesia (the islands included in a triangular area marked by Hawaii to the north, Easter Island to the east, and New Zealand to the southwest). In Melanesia, one could acquire mana by chance, or by working hard to get it. In Polynesia, however, mana wasn't potentially available to everyone but was attached to political offices. Chiefs and nobles had more mana than ordinary people did.

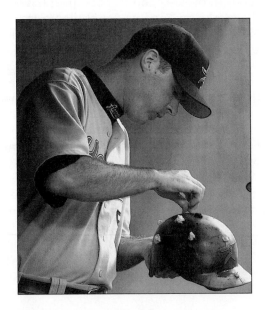

Mana is a supernatural force or power, which people may manipulate for their own ends. Mana can reside in people, animals, plants, and objects—even bubble gum. Illustrating baseball magic, pitcher Scott Elarton covers the helmet of teammate Craig Biggio with wads of lucky gum during a game against Detroit on July 14, 2000. Do you own anything that contains mana?

So charged with mana were the highest chiefs that contact with them was dangerous to the commoners. The mana of chiefs flowed out of their bodies wherever they went. It could infect the ground, making it dangerous for others to walk in the chief's footsteps. It could permeate the containers and utensils chiefs used in eating. Contact between chief and commoners was dangerous because mana could have an effect like an electric shock. Because high chiefs had so much mana, their bodies and possessions were **taboo** (set apart as sacred and off-limits to ordinary people). Contact between a high chief and commoners was forbidden. Because ordinary people couldn't bear as much sacred current as royalty could, when commoners were accidentally exposed, purification rites were necessary.

One function of religion is to explain. A belief in souls explains what happens in sleep, trance, and death. Melanesian mana explains differential success that people can't understand in ordinary, natural terms. People fail at hunting, war, or gardening not because they are lazy, stupid, or inept but because success comes—or doesn't come—from the supernatural world.

The beliefs in spiritual beings (e.g., animism) and supernatural forces (e.g., mana) fit within the definition of religion given at the beginning of this chapter. Most religions include both spirits and impersonal forces. Likewise the supernatural beliefs of contemporary North Americans include beings (gods, saints, souls, demons) and forces (charms, talismans, crystals, and sacred objects).

Magic and Religion

Magic refers to supernatural techniques intended to accomplish specific aims. These techniques include spells, formulas, and incantations used with deities or with impersonal forces. Magicians use *imitative magic* to produce a desired effect by imitating it. If magicians wish to injure or kill someone, they may imitate that effect on an image of the victim. Sticking pins in "voodoo dolls" is an example. With *contagious magic,* whatever is done to an object is believed to affect a person who once had contact with it. Sometimes practitioners of contagious magic use body products from prospective victims—their nails or hair, for example. The spell performed on the body product is believed to reach the person eventually and work the desired result.

We find magic in societies with diverse religious beliefs. It can be associated with animism, mana, polytheism, or monotheism. Magic is neither simpler nor more primitive than animism or the belief in mana.

Uncertainty, Anxiety, Solace

Religion and magic don't just explain things and help people accomplish goals. They also enter the realm of human feelings. In other words, they serve emotional needs as well as cognitive (e.g., explanatory) ones. For example, supernatural beliefs and practices can help reduce anxiety. Magical techniques can dispel doubts that arise when outcomes are beyond human control. Similarly, religion helps people face death and endure life crises.

Although all societies have techniques to deal with everyday matters, there are certain aspects of people's lives over which they lack control. When people face uncertainty and danger, according to Malinowski, they turn to magic.

Malinowski found that the Trobriand Islanders used magic when sailing, a hazardous activity. He proposed that because people can't control matters such as wind, weather, and the fish supply, they turn to magic. People may call on magic when they come to a gap in their knowledge or powers of practical control yet have to continue in a pursuit (Malinowski 1931/1978).

According to Malinowski, magic is used to establish control, but religion "is born out of . . . the real tragedies of human life" (Malinowski 1931/1978, p. 45). Religion offers emotional comfort, particularly when people face a crisis. Malinowski saw tribal religions as concerned mainly with organizing, commemorating, and helping people get through such life events as birth, puberty, marriage, and death.

Rituals

Several features distinguish **rituals** from other kinds of behavior (Rappaport 1974, 1999). Rituals are formal—stylized, repetitive, and stereotyped. People perform them in special (sacred) places and at set times. Rituals include *liturgical orders*—sequences of words and actions invented prior to the current performance of the ritual in which they occur.

These features link rituals to plays, but there are important differences. Plays have audiences rather than participants. Actors merely *portray* something, but ritual performers—who make up congregations—are *in earnest*. Rituals convey information about the participants and their traditions. Repeated year after year, generation after generation, rituals translate enduring messages, values, and sentiments into action.

Rituals are *social* acts. Inevitably, some participants are more committed than others to the beliefs that lie behind the rites. However, just by taking part in a joint public act, the performers signal that they accept a common social and moral order, one that transcends their status as individuals.

Rites of Passage

Magic and religion, as Malinowski noted, can reduce anxiety and allay fears. Ironically, beliefs and rituals can also *create* anxiety and a sense of insecurity and danger (Radcliffe-Brown 1962/1965). Anxiety may arise *because* a rite exists. Indeed, participation in a collective ritual may build up stress, whose common reduction, through the completion of the ritual, enhances the solidarity of the participants.

Rites of passage, e.g., the collective circumcision of teenagers, can be very stressful. The traditional vision quests of Native Americans, particularly the Plains Indians, illustrate **rites of passage** (customs associated with the transition from one place or stage of life to another), which are found throughout the world. Among the Plains Indians, to move from boyhood to manhood, a youth temporarily separated from his community. After a period of isolation in the wilderness, often featuring fasting and drug consumption, the young man would see a vision, which would become his guardian spirit. He would then return to his community as an adult.

The rites of passage of contemporary societies include confirmations, baptisms, bar and bat mitzvahs, and fraternity hazing. Passage rites involve changes in social status, such as from boyhood to manhood and from non-member to sorority sister. More generally, a rite of passage may mark any change in place, condition, social position, or age.

All rites of passage have three phases: separation, liminality, and incorporation. In the first phase, people withdraw from the group and begin moving from one place or status to another. In the third phase, they reenter society, having completed the rite. The *liminal* phase is the most interesting. It is the period between states, the limbo during which people have left one place or state but haven't yet entered or joined the next (Turner 1969/1974).

Liminality always has certain characteristics. Liminal people occupy ambiguous social positions. They exist apart from ordinary distinctions and expectations, living in a time out of time. They are cut off from normal

Liminal people, like these Xavante Indian boys in Brazil, are temporarily set apart from ordinary distinctions and expectations. Their liminal status may be marked by a variety of contrasts with ordinary life, such as dietary restrictions or confinement to an initiation hut of the sort shown here. When was the last time you were liminal?

TABLE 9-1	Oppositions between Liminality and Normal Social Life
Liminality	**Normal Social Structure**
transition	state
homogeneity	heterogeneity
communitas	structure
equality	inequality
anonymity	names
absence of property	property
absence of status	status
nakedness or uniform dress	dress distinctions
sexual continence or excess	sexuality
minimization of sex distinctions	maximization of sex distinctions
absence of rank	rank
humility	pride
disregard of personal appearance	care for personal appearance
unselfishness	selfishness
total obedience	obedience only to superior rank
sacredness	secularity
sacred instruction	technical knowledge
silence	speech
simplicity	complexity
acceptance of pain and suffering	avoidance of pain and suffering

Source: Adapted from Turner 1969/1974. Copyright © 1969 by Victor W. Turner. By permission of Aldine de Gruyter, New York.

social contacts. A variety of contrasts may demarcate liminality from regular social life. For example, among the Ndembu of Zambia, a chief underwent a rite of passage before taking office. During the liminal period, his past and future positions in society were ignored, even reversed. He was subjected to a variety of insults, orders, and humiliations.

Unlike the vision quest and the Ndembu initiation, which are individual experiences, passage rites are often collective. Several individuals—boys being circumcised, fraternity or sorority initiates, men at military boot camps, football players in summer training camps, women becoming nuns—pass through the rites together as a group. Table 9-1 summarizes the contrasts or oppositions between liminality and normal social life.

Most notable is a social aspect of *collective liminality* called **communitas** (Turner 1969/1974), an intense community spirit, a feeling of great social solidarity, equality, and togetherness. People experiencing liminality together form a community of equals. The social distinctions that have existed before or will exist afterward are temporarily forgotten. Liminal people experience the same treatment and conditions and must act alike. Liminality may be marked ritually and symbolically by *reversals* of ordinary behavior. For example, sexual taboos may be intensified, or conversely, sexual excess may be encouraged.

Liminality is basic to every passage rite. Furthermore, in certain societies, including our own, liminal symbols may be used to set off one (religious) group from another, and from society as a whole. Such "permanent liminal groups" (e.g., sects, brotherhoods, and cults) are found most characteristically in complex societies—nation-states. Such liminal features as humility, poverty, equality, obedience, sexual abstinence, and silence may be required for all sect or cult members. Those who join such a group agree to its rules. As if they were undergoing a passage rite—but in this case a never-ending one—they may rid themselves of their previous possessions and cut themselves off from former social links, including those with family members.

Identity as a member of the group is expected to transcend individuality. Cult members often wear uniform clothing. They may try to reduce distinctions based on age and gender by using a common hair style (shaved head, short hair, or long hair). The Heaven's Gate cult, whose mass suicide garnered headlines in 1997, even used castration to increase *androgyny* (similarity between males and females). With such cults (as in the military), the individual, so important in American culture, is submerged in the collective. This is one reason Americans are so fearful and suspicious of "cults." In a variety of contexts, liminal features signal the distinctiveness or sacredness of groups, persons, settings, and events. Liminal symbols mark entities and circumstances as extraordinary—outside and beyond ordinary social space and routine social events.

Totemism

Rituals serve the social function of creating temporary or permanent solidarity among people—forming a social community. We see this also in practices known as totemism. Totemism was important in the religions of the Native Australians. *Totems* could be animals, plants, or geographical features. In each tribe, groups of people had particular totems. Members of each totemic group believed themselves to be descendants of their totem. They customarily neither killed nor ate it, but this taboo was lifted once a year, when people assembled for ceremonies dedicated to the totem. These annual rites were believed to be necessary for the totem's survival and reproduction.

Totemism uses nature as a model for society. The totems are usually animals and plants, which are part of nature. People relate to nature through their totemic association with natural species. Because each group has a different totem, social differences mirror natural contrasts. Diversity in the natural order becomes a model for diversity in the social order. However, although totemic plants and animals occupy different niches in nature, on another level they are united because they all are part of nature. The unity of the human social order is enhanced by symbolic association with and imitation of the natural order (Durkheim 1912/1961; Lévi-Strauss 1963; Radcliffe-Brown 1962/1965).

One role of religious rites and beliefs is to affirm, and thus maintain, the solidarity of a religion's adherents. Totems are sacred emblems symbolizing common identity. This is true not just among Native Australians, but also among Native American groups of the North Pacific coast of North America, whose totem poles are well known. Their totemic carvings, which commemorated, and told visual stories about, ancestors, animals and spirits, were also associated with ceremonies. In totemic rites, people gather together to honor their totem. In so doing, they use ritual to maintain the social oneness that the totem symbolizes.

SOCIAL CONTROL

Religion has meaning for people. It helps them cope with adversity and tragedy. It offers hope that things will get better. Lives can be transformed through spiritual healing or rebirth. Sinners can repent and be saved—or they can go on sinning and be damned. If the faithful truly internalize a system of religious rewards and punishments, their religion becomes a powerful means of controlling their beliefs, behavior, and what they teach their children.

Many people engage in religious activity because it seems to work. Prayers get answered. Faith healers heal. Sometimes it doesn't take much to convince the faithful that religious actions are efficacious. Many American Indian people in southwestern Oklahoma use faith healers at high monetary costs, not just because it makes them feel better about the uncertain, but because it works (Lassiter 1998). Each year legions of Brazilians visit a church, Nosso Senhor do Bomfim, in the city of Salvador, Bahia. They vow to repay "Our Lord" (Nosso Senhor) if healing happens. Showing that the vows work, and are repaid, are the thousands of *ex votos*, plastic impressions of every conceivable body part, that adorn the church, along with photos of people who have been cured.

Religion can work by getting inside people and mobilizing their emotions—their joy, their wrath, their righteousness. Émile Durkheim (1912/1961), a prominent French social theorist and scholar of religion, described the collective "effervescence" that can develop in religious contexts. Intense emotion bubbles up. People feel a deep sense of shared joy, meaning, experience, communion, belonging, and commitment to their religion.

The power of religion affects action. When religions meet, they can coexist peacefully, or their differences can be a basis for enmity and disharmony, even battle. Religious fervor has inspired Christians on crusades against the infidel and has led Muslims to wage jihads, holy wars against non-Islamic peoples. Throughout history, political leaders have used religion to promote and justify their views and policies.

By late September 1996, the Taliban Movement had firmly imposed an extreme form of social control in the name of religion on Afghanistan and its people. Led by Muslim clerics, the Taliban aimed to create their version of an Islamic society modeled on the teachings of the Koran (Burns 1997). Various repressive measures were instituted. The Taliban barred women from work and girls from school. Females past puberty were prohibited from talking to unrelated men. Women needed an approved reason, such as shopping for food, to leave their homes. Men, who were required to grow bushy beards, also faced an array of bans—against playing cards, listening to music, keeping pigeons, and flying kites.

To enforce their decrees, the Taliban sent armed enforcers throughout the country. These agents took charge of "beard checks" and other forms of scrutiny on behalf of a religious police force known as the General Department for the Preservation of Virtue and the Elimination of Vice (Burns 1997). By late Fall 2001 the Taliban had been overthrown, with a new interim government established in Kabul, the Afghan capital, on December 22. The collapse of the Taliban followed American bombing of Afghanistan in response to the September 11, 2001 attacks on New York's World Trade Center and Washington's Pentagon. As the Taliban yielded Kabul to victorious northern alliance forces, local men flocked to barbershops to have their beards trimmed or shaved. They were using a key Taliban symbol to celebrate the end of repression in religion's name.

Discrimination on the basis of religion is a familiar theme in national and world history. How may religious leaders mobilize communities and, in so doing, gain support for their own policies? One way is by persuasion; another is by instilling hatred or fear. Consider witchcraft accusations. Witch hunts can be powerful means of social control by creating a climate of danger and insecurity that affects everyone, not just the people who are

Members of different religions can coexist peacefully, or be in a state of disharmony, enmity, or battle. Religious fervor has inspired Christians on crusades against the infidel and has led Muslims to wage jihads, holy wars against non-Islamic peoples. During an October 21, 2001, gathering of Sunni Muslims at a mosque in Peshawar, Pakistan, men urge support for a Taliban-backed anti-American jihad.

likely targets. No one wants to seem deviant, to be accused of being a witch. In state societies, witch hunts often take aim at people who can be accused and punished with least chance of retaliation. During the great European witch craze, during the fifteenth, sixteenth, and seventeenth centuries (Harris 1974), most accusations and convictions were against poor women with little social support.

Witchcraft accusations are often directed at socially marginal or anomalous individuals. Among the Betsileo of Madagascar, for example, who prefer patrilocal postmarital residence, men living in their wife's or their mother's village violate a cultural norm. Linked to their anomalous social position, just a bit of unusual behavior (e.g., staying up late at night) on their part is sufficient for them to be called witches and avoided as a result. In tribes and peasant communities, people who stand out economically, especially if they seem to be benefiting at the expense of others, often face witchcraft accusations, leading to social ostracism or punishment. In this case witchcraft accusation becomes a **leveling mechanism**, a custom or social action that operates to reduce differences in wealth and thus to bring standouts in line with community norms—another form of social control.

To ensure proper behavior, religions offer rewards, e.g., the fellowship of the religious community, and punishments, e.g., the threat of being cast out or excommunicated. "The Lord giveth and the Lord taketh away." Many religions promise rewards for the good life and punishment for the bad. Your physical, mental, moral, and spiritual health, now and forever, may depend on your beliefs and behavior. For example, if you don't pay enough attention to the ancestors, they may snatch your kids from you.

Religions, especially the formal organized ones typically found in state societies, often prescribe a code of ethics and morality to guide behavior. The Judaic Ten Commandments laid down a set of prohibitions against killing, stealing, adultery, and other misdeeds. Crimes are breaches of secular laws, as sins are breaches of religious strictures. Some rules (e.g., the Ten Commandments) proscribe or prohibit behavior; others prescribe behavior. The Golden Rule, for instance, is a religious guide to do unto others as you would have them do unto you. Moral codes are ways of maintaining order and stability. Codes of morality and ethics are constantly repeated in religious sermons, catechisms, and the like. They become internalized psychologically. They guide behavior and produce regret, guilt, shame, and the need for forgiveness, expiation, and absolution when they are not followed.

Religions also maintain social control by stressing the temporary and fleeting nature of this life. They promise rewards (and/or punishment) in an afterlife (Christianity) or reincarnation (Hinduism and Buddhism). Such beliefs serve to reinforce the status quo. People can accept what they have now, knowing they can expect something better in the afterlife or the next life, if they follow religious guidelines. Under slavery in the American South, the masters taught portions of the Bible, such as the story of Job, that stressed compliance. The slaves, however, seized on the story of Moses, the promised land, and deliverance.

KINDS OF RELIGION

Religion is a cultural universal. But religions are parts of particular cultures, and cultural differences show up systematically in religious beliefs and practices. For example, the religions of stratified, state societies differ from those of societies with less marked social contrasts and power differentials.

Considering several societies, Wallace (1966) identified four types of religion: shamanic, communal, Olympian, and monotheistic (Table 9-2). The simplest type is shamanic religion. Unlike priests, **shamans** aren't full-time religious officials but part-time religious figures who mediate between people and supernatural beings and forces. All societies have medico-magico-religious specialists. *Shaman* is the general term encompassing curers ("witch doctors"), mediums, spiritualists, astrologers, palm readers, and other diviners. Wallace found shamanic religions to be most characteristic of foraging societies, particularly those found in the northern latitudes, such as the Inuit and the native peoples of Siberia.

Although they are only part-time specialists, shamans often set themselves off symbolically from ordinary people by assuming a different or ambiguous sex or gender role. (In nation-states, priests, nuns, and vestal virgins do something similar by taking vows of celibacy and chastity.) Transvestism is one way of being sexually ambiguous. Among the Chukchee of Siberia (Bogoras 1904), where coastal populations fished and interior groups hunted, male shamans copied the dress, speech, hair arrangements, and life styles of women. These shamans took other men as husbands and sex partners and received respect for their supernatural and curative expertise. Female shamans could join a fourth gender, copying men and taking wives.

TABLE 9-2	Wallace's Typology of Religions		
Type of Religion	Type of Practitioner	Conception of Supernatural	Type of Society
Monotheistic	Priests, ministers, etc.	Supreme being	States
Olympian	Priesthood	Hierarchical pantheon with powerful deities	Chiefdoms and archaic states
Communal	Part-time specialists; occasional community-sponsored events, including collective rites of passage	Several deities with some control over nature	Food-producing tribes
Shamanic	Shaman is a part-time practitioner	Zoomorphic (plants and animals)	Foraging bands

Communal religions have, in addition to shamans, community rituals such as harvest ceremonies and collective rites of passage. Although communal religions lack *full-time* religious specialists, they believe in several deities (**polytheism**) who control aspects of nature. Although some hunter-gatherers, including Australian totemites, have communal religions, these religions are more typical of farming societies.

Olympian religions, which arose with state organization and marked social stratification, add full-time religious specialists—professional *priest-hoods*. Like the state itself, the priesthood is hierarchically and bureaucratically organized. The term *Olympian* comes from Mount Olympus, home of the classical Greek gods. Olympian religions are polytheistic. They include powerful anthropomorphic gods with specialized functions, for example, gods of love, war, the sea, and death. Olympian *pantheons* (collections of supernatural beings) were prominent in the religions of many nonindustrial nation-states, including the Aztecs of Mexico, several African and Asian kingdoms, and classical Greece and Rome. Wallace's fourth type—**monotheism**—also has priesthoods and notions of divine power, but it views the supernatural differently. In monotheism, all supernatural phenomena are manifestations of, or are under the control of, a single eternal, omniscient, omnipotent, and omnipresent supreme being.

Robert Bellah (1978) coined the term "world-rejecting religion" to describe most forms of Christianity. The first world-rejecting religions arose in ancient civilizations, along with literacy and a specialized priesthood. These religions are so-named because of their tendency to reject the natural (mundane, ordinary, material, secular) world and to focus instead on a higher (sacred, transcendent) realm of reality. The divine is a domain of exalted morality to which humans can only aspire. Salvation through fusion with the supernatural is the main goal of such religions.

RELIGION AND CHANGE

Religious fundamentalists seek order based on strict adherence to purportedly traditional standards, beliefs, rules, and customs. Christian and Islamic fundamentalists recognize, decry, and attempt to redress change, yet they also contribute to change. In a worldwide process, new religions challenge established churches. In the United States, for example, conservative Christian TV hosts have become influential broadcasters and opinion shapers. In Latin America evangelical Protestantism is winning millions of converts from Roman Catholicism.

Religion helps maintain social order, but it can also be an instrument not just of change, but also of revolution. As a response to conquest or foreign domination, for example, religious leaders often undertake to alter or revitalize a society. In an "Islamic Revolution," Iranian ayatollahs marshaled religious fervor to create national solidarity and radical change. We call such movements nativistic movements (Linton 1943) or *revitalization movements* (Wallace 1956).

Revitalization Movements

Revitalization movements are social movements that occur in times of change, in which religious leaders emerge and undertake to alter or revitalize a society. Christianity originated as a revitalization movement. Jesus was one of several prophets who preached new religious doctrines while the Middle East was under Roman rule. It was a time of social unrest, when a foreign power ruled the land. Jesus inspired a new, enduring, and major religion. His contemporaries were not so successful.

The Handsome Lake religion arose around 1800 among the Iroquois of New York State (Wallace 1969). Handsome Lake, the founder of this revitalization movement, was a leader of one of the Iroquois tribes. The Iroquois had suffered because of their support of the British against the American colonials. After the colonial victory and a wave of immigration to their homeland, the Iroquois were dispersed on small reservations. Unable to pursue traditional horticulture and hunting in their homeland, the Iroquois became heavy drinkers and quarreled among themselves.

Handsome Lake was a heavy drinker who started having visions from heavenly messengers. The spirits warned him that unless the Iroquois changed their ways, they would be destroyed. His visions offered a plan for coping with the new order. Witchcraft, quarreling, and drinking would end. The Iroquois would copy European farming techniques, which, unlike traditional Iroquois horticulture, stressed male rather than female labor. Handsome Lake preached that the Iroquois should also abandon their communal long houses and matrilineal descent groups for more permanent marriages and individual family households. The teachings of Handsome Lake produced a new church and religion, one that still has members in New York and Ontario. This revitalization movement helped the Iroquois adapt to and survive in a modified environment. They eventually gained a reputation among their non-Indian neighbors as sober family farmers.

Cargo Cults

Like the Handsome Lake religion just discussed, cargo cults are revitalization movements. Such movements may emerge when natives have regular contact with industrial societies but lack their wealth, technology, and living standards. Some such movements attempt to *explain* European domination and wealth and to achieve similar success magically by mimicking European behavior and manipulating symbols of the desired life style. The **cargo cults** of Melanesia and Papua New Guinea weave Christian doctrine with aboriginal beliefs. They take their name from their focus on cargo—European goods of the sort natives have seen unloaded from the cargo holds of ships and airplanes.

In one early cult, members believed that the spirits of the dead would arrive in a ship. These ghosts would bring manufactured goods for the natives and would kill all the whites. More recent cults replaced ships with airplanes (Worsley 1959/1985). Many cults have used elements of European

A cargo cult in Vanuatu, a country in Melanesia. Boys and men march with spears, imitating British colonial soldiers. Does anything in your own society remind you of a cargo cult?

culture as sacred objects. The rationale is that Europeans use these objects, have wealth, and therefore must know the "secret of cargo." By mimicking how Europeans use or treat objects, natives hope also to come upon the secret knowledge needed to gain cargo.

For example, having seen Europeans' reverent treatment of flags and flagpoles, the members of one cult began to worship flagpoles. They believed the flagpoles were sacred towers that could transmit messages between the living and the dead. Other natives built airstrips to entice planes bearing canned goods, portable radios, clothing, wristwatches, and motorcycles. Near the airstrips they made effigies of towers, airplanes, and radios. They talked into the cans in a magical attempt to establish radio contact with the gods.

Some cargo cult prophets proclaimed that success would come through a reversal of European domination and native subjugation. The day was near, they preached, when natives, aided by God, Jesus, or native ancestors, would turn the tables. Native skins would turn white, and those of Europeans would turn brown; Europeans would die or be killed.

Cargo cults blend aboriginal and Christian beliefs. Melanesian myths told of ancestors shedding their skins and changing into powerful beings and of dead people returning to life. Christian missionaries, who had been in Melanesia since the late nineteenth century, also spoke of resurrection.

The cults' preoccupation with cargo is related to traditional Melanesian big-man systems. In Chapter 7, "Political Systems," we saw that a Melanesian big man had to be generous. People worked for the big man, helping him amass wealth, but eventually he had to give a feast and give away all that wealth.

Because of their experience with big-man systems, Melanesians believed that all wealthy people eventually had to give their wealth away. For decades they had attended Christian missions and worked on plantations. All the while they expected Europeans to return the fruits of their labor as their own big men did. When the Europeans refused to distribute the wealth or even to let natives know the secret of its production and distribution, cargo cults developed.

Like arrogant big men, Europeans would be leveled, by death if necessary. However, natives lacked the physical means of doing what their traditions said they should do. Thwarted by well-armed colonial forces, natives resorted to magical leveling. They called on supernatural beings to intercede, to kill or otherwise deflate the European big men and redistribute their wealth.

Cargo cults are religious responses to the expansion of the world capitalist economy. However, this religious mobilization had political and economic results. Cult participation gave Melanesians a basis for common interests and activities and thus helped pave the way for political parties and economic interest organizations. Previously separated by geography, language, and customs, Melanesians started forming larger groups as members of the same cults and followers of the same prophets. The cargo cults paved the way for political action through which the indigenous peoples eventually regained their autonomy.

A New Age

Among the changes involving religion in contemporary North America is a certain decline in formal organized religions and a rise of secularism. Between 1972 and 1998, the percentage of Americans saying they never attend church rose from 14 to 33 percent. The number saying they lacked religious beliefs or adhered to something other than Christianity or Judaism tripled from 5 to 16 percent (Edsall 2001). A similar shift has occurred in Canada. Atheists and "secular humanists" are not just bugaboos for religious conservatives. They really do exist, and they, too, are organized. Like members of religious groups, they use varied media, including print and the Internet, to communicate among themselves. Just as Buddhists can peruse *Tricycle: The Buddhist Review*, secular humanists can find their views validated in *Free Inquiry*, a quarterly identifying itself as "the international secular humanist magazine." Secular humanists speak out against organized religion and its "dogmatic pronouncements" and "supernatural or spiritual agendas" and the "obscurantist views" of religious leaders who presume "to inform us of God's views" by appealing to sacred texts (Steinfels 1997).

Even as our society appears to be growing more secular, some middle-class people have also turned to spiritualism, in search of the meaning of life. Spiritual orientations serve as the basis of new social movements. Some white people have appropriated the symbols, settings, and purported religious practices of Native Americans and, in Australia, of Native Australians, for New Age religions. Many natives have strongly protested the use of their sacred property and places by such groups.

New religious movements have varied origins. Some have been influenced by Christianity, others by Eastern (Asian) religions, and still others by mysticism and spiritualism. Religion also evolves in tandem with science and technology. For example, the Raelian Movement, a religious group centered in Switzerland and Montreal, promotes cloning as a way of achieving "eternal life. Raelians believe that extraterrestrials called "Elohim" artificially created all life on earth. The group has established a company called Valiant Venture Ltd., which offers infertile and homosexual couples the opportunity to have a child cloned from one of the spouses (Ontario Consultants on Religious Tolerance 1996).

In the United States the official recognition of a religion entitles it to a modicum of respect and certain benefits, such as exemption from taxation on its income and property (as long as it does not engage in political activity). Not all would-be religions receive official recognition. For example, Scientology is recognized as a church in the United States but not in Germany. In 1997 United States government officials spoke out against Germany's persecution of Scientologists as a form of "human rights abuse." Germans protested vehemently, calling Scientology a dangerous nonreligious political movement, with between 30,000 and 70,000 German members.

SECULAR RITUALS

In concluding this discussion of religion, we may recognize some problems with the definition of religion given at the beginning of this chapter. The first problem: If we define religion with reference to supernatural beings, powers, and forces, how do we classify ritual-like behavior that occurs in secular contexts? Some anthropologists believe there are both sacred and secular rituals. Secular rituals include formal, invariant, stereotyped, earnest, repetitive behavior and rites of passage that take place in nonreligious settings.

A second problem: If the distinction between the supernatural and the natural is not consistently made in a society, how can we tell what is religion and what isn't? The Betsileo of Madagascar, for example, view witches and dead ancestors as real people who play roles in ordinary life. However, their occult powers are not empirically demonstrable.

A third problem: The behavior considered appropriate for religious occasions varies tremendously from culture to culture. One society may consider drunken frenzy the surest sign of faith, whereas another may inculcate quiet reverence. Who is to say which is "more religious"?

Some anthropologists insist that rituals are distinguished from other behavior by special emotions, nonutilitarian intentions, and supernatural entities. However, others define ritual more broadly. Writing about football, W. Arens (1981) points out that behavior can simultaneously have sacred and secular aspects. On one level, football is "simply a sport"; on another, it is a public ritual.

In the context of comparative religion, this isn't surprising. The French sociologist/anthropologist. Émile Durkheim (1912/1961) pointed out long ago that almost everything from the sublime to the ridiculous has in some societies been treated as sacred. The distinction between sacred and profane doesn't depend on the intrinsic qualities of the sacred symbol. In Australian totemism, for example, sacred beings include such humble creatures as ducks, frogs, rabbits, and grubs, whose inherent qualities could hardly have given rise to the religious sentiment they inspire. If frogs and grubs can be elevated to a sacred level, why not, for example, a sports experience? Olympic and World Cup contests are certainly capable of generating fervor reminiscent of religion.

Many Americans believe that recreation and religion are separate domains. From my field work in Brazil and Madagascar and my reading about other societies, I believe that this separation is both ethnocentric and false. Madagascar's tomb-centered ceremonies are times when the living and the dead are joyously reunited, when people get drunk, gorge themselves, and enjoy sexual license. Perhaps the gray, sober, ascetic, and moralistic aspects of many religious events in the United States, in taking the "fun" out of religion, force us to find our religion in fun. Many contemporary people seek in such apparently secular contexts as sporting events and rock concerts what others find in religious rites, beliefs, and ceremonies.

S u m m a r y

1. Religion, a cultural universal, consists of belief and behavior concerned with supernatural beings, powers, and forces. Religion also encompasses the feelings and meanings associated with such beliefs and behavior. Anthropological studies have revealed many expressions and functions of religion.

2. Tylor considered animism—the belief in spirits or souls—to be religion's earliest and most basic form. He focused on religion's explanatory role, arguing that religion would eventually disappear as science provided better explanations. Besides animism, yet another view of the supernatural also occurs in nonindustrial societies, seeing the supernatural as a domain of raw, impersonal power or force (called

mana in Polynesia and Melanesia). People can manipulate and control mana under certain conditions.

3. When ordinary technical and rational means of doing things fail, people may turn to magic. Often they use magic when they lack control over outcomes. Religion offers comfort and psychological security at times of crisis. On the other hand, rites can also create anxiety. Rituals are formal, invariant, stylized, earnest acts in which people subordinate their particular beliefs to a social collectivity. Rites of passage have three stages: separation, liminality, and incorporation. Such rites can mark any change in social status, age, place, or social condition. Collective rites are often cemented by communitas, a feeling of intense solidarity.

4. Religion establishes and maintains social control through a series of moral and ethical beliefs and real and imagined rewards and punishments, internalized in individuals. Religion also achieves social control by mobilizing its members for collective action.

5. Wallace defines four types of religion: shamanic, communal, Olympian, and monotheistic. Each has its characteristic ceremonies and practitioners. Religion helps maintain social order, but it can also promote change. Revitalization movements blend old and new beliefs and have helped people adapt to changing conditions.

6. There are secular as well as sacred rituals. Contemporary people may seek in such apparently secular contexts as sporting events and rock concerts what others find in religious rites, beliefs, and ceremonies.

Case Study
Azande

This chapter has discussed ways in which religious beliefs may serve to establish social control and to provide comfort and answers in times of crisis. In *Culture Sketches* by Holly Peters-Golden read the chapter on the Azande: Witchcraft and Oracles in Africa. Witchcraft among the Azande traditionally served as an effective means of social control. What are the major institutions and beliefs in your own societies that function similarly? Think about the ways in which members of your society are compelled to behave in socially acceptable ways. Is religion among them? There is a "logic" to the Azande belief in witchcraft and the causality of misfortune. Do you employ logic that is similar or different when explaining negative events? Are there several different "systems of logic" that may be invoked, depending on the circumstances?

Sacred Cattle in India

The people of India worship zebu cattle, which are protected by the Hindu doctrine of *ahimsa*, a principle of nonviolence that forbids the killing of animals generally. Western economic development experts occasionally (and erroneously) cite the Hindu cattle taboo to illustrate the idea that religious beliefs can stand in the way of rational economic decisions. Hindus seem to be irrationally ignoring a valuable food (beef) because of their cultural or religious traditions.

The economic developers also comment that Indians don't know how to raise proper cattle. They point to the scraggly zebus that wander about town and country. Western techniques of animal husbandry grow bigger cattle that produce more beef and milk. Western planners lament that Hindus are set in their ways. Bound by culture and tradition, they refuse to develop rationally.

These assumptions are both ethnocentric and wrong. Sacred cattle actually play an important adaptive role in an Indian ecosystem that has evolved over thousands of years (Harris 1974, 1978). Peasants' use of cattle to pull plows and carts is part of the technology of Indian agriculture. Indian peasants have no need for large, hungry cattle of the sort that economic developers, beef marketers, and North American cattle ranchers prefer. Scrawny animals pull plows and carts well enough but don't eat their owners out of house and home. How could peasants with limited land and marginal diets feed supersteers without taking food away from themselves?

Indians use cattle manure to fertilize their fields. Not all the manure is collected, because peasants don't spend much time watching their cattle, which wander and graze at will during certain seasons. In the rainy season, some of the manure that cattle deposit on the hillsides washes down to the fields. In this way, cattle also fertilize the fields indirectly. Furthermore, in a country where fossil fuels are scarce, dry cattle dung, which burns slowly and evenly, is a basic cooking fuel.

Far from being useless, as the development experts contend, sacred cattle are essential to Indian cultural adaptation. Biologically adapted to poor pasture land and a marginal environment, the scraggly zebu provides fertilizer and fuel, is indispensable in farming, and is affordable for peasants. The Hindu doctrine of ahimsa puts the full power of organized religion behind the command not to destroy a valuable resource even in times of extreme need.

We see then yet another domain in which religion plays a prominent role—cultural ecology. Behavior motivated by religious beliefs may help people survive by conserving their material resources, thus functioning as part of a group's cultural adaptation to its environment.

The Modern World System

Although field work in small communities is anthropology's hallmark, isolated groups are impossible to find today. Truly isolated societies have probably never existed. For thousands of years, human groups have been in contact with one another. Local societies have always participated in a larger system, which today has global dimensions—we call it the *modern world system,* by which we mean a world in which nations are economically and politically interdependent.

City, nation, and world increasingly invade local communities. Today, if anthropologists want to study a fairly isolated society, they must journey to the highlands of Papua New Guinea or the tropical forests of South America. Even in those places they will probably encounter missionaries or prospectors. In contemporary Australia, sheep owned by people who speak English graze where totemic ceremonies once were held. Farther into the outback some descendants of those totemites may be working in a film crew making *Crocodile Dundee IV* or *Survivor VI*. A Hilton hotel stands in the capital of faraway Madagascar, and a paved highway now has an exit for Arembepe, the Brazilian fishing community I have been studying since 1962. When and how did the modern world system begin?

The world system and the relations between the countries within that system are shaped by the world capitalist economy. World-system theory can be traced to the French social historian Fernand Braudel. In his three-volume work *Civilization and Capitalism, 15th–18th Century* (1981, 1982, 1992), Braudel argues that society consists of parts assembled into an interrelated system. Societies are subsystems of bigger systems, with the world system the largest.

The modern world system rests on the world capitalist economy. Shown here is a Honda motorcycle plant, the world's largest such plant, in Bangkok, Thailand. Is Honda a Thai firm? Where do you imagine such motorcycles are sold?

THE EMERGENCE OF THE WORLD SYSTEM

As Europeans took to ships, developing a transoceanic trade-oriented economy, people throughout the world entered Europe's sphere of influence. In the fifteenth century Europe established regular contact with Asia, Africa, and eventually the New World (the Caribbean and the Americas). Christopher Columbus's first voyage from Spain to the Bahamas and the Caribbean in 1492 was soon followed by additional voyages. These journeys opened the way for a major exchange of people, resources, diseases, and ideas, as the Old and New Worlds were forever linked (Crosby 1972; Diamond 1997; Fagan 1998; Viola and Margolis 1991). Led by Spain and Portugal, Europeans extracted silver and gold, conquered the natives (taking some as slaves), and colonized their lands.

Previously in Europe as throughout the world, rural people had produced mainly for their own needs, growing their own food and making clothing, furniture, and tools from local products. Production beyond immediate needs was undertaken to pay taxes and to purchase trade items such as salt and iron. As late as 1650 the English diet, like diets in most of the world today, was based on locally grown starches (Mintz 1985). In the 200 years that followed, however, the English became extraordinary consumers of imported goods. One of the earliest and most popular of those goods was sugar (Mintz 1985).

Sugarcane was originally domesticated in Papua New Guinea, and sugar was first processed in India. Reaching Europe via the Middle East and the eastern Mediterranean, it was carried to the New World by Columbus (Mintz 1985). The climate of Brazil and the Caribbean proved ideal for growing sugarcane, and Europeans built plantations there to supply the growing demand for sugar. This led to the development in the seventeenth century of a plantation economy based on a single cash crop—a system known as monocrop production.

The demand for sugar in a growing international market spurred the development of the transatlantic slave trade and New World plantation economies based on slave labor. By the eighteenth century, an increased English demand for raw cotton led to rapid settlement of what is now the southeastern United States and the emergence there of another slave-based monocrop production system. Like sugar, cotton was a key trade item that fueled the growth of the world system.

The increasing dominance of international trade led to the **capitalist world economy** (Wallerstein 2000), a single world system committed to production for sale or exchange, with the object of maximizing profits rather than supplying domestic needs. **Capital** refers to wealth or resources invested in business, with the intent of producing a profit; the defining attribute of capitalism is economic orientation to the world market for profit.

The key claim of world-system theory is that an identifiable social system, based on wealth and power differentials, extends beyond individual states and nations. That system is formed by a set of economic and political relations that has characterized much of the globe since the sixteenth century, when the Old World established regular contact with the New World.

According to Wallerstein (1982, 2000), the nations within the world system occupy three different positions of economic and political power: core, periphery, and semiperiphery. The geographic center or **core,** the dominant position in the world system, includes the strongest and most powerful nations. In core nations, "the complexity of economic activities and the level of capital accumulation is the greatest" (Thompson 1983, p. 12). With its sophisticated technologies and mechanized production, the core churns out products that flow mainly to other core nations. Some also go to the periphery and semiperiphery. According to Arrighi (1995), the core monopolizes the most profitable activities, especially the control of world finance.

Semiperiphery and **periphery** nations, which roughly correspond to what is usually called the Third World, have less power, wealth, and influence than the core does. The semiperiphery is intermediate between the core and the periphery. Contemporary nations of the semiperiphery are industrialized. Like core nations, they export both industrial goods and commodities, but they lack the power and economic dominance of core nations. Thus Brazil, a semiperiphery nation, exports automobiles to Nigeria and auto engines, orange juice extract, and coffee to the United States.

Economic activities in the periphery are less mechanized and use human labor more intensively than do those in the semiperiphery. The periphery produces raw materials and agricultural commodities for export to the core and the semiperiphery. In the modern world, however, industrialization has reached even peripheral nations. Trade and other forms of economic relations between core and periphery tend to benefit capitalists in the core at the expense of the periphery (Shannon 1996; Hall, ed., 1999; Kardulias 1999).

INDUSTRIALIZATION

By the eighteenth century the stage had been set for the **Industrial Revolution**—the historical transformation (in Europe, after 1750) of "traditional" into "modern" societies through industrialization of the economy. Industrialization required capital for investment. The established system of transoceanic trade and commerce supplied this capital from the enormous profits it generated. Wealthy people sought investment opportunities and eventually found them in machines and engines to drive machines. Industrialization increased production in both farming and manufacturing. Capital and scientific innovation fueled invention.

In the home-handicraft, or domestic, system of production, an organizer supplied raw materials to workers in their homes and collected their products. Family life and work were intertwined, as in this English scene. Is there a modern equivalent to the domestic system of production?

European industrialization developed from (and eventually replaced) the *domestic system* of manufacture (or home handicraft system). In this system, an organizer-entrepreneur supplied the raw materials to workers in their homes and collected the finished products from them. The entrepreneur, whose sphere of operations might span several villages, owned the materials, paid for the work, and arranged the marketing.

Causes of the Industrial Revolution

The Industrial Revolution began with cotton products, iron, and pottery. These were widely used goods whose manufacture could be broken down into simple routine motions that machines could perform. When manufacturing moved from homes to factories, where machinery replaced handwork, agrarian societies evolved into industrial ones. As factories produced cheap staple goods, the Industrial Revolution led to a dramatic increase in production. Industrialization fueled urban growth and created a new kind of city, with factories crowded together in places where coal and labor were cheap.

The Industrial Revolution began in England rather than in France. Why? Unlike the English, the French didn't have to transform their domestic manufacturing system by industrializing. Faced with an increased need for products, with a late eighteenth-century population at least twice that of Great Britain, France could simply augment its domestic system of production by drawing in new homes. Thus, the French were able to increase production *without innovating*—they could enlarge the existing system rather than adopt a new one. To meet mounting demand for staples—at home and in the colonies—England had to industrialize.

Britain's population doubled during the eighteenth century (particularly after 1750) and did so again between 1800 and 1850. This demographic explosion fueled consumption, but British entrepreneurs couldn't meet the increased demand with the traditional production methods. This spurred experimentation, innovation, and rapid technological change.

English industrialization drew on national advantages in natural resources. Britain was rich in coal and iron ore, and had navigable waterways and easily negotiated coasts. It was a seafaring island-nation located at the crossroads of international trade. These features gave Britain a favored position for importing raw materials and exporting manufactured goods. Another factor in England's industrial growth was the fact that much of its eighteenth-century colonial empire was occupied by English settler families who looked to the mother country as they tried to replicate European civilization in the New World. These colonies bought large quantities of English staples.

It has also been argued that particular cultural values and religion contributed to industrialization. Many members of the emerging English middle class were Protestant nonconformists. Their beliefs and values encouraged industry, thrift, the dissemination of new knowledge, inventiveness, and willingness to accept change (Weber 1904/1958).

STRATIFICATION

The socioeconomic effects of industrialization were mixed. English national income tripled between 1700 and 1815 and increased thirty times more by 1939. Standards of comfort rose, but prosperity was uneven. At first, factory workers got wages higher than those available in the domestic system. Later, owners started recruiting labor in places where living standards were low and labor (including that of women and children) was cheap.

Social ills worsened with the growth of factory towns and industrial cities, amid conditions like those Charles Dickens described in *Hard Times*. Filth and smoke polluted the nineteenth-century cities. Housing was crowded and unsanitary, with insufficient water and sewage disposal facilities. People experienced rampant disease and rising death rates. This was the world of Ebenezer Scrooge, Bob Cratchit, Tiny Tim—and Karl Marx.

Industrial Stratification

The social theorists Karl Marx and Max Weber focused on the stratification systems associated with industrialization. From his observations in England and his analysis of nineteenth-century industrial capitalism, Marx (Marx and Engels 1848/1976) saw socioeconomic stratification as a sharp and simple division between two opposed classes: the bourgeoisie (capitalists) and the proletariat (propertyless workers). The bourgeoisie traced its origins to overseas ventures and the world capitalist economy, which had transformed the social structure of northwestern Europe, creating a wealthy commercial class.

Industrialization shifted production from farms and cottages to mills and factories, where mechanical power was available and where workers could be assembled to operate heavy machinery. The **bourgeoisie** were the owners of the factories, mines, large farms, and other means of production. The **working class, or proletariat,** was made up of people who had to sell their labor to survive. With the decline of subsistence production and with the rise of urban migration and the possibility of unemployment, the bourgeoisie came to stand between workers and the means of production.

Industrialization hastened the process of *proletarianization*—the separation of workers from the means of production. The bourgeoisie also came to dominate the means of communication, the schools, and other key institutions. Marx viewed the nation-state as an instrument of oppression and religion as a method of diverting and controlling the masses.

Class consciousness (recognition of collective interests and personal identification with one's economic group) was a vital part of Marx's view of class. He saw bourgeoisie and proletariat as socioeconomic divisions with radically opposed interests. Marx viewed classes as powerful collective forces that could mobilize human energies to influence the course of history. Finding strength through common experience, he said workers would develop organizations to protect their interests and increase their share of industrial profits.

And so they did. During the nineteenth century trade unions and social-ist parties emerged to express a rising anticapitalist spirit. The concerns of the English labor movement were to remove young children from factories and limit the hours during which women and children could work. The pro-file of stratification in industrial core nations gradually took shape. Capital-ists controlled production, but labor was organizing for better wages and working conditions. By 1900 many governments had factory legislation and social-welfare programs. Mass living standards in core nations rose as pop-ulation grew.

The modern capitalist world system maintains the distinction between those who own the means of production and those who don't. The class di-vision into capitalists and propertyless workers is now worldwide. Never-theless, modern stratification systems aren't simple and dichotomous. They include (particularly in core and semiperiphery nations) a middle class of skilled and professional workers. Gerhard Lenski (1966) argues that social equality tends to increase in advanced industrial societies. The masses im-prove their access to economic benefits and political power. In Lenski's scheme, the shift of political power to the masses reflects the growth of the middle class, which reduces the polarization between owning and work-ing classes. The proliferation of middle-class occupations creates oppor-tunities for social mobility. The stratification system grows more complex (Giddens 1973).

Faulting Marx for an overly simple and exclusively economic view of stratification, Weber (1992/1968) defined three dimensions of social stratifi-cation: wealth (economic status), power (political status), and prestige (so-cial status). Although, as Weber showed, wealth, power, and prestige are separate components of social ranking, they tend to be correlated. Weber also believed that social identities based on ethnicity, religion, race, na-tionality, and other attributes could take priority over class (social identity based on economic status). In addition to class contrasts, the modern world system is cross-cut by status groups such as ethnic and religious groups and nations (Shannon 1996). Class conflicts tend to occur within na-tions, and nationalism has prevented global class solidarity, particularly of proletarians.

Although the capitalist class dominates politically in most countries, the leaders of core nations have found it to be in their interest to allow prole-tarians to organize and make demands. Growing wealth has made it easier for core nations to grant higher wages (Hopkins and Wallerstein 1982). However, the improvement in core workers' living standards wouldn't have occurred without the world system. The added surplus that comes from the periphery allows core capitalists to maintain their profits while satisfying the demands of core workers. In the periphery, wages and living standards are much lower. The current *world stratification system* features a substan-tial contrast between both capitalists and workers in the core nations and workers on the periphery.

With the expansion of the world capitalist economy, people on the periphery have been removed from the land by large landowners and agribusiness interests. One result is increased poverty, including food shortages. Displaced people can't earn enough to buy the food they can no longer grow.

Malaysian Factory Women

Malaysia, a former British colony, has undergone successive waves of integration into the world system. The Malays have known sea trade, conquest, the influx of British and Chinese capital, and immigration from China and India. For centuries Malaysia has thus been part of the world system. Recently, in response to rural discontent over poverty and landlessness as some 10,000 families per year are pushed off the land, the Malaysian government has promoted export-oriented industry to bring rural Malays into the capitalist system. Since 1970 transnational companies have been installing labor-intensive manufacturing operations in rural Malaysia. Between 1970 and 1980 agriculture's contribution to the national labor force fell from 53 to 41 percent as manufacturing jobs proliferated.

The industrialization of Malaysia is part of a global strategy. To escape the mounting labor costs in the core, corporations headquartered in Japan, Western Europe, and the United States have been moving labor-intensive factories to the periphery. Malaysia now has hundreds of Japanese and American subsidiaries, which mainly produce garments, foodstuffs, and electronics components. In electronics plants in rural Malaysia, thousands of young women from peasant families assemble microchips and microcomponents for transistors and capacitors. Aihwa Ong (1987) did a study of electronics assembly workers in an area where 85 percent of the workers were young unmarried females from nearby villages.

Ong found that factory discipline and social relations contrasted strongly with traditional community life. Previously, agricultural cycles and daily Islamic prayers, rather than production quotas and work shifts, had framed the rural economy and social life. Villagers had planned and done their own work, without bosses. In factories, however, village women had to cope with a rigid work routine and constant supervision by men.

Factory relations of production featured a hierarchy, pay scale, and division of labor based on ethnicity and gender. Japanese men filled top management, while Chinese men were the engineers and production supervisors. The Malay men also worked as supervisors of the factory workforce, which consisted of nonunion female semiskilled workers from poor Malay peasant families.

The Japanese firms in rural Malaysia were paternalistic. Managers assured village parents that they would care for their daughters as though they were their own. Unlike the American firms, the Japanese subsidiaries worked hard at maintaining good relations with rural elders. Management gave money for village events, visited workers' home communities, and invited parents to the plant for receptions. In return, village elders accorded high status to the Japanese managers. The elders colluded with the managers to urge young women to accept and stay with factory work.

The discipline, diligence, and obedience that factories value is learned in local schools, where uniforms help prepare girls for the factory dress code. Peasant women wear loose, flowing tunics, sarongs, and sandals, but factory workers must don tight overalls and heavy rubber gloves, in which they feel constrained and controlled.

Assembling electronics components requires precise, concentrated labor. Demanding and depleting, labor in these factories illustrates the separation of intellectual and manual activity that Marx considered the defining feature of industrial work. One woman said about her bosses, "They exhaust us very much, as if they do not think that we too are human beings" (Ong 1987, p. 202). Nor does factory work bring women a substantial financial reward, given low wages, job uncertainty, and family claims on wages. Young women typically work just a few years. Production quotas, three daily shifts, overtime, and surveillance take their toll in mental and physical exhaustion.

One response to factory relations of production is spirit possession, which Ong interprets as an unconscious protest against labor discipline and male control of the industrial setting. Sometimes possession takes the form of mass hysteria. Spirits have simultaneously invaded as many as 120 factory workers. Weretigers (the Malay equivalent of the werewolf) arrive to avenge the construction of a factory on aboriginal burial grounds. Disturbed earth and grave spirits swarm on the shop floor. First the women see the spirits; then their bodies are invaded. The women become violent and scream abuses. The weretigers send the women into sobbing, laughing, and shrieking fits. To deal with possession, factories employ local medicine men, who sacrifice chickens and goats to fend off the spirits. This solution works only some of the time; possession still goes on. Factory women continue to act as vehicles to express the anger of avenging ghosts and their own frustrations.

Ong argues that spirit possession expresses anguish at and resistance to capitalist relations of production. By engaging in this form of rebellion, however, factory women avoid a direct confrontation with the source of their distress. Ong concludes that spirit possession, while expressing repressed resentment, doesn't do much to modify factory conditions. (Other tactics, such as unionization, would do more.) Spirit possession may even help maintain the current system by operating as a safety valve for accumulated tensions.

Open and Closed Class Systems

Inequalities, which are built into the structure of state societies, tend to persist across the generations. The extent to which they do or don't is a measure of the openness of the stratification system, the ease of social mobility it permits. Within the world capitalist economy, stratification has taken many forms, including caste, slavery, and class systems.

Slavery is the most extreme, coercive, and abusive form of legalized inequality. Although proletarians, such as these "white slaves of England," also lacked control over the means of production, they did have some control over where they worked. In what other ways do proletarians differ from slaves?

Caste systems are closed, hereditary systems of stratification that are often dictated by religion. Hierarchical social status is ascribed at birth, so that people are locked into their parents' social position. Caste lines are clearly defined, and legal and religious sanctions are applied against those who seek to cross them.

In **slavery**, the most inhumane, coercive, and degrading form of legal stratification, people who are conquered or stolen from their homelands become someone's property. In the Atlantic slave trade millions of human beings were treated as commodities. The plantation systems of the Caribbean, the southeastern United States, and Brazil were based on forced slave labor. Slaves lacked control over the means of production. They were like proletarians in this respect. But proletarians at least are legally free. Unlike slaves, they have some control over where they work, how much they work, for whom they work, and what they do with their wages. Slaves, in contrast, were forced to live and work at their master's whim. Defined as lesser—or less than—human beings, slaves lacked legal rights. They could be sold and resold; their families were split apart. Slaves, unlike the poorest nonslaves, had nothing to sell—not even their own labor (Mintz 1985).

Vertical mobility is an upward or downward change in a person's social status. A truly **open class system** would facilitate mobility. Individual achievement and personal merit would determine social rank. Hierarchical social statuses would be achieved on the basis of people's efforts. Ascribed statuses (family background, ethnicity, gender, religion) would be less important. Open class systems would have blurred class lines and a wide range of status positions. Compared with nonindustrial states and contemporary peripheral and semiperipheral nations, core industrial nations tend to have more open class systems.

THE WORLD SYSTEM TODAY

World-system theory stresses the existence of a global culture. It emphasizes historical contacts, linkages, and power differentials between local people and international forces. The major forces influencing cultural interaction during the past 500 years have been commercial expansion, industrial capitalism, and the differential power of colonial and core nations (Wolf 1982; Wallerstein 1982, 2000). As state formation had done previously, industrialization accelerated local participation in larger networks. According to Bodley (1985), perpetual expansion (whether in population or consumption) is the distinguishing feature of industrial economic systems. Bands and tribes are small, self-sufficient, subsistence-based systems. Industrial economies, by contrast, are large, highly specialized systems in which market exchanges occur with profit as the primary motive (Bodley 1985).

After 1870 European business initiated a concerted search for more secure markets in Asia, Africa, and other less-developed areas. This process led to European imperialism in Africa, Asia, and Oceania. **Imperialism** (*colonialism* is a near synonym) refers to a policy of extending the rule of a nation or empire, such as the British empire, over foreign nations and of taking and holding foreign colonies. *Colonialism* is the political, social, economic, and cultural domination of a territory and its people by a foreign power for an extended time. European imperial expansion was aided by improved transportation, which brought huge new areas within easy reach. Europeans colonized vast areas of previously unsettled or sparsely settled lands in the interior of North and South America and Australia. The new colonies purchased masses of goods from the industrial centers and shipped

TABLE 10-1	Ascent and Decline of Nations within the World System	
Periphery to Semiperiphery	Semiperiphery to Core	Core to Semiperiphery
United States (1800–1860)	United States (1860–1900)	Spain (1620–1700)
Japan (1868–1900)	Japan (1945–1970)	
Taiwan (1949–1980)	Germany (1870–1900)	
S. Korea (1953–1980)		

Source: From Shannon 1989, p. 130. Reprinted by permission of author.

back wheat, cotton, wool, mutton, beef, and leather. If the first phase of colonialism had been exploration and exploitation of the New World after Columbus, a new second phase began as European nations competed for colonies between 1875 and 1914, setting the stage for World War I.

Industrialization appeared first in England and then in many other nations in a process that continues today (Table 10-1). By 1900, the United States had become a core nation within the world system and had overtaken Great Britain in iron, coal, and cotton production. In a few decades (1868–1900), Japan had changed from a medieval handicraft economy to an industrial one, joining the semiperiphery by 1900 and moving to the core between 1945 and 1970. Figure 10-1 is a map showing the modern world system.

Twentieth-century industrialization added hundreds of new industries and millions of new jobs. Production increased, often beyond immediate demand, spurring strategies, such as advertising, to sell everything industry could churn out. Mass production gave rise to a culture of consumption, which valued acquisitiveness and conspicuous consumption (Veblen 1934). Industrialization entailed a shift from reliance on renewable resources to the use of fossil fuels. Fossil fuel energy, stored over millions of years, was being rapidly depleted to support a previously unknown and probably unsustainable level of consumption (Bodley 1985). Table 10-2 compares energy consumption in various types of societies. Americans are the world's foremost consumers of nonrenewable resources. In energy terms, the average American, drawing on 275,000 calories of energy each day, is about 35 times more expensive than the average forager or tribesperson, averaging just 8,000 daily calories. Since 1900, the United States has tripled its per capita energy use. It has also increased its total energy consumption thirtyfold.

Industrial Degradation

Today's industrialization extends to the Third World. Factory labor now characterizes many societies in Latin America, Africa, the Pacific, and Asia. One effect of the spread of industrialization has been the destruction of indigenous economies, ecologies, and populations.

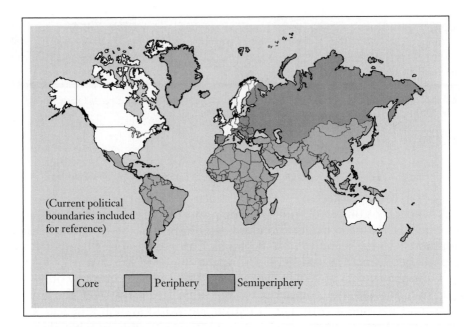

FIGURE 10-1 The world system today.
Source: From Shannon 1996. Reprinted by permission of Westview Press. Copyright Westview Press 1996, Boulder, CO.

TABLE 10-2	Energy Consumption in Various Contexts
Type of Society	Daily Kilocalories per Person
Bands and tribes	4,000–12,000
Preindustrial states	26,000 (maximum)
Early industrial states	70,000
Americans in 1970	230,000
Americans in 1990	275,000

Source: From Bodley 1985. Reprinted by permission of Mayfield Publishing, Mountain View, CA.

Two centuries ago, as industrialization was developing, 50 million people still lived beyond the periphery in politically independent bands, tribes, and chiefdoms. Occupying vast areas, those nonstate societies, although not totally isolated, were only marginally affected by nation-states and the world capitalist economy. In 1800 bands, tribes, and chiefdoms controlled half the globe and 20 percent of its population (Bodley, ed. 1988). Industrialization tipped the balance in favor of states.

As industrial states have conquered, annexed, and "developed" nonstates, there has been genocide on a grand scale. *Genocide* is the physical

As industrialization spreads, environmental resources, such as forests and their biodiversity, may be threatened. These Nigerian children collect fuel wood from the forest. How might urban growth affect deforestation?

destruction of ethnic groups by murder, warfare, and introduced diseases. Bodley (1988) estimates that an average of 250,000 indigenous people perished annually between 1800 and 1950. The causes included foreign diseases (to which natives had no resistance), warfare, slavery, land grabbing, and other forms of dispossession and impoverishment.

Many native groups have been incorporated within nation-states, in which they have become ethnic minorities. Some such groups have been able to recoup their population. Many indigenous peoples survive and maintain their ethnic identity despite having lost their ancestral cultures to varying degrees (partial ethnocide). And many descendants of tribespeople live on as culturally distinct and self-conscious colonized peoples, many of whom aspire to autonomy. As the original inhabitants of their territories, they are called **indigenous peoples.**

Around the world many contemporary nations are repeating—at an accelerated rate—the process of resource depletion that started in Europe and the United States during the Industrial Revolution. Fortunately, however, today's world has some environmental watchdogs that did not exist during the first centuries of the Industrial Revolution. Given national and international cooperation and sanctions, the modern world may benefit from the lessons of the past.

S u m m a r y

1. Local societies increasingly participate in wider systems—regional, national, and global. Columbus's voyages opened the way for a major exchange between the Old and New Worlds. Seventeenth-century plantation economies in the Caribbean and Brazil were based on sugar. In the eighteenth century, plantation economies based on cotton arose in the southeastern United States.

2. The capitalist world economy depends on production for sale, with the goal of maximizing profits. World capitalism has political and economic specialization at the core, semiperiphery, and periphery. Since the sixteenth century, the particular countries fulfilling those roles have changed.

3. The Industrial Revolution began in England around 1760. Transoceanic commerce supplied capital for industrial investment. Industrialization hastened the separation of workers from the means of production. Marx saw a sharp division between the bourgeoisie and the proletariat. Class consciousness was a key feature of Marx's view of this stratification. Weber believed that social solidarity based on ethnicity, religion, race, or nationality could take priority over class. Today's capitalist world system maintains the contrast between those who own the means of production and those who don't, but the division is now worldwide and involves the categories Weber foresaw. Nationalism has prevented global class solidarity. There is a substantial contrast between not only capitalists but workers in the core nations and workers on the periphery.

4. Modern stratification systems also include a middle class of skilled and professional workers. The extent to which inequalities persist across the generations is a measure of the openness of the class system, the ease of social mobility it permits. Under world capitalism, stratification has taken many forms, some of them extreme, including caste, slavery, and class systems.

5. The major forces influencing cultural interaction during the past 500 years have been commercial expansion and industrial capitalism. In the nineteenth century, industrialization spread to Belgium, France, Germany, and the United States. After 1870, businesses began a concerted search for more secure markets. This process led to European imperialism in Africa, Asia, and Oceania. By 1900 the United States had become a core nation. Mass production gave rise to a culture that valued acquisitiveness and conspicuous consumption. One effect of industrialization has been the destruction of indigenous economies, ecologies, and populations. Another has been the accelerated rate of resource depletion.

Case Study
Ju/'hoansi

This chapter has discussed consequences of the spread of the industrial world system. Many foraging societies find their ways of life threatened. Two or three decades ago, the Ju/'hoansi maintained much more traditional lifestyles. They now find themselves fully drawn into a market economy, affected not only by institutions such as schools and hospitals, but also by militarization, civil war, sedentism, resettlement, and governmental control. In *Culture Sketches* by Holly Peters-Golden read the chapter on Ju/'hoansi: Reciprocity and Sharing. Which effects of the modern world system are demonstrated in contemporary Ju/'hoansi life? The Ju/'hoansi tradition is one of egalitarianism and reciprocity. It is reported that the Dobe Ju/'hoansi still hold those values above all else. Do you think they can integrate their belief that no one should be denied the necessities of life with the demands of their modern situation? Why or why not?

Troubles in Swooshland

Famous for its Swoosh, Nike is the world's leading manufacturer of athletic shoes. Nike subcontracts its shoe-making to factories in Vietnam, Indonesia, China, Thailand, and Pakistan. Most of the 530,000 workers in these factories are women between the ages of 15 and 28.

In 1996, the CBS television program "48 Hours" ran a segment critical of work conditions at Nike factories in Vietnam. The practices of Nike's Asian subcontractors, and of Nike itself, were questioned by international media, labor, and human rights groups. Publicity centered on the shoes' being produced by very cheap Asian labor then sold in North America for up to $100 a pair. Disturbed by the CBS report, a group of Vietnamese Americans organized to form a new NGO (nongovernmental organization), Vietnam Labor Watch. With the company's cooperation, this group carried out a study of Nike's Vietnamese operations.

They confirmed that wages and working conditions were problematic. Across Asia, the wages paid to Nike workers averaged $1.84 per day. In Vietnam's Ho Chi Minh City, where the cost of three simple meals was $2.10 per day, Nike factory workers made only $1.60 per day. Health was also a concern, and so was factory safety. According to law, factory doors must be kept open during operating hours, a precaution against fire. In fact, doors were often closed. Workers also had to endure overheated factories with bad air.

Nike's young female workers, like those in the Malaysian electronics factories described in this chapter, had to wear uniforms. Adding to their regimentation was a military boot camp atmosphere. Workers were allowed only one toilet break and two chances to drink per eight hours. There were complaints of physical abuse and sexual harassment by male supervisors and insults by foreign supervisors (Koreans).

Prior to 1996, Nike already had a Code of Conduct, but the company had no effective way of ensuring that its contractors would abide by the code. In theory the Vietnamese workers should have been protected both by Nike's Code of Conduct and by Vietnam's labor standards and laws. But the study by Vietnam Labor Watch (1997) found that many labor laws were being broken. Nike workers in Ho Chi Minh City weren't receiving proper overtime pay, and many were working well over the legal limit of 200 overtime hours per year. Workers were threatened with punishment or firing if they refused requests to work overtime. The factory needed to keep running to meet production quotas.

After more than a year of negative publicity and accusations by human rights and labor groups, Nike announced a new policy on May 12, 1998. Nike chairman and CEO Philip Knight proposed "major changes" to Nike's overseas operations. The new policy would institute a minimal age of 18 for shoe workers, and 16 for workers in Nike's apparel and athletic equipment (e.g., soccer ball) factories. The previous minimum age for shoe workers had been 16, but younger women had sometimes been hired.

The new policy would also improve factory safety by implementing U.S. standards. Nike committed to "adopting U.S. Occupational Safety and Health Administration (OSHA) indoor air quality standards for all footwear factories" (http://www.corpwatch.org/trac/nike/announce/clr.html).

In addition, Nike committed to "expanding its current independent monitoring programs to include nongovernmental organizations (NGOs), foundations, and educational institutions and making summaries of the findings public" (http://www.corpwatch.org/trac/nike/announce/clr.html).

The Malaysian factory women described in the chapter used spirit possession to vent their frustration over working conditions. The Vietnamese Nike workers did something more effective. They employed labor union tactics, including strikes and frequent work stoppages and slowdowns. These practices were in response to disputes about overtime pay, arbitrary firings, and abusive treatment. The Vietnamese workers also enlisted the support of NGOs, international labor organizations, and concerned Vietnamese Americans. Some of their efforts have already paid off.

Colonialism and Development

In the last chapter we saw that after 1870 Europe began a concerted search for markets in Asia and Africa, leading to European imperialism in Africa, Asia, and Oceania. *Imperialism* refers to a policy of extending the rule of a nation or empire, such as the British empire, over foreign nations and of taking and holding foreign colonies. **Colonialism** is the political, social, economic, and cultural domination of a territory and its people by a foreign power for an extended time.

COLONIALISM

Imperialism goes back to early states, including Egypt in the Old World and the Incas in the New. A Greek empire was forged by Alexander the Great, as Julius Caesar and his successors spread the Roman empire. More recent examples include the British, French, and Soviet empires (Scheinman 1980).

If imperialism is almost as old as the state, colonialism can be traced back to the Phoenicians, who established colonies along the eastern Mediterranean by 3,000 years ago. The ancient Greeks and Romans were avid colonizers, as well as empire builders.

Modern colonialism began with the European "Age of Discovery"—of the Americas and of a sea route to the Far East. After 1492, European nations founded colonies abroad. In South America, Portugal ruled over Brazil. The Spanish, the original conquerors of the Aztecs and the Incas, explored the New World widely, the Caribbean, Mexico, the southern portions of what was to become the United States and Central and South America.

Rebellions and wars aimed at independence for American nations ended the first phase of European colonialism by the early nineteenth century. Brazil declared independence from Portugal in 1822. By 1825 most of

Spain's colonies were politically independent. Spain held onto Cuba and the Philippines until 1898, but otherwise withdrew from the colonial field.

British Colonialism

At its peak about 1914, the British empire covered a fifth of the world's land surface and ruled a fourth of its population (see Figure 11-1). Like several other European nations, Britain had two stages of colonialism. The first began with the Elizabethan voyages of the sixteenth century. During the seventeenth century, Britain acquired most of the eastern coast of North America, Canada's St. Lawrence basin, islands in the Caribbean, slave stations in Africa, and interests in India.

The British shared the exploration of the New World with the Spanish, Portuguese, French, and Dutch. The British by and large left Mexico, along with Central and South America, to the Spanish and the Portuguese. The end of the Seven Years' War in 1763 forced a French retreat from most of Canada and India, where France had previously competed with Britain (Farr 1980, Cody 1998).

The American revolution ended the first stage of British colonialism. A second colonial empire, on which the "sun never set," rose from the ashes of the first. Beginning in 1788, but intensifying after 1815, the British settled Australia, and Britain had acquired Dutch South Africa by 1815. The establishment of Singapore in 1819 provided a base for a British trade network that extended to much of South Asia and along the coast of China. By this time, the empires of Britain's traditional rivals, particularly Spain, had been severely diminished in scope. Britain's position as imperial power and the world's leading industrial nation was unchallenged (Farr 1980, Cody 1998).

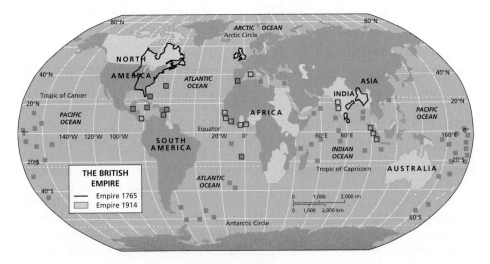

FIGURE 11-1   Map of British empire in 1914.

During the Victorian Era (1837–1901), while Britain's acquisition of territory and of further trading concessions continued apace, Prime Minister Benjamin Disraeli implemented a foreign policy justified by a view of imperialism as shouldering "the white man's burden"—a phrase coined by the poet Rudyard Kipling. People in the empire were seen as unable to govern themselves, so that British guidance was needed to civilize and Christianize them. This paternalistic and racist doctrine served to legitimize Britain's acquisition and control of parts of central Africa and Asia (Cody 1998).

After World War II, the British Empire began to fall apart, with nationalist movements for independence. India became independent in 1947, as did Ireland in 1949. Decolonization in Africa and Asia accelerated during the late 1950s. Today, the ties that remain between Britain and its former colonies are mainly linguistic or cultural rather than political (Cody 1998).

Indochina fell fully under French colonial control in 1893. In this historical photo from the 1920s, a Frenchman sits in a rickshaw (pousse-pousse). What does this mode of transit say to you about colonialism?

French Colonialism

French colonialism also had two phases. The first began with the explorations of the early 1600s. Prior to the French revolution in 1789, missionaries, explorers, and traders led French expansion. They carved out niches for France in Canada, the Louisiana territory, several Caribbean islands, and parts of India, which were lost along with Canada to Great Britain in 1763 (Harvey 1980).

The foundations of the second French empire were established between 1830 and 1870, the French manifestation of the more general European imperialism that followed the spread of industrialization and the search for new markets, raw materials, and cheap labor. If in Great Britain the sheer drive for profit led expansion, French colonialism was spurred more by the state, church, and armed forces than by pure business interests. France acquired Algeria and part of what eventually became Indochina (Cambodia, Laos, and Vietnam). By 1914 the French empire covered 4 million square miles and included some 60 million people (see Figure 11-2). By 1893 French rule had been fully established in Indochina, and Tunisia and Morocco became French protectorates (Harvey 1980).

To be sure the French, like the British, had substantial business interests in their colonies, but they also sought, again like the British, international glory and prestige. The French promulgated a *mission civilisatrice*, their equivalent of Britain's "white man's burden." The goal was to implant French culture, language, and religion, Roman Catholicism, throughout the colonies (Harvey 1980).

The French used two forms of colonial rule: *indirect rule,* governing through native leaders and established political structures, in areas with long histories of state organization, such as Morocco and Tunisia; and *direct*

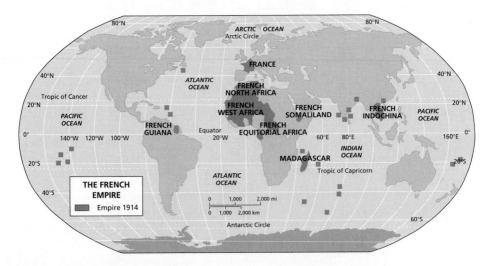

FIGURE 11-2   Map of the French empire at its height around 1914.

rule by French officials in many areas of Africa, where the French imposed new government structures to control diverse societies, many of them previously stateless. Like the British empire, the French empire began to disintegrate after World War II. France fought long—and ultimately futile—wars to keep its empire intact in Indochina and Algeria (Harvey 1980).

Colonialism and Identity

Many geopolitical labels in the news today had no equivalent meaning before colonialism. Whole countries, along with social groups and divisions within them, were colonial inventions. In West Africa, for example, by geographic logic, several adjacent countries could be one (Togo, Ghana, Ivory Coast, Guinea, Guinea-Bissau, Sierra Leone, Liberia). Instead, they are separated by linguistic, political, and economic contrasts promoted under colonialism, sometimes inciting "tribalism."

Hundreds of ethnic groups and "tribes" are colonial constructions (see Ranger 1996). The Sukuma of Tanzania, for instance, were first registered as a single tribe by the colonial administration. Then missionaries standardized a series of dialects into a single Sukuma language into which they translated the Bible and other religious texts. Thereafter, those texts were taught in missionary schools and to European foreigners and other non-Sukuma speakers. Over time this standardized the Sukuma language and ethnicity (Finnstrom 1997).

As in most of East Africa, in Rwanda and Burundi farmers and herders live in the same areas and speak the same language. Historically they have shared the same social world, although their social organization is "extremely hierarchical," almost "castelike" (Malkki 1995, p. 24). There has been a tendency to see the pastoral Tutsis as superior to the agricultural Hutus. Tutsis have been presented as nobles, Hutus as commoners. Yet when distributing identity cards in Rwanda, the Belgian colonizers simply identified all people with more than ten heads of cattle as Tutsi. Owners of fewer cattle were registered as Hutus (Bjuremalm 1997). Years later, these arbitrary colonial registers were used systematically for "ethnic" identification during the mass killings that took place in Rwanda in 1994.

DEVELOPMENT

During the Industrial Revolution, a strong current of thought viewed industrialization as a beneficial process of organic development and progress. Many economists still assume that industrialization increases production and income. They seek to create in Third World ("developing") countries a process like the one that first occurred spontaneously in eighteenth-century Great Britain.

We have seen that Great Britain used the notion of a "white man's burden" to justify its imperialist expansion and that France claimed to be involved in a *mission civilisatrice*, a civilizing mission, in its colonies. Both these ideas illustrate an **intervention philosophy,** an ideological justification for outsiders to guide native peoples in specific directions. Economic development plans also have intervention philosophies. John Bodley (1988) argues that the basic belief behind interventions—whether by colonialists, missionaries, governments, or development planners—has been the same for more than 100 years. This belief is that industrialization, modernization, Westernization, and individualism are desirable evolutionary advances and that development schemes that promote them will bring long-term benefits to local people. In a more extreme form, intervention philosophy may pit the assumed wisdom of enlightened colonial or other First World planners against the purported conservatism, ignorance, or "obsolescence" of "inferior" local people.

Anthropologists dispute such views. We know that for thousands of years bands and tribes have done "a reasonable job of taking care of themselves" (Bodley, ed. 1988, p. 93). Many problems people face today have been caused by their having been subsumed within nation-states and by their increasing dependence on the world cash economy.

Conflicts between governments and local people often arise when outside interests exploit resources on tribal lands. Driven by deficits and debts, governments seek to wrest as much wealth as possible from the territory they administer. The result has been the worldwide intrusion on indigenous peoples and their local ecosystems by highway construction, mining, hydroelectric projects, ranching, lumbering, agribusiness, and planned colonization (Bodley, ed. 1988; Bodley 1999, 2000).

Studying people at the local level, ethnographers have a unique view of the impact of national and international planning on intended "beneficiaries." Local-level research often reveals inadequacies in the measures that economists use to assess development and a nation's economic health. For example, per capita income and gross national product don't measure the distribution of wealth. Because the first is an average and the second is a total, they may rise as the rich get richer and the poor get poorer.

Applied anthropology refers to the application of anthropological perspectives, theory, methods, and data to identify, assess, and solve social problems. **Development anthropology** is the branch of applied anthropology that focuses on social issues in, and the cultural dimension of, economic development. Development anthropologists should not just carry out development policies planned by others; they are as qualified as economists are to make policy. (For more detailed discussions of the role of anthropologists in economic development see Escobar [1995] and Robertson [1995]).

Ethical dilemmas often confront development anthropologists (Escobar 1991, 1995). Our respect for cultural diversity is often offended because efforts to extend industry and technology may entail profound cultural changes. Foreign aid doesn't usually go where need and suffering are greatest. It is spent on political, economic, and strategic priorities as national leaders and powerful interest groups perceive them. Planners' interests don't always coincide with the best interests of the local people. Although the aim of most development projects is to enhance the quality of life, living standards often decline in the target area (Bodley, ed. 1988).

The Greening of Java

Anthropologist Richard Franke (1977) conducted a study of discrepancies between goals and results in a scheme to promote social and economic change in Java, Indonesia. Experts and planners of the 1960s and 1970s assumed that as small-scale farmers got modern technology and more productive crop varieties, their lives would improve. The media publicized new, high-yielding varieties of wheat, maize, and rice. These new crops, along with chemical fertilizers, pesticides, and new cultivation techniques, were hailed as the basis of a **green revolution.** This "revolution" was expected to increase the world's food supply and thus improve the diets and living conditions of victims of poverty, particularly in land-scarce, overcrowded regions.

The green revolution was an economic success. It did increase the global food supply. New strains of wheat and rice doubled or tripled farm supplies in many Third World countries. Thanks to the green revolution, world food prices declined by more than 20 percent during the 1980s (Stevens 1992). But its social effects were not what its advocates had intended, as we learn from Javanese experience.

Java received a genetic cross between rice strains from Taiwan and Indonesia—a high-yielding "miracle" rice known as IR-8. This hybrid could raise the productivity of a given plot by at least half. Governments throughout southern Asia, including Indonesia, encouraged the cultivation of IR-8, along with the use of chemical fertilizers and pesticides.

The Indonesian island of Java, one of the most densely populated places in the world (over 700 people per square kilometer), was a prime target for the green revolution. Java's total crop was insufficient to supply its people with minimal daily requirements of calories (2,150) and protein (55 grams). In 1960 Javanese agriculture supplied 1,950 calories and 38 grams of protein per capita. By 1967 these already inadequate figures had fallen to 1,750 calories and 33 grams. Could miracle rice, by increasing crop yields 50 percent, reverse the trend?

Java shares with many other underdeveloped nations a history of socioeconomic stratification and colonialism. Indigenous contrasts in wealth and power were intensified by Dutch colonialism. Although Indonesia gained political independence from the Netherlands in 1949, internal stratification continued. Today, contrasts between the wealthy (government employees, business people, large landowners) and the poor (small-scale peasants) exist even in small farming communities. Stratification led to problems during Java's green revolution.

In 1963 the University of Indonesia's College of Agriculture launched a program in which students went to live in villages. They worked with peasants in the fields and shared their knowledge of new agricultural techniques while learning from the peasants. The program was a success. Yields in the affected villages increased by half. The program, directed by the Department of Agriculture, was expanded in 1964; nine universities and 400 students joined. These intervention programs succeeded where others had failed because the outside agents recognized that economic development rests not only on technological change but on political change as well. Students could observe firsthand how interest groups resisted attempts by peasants to improve their lot. Once, when local officials stole fertilizer destined for peasant fields, students got it back by threatening in a letter to turn evidence of the crime over to higher-level officials.

The combination of new work patterns and political action was achieving promising results when, in 1965–66, there was an insurrection against the government. In the eventual military takeover, Indonesia's President Sukarno was ousted and replaced by President Suharto, who ruled Indonesia until 1998. Efforts to increase agricultural production resumed soon after Suharto took control. However, the new government assigned the task to multinational corporations based in Japan, West Germany, and Switzerland rather than to students and peasants. These industrial firms were to supply miracle rice and other high-yielding seeds, fertilizers, and pesticides. Peasants adopting the whole green revolution kit were eligible for loans that would allow them to buy food and other essentials in the lean period just before harvesting.

Java's green revolution soon encountered problems. One pesticide, which had never been tested in Java, killed the fish in the irrigation canals and thus destroyed an important protein resource. One development agency turned out to be a fraud, set up to benefit the military and government officials.

Java's green revolution also encountered problems at the village level because of entrenched interests. Traditionally, peasants had fed their families by taking temporary jobs, or borrowing, from wealthier villagers before the harvest. Having accepted loans, the peasants were obliged to work for wages lower than those paid on the open market. Low-interest loans would have made peasants less dependent on wealthy villagers, thus depriving local patrons of cheap labor.

Local officials were put in charge of spreading information about how the program worked. Instead they limited peasant participation by withholding information. Wealthy villagers also discouraged peasant participation more subtly: They raised doubts about the effectiveness of the new techniques and about the wisdom of taking government loans when familiar patrons were nearby. Faced with the thought that starvation might follow if innovation failed, peasants were reluctant to take risks—an understandable reaction.

Production increased, but wealthy villagers rather than small-scale farmers reaped the benefits of the green revolution. Just 20 percent of one village's 151 households participated in the program. However, because they were the wealthiest households, headed by people who owned the most land, 40 percent of the land was being cultivated by means of the new system. Some large-scale landowners used their green revolution profits at the peasants' expense. They bought up peasants' small plots and purchased labor-saving machinery, including rice-milling machines and tractors. As a result, the poorest peasants lost both their means of subsistence—land— and local work opportunities. Their only recourse was to move to cities, where a growing pool of unskilled laborers depressed already low wages.

In a complementary view of the green revolution's social effects, Ann Stoler (1977) focused on gender and stratification. She took issue with Esther Boserup's (1970) contention that colonialism and development inevitably hurt Third World women more than men by favoring commercial agriculture and excluding women from it. Stoler found that the green revolution had permitted some women to gain power over other women and men. Javanese women were not a homogeneous group but varied by class. Stoler found that whether the green revolution helped or harmed Javanese women depended on their position in the class structure. The status of landholding women rose as they gained control over more land and the labor of more poor women. The new economy offered wealthier women higher profits, which they used in trading. Poor women suffered along with poor men as traditional economic opportunities declined. Nevertheless, the poor women fared better than did the poor men, who had no access at all to off-farm work.

These studies of the local effects of the green revolution reveal results different from those foreseen by policy makers, planners, and the media. Again we see the unintended and often undesirable effects of development programs that ignore traditional social, political, and economic divisions. New technology, no matter how promising, does not inevitably help the intended beneficiaries. It may very well hurt them if vested interests interfere. In Java, a development program designed to alleviate poverty actually increased it. Agricultural production became profit-oriented, machine-based, and chemical-dependent. Local autonomy diminished as linkages with the world system increased. Production rose, as the rich got richer and poverty increased.

Equity

A commonly stated goal of development policy today is to promote equity. **Increased equity** means reduced poverty and a more even distribution of wealth. However, if projects are to increase equity, they must have the support of reform-minded governments. Wealthy and powerful people typically resist projects that threaten their vested interests.

Some types of development projects, particularly irrigation schemes, are more likely than others to widen wealth disparities, that is, to have a negative equity impact. An initial uneven distribution of resources (particularly land) often becomes the basis for greater skewing after the project. The social impact of new technology tends to be more severe, contributing negatively to quality of life and to equity, when inputs are channeled to or through the rich, as in Java's green revolution.

Many fisheries projects have also had negative equity results. In Bahia, Brazil (Kottak 1999), sailboat owners (but not nonowners) got loans to buy motors for their boats. To repay the loans, the owners increased the percentage of the catch they took from the men who fished in their boats. Over the years, they used their rising profits to buy larger and more expensive boats. The result was stratification—the creation of a group of wealthy people within a formerly egalitarian community. These events hampered individual initiative and interfered with further development of the fishing industry. With new boats so expensive, ambitious young men who once would have sought careers in fishing no longer had any way to obtain their own boats. They sought wage labor on land instead. To avoid such results, credit-granting agencies must seek out enterprising young fishers rather than giving loans only to owners and established business people.

STRATEGIES FOR INNOVATION

Development anthropologists, who are concerned with social issues in, and the cultural dimension of, economic development, must work closely with local people to assess and help them realize their own wishes and needs for change. Too many true local needs cry out for a solution to waste money funding development projects in area A that are inappropriate there but needed in area B, or that are unnecessary anywhere. Development anthropology can help sort out the needs of the As and Bs and fit projects accordingly. Projects that put people first by consulting with them and responding to their expressed needs must be identified (Cernea, ed. 1991). Thereafter, development anthropologists can work to ensure socially compatible ways of implementing a good project.

In a comparative study of sixty-eight rural development projects from all around the world, I found the *culturally compatible* economic development projects to be twice as successful financially as the incompatible ones (Kottak 1990*b*, 1991). This finding shows that using anthropological expertise in planning to ensure cultural compatibility is cost-effective. To maximize social and economic benefits, projects must (1) be culturally compatible, (2) respond to locally perceived needs, (3) involve men and women in planning and carrying out the changes that affect them, (4) harness traditional organizations, and (5) be flexible.

Overinnovation

In my comparative study, the compatible and successful projects avoided the fallacy of **overinnovation** (too much change). We would expect people to resist development projects that require major changes in their daily lives. People usually want to change just enough to keep what they have. Motives for modifying behavior come from the traditional culture and the small concerns of ordinary life. Peasants' values are not such abstract ones as "learning a better way," "progressing," "increasing technical know-how,"

To maximize benefits, development projects should be culturally compatible and respond to locally perceived needs for change. What else should they do? This Zambian farm club, which draws on traditional social organization, plants cabbages.

"improving efficiency," or "adopting modern techniques." (Those phrases exemplify intervention philosophy.)

Instead, their objectives are down-to-earth and specific ones. People want to improve yields in a rice field, amass resources for a ceremony, get a child through school, or have enough cash to pay the tax bill on time. The goals and values of subsistence producers differ from those of people who produce for cash, just as they differ from the intervention philosophy of development planners. Different value systems must be considered during planning.

In the comparative study, the projects that failed were usually both economically and culturally incompatible. For example, one South Asian project promoted the cultivation of onions and peppers, expecting this practice to fit into a preexisting labor-intensive system of rice-growing. Cultivation of these cash crops wasn't traditional in the area. It conflicted with existing crop priorities and other interests of farmers. Also, the labor peaks for pepper and onion production coincided with those for rice, to which the farmers gave priority.

Throughout the world, project problems have arisen from inadequate attention to, and consequent lack of fit with, local culture. Another naive and incompatible project was an overinnovative scheme in Ethiopia. Its major fallacy was to try to convert nomadic herders into sedentary cultivators. It ignored traditional land rights. Outsiders—commercial farmers—were to get much of the herders' territory. The pastoralists were expected to settle down and start farming. This project helped wealthy outsiders instead of the local people. The planners naively expected free-ranging herders to give up a generations-old way of life to work three times harder growing rice and picking cotton.

Underdifferentiation

The fallacy of **underdifferentiation** is the tendency to view "the less-developed countries" as more alike than they are. Development agencies have often ignored cultural diversity (e.g., between Brazil and Burundi) and adopted a uniform approach to deal with very different sets of people. Neglecting cultural diversity, many projects also have tried to impose incompatible property notions and social units. Most often, the faulty social design assumes either (1) individualistic productive units that are privately owned by an individual or couple and worked by a nuclear family or (2) cooperatives that are at least partially based on models from the former Eastern bloc and Socialist countries.

One example of faulty Euro-American models (the individual and the nuclear family) was a West African project designed for an area where the extended family was the basic social unit. The project succeeded despite its faulty social design because the participants used their traditional extended family networks to attract additional settlers. Eventually, twice as many people as planned benefited as extended family members flocked to the project area. Here, settlers modified the project design that had been imposed on them by following the principles of their traditional society.

The second dubious foreign social model that is common in development strategy is the cooperative. In the comparative study of rural development projects, new cooperatives fared badly. Cooperatives succeeded only when they harnessed preexisting local-level communal institutions. This is a corollary of a more general rule: Participants' groups are most effective when they are based on traditional social organization or on a socioeconomic similarity among members.

Neither foreign social model—the nuclear family farm nor the cooperative—has an unblemished record in development. An alternative is needed: greater use of Third World social models for Third World development. These are traditional social units, such as the clans, lineages, and other extended kin groups of Africa, Oceania, and many other nations, with their communally held estates and resources. The most humane and productive strategy for change is to base the social design for innovation on traditional social forms in each target area.

Third World Models

Many governments are not genuinely, or realistically, committed to improving the lives of their citizens. Interference by major powers has also kept governments from enacting needed reforms. In highly stratified societies,

In Bangladesh, women count money at a weekly meeting where loans from the female-run Grameen Credit Bank are repaid. Groups promoting development can be particularly effective when they are based on traditional social organization or on a socioeconomic similarity among members.

particularly in Latin America, the class structure is very rigid. Movement of individuals into the middle class is difficult. It is equally hard to raise the living standards of the lower class as a whole. These nations have a long history of government control by antidemocratic leaders and powerful interest groups, which tend to oppose reform.

In some nations, however, the government acts more as an agent of the people. Madagascar provides an example. As in many areas of Africa, precolonial states had developed in Madagascar before its conquest by the French in 1895. The people of Madagascar, the Malagasy, had been organized into descent groups before the origin of the state. The Merina, creators of the major precolonial state of Madagascar, wove descent groups into its structure, making members of important groups advisers to the king and thus giving them authority in government. The Merina state made provisions for the people it ruled. It collected taxes and organized labor for public works projects. In return, it redistributed resources to peasants in need. It also granted them some protection against war and slave raids and allowed them to cultivate their rice fields in peace. The government maintained the water works for rice cultivation. It opened to ambitious peasant boys the chance of becoming, through hard work and study, state bureaucrats.

Throughout the history of the Merina state—and continuing in modern Madagascar—there have been strong relationships between the individual, the descent group, and the state. Local Malagasy communities, where residence is based on descent, are more cohesive and homogeneous than are communities in Java or Latin America. Madagascar gained political independence from France in 1960. Although it was still economically dependent on France when I first did research there in 1966–67, the new government had an economic development policy aimed at increasing the ability of the Malagasy to feed themselves. Government policy emphasized increased production of rice, a subsistence crop, rather than cash crops. Furthermore, local communities, with their traditional cooperative patterns and solidarity based on kinship and descent, were treated as partners in, not obstacles to, the development process.

In a sense, the descent group is preadapted to equitable national development. In Madagascar, members of local descent groups have customarily pooled their resources to educate their ambitious members. Once educated, these men and women gain economically secure positions in the nation. They then share the advantages of their new positions with their kin. For example, they give room and board to rural cousins attending school and help them find jobs.

Malagasy administrations appear generally to have shared a commitment to democratic economic development. Perhaps this is because government officials are of the peasantry or have strong personal ties to it. By contrast, in Latin American countries, the elites and the lower class have different origins and no strong connections through kinship, descent, or marriage.

Furthermore, societies with descent-group organization contradict an assumption that many social scientists and economists seem to make. It is not inevitable that as nations become more tied to the world capitalist economy, native forms of social organization will break down into nuclear family organization, impersonality, and alienation. Descent groups, with their traditional communalism and corporate solidarity, have important roles to play in economic development.

Realistic development promotes change but not overinnovation. Many changes are possible if the aim is to preserve local systems while making them work better. Successful economic development projects respect, or at least don't attack, local cultural patterns. Effective development draws on indigenous cultural practices and social structures.

S u m m a r y

1. Imperialism is the policy of extending the rule of a nation or empire over other nations and of taking and holding foreign colonies.
   Colonialism is the domination of a territory and its people by a foreign power for an extended time. European colonialism had two main phases. The first started in 1492 and lasted through 1825. For Britain this phase ended with the American revolution. For France it ended when Britain won the Seven Years' War, forcing the French to abandon

Canada and India. For Spain, it ended with Latin American independence. The second phase of European colonialism extended approximately from 1850 to 1950. The British and French empires were at their height around 1914, when European empires controlled 85 percent of the world. Britain and France had colonies in Africa, Asia, Oceania, and the New World.

2. Many geopolitical labels and identities were created under colonialism that had little or nothing to do with existing social demarcations. The new ethnic or national divisions were colonial inventions, sometimes aggravating conflicts.

3. Like colonialism, economic development has an intervention philosophy that provides a justification for outsiders to guide native peoples toward particular goals. Development is usually justified by the idea that industrialization and modernization are desirable evolutionary advances. Yet many problems faced by Third World peoples have been caused by their incorporation in the world cash economy. Roads, mining, hydroelectric projects, ranching, lumbering, and agribusiness threaten indigenous peoples and their ecosystems.

4. Development anthropology focuses on social issues in, and the cultural dimension of, economic development. Development projects typically promote cash employment and new technology at the expense of subsistence economies. Research in Java found the green revolution was failing. It promoted the new technology while ignoring peasant political organization.

5. Not all governments seek to increase equality and end poverty. Resistance by elites to reform is typical and hard to combat. At the same time, local people rarely cooperate with projects requiring major and risky changes in their daily lives. Many projects seek to impose inappropriate property notions and incompatible social units on their intended beneficiaries. The best strategy for change is to base the social design for innovation on traditional social forms in each target area.

Case Study
Haiti

This chapter has discussed the far-reaching and long-lasting results of colonialism. In *Culture Sketches* by Holly Peters-Golden read the chapter on Haiti: A Nation in Turmoil. How do you think Haiti's colonial past has contributed to its contemporary situation? What sorts of problems does Haiti face owing to development or lack thereof? How does Haiti compare to some other examples mentioned in this chapter?

Culturally Appropriate Marketing

Innovation succeeds best when it is culturally appropriate. This axiom of applied anthropology could guide the international spread not only of development projects but also of businesses, such as fast food. Each time McDonald's or Burger King expands to a new nation, it must devise a culturally appropriate strategy for fitting into the new setting.

McDonald's has been successful internationally, with more than a quarter of its sales outside the United States. One place where McDonald's is expanding successfully is Brazil, where some fifty million middle-class people, most living in densely packed cities, provide a concentrated market for a fast-food chain. Still, it took McDonald's some time to find the right marketing strategy for Brazil.

In 1980 when I visited Brazil after a seven-year absence, I first noticed, as a manifestation of Brazil's growing participation in the world economy, the appearance of two McDonald's restaurants in Rio de Janeiro. There wasn't much difference between Brazilian and American McDonald's. The restaurants looked alike. The menus was more or less the same, as was the taste of the quarter-pounders. I picked up an artifact, a white paper bag with yellow lettering, exactly like the take-out bags then used in American McDonald's. An advertising device, it carried several messages about how Brazilians could bring McDonald's into their lives. However, it seemed to me that McDonald's Brazilian ad campaign was missing some important points about how fast food should be marketed in a culture that values large, leisurely lunches.

The bag proclaimed, "You're going to enjoy the [McDonald's] difference," and listed several "favorite places where

you can enjoy McDonald's products." This list confirmed that the marketing people were trying to adapt to Brazilian middle-class culture, but they were making some mistakes. "When you go out in the car with the kids" transferred the uniquely developed North American cultural combination of highways, affordable cars, and suburban living to the very different context of urban Brazil. A similar suggestion was "traveling to the country place." Even Brazilians who own country places can't find McDonald's, still confined to the cities, on the road. The ad creator had apparently never attempted to drive up to a fast-food restaurant in a neighborhood with no parking spaces.

Several other suggestions pointed customers toward the beach, where *cariocas* (Rio natives) do spend much of their leisure time. One could eat McDonald's products "after a dip in the ocean," "at a picnic at the beach," or "watching the surfers." These suggestions ignored the Brazilian custom of consuming cold things, such as beer, soft drinks, ice cream, and ham and cheese sandwiches, at the beach. Brazilians don't consider a hot, greasy hamburger proper beach food. They view the sea as "cold" and hamburgers as "hot"; they avoid "hot" foods at the beach.

Also culturally dubious was the suggestion to eat McDonald's hamburgers "lunching at the office." Brazilians prefer their main meal at midday, often eating at a leisurely pace with business associates. Many firms serve ample lunches to their employees. Other workers take advantage of a two-hour lunch break to go home to eat with the spouse and children. Nor did it make sense to suggest that children should eat hamburgers for lunch, since most kids attend school for half-day sessions and have lunch at home. Two other suggestions—"waiting for the bus" and "in the beauty parlor"—did describe common aspects of daily life in a Brazilian city. However, these settings have not proved especially inviting to hamburgers or fish filets.

The homes of Brazilians who can afford McDonald's products have cooks and maids to do many of the things that fast-food restaurants do in the United States. The suggestion that McDonald's products be eaten "while watching your favorite television program" is culturally appropriate, because Brazilians watch TV a lot. However, Brazil's consuming classes can ask the cook to make a snack when hunger strikes. Indeed, much televiewing occurs during the light dinner served when the husband gets home from the office.

Most appropriate to the Brazilian lifestyle was the suggestion to enjoy McDonald's "on the cook's day off." Throughout Brazil, Sunday is that day. The Sunday pattern for middle-class families is a trip to the beach, liters of beer, a full midday meal around 3 P.M., and a light evening snack. McDonald's has found its niche in the Sunday evening meal, when families flock to the fast-food restaurant, and it is to this market that its advertising is now appropriately geared.

McDonald's is expanding rapidly in Brazilian cities, and in Brazil as in North America, teenage appetites are fueling the fast-food explosion. As McDonald's outlets appeared in urban neighborhoods, Brazilian teenagers used them for after-school snacks, while families had evening meals there. As an anthropologist could have predicted, the fast-food industry has not revolutionized Brazilian food and meal customs. Rather, McDonald's is succeeding because it has adapted to preexisting Brazilian cultural patterns.

The main contrast with North America is that the Brazilian evening meal is lighter. McDonald's now caters to the evening meal rather than to lunch. Once McDonald's realized that more money could be made by fitting in with, rather than trying to Americanize, Brazilian meal habits, it started aiming its advertising at that goal.

Cultural Exchange and Survival

This book has examined many aspects of increasing participation by local societies in wider systems—regional, national, colonial, and global. Since the 1920s anthropologists have been investigating the changes that arise from contact between industrial and nondustrial societies. Studies of "social change" and "acculturation" are abundant. British and American ethnographers, respectively, have used these terms to describe the same process. *Acculturation* refers to changes that result when groups come into continuous firsthand contact—changes in the cultural patterns of either or both groups (Redfield, Linton, and Herskovits 1936, p. 149).

CONTACT AND DOMINATION

Acculturation differs from diffusion, or cultural borrowing, which can occur without firsthand contact. For example, most North Americans who eat hot dogs ("frankfurters") have never been to Frankfurt, nor have most North American Toyota owners or sushi eaters ever visited Japan. Although acculturation can be applied to any case of cultural contact and change, the term has most often described **Westernization**—the influence of Western expansion on native societies. Thus natives who wear store-bought clothes, learn Indo-European languages, and otherwise adopt Western customs are called acculturated. Acculturation may be voluntary or forced.

Different degrees of destruction, domination, resistance, survival, adaptation, and modification of native cultures may follow interethnic contact. In cases in which contact between the indigenous societies and more powerful outsiders leads to destruction—a situation that is particularly characteristic of colonialist and expansionist eras—a "shock phase" often follows the initial encounter (Bodley, ed. 1988). Outsiders may attack or exploit the native people. Such exploitation may increase mortality, disrupt subsistence, fragment kin groups, damage social support systems, and inspire new religious movements, such as the cargo cults examined in Chapter 9, "Religion" (Bodley, ed. 1988). During the shock phase, there may be civil repression backed by military force. Such factors may lead to the tribe's cultural collapse (*ethnocide*) or its physical extinction (*genocide*).

Outsiders often attempt to remake native landscapes and cultures in their own image. Political and economic colonialists have tried to redesign conquered and dependent lands, peoples, and cultures, imposing their cultural standards on others. The aim of many agricultural development projects, for example, seems to have been to make the world as much like Iowa as possible, complete with mechanized farming and nuclear family ownership—despite the fact that these models may be inappropriate for settings outside the North American heartland.

Development and Environmentalism

Today it is often multinational corporations, usually based in core nations, rather than the governments of those nations, that are changing the nature of Third World economies. Governments of many peripheral and semiperipheral nations, such as Brazil, have supported the predatory enterprises of some corporations that seek cheap labor and raw materials in their countries, where economic development has often contributed to ecological devastation.

Simultaneously, environmentalists from core nations increasingly state their case, promoting conservation, to the rest of the world. Akbar Ahmed (1992) finds the non-Western world to be cynical about Western ecological morality, seeing it as yet another imperialist message. "The Chinese have cause to snigger at the Western suggestion that they forgo the convenience of the fridge to save the ozone layer" (Ahmed 1992, p. 120). Brazilians complain that northerners talk about global needs and saving the Amazon after having destroyed their own forests for First World economic growth.

In the last chapter we saw that development projects usually fail if they try to replace native forms with culturally alien property concepts and productive units. A strategy that incorporates the native forms is more effective than the fallacies of overinnovation and underdifferentiation. The same caveats would seem to apply to an intervention philosophy that seeks to impose global ecological morality without due attention to cultural variation and autonomy. Countries and societies may resist interventionist philosophies aimed at either development or globally justified environmentalism.

A clash of cultures related to environmental change may occur when *development threatens indigenous peoples and their environments*. Hundreds of native groups throughout the world, including the Kayapó Indians of Brazil and the Kaluli of Papua New Guinea (see the box at the end of the chapter), have been threatened by plans and forces, such as dam construction or commercially driven deforestation, that would *destroy* their homelands.

A second clash of cultures related to environmental change occurs when *external regulation threatens indigenous peoples.* Native groups may actually be threatened by environmental plans that seek to *save* their homelands. Sometimes outsiders expect local people to give up many of their customary economic and cultural activities without clear substitutes, alternatives, or incentives. The traditional approach to conservation has been to restrict access to protected areas, hire park guards, and punish violators. Ironically, well-meaning conservation efforts can be as insensitive as development schemes that promote radical changes without involving local people in planning and carrying out the policies that affect them. When people are asked to give up the basis of their livelihood, they usually resist.

Religious Change

Religious proselytizing can promote ethnocide, as native beliefs and practices are replaced by Western ones. Sometimes a religion and associated customs are replaced by ideology and behavior more compatible with Western culture. One example is the Handsome Lake religion (as described in the chapter on religion), which led the Iroquois to copy European farming techniques, stressing male rather than female labor. The Iroquois also gave up their communal longhouses and matrilineal descent groups for nuclear family households. The teachings of Handsome Lake led to a new church and religion. This revitalization movement helped the Iroquois survive in a drastically modified environment, but much ethnocide was involved.

Handsome Lake was a native who created a new religion, drawing on Western models. More commonly, missionaries and proselytizers representing the major world religions, especially Christianity and Islam, are the proponents of religious change. Protestant and Catholic missionization continues even in remote corners of the world. Evangelical Protestantism, for example, is advancing in Peru, Brazil, and other parts of Latin America. It challenges an often jaded Catholicism that has too few priests and that is sometimes seen mainly as women's religion.

Sometimes the political ideology of a nation-state is pitted against traditional religion. Officials of the former Soviet empire discouraged Catholicism, Judaism, and Islam. In Central Asia, Soviet dominators destroyed Muslim mosques and discouraged religious practice. On the other hand, governments often use their power to advance a religion, such as Islam in Iran or Sudan.

A military government seized power in Sudan in 1989. It immediately launched a campaign to change that country of more than 25 million people, where one-third are not Muslims, into an Islamic nation. Declaring a *jihad* (holy war) against non-Muslims, the government sought to extend Islam and the Arabic language to the non-Muslim south. This was an area of Christianity and tribal religions that had resisted the central government for a decade (Hedges 1992*a*). Resistance continues.

RESISTANCE AND SURVIVAL

Systems of domination—whether political, economic, cultural, or religious—have their more muted aspects along with their public dimensions. In studying systems of domination, we must pay attention to what lies beneath the surface of evident, public behavior. In public the oppressed may seem to accept their own domination, but they always question it offstage. James Scott (1990) uses the terms **public transcript** and **hidden transcript** to describe, respectively, the open, public interactions between dominators and oppressed—the outer shell of power relations—and the critique of power that goes on offstage—where the power holders can't see or hear it.

In public, the elites and the oppressed observe the etiquette of power relations. The dominants act like haughty masters while their subordinates show humility and defer. Antonio Gramsci (1971) developed the concept of **hegemony** for a stratified social order in which subordinates comply with domination by internalizing their rulers' values and accepting the "naturalness" of domination (this is the way things were meant to be). According to Pierre Bourdieu (1977, p. 164), every social order tries to make its own arbitrariness (including its oppression) seem natural. All hegemonic ideologies offer explanations about why the existing order is in everyone's interest. Often promises are made (things will get better if you're patient). Gramsci and others use the idea of hegemony to explain why people conform even without coercion.

Hegemony, the internalization of a dominant ideology, is one way to curb resistance. Another way is to let subordinates know they will eventually gain power—as young people usually foresee when they let their elders dominate them. Another way of curbing resistance is to separate or isolate subordinates and supervise them closely. According to Michel Foucault (1979), describing control over prisoners, solitude (as in solitary confinement) is one effective way to induce submission.

Weapons of the Weak

Often, situations that seem to be hegemonic do have active resistance, but it is individual and disguised rather than collective and defiant. Scott (1985) uses Malay peasants, among whom he did field work, to illustrate small-scale acts of resistance—which he calls "weapons of the weak." The Malay peasants used an indirect strategy to resist an Islamic tithe (religious tax). The goods (usually rice) that peasants had to give went to the provincial capital. In theory, the tithe would come back as charity to the peasants, but it never did. Peasants didn't resist the tithe by rioting, demonstrating, or protesting. Instead they used a "nibbling" strategy, based on small acts of resistance. For example, they failed to declare their land or lied about the amount they farmed. They underpaid or delivered rice paddy contaminated with water, rocks, or mud, to add weight. Because of this resistance, only 15 percent of what was due was actually paid (Scott 1990, p. 89).

Subordinates also use various strategies to resist *publicly,* but again, usually in disguised form. Discontent may be expressed in public rituals and language, including metaphors, euphemisms, and folk tales. For example, trickster tales (such as the Brer Rabbit stories told by slaves in the southern United States) celebrate the wiles of the weak as they triumph over the strong.

Resistance is most likely to be expressed openly when the oppressed are allowed to assemble. The hidden transcript may be publicly revealed on such occasions. People see their dreams and anger shared by others with whom they haven't been in direct contact. The oppressed may draw courage from the crowd, from its visual and emotional impact and its anonymity. Sensing danger, the elites discourage such public gatherings. They try to limit and control holidays, funerals, dances, festivals, and other occasions that might unite the oppressed. Thus in the southern United States gatherings of five or more slaves were forbidden unless a white person was present.

Factors that interfere with community formation—such as geographic, linguistic, and ethnic separation—also work to curb resistance. Consequently, southern U.S. plantation owners sought slaves with diverse cultural and linguistic backgrounds. Despite the measures used to divide them, the slaves resisted, developing their own popular culture, linguistic codes, and religious vision. The masters taught portions of the Bible that stressed compliance, but the slaves seized on the story of Moses, the promised land, and deliverance. The cornerstone of slave religion became the idea of a reversal in the conditions of whites and blacks. Slaves also resisted directly, through sabotage and flight. In many New World areas slaves managed to establish free communities in the hills and other remote areas (Price, ed. 1973).

Hidden transcripts tend to be publicly expressed at certain times (festivals and *Carnavals*) and in certain places (for example, markets). Because of its costumed anonymity, Carnaval is an excellent arena for expressing normally suppressed speech and aggression—antihegemonic discourse. (*Discourse* includes talk, speeches, gestures, and actions.) Carnavals celebrate freedom through immodesty, dancing, gluttony, and sexuality (DaMatta 1991). Carnaval may begin as a playful outlet for frustrations built up during the year. Over time it may evolve into a powerful annual critique of domination and a threat to the established order (Gilmore 1987). (Recognizing that ceremonial license could turn into political defiance, the Spanish dictator Francisco Franco outlawed Carnaval.)

Cultural Imperialism

Cultural imperialism refers to the spread or advance of one culture at the expense of others, or its imposition on other societies, which it modifies, replaces, or destroys—usually because of differential economic or political influence. Thus, children in the French colonial empire learned French history, language, and culture from standard textbooks also used in France. Tahitians, Malagasy, Vietnamese, and Senegalese learned the French language by reciting from books about "our ancestors the Gauls."

Because of its costumed anonymity, *Carnaval* is an excellent arena for expressing normally suppressed speech. This is vividly symbolized by these Carnaval head-dresses in Trinidad. Is there anything like Carnaval in your society?

To what extent is modern technology, especially the mass media, an agent of cultural imperialism? Some commentators see modern technology as erasing cultural differences, as homogeneous products reach more people worldwide. But others see a role for modern technology in allowing social groups (local cultures) to express themselves (Marcus and Fischer 1999). Modern radio and TV, for example, constantly bring local happenings (for example, a "chicken festival" in Iowa) to the attention of a larger public. The North American media play a role in stimulating local activities of many sorts. Similarly in Brazil, local practices, celebrations, and perform-ances are changing in the context of outside forces, including the mass me-dia and tourism.

In the Brazilian town of Arembepe, TV coverage has stimulated partici-pation in a traditional annual performance, the *Chegança*. This is a fisher-men's danceplay, that reenacts the Portuguese discovery of Brazil. Arembepeiros have traveled to the state capital to perform the Chegança be-fore television cameras, for a TV program featuring traditional perform-ances from many rural communities.

One national Brazilian Sunday-night variety program (*Fantástico*) is es-pecially popular in rural areas because it shows such local events. In several towns along the Amazon River, annual folk ceremonies are now staged more lavishly for TV cameras. In the Amazon town of Parantíns, for example, boatloads of tourists arriving any time of year are shown a videotape of the town's annual Bumba Meu Boi festival. This is a costumed performance mimicking bull-fighting, parts of which have been shown on *Fantástico*. This pattern, in which communities preserve, revive, and intensify the scale of traditional ceremonies to perform for TV and tourists, is expanding.

Brazilian television has also played a "top-down" role by spreading the popularity of holidays such as Carnaval and Christmas (Kottak 1990a). TV has aided the national spread of Carnaval beyond its traditional urban centers. Still, local reactions to the nationwide broadcasting of Carnaval and its trappings (elaborate parades, costumes, and frenzied dancing) are not simple or uniform responses to external stimuli.

Rather than direct adoption of Carnaval, local Brazilians respond in various ways. Often they don't take up Carnaval itself but modify their local festivities to fit Carnaval images. Others actively spurn Carnaval. One example is Arembepe, where Carnaval has never been important, probably because of its calendrical closeness to the main local festival, which is held in February to honor Saint Francis of Assisi. In the past, villagers couldn't afford to celebrate both occasions. Now, not only do the people of Arembepe reject Carnaval, they are also increasingly hostile to their own main festival. Arembepeiros resent the fact that Saint Francis has become "an outsiders' event," because it draws thousands of tourists to Arembepe each February. The villagers think that commercial interests and outsiders have appropriated Saint Francis.

In opposition to these trends, many Arembepeiros now say they like and participate more in the traditional June festivals honoring Saint John, Saint Peter, and Saint Anthony. In the past these were observed on a much smaller scale than was the festival for Saint Francis. Arembepeiros celebrate them now with a new vigor and enthusiasm, as they react to outsiders and their celebrations, real and televised.

MAKING AND REMAKING CULTURE

Any media-borne image, such as Carnaval, can be analyzed in terms of its nature and effects. It can also be analyzed as a **text**—something that is creatively "read," interpreted, and assigned meaning by each person who receives it. Carnaval images in Brazil illustrate some ways in which "readers" derive their own meanings and feelings from a text. Such meanings may be very different from what the creators of the text imagined. (The reading or meaning that the creators intended—or the one that the elites consider to be the intended or correct meaning—can be called the *hegemonic reading*.)

"Readers" of media messages constantly produce their own meanings. They may resist or oppose the hegemonic meanings of a text, or they may seize on the antihegemonic aspects of a text. We saw this process when American slaves preferred the Biblical story of Moses and deliverance to the hegemonic lessons of obedience that their masters taught.

Popular Culture

In his book *Understanding Popular Culture* (1989), John Fiske views each individual's use of popular culture as a creative act (an original "reading" of a text). (For example, Madonna, the Grateful Dead, or *Star Wars* mean something different to each of their fans.) As Fiske puts it, "the meanings I make from a text are pleasurable when I feel that they are *my* meanings and that they relate to *my* everyday life in a practical, direct way" (1989, p. 57). All of us can creatively "read" magazines, books, music, television, films, celebrities, and other popular culture products.

Individuals also draw on popular culture to express resistance. Through their use of popular culture, people can symbolically resist the unequal power relations they face each day—in the family, at work, and in the classroom. Forms and readings of popular culture (from rap music to comedy) can express discontent and resistance by groups that are or feel oppressed.

Indigenizing Popular Culture

To understand culture change, it is important to recognize that meaning may be locally manufactured. People assign their own meanings and value to the texts, messages, and products they receive. Those meanings reflect their cultural backgrounds and experiences. When forces from world centers enter new societies, they are **indigenized**—modified to fit the local culture. This is true of cultural forces as various as fast food (see the box in the last chapter), music, housing styles, science, terrorism, celebrations, and political ideas and institutions (Appadurai 1990).

Consider the reception of the movie *Rambo* in Australia as an example of how popular culture may be indigenized Michaels (1986) found *Rambo* to be very popular among aborigines in the deserts of central Australia, who had manufactured their own meanings from the film. Their "reading" was very different from the one imagined by the movie's creators and by most Americans. The Native Australians saw Rambo as a representative of the Third World battling the white officer class. This reading expressed their negative feelings about white paternalism and existing race relations. The Native Australians also imagined that there were tribal ties and kin links between Rambo and the prisoners he was rescuing. All this made sense, based on their experience. Native Australians are disproportionately represented in Australian jails. Their most likely liberator would be someone with a personal link to them. These readings of *Rambo* were relevant meanings produced *from* the text, not *by* it (Fiske 1989).

A World System of Images

All societies express imagination—in dreams, fantasies, songs, myths, and stories. Today, however, more people in many more places imagine "a wider set of 'possible' lives than they ever did before. One important source of this

When products and images enter new settings, they are typically indigenized—modified to fit the local culture. Jeans Street, in Bandung, Indonesia, is a strip of stores, vendors, and restaurants catering to young people interested in Western pop culture. How is the poster of Batman and Robin indigenized?

change is the mass media, which present a rich, ever-changing store of possible lives . . ." (Appadurai 1991, p. 197). The United States as a media center has been joined by Canada, Japan, Western Europe, Brazil, Mexico, Nigeria, Egypt, India, and Hong Kong.

As print has done for centuries (Anderson 1991), the electronic mass media can also spread, even help create, national and ethnic identities. Like print, television and radio can diffuse the cultures of countries within their own boundaries, thus enhancing national cultural identity. For example, millions of Brazilians who were formerly cut off (by geographic isolation or illiteracy) from urban and national events and information now participate in a national communication system, through TV networks (Kottak 1990*a*).

Cross-cultural studies of television contradict a belief Americans ethnocentrically hold about televiewing in other countries. This misconception is that American programs inevitably triumph over local products. This doesn't happen when there is appealing local competition. In Brazil, for example, the most popular network (TV Globo) relies heavily on native productions. TV Globo's most popular programs are *telenovelas,* locally made serials that are similar to American soap operas. Globo plays each night to the world's largest and most devoted audience (60 to 80 million viewers throughout the nation). The programs that attract this horde are made by Brazilians, for Brazilians. Thus it is not North American culture but a new pan-Brazilian national culture which Brazilian TV is propagating. Brazilian productions also compete internationally. They are exported to over 100 countries, spanning Latin America, Europe, Asia, and Africa.

We may generalize that programming that is culturally alien won't do very well anywhere, when a quality local choice is available. Confirmation comes from many countries. National productions are highly popular in Japan, Mexico, India, Egypt, and Nigeria. In a survey during the mid-1980s, 75 percent of Nigerian viewers preferred local productions. Only 10 percent favored imports, and the remaining 15 percent liked the two options equally. Local productions are successful in Nigeria because "they are filled with everyday moments that audiences can identify with. These shows are locally produced by Nigerians" (Gray 1986). Thirty million people watched one of the most popular series, *The Village Headmaster*, each week. That program brought rural values to the screens of urbanites who had lost touch with their rural roots (Gray 1986).

The mass media can also play a role in maintaining ethnic and national identities among people who lead transnational lives. As groups move, they stay linked to each other and to their homeland through the media. Diasporas have enlarged the markets for media and travel services targeted at specific ethnic, national, or religious audiences. For a fee, a PBS station in Fairfax, Virginia, offers more than thirty hours a week to immigrant groups in the D.C. area, to make programs in their own languages (*New York Times*, December 18, 1992).

A Transnational Culture of Consumption

Another key transnational force is finance. Multinational corporations and other business interests look beyond national boundaries for places to invest and draw profits. As Appadurai (1991, p. 194) puts it, "money, commodities, and persons unendingly chase each other around the world." Residents of many Latin American communities now depend on outside cash, remitted from international labor migration. Also, the economy of the United States is increasingly influenced by foreign investment, especially from Britain, Canada, Germany, the Netherlands, and Japan (Rouse 1991). The American economy has also increased its dependence on foreign labor—through both the immigration of laborers and the export of jobs.

Contemporary global culture is driven by flows of people, technology, finance, information, and ideology (Appadurai 1990). Business, technology, and the media have increased the craving for commodities and images throughout the world. This has forced most nation-states to open to a global culture of consumption. Almost everyone today participates in this culture. Few people have never seen a T-shirt advertising a Western product. American and English rock stars' recordings blast through the streets of Rio de Janeiro, while taxi drivers from Toronto to Madagascar play Brazilian *lambada* tapes. Peasants and tribal people participate in the modern world system not only because they have been hooked on cash, but also because their products and images are appropriated by world capitalism (Gottdiener, ed.

Business and the media have increased the craving for products
throughout the world. Here, exiting a shopping mall, a German man
takes home a Barbie doll.

2000; Marcus and Myers, eds. 1995; Root 1996). They are commercialized
by others (like the San in the movie *The Gods Must Be Crazy*). Furthermore,
indigenous peoples also market their own images and products, through
outlets such as Cultural Survival. David Maybury-Lewis's ten-program 1992
TV series *Millennium (Tribal Wisdom and the Modern World)* was designed to
remedy misconceptions about tribal people, to help ensure their autonomy
and survival.

PEOPLE IN MOTION

The linkages in the modern world system have both enlarged and erased old
boundaries and distinctions. Arjun Appadurai (1990, p. 1) characterizes today's world as a "translocal" "interactive system" that is "strikingly new."
Whether as refugees, migrants, tourists, pilgrims, proselytizers, laborers,
business people, development workers, employees of nongovernmental
organizations (NGOs), politicians, soldiers, sports figures, or media-borne
images, people travel more than ever.

So important is transnational migration that many Mexican villagers
find "their most important kin and friends are as likely to be living hundreds
or thousands of miles away as immediately around them" (Rouse 1991).
Most migrants maintain their ties with their native land (phoning, visiting,
sending money, watching "ethnic TV"). In a sense, they live multilocally—in

different places at once. Dominicans in New York City, for example, have been characterized as living "between two islands"—Manhattan and the Dominican Republic (Grasmuck and Pessar 1991). Many Dominicans—like migrants from other countries—migrate to the United States temporarily, seeking cash to transform their life styles when they return to the Caribbean.

With so many people "in motion," the unit of anthropological study expands from the local community to the **diaspora**—the offspring of an area who have spread to many lands. Anthropologists increasingly follow descendants of the communities they have studied as they move from rural to urban areas and across national boundaries. For the 1991 annual meeting of the American Anthropological Association in Chicago, the anthropologist Robert Kemper organized a session of presentations about long-term ethnographic field work. Kemper's own long-time research focus has been the Mexican village of Tzintzuntzan, which, with his mentor George Foster, Kemper has studied for decades. However, their database now includes not just Tzintzuntzan, but its descendants all over the world. Given the Tzintzuntzan diaspora, Kemper was even able to use some of his time in Chicago to visit people from Tzintzuntzan who had established a colony there. In today's world, as people move, they take their traditions and their anthropologists along with them.

Postmodernity describes our time and situation—today's world in flux, these people on the move who have learned to manage multiple identities depending on place and context. In its most general sense, **postmodern** refers to the blurring and breakdown of established canons (rules or standards), categories, distinctions, and boundaries. The word is taken from **postmodernism**—a style and movement in architecture that succeeded modernism, beginning in the 1970s. Postmodern architecture rejected the rules, geometric order, and austerity of modernism. Modernist buildings were expected to have a clear and functional design. Postmodern design is "messier" and more playful. It draws on a diversity of styles from different times and places—including popular, ethnic, and non-Western cultures. Postmodernism extends "value" well beyond classic, elite, and Western cultural forms. *Postmodern* is now used to describe comparable developments in music, literature, and visual art. From this origin, *postmodernity* describes a world in which traditional standards, contrasts, groups, boundaries, and identities are opening up, reaching out, and breaking down.

New kinds of political and ethnic units are emerging. In some cases, cultures and ethnic groups have banded together in larger associations. There is a growing pan-Indian identity (Nagel 1996) and an international Pantribal movement as well. Thus in June 1992 the World Conference of Indigenous Peoples met in Rio de Janeiro concurrently with UNCED (the United Nations Conference on the Environment and Development). Along with diplomats, journalists, and environmentalists came 300 representatives of the tribal diversity that survives in the modern world—from Lapland to Mali (Brooke 1992).

Working to promote cultural survival is a growing international Pan-tribal movement. In June 1992 the World Conference of Indigenous Peoples met in Rio de Janeiro. Along with diplomats, journalists, and environmentalists came 300 representatives of the tribal diversity that survives in the modern world.

S u m m a r y

1. Different degrees of destruction, domination, resistance, survival, and modification of native cultures may follow interethnic contact. This may lead to the tribe's cultural collapse (ethnocide) or its physical extinction (genocide). Multinational corporations have fueled economic development and ecological devastation. Either development or external regulation may pose a threat to indigenous peoples, their cultures, or their environments. The most effective conservation strategies pay attention to the needs, incentives, and customs of people living in the affected area.

2. "Public transcript" refers to the open, public interactions between the dominators and the oppressed. "Hidden transcript" describes the critique of power that goes on offstage, where the power holders can't see it. Discontent may also be expressed in public rituals and language. Hegemony describes a stratified social order in which subordinates comply with domination by internalizing its values and accepting its "naturalness." Often, situations that appear hegemonic have resistance that is individual and disguised rather than collective and defiant.

3. Cultural imperialism refers to the spread of one culture and its imposition on other societies, which it modifies, replaces, or destroys— usually because of differential economic or political influence. Some worry that modern technology, including the mass media, is destroying traditional cultures. But others see an important role for new technology in allowing local cultures to express themselves.

4. The term "text" is used here to describe anything that can be creatively "read," interpreted, and assigned meaning by someone who receives it. People may resist the hegemonic meaning of a text. Or they may seize on its antihegemonic aspects. When forces from world centers enter new societies, they are indigenized. Like print, the electronic mass media can help diffuse a national culture within its own boundaries. The media also play a role in preserving ethnic and national identities among people who lead transnational lives.

5. People travel more than ever. But migrants also maintain ties with home, so they live multilocally. With so many people "in motion," the unit of anthropological study expands from the local community to the diaspora. Postmodernity describes this world in flux, such people on the move who manage multiple social identities depending on place and context. New kinds of political and ethnic units are emerging as others break down or disappear.

Case Study
Yanomamo

This chapter discusses the potentially grave consequences of economic development and environmental degradation. Outside exploitation poses a threat to indigenous peoples. In *Culture Sketches* by Holly Peters-Golden read the chapter on the Yanomamo: Challenges in the Rainforest. What are some challenges faced by the Yanomamo (a.k.a. Yanomami)? What is the anthropologist's role in conflicts between indigenous peoples and the governments of the countries in which they live? Should an anthropologist be an objective observer, an advocate, or neither of these? What are some difficulties involved in choosing a position?

Voices of the Rainforest

The government of Papua New Guinea has approved oil exploration by American, British, Australian, and Japanese companies in the rainforest habitat of the Kaluli and other indigenous peoples. The forest degradation that usually accompanies logging, ranching, road building, and drilling endangers plants, animals, peoples, and cultures. Lost along with trees are songs, myths, words, ideas, artifacts, and techniques— the cultural knowledge and practices of rainforest people such as the Kaluli, whom the anthropologist and ethnomusicologist Steven Feld has been studying for many years.

Feld teamed up with Mickey Hart of the Grateful Dead in a project designed to promote the cultural survival of the Kaluli through their music. For years Hart has worked to preserve musical diversity through educational funding, concert promotion, and recording, including a successful series called "The World" on the Rykodisc label. "Voices of the Rainforest" was the first CD completely devoted to indigenous music from Papua New Guinea. In one hour it encapsulates twenty-four hours of a day in Kaluli life in Bosavi village. The recording permits a form of cultural survival and diffusion in a high-quality commercial product. Bosavi is presented as a "soundscape" of blended music and natural environmental sounds. Kaluli weave the natural sounds of birds, frogs, rivers, and streams into their texts, melodies, and rhythms. They sing and whistle with birds and waterfalls. They compose instrumental duets with birds and cicadas.

"Voices of the Rainforest" has been marketed as "world music." This term is intended to point up musical diversity, the fact that music originates from all world regions and all societies. Our postmodern world (see the discussion in the chapter) recognizes more than one canon (standard for excellence). In the postmodern view, "tribal" music joins Western "classical" music as a form of artistic expression worth performing, hearing, and preserving. Hart's series offers musics of non-Western origin as well as those of ethnically dominated

groups of the Western world. Like Paul Simon's recordings "Graceland" and "Rhythm of the Saints," which draw on African and Brazilian music, a "world music" record series helps blur the boundaries between the exotic and the familiar. The local and the global unite in a transnational popular culture.

In "Voices of the Rainforest," Feld and Hart excised all "modern" and "dominant" sounds from their recording. Gone are the world system sounds that Kaluli villagers now hear every day. The recording temporarily silences the "machine voices": the tractor that cuts the grass on the local airstrip, the gas generator, the sawmill, the helicopters, and light planes buzzing to and from the oil-drilling areas. Gone, too, are the village church bells, Bible readings, evangelical prayers and hymns, and the voices of teachers and students at an English-only school.

Initially, Feld anticipated criticism for attempting to create an idealized Kaluli "soundscape" insulated from invasive forces and sounds. Among the Kaluli he expected varied opinions about the value of his project:

> It is a soundscape world that some Kaluli care little about, a world that other Kaluli momentarily choose to forget, a world that some Kaluli are increasingly nostalgic and uneasy about, a world that other Kaluli are still living and creating and listening to. It is a sound world that increasingly fewer Kaluli will actively know about and value, but one that increasingly more Kaluli will only hear on cassette and sentimentally wonder about. (Feld 1991, p. 137)

Despite these concerns, Feld was met with an overwhelmingly positive response when he returned to Papua New Guinea armed with a boombox and the recording. The Education Department has put copies of the recording into every high school library. The people of Bosavi also reacted very favorably. Not only did they appreciate the recording, they have also been able to build a much-needed community school with

the "Voices of the Rainforest" royalties that have been donated to the Bosavi Peoples Fund.

Source: Based on Steven Feld, "Voices of the Rainforest," *Public Culture* 4, no. 1 (1991), pp. 131–140.

Chapter 18

Applied Anthropology

THEORY AND PRACTICE
  Applied Anthropology and the Subdisciplines
ANTHROPOLOGY AND EDUCATION
URBAN ANTHROPOLOGY
  Urban versus Rural
MEDICAL ANTHROPOLOGY
ANTHROPOLOGY AND BUSINESS
CAREERS IN ANTHROPOLOGY
THE CONTINUANCE OF DIVERSITY
Box: Hot Asset in Corporate: Anthropology Degrees

Anthropology can reduce ethnocentrism by instilling an appreciation of cultural diversity. Its broadening, educational role affects the knowledge, values, and attitudes of people exposed to anthropology. Now we focus on the question: What contributions can anthropology make in identifying and solving problems stirred up by contemporary currents of economic, social, and cultural change?

Anthropology's foremost professional organization, the American Anthropological Association (AAA), has formally acknowledged a public service role by recognizing that anthropology has two dimensions: (1) theoretical/academic anthropology and (2) practicing or applied anthropology. **Applied anthropology** refers to the application of anthropological perspectives, theory, methods, and data to identify, assess, and solve social problems. As Erve Chambers (1987, p. 309) states it, applied anthropology is the "field of inquiry concerned with the relationships between anthropological knowledge and the uses of that knowledge in the world beyond anthropology."

Applied anthropologists, who are also known as *practicing anthropologists*, work (regularly or occasionally, full-time or part-time) for nonacademic clients. These include governments, development agencies, nongovernmental organizations (NGOs), tribal and ethnic associations, interest groups, businesses, and social-service and educational agencies. Applied anthropologists work for groups that promote, manage, and assess programs aimed at influencing human social conditions. The scope of applied anthropology includes change and development abroad and social problems and policies in North America.

Modern applied anthropology differs from an earlier version that mainly served the goals of colonial regimes. Application was a central concern of early anthropology in Great Britain (in the context of colonialism) and the United States (in the context of Native American policy). Before turning to the new, we should consider some dangers of the old.

In the context of the British empire, specifically its African colonies, Malinowski (1929) proposed that "practical anthropology" (his term for colonial applied anthropology) should focus on Westernization, the diffusion of European culture into tribal societies. He contended that anthropologists should and could avoid politics by concentrating on facts and processes. He was actually expressing his own political views; he questioned neither the legitimacy of colonialism nor the anthropologist's role in making it work. Malinowski saw nothing wrong with aiding colonial regimes by studying land tenure and land use to decide how much of their land natives should keep and how much Europeans should get. Malinowski's views exemplify a historical association between anthropology, particularly in Europe, and colonialism (Maquet 1964).

Colonial anthropologists faced, as do some of their modern counterparts (Escobar 1991, 1995), problems posed by their inability or reluctance to set or influence policy and the difficulty of criticizing programs in which they have participated. Anthropology's professional organizations have addressed some of these problems by establishing codes of ethics and ethics committees. As Tice (1997) notes, attention to such ethical issues is paramount in the teaching of applied anthropology today.

THEORY AND PRACTICE

One of the applied anthropologist's most valuable research tools is the ethnographic method. Ethnographers study societies firsthand, living with and learning from ordinary people. Ethnographers are participant observers, taking part in the events they study in order to understand native thought and behavior. Ethnographic techniques guide applied anthropologists in both foreign and domestic settings.

Other "expert" participants in social-change programs may be content to converse with officials, read reports, and copy statistics. The applied anthropologist's first request is likely to be some variant of "take me to your villagers." We know that local people must play an active role in the changes that affect them and that "the people" have information that "the experts" lack.

Anthropological theory—the field's body of findings and generalizations—also guides applied anthropology. Anthropology's holistic perspective—its interest in biology, society, culture, and language—permits the evaluation of many issues that affect people. Anthropology's systemic perspective recognizes that changes don't occur in a vacuum. A project or program always has multiple effects, some unforeseen. For example, dozens of economic development projects intended to increase productivity through irrigation have worsened public health by creating waterways where diseases thrive. In an American example of unintended consequences, a program aimed at enhancing teachers' appreciation of cultural differences led to ethnic stereotyping (Kleinfeld 1975). Specifically, Native American students did not welcome teachers' frequent comments about their Indian heritage. The students felt set apart from their classmates and saw this attention to their ethnicity as patronizing and demeaning.

Theory aids practice and practice amplifies theory. As we compare social-change policy and projects, our understanding of cause and effect increases. We add new generalizations about culture change to those discovered in traditional and ancient societies.

Applied Anthropology and the Subdisciplines

Applied anthropologists come from all four subdisciplines. Biological anthropologists work in the fields of public health, nutrition, genetic counseling, substance abuse, epidemiology, aging, and mental illness. They apply their knowledge of human anatomy and physiology to the improvement of automobile safety standards and to the design of airplanes and spacecraft. In forensic work, biological anthropologists help police identify skeletal remains. Similarly, forensic archaeologists reconstruct crimes by analyzing physical evidence.

An important role for applied archaeologists has been created by legislation requiring surveys of prehistoric and historic sites threatened by dams, highways, construction, and other projects supported by federal funds. To save as much as possible of the past when actual sites cannot be preserved is the work of *cultural resource management* (CRM). Applied cultural anthropologists sometimes work with the applied archaeologists, assessing the human problems generated by the change and determining how they can be reduced.

Cultural anthropologists work with social workers, business people, advertising professionals, factory workers, nurses, physicians, gerontologists, mental-health professionals, school personnel, and economic development experts. Linguistic anthropology, particularly sociolinguistics, aids education. Knowledge of linguistic differences is important in an increasingly multicultural society whose populace grows up speaking many languages and dialects. Because linguistic differences may affect children's schoolwork and teachers' evaluations, many schools of education now require courses in sociolinguistics.

ANTHROPOLOGY AND EDUCATION

Anthropology and education refers to anthropological research in classrooms, homes, and neighborhoods (see Spindler, ed. 2000). Some of the most interesting research has been done in classrooms, where anthropologists

Children in a primary school class in Bangladesh. If you were an applied anthropologist trying to improve education in Bangladesh, how would you design your research? Assume this classroom would be part of your study.

observe interactions among teachers, students, parents, and visitors. Jules Henry's classic account of the American elementary school classroom (1955) shows how students learn to conform to and compete with their peers. Anthropologists also follow students from classrooms into their homes and neighborhoods, viewing children as total cultural creatures whose enculturation and attitudes toward education belong to a context that includes family and peers.

Sociolinguists and cultural anthropologists work side by side in education research. For example, in a study of Puerto Rican seventh-graders in the urban Midwest (Hill-Burnett 1978), anthropologists uncovered some misconceptions held by teachers. The teachers had mistakenly assumed that Puerto Rican parents valued education less than did non-Hispanics, but in-depth interviews revealed that the Puerto Rican parents valued it more.

The anthropologists also found that certain practices were preventing Hispanics from being adequately educated. For example, the teachers' union and the board of education had agreed to teach "English as a foreign language." However, they had provided no bilingual teachers to work with Spanish-speaking students. The school was assigning all students (including non-Hispanics) with low reading scores and behavior problems to the English-as-a-foreign-language classroom. This educational disaster brought together in the classroom a teacher who spoke no Spanish, children who barely spoke English, and a group of English-speaking students with reading and behavior problems. The Spanish speakers were falling behind not just in reading but in all subjects. They could at least have kept up in the other subjects if a Spanish speaker had been teaching them science, social studies, and math until they were ready for English-language instruction in those areas.

URBAN ANTHROPOLOGY

By 2025 the developing nations will account for 85 percent of the world's population, compared with 77 percent in 1992 (Stevens 1992). Solutions to future problems will depend increasingly on understanding non-Western cultural backgrounds. The fastest population growth rates are in Third World cities. The world had only 16 cities with more than a million people in 1900, but there were 276 such cities in 1990. By 2025, 60 percent of the global population will be urban, compared with 37 percent in 1990 (Stevens 1992).

If current trends continue, urban population increase and the concentration of people in slums will be accompanied by rising rates of crime and water, air, and noise pollution. These problems will be most severe in the less-developed countries. Most (97 percent) of the projected world population increase will occur in developing countries, 34 percent in Africa alone (Lewis 1992). Global population growth continues to affect the northern hemisphere, especially through international migration.

As industrialization and urbanization spread globally, anthropologists increasingly study these processes and the social problems they create. Urban anthropology, which has theoretical (basic research) and applied dimensions, is the cross-cultural and ethnographic study of global urbanization and life in cities. The United States and Canada have also become popular arenas for urban anthropological research on topics such as ethnicity, poverty, class, and subcultural variations (Mullings, ed. 1987).

Urban versus Rural

Recognizing that a city is a social context that is very different from a tribal or peasant village, an early student of Third World urbanization, the anthropologist Robert Redfield, focused on contrasts between rural and urban life. He contrasted rural communities, whose social relations are on a face-to-face basis, with cities, where impersonality characterizes many aspects of life. Redfield (1941) proposed that urbanization be studied along a rural-urban continuum. He described differences in values and social relations in four sites that spanned such a continuum. In Mexico's Yucatán peninsula, Redfield compared an isolated Maya-speaking Indian community, a rural peasant village, a small provincial city, and a large capital. Several studies in Africa (Little 1971) and Asia were influenced by Redfield's view that cities are centers through which cultural innovations spread to rural and tribal areas.

In any nation, urban and rural represent different social systems. However, cultural diffusion occurs as people, products, and messages move from one to the other. Migrants bring rural practices and beliefs to town and take urban patterns back home. The experiences and social forms of the rural area affect adaptation to city life. For example, principles of tribal organization, including descent, provide migrants to African cities with coping mechanisms that Latin American peasants lack. City folk also develop new institutions to meet specific urban needs (Mitchell 1966).

Chapter 11, "Colonialism and Development," made the case for the systematic incorporation of native social forms (e.g., descent groups) in programs and policies aimed at change in rural areas. The same strategy applies to urban programs. An applied anthropology approach to urban planning would start by identifying key social groups in the urban context. After identifying those groups, the anthropologist would elicit their wishes for change and translate those needs to funding agencies. The next role would be to work with the agencies and the people to ensure that the change is implemented correctly and that it corresponds to what the people said they wanted at the outset. The most humane and productive strategy for change is to base the social design for innovation on traditional social forms in each target area, whether rural or urban.

Relevant African urban groups include ethnic associations, occupational groups, social clubs, religious groups, and burial societies. Through membership in these groups, urban Africans have wide networks of personal contacts and support. Ethnic or "tribal" associations are common both in West and East Africa (Little 1965; Banton 1957). These groups also maintain links with, and provide cash support and urban lodging for, their rural relatives.

The ideology of such associations is that of a gigantic kin group. The members call one another "brother" and "sister." As in an extended family, rich members help their poor relatives. When members fight among themselves, the group acts as judge. A member's improper behavior can lead to expulsion—an unhappy fate for a migrant in a large ethnically heterogeneous city.

Modern North American cities also have kin-based ethnic associations. One example comes from Los Angeles, which has the largest Samoan immigrant community (12,000 people) in the United States. Samoans in Los Angeles draw on their traditional system of *matai* (matai means chief; the matai system now refers to respect for elders) to deal with modern urban problems. One example: In 1992, a white policeman shot and killed two unarmed Samoan brothers. When a judge dismissed charges against the officer, local leaders used the matai system to calm angry youths (who have formed gangs, like other ethnic groups in the Los Angeles area). Clan leaders and elders organized a well-attended community meeting, in which they urged young members to be patient.

The Samoans used the American judicial system. They brought a civil case against the officer in question and pressed the U.S. Justice Department

Kin-modeled associations help reduce the stress of urban life on migrants. In Los Angeles, youths of many national backgrounds, like these Cambodians, have formed gangs. If you were an applied anthropologist designing a program for this neighborhood, what role do you think such gangs would play in it?

to initiate a civil-rights case in the matter (Mydans 1992*b*). One role for the urban applied anthropologist is to help relevant social groups deal with larger urban institutions, such as legal and social service agencies with which recent migrants, in particular, may be unfamiliar.

MEDICAL ANTHROPOLOGY

Medical anthropology is both academic/theoretical and applied/practical. It is a field that includes both biological and sociocultural anthropologists. Medical anthropology is discussed in this chapter because of its many applications. Medical anthropologists examine such questions as which diseases affect different populations, how illness is socially constructed, and how one treats illness in effective and culturally appropriate ways.

This growing field considers the sociocultural context and implications of disease and illness. **Disease** refers to a scientifically identified health threat caused by a bacterium, virus, fungus, parasite, or other pathogen. **Illness** is a condition of poor health perceived or felt by an individual (Inhorn and Brown 1990). Cross-cultural research shows that perceptions of good and bad health, along with health threats and problems, are culturally constructed. Various ethnic groups and cultures recognize different illnesses, symptoms, and causes and have developed different health care systems and treatment strategies.

Disease also varies among societies. Traditional and ancient foragers, because of their small numbers, mobility, and relative isolation from other groups, lacked most of the epidemic infectious diseases that affect agrarian and urban societies (Inhorn and Brown 1990; Cohen and Armelagos, eds. 1984). Epidemic diseases such as cholera, typhoid, and bubonic plague thrive in dense populations, and thus among farmers and city dwellers. The spread of malaria has been linked to population growth and deforestation associated with food production.

Certain diseases have spread with economic development. *Schistosomiasis* or bilharzia (liver flukes) is probably the fastest-spreading and most dangerous parasitic infection now known (Heyneman 1984). It is propagated by snails that live in ponds, lakes, and waterways, usually ones created by irrigation projects. A study done in a Nile Delta village in Egypt (Farooq 1966) illustrated the role of culture (religion) in the spread of schistosomiasis. The disease was more common among Muslims than among Christians because of an Islamic practice called *wudu*, ritual ablution (bathing) before prayer. The applied anthropology approach to reducing such diseases is to see if natives perceive a connection between the vector (e.g., snails in the water) and the disease. If not, such information may be provided by enlisting active local groups, schools, and the media.

In eastern Africa, AIDS and other sexually transmitted diseases (STDs) have spread along highways, via encounters between male truckers and female prostitutes. STDs are also spread through prostitution as young men from rural areas seek wage work in cities, labor camps, and mines. When the men return to their natal villages, they infect their wives (Larson 1989; Miller and Rockwell, eds. 1988). Cities are also prime sites of STD transmission in Europe, Asia, and North and South America.

The kind of and incidence of disease varies among societies, and cultures interpret and treat illness differently. Standards for sick and healthy bodies are cultural constructions that vary in time and space (Martin 1992). Still, all societies have what George Foster and Barbara Anderson call "disease-theory systems" to identify, classify, and explain illness. According to Foster and Anderson (1978), there are three basic theories about the causes of illness: personalistic, naturalistic, and emotionalistic. **Personalistic disease theories** blame illness on agents, such as sorcerers, witches, ghosts, or ancestral spirits. **Naturalistic disease theories** explain illness in impersonal terms. One example is Western medicine or *biomedicine*, which aims to link illness to scientifically demonstrated agents which bear no personal malice toward their victims. Thus Western medicine attributes illness to organisms (e.g., bacteria, viruses, fungi, or parasites), accidents, or toxic materials. Other naturalistic ethnomedical systems blame poor health on unbalanced body fluids. Many Latin societies classify food, drink, and environmental conditions as "hot" or "cold." People believe their health suffers when they eat or drink hot or cold substances together or under inappropriate conditions. For example, one shouldn't drink something cold after a hot bath or eat a pineapple (a "cold" fruit) when one is menstruating (a "hot" condition).

Emotionalistic disease theories assume that emotional experiences cause illness. For example, Latin Americans may develop *susto*, an illness caused by anxiety or fright (Bolton 1981; Finkler 1985). Its symptoms (lethargy, vagueness, distraction) are similar to those of "soul loss," a diagnosis of similar symptoms made by people in Madagascar. Modern psychoanalysis also focuses on the role of the emotions in physical and psychological well-being.

All societies have **health care systems** consisting of beliefs, customs, specialists, and techniques aimed at ensuring health and at preventing, diagnosing, and curing illness. A society's illness-causation theory is important for treatment. When illness has a personalistic cause, shamans and other magicoreligious specialists may be good curers. They draw on varied techniques (occult and practical), which comprise their special expertise. A shaman may cure soul loss by enticing the spirit back into the body. Shamans may ease difficult childbirths by asking spirits to travel up the birth canal to guide the baby out (Lévi-Strauss 1967). A shaman may cure a cough by counteracting a curse or removing a substance introduced by a sorcerer.

If there is a "world's oldest profession" besides hunter and gatherer, it is **curer,** often a shaman. The curer's role has some universal features (Foster and Anderson 1978). Thus curers emerge through a culturally defined process of selection (parental prodding, inheritance, visions, dream instructions) and training (apprentice shamanship, medical school). Eventually, the curer is certified by older practitioners and acquires a professional image. Patients believe in the skills of the curer, whom they consult and compensate.

We should not lose sight, ethnocentrically, of the difference between **scientific medicine** and Western medicine per se (Lieban 1977). Despite advances in pathology, microbiology, biochemistry, surgery, diagnostic technology, and applications, many Western medical procedures have little justification in logic or fact. Overprescription of drugs, unnecessary surgery, and the impersonality and inequality of the physician-patient relationship are questionable features of Western medical systems. Also, overuse of antibiotics, not just for people, but also in animal feed, seems to be triggering an explosion of resistant microorganisms, which may pose a long-term global public health hazard.

Still, biomedicine surpasses tribal treatment in many ways. Although medicines such as quinine, coca, opium, ephedrine, and rauwolfia were discovered in nonindustrial societies, thousands of effective drugs are available today to treat myriad diseases. Preventive health care improved during the twentieth century. Today's surgical procedures are safer and more effective than those of traditional societies.

How do Western medicine and scientific medicine differ? Clinics bring antibiotics, minor surgery, and preventive medicine to rural people in Congo. What kind of medicine is being shown here? How can it coexist with the native healing system?

But industrialization has spawned its own health problems. Modern stressors include noise, air, and water pollution, poor nutrition, dangerous machinery, impersonal work, isolation, poverty, homelessness, and substance abuse. Health problems in industrial nations are as much caused by economic, social, political, and cultural factors as by pathogens. In modern North America, for example, poverty contributes to many illnesses, including arthritis, heart conditions, back problems, and hearing and vision impairment. Poverty is also a factor in the differential spread of infectious diseases.

Medical anthropologists have served as cultural interpreters in public health programs, which must pay attention to native theories about the nature, causes, and treatment of illness. Successful health interventions cannot simply be forced on communities. They must fit into local cultures and be accepted by local people. When Western medicine is introduced, people usually retain many of their old methods while also accepting new ones (see Green 1987/1992). Native curers may go on treating certain conditions (spirit possession), whereas M.D.s may deal with others. If both modern and traditional specialists are consulted and the patient is cured, the native curer may get as much or more credit than the physician.

A more personal treatment of illness that emulates the non-Western curer-patient-community relationship could probably benefit Western systems. Western medicine tends to draw a rigid line between biological and psychological causation. Non-Western theories usually lack this sharp distinction, recognizing that poor health has intertwined physical, emotional, and social causes. The mind-body opposition is part of Western folk taxonomy, not of science (see also Brown 1998, Helman 2001, Joralemon 1999, Strathern and Stewart 1999).

ANTHROPOLOGY AND BUSINESS

Carol Taylor (1987) discusses the value of an "anthropologist-in-residence" in a large, complex organization, such as a hospital or a business. A free-ranging ethnographer can be a perceptive oddball when information and decisions usually move through a rigid hierarchy. If allowed to observe and converse freely with all types and levels of personnel, the anthropologist may acquire a unique perspective on organizational conditions and problems. Also, high-tech companies, such as Xerox, IBM, and Apple, have employed anthropologists in various roles. Closely observing how people actually use computer products, anthropologists work with engineers to design products that are more user-friendly.

For many years anthropologists have used ethnography to study business settings (Arensberg 1987). For example, ethnographic research in an auto factory may view workers, managers, and executives as different social categories participating in a common social system. Each group has characteristic attitudes, values, and behavior patterns. These are transmitted through *microenculturation*, the process by which people learn particular roles in a limited social system. The free-ranging nature of ethnography takes the anthropologist back and forth from worker to executive. Each is an individual with a personal viewpoint and a cultural creature whose

Professor Marietta Baba of Michigan State University does applied anthropology at an automotive supply plant in Detroit. What issues might interest her in this setting?

perspective is, to some extent, shared with other members of a group. Applied anthropologists have acted as "cultural brokers," translating managers' goals or workers' concerns to the other group.

For business, key features of anthropology include: (1) ethnography and observation as ways of gathering data, (2) cross-cultural expertise, and (3) focus on cultural diversity (Ferraro 2001). An important business application of anthropology has to do with knowledge of how consumers use products. Businesses hire anthropologists because of the importance of observation in natural settings and the focus on cultural diversity. Thus, Hallmark cards has hired anthropologists to observe parties, holidays, and celebrations of ethnic groups to improve its ability to design cards for targeted audiences. Anthropologists go into people's homes to see how they actually use products. (See the box at the end of the chapter.)

CAREERS IN ANTHROPOLOGY

Many college students find anthropology interesting and consider majoring in it. However, their parents or friends may discourage them by asking, "What kind of job are you going to get with an anthropology major?" The purpose of this section is to answer that question. The first step in answering "What do you do with an anthropology major?" is to consider the more general question, "What do you do with any college major?" The answer is "Not much, without a good bit of effort, thought, and planning." A survey of graduates of the literary college of the University of Michigan showed that few had jobs that were clearly linked to their majors. Medicine, law, and many other professions require advanced degrees. Although many colleges offer bachelor's degrees in engineering, business, accounting, and social work, master's degrees are often needed to get the best jobs in those fields. Anthropologists, too, need an advanced degree, almost always a Ph.D., to find gainful employment in academic, museum, or applied anthropology.

A broad college education, and even a major in anthropology, can be an excellent foundation for success in many fields. A recent survey of women executives showed that most had not majored in business but in the social sciences or humanities. Only after graduating did they study business, obtaining a master's degree in business administration. These executives felt that the breadth of their college educations had contributed to their business careers. Anthropology majors go on to medical, law, and business schools and find success in many professions that often have little explicit connection to anthropology.

Anthropology's breadth provides knowledge and an outlook on the world that are useful in many kinds of work. For example, an anthropology major combined with a master's degree in business is excellent preparation for work in international business. Breadth is anthropology's hallmark. Anthropologists study people biologically, culturally, socially, and linguistically, across time and space, in developed and underdeveloped nations, in simple and complex settings. Most colleges have anthropology courses that compare cultures and others that focus on particular world areas, such as Latin America, Asia, and Native North America. The knowledge of foreign areas acquired in such courses can be useful in many jobs. Anthropology's comparative outlook, its longstanding Third World focus, and its appreciation of diverse life styles combine to provide an excellent foundation for overseas employment.

Even for work in North America, the focus on culture is valuable. Every day we hear about cultural differences and about social problems whose solutions require a multicultural viewpoint—an ability to recognize and reconcile ethnic differences. Government, schools, and private firms constantly deal with people from different social classes, ethnic groups, and tribal backgrounds. Physicians, attorneys, social workers, police officers, judges, teachers, and students can all do a better job if they understand social differences in a part of the world such as ours that is one of the most ethnically diverse in history.

Knowledge about the traditions and beliefs of the many social groups within a modern nation is important in planning and carrying out programs that affect those groups. Attention to social background and cultural categories helps ensure the welfare of affected ethnic groups, communities, and neighborhoods. Experience in planned social change—whether community organization in North America or economic development overseas—shows that a proper social study should be done before a project or policy is implemented. When local people want the change and it fits their lifestyle and traditions, it will be more successful, beneficial, and cost-effective. There will be not only a more humane but a more economical solution to a real social problem.

People with anthropology backgrounds are doing well in many fields. Even if one's job has little or nothing to do with anthropology in a formal or obvious sense, a background in anthropology provides a useful orientation when we work with our fellow human beings. For most of us, this means every day of our lives.

THE CONTINUANCE OF DIVERSITY

Anthropology has a crucial role to play in promoting a more humanistic vision of social change, one that respects the value of cultural diversity. The existence of anthropology is itself a tribute to the continuing need to understand social and cultural similarities and differences. Anthropology teaches us that the adaptive responses of humans can be more flexible than can those of other species because our main adaptive means are sociocultural and can change. However, anthropology also teaches us that the cultural forms, institutions, values, and customs of the past always influence subsequent adaptation, producing continued diversity and giving a certain uniqueness to the actions and reactions of different groups. Thus the recognition of diversity promoted by anthropology is itself an adaptive means in today's world.

Let us hope that vigorous cultural differences will endure and that the free and open investigation of human diversity will continue also. With our knowledge and our awareness of our professional responsibilities, let us work to keep anthropology, the study of humankind, the most humanistic of all the sciences.

S u m m a r y

1. Applied anthropology uses anthropological perspectives, theory, methods, and data to identify, assess, and solve problems. Applied anthropologists have a range of employers. Examples: development and government agencies, NGOs, tribal, ethnic, and interest groups, businesses, social service and educational agencies. Applied anthropologists come from all four subfields. Ethnography is one of applied anthropology's most valuable research tools. Another is the comparative, cross-cultural perspective. A systemic perspective recognizes that changes have multiple consequences, some unintended.

2. Anthropology and education researchers work in classrooms, homes, and other settings relevant to education. Their studies may lead to policy recommendations. Both academic and applied anthropologists study migration from rural areas to cities and across national boundaries. Although rural and urban are different social systems, there is cultural diffusion from one to the other. Rural and tribal social forms affect adjustment to the city.

3. Medical anthropology is the cross-cultural study of health problems and conditions, disease, illness, disease theories, and health care systems. Medical anthropology includes biological and cultural anthropologists and has theoretical (academic) and applied dimensions. In a given setting, the characteristic diseases reflect diet, population density, economy, and social complexity. Native theories of illness may be personalistic, naturalistic, or emotionalistic.

4. In applying anthropology to business, the key features are: (1) ethnography and observation as ways of gathering data, (2) cross-cultural expertise, and (3) focus on cultural diversity. A broad college education, including anthropology and foreign-area courses, offers an excellent background for many fields. Anthropology's comparative outlook and cultural relativism provide an excellent orientation for overseas employment. Even for work in North America, a focus on culture and cultural diversity is valuable.

Anthropology majors attend medical, law, and business schools and succeed in many fields, some of which have little explicit connection with anthropology.

5. Experience with social-change programs, whether in North America or abroad, offers a common lesson. When local people want a change, and when that change fits their lifestyle and traditions, the change is most likely to be successful, beneficial, and cost-effective.

Case Study
Ojibwa

Urban anthropology, one applied field presented in this chapter, discusses differences between rural and urban life and the process of change through urbanization. In *Culture Sketches* by Holly Peters-Golden read the chapter on the Ojibwa: "The People" Endure. What sorts of changes have occurred in Ojibwa life through urbanization? Might the move from reservation to city, for Native Americans, be different from urbanization experienced by other social groups? Why or why not?

Hot Asset in Corporate: Anthropology Degrees

An important business application of anthropology has to do with knowledge of how consumers use products. Businesses hire anthropologists because of the importance of observation in natural settings and the focus on cultural diversity. Thus, as we see in the following article, Hallmark cards has hired anthropologists to observe parties, holidays, and celebrations of ethnic groups to improve its ability to design cards for targeted audiences. Anthropologists go into people's homes to see how they actually use products. This permits better product design and more effective advertising.

Don't throw away the MBA degree yet.

But as companies go global and crave leaders for a diverse workforce, a new hot degree is emerging for aspiring executives: anthropology.

The study of man is no longer a degree for museum directors. Citicorp created a vice presidency for anthropologist Steve Barnett, who discovered early warning signs to identify people who don't pay credit card bills.

Not satisfied with consumer surveys, Hallmark is sending anthropologists into the homes of immigrants, attending holidays and birthday parties to design cards they'll want.

No survey can tell engineers what women really want in a razor, so marketing consultant Hauser Design sends anthropologists into bathrooms to watch them shave their legs.

Unlike MBAs, anthropology degrees are rare: one undergraduate degree for every 26 in business and one anthropology Ph.D. for every 235 MBAs.

Textbooks now have chapters on business applications. The University of South Florida has created a course of study for anthropologists headed for commerce.

Motorola corporate lawyer Robert Faulkner got his anthropology degree before going to law school. He says it becomes increasingly valuable as he is promoted into management.

"When you go into business, the only problems you'll have are people problems," was the advice given to teenager Michael Koss by his father in the early 1970s.

Koss, now 44, heeded the advice, earned an anthropology degree from Beloit College in 1976, and is today CEO of the Koss headphone manufacturer.

Katherine Burr, CEO of The Hanseatic Group, has masters in both anthropology and business from the University of New Mexico. Hanseatic was among the first money management programs to predict the Asian crisis and last year produced a total return of 315 percent for investors.

"My competitive edge came completely out of anthropology," she says. "The world is so unknown, changes so rapidly. Preconceptions can kill you."

Companies are starving to know how people use the Internet or why some pickups, even though they are more powerful, are perceived by consumers as less powerful, says Ken Erickson, of the Center for Ethnographic Research.

It takes trained observation, Erickson says. Observation is what anthropologists are trained to do.

Source: Del Jones, "Hot Asset in Corporate: Anthropology Degrees," *USA Today,* February 18, 1999, p. B1.

Glossary

acculturation: The exchange of cultural features that results when groups come into continuous firsthand contact; the original cultural patterns of either or both groups may be altered, but the groups remain distinct.

achieved status: Social status that comes through talents, actions, efforts, activities, and accomplishments, rather than ascription.

adaptation: The process by which organisms cope with environmental stresses.

African-American English Vernacular (AAEV): See *Black English Vernacular.*

age set: Group uniting all men or women (usually men) born during a certain time span; this group controls property and often has political and military functions.

agnates: Members of the same patrilineal descent group.

agriculture: Nonindustrial system of plant cultivation characterized by continuous and intensive use of land and labor.

androgyny: Similarities (e.g., in dress, adornment, or body features) between males and females.

animism: Belief in souls or doubles.

anthropology and education: Anthropological research in classrooms, homes, and neighborhoods, viewing students as total cultural creatures whose enculturation and attitudes toward education belong to a larger context that includes family, peers, and society.

apical ancestor: In a descent group, the individual who stands at the apex, or top, of the common genealogy.

applied anthropology: The application of anthropological data, perspectives, theory, and methods to identify, assess, and solve contemporary social problems.

archaeological anthropology: The branch of anthropology that reconstructs, describes, and interprets human behavior and cultural patterns through material remains; best known for the study of prehistory. Also known as "archaeology."

archaic state: Nonindustrial state.

ascribed status: Social status (e.g., race or gender) that people have little or no choice about occupying.

assimilation: The process of change that a minority group may experience when it moves to a country where another culture dominates; the minority is incorporated into the dominant culture to the point that it no longer exists as a separate cultural unit.

balanced reciprocity: See *generalized reciprocity.*

band: Basic unit of social organization among foragers. A band includes fewer than one hundred people; it often splits up seasonally.

berdaches: Among the Crow Indians, members of a third gender, for whom certain ritual duties were reserved.

big man: Figure often found among tribal horticulturalists and pastoralists. The big man occupies no office but creates his reputation through entrepreneurship and generosity to others. Neither his wealth nor his position passes to his heirs.

bilateral kinship calculation: A system in which kinship ties are calculated equally through both sexes: mother and father, sister and brother, daughter and son, and so on.

binary opposition: Pairs of opposites, such as good-evil and old-young, produced by converting differences of degree into qualitative distinctions; important in structuralism.

biological anthropology: The branch of anthropology that studies human biological diversity in time and space—for instance, hominid evolution, human genetics, human biological adaptation; also includes primatology (behavior and evolution of monkeys and apes). Also called *physical anthropology.*

biological determinists: Those who argue that human behavior and social organization are biologically determined.

biological kin types: Actual genealogical relationships, designated by letters and symbols (e.g., FB), as opposed to the kin terms (e.g., uncle) used in a particular society.

biomedicine: Western medicine, which attributes illness to scientifically demonstrated agents—biological organisms (e.g., bacteria, viruses, fungi, or parasites) or toxic materials.

biopsychological equality: The premise that although individuals differ in emotional and intellectual capacities, all human populations have equivalent capacities for culture.

Black English Vernacular (BEV): The rule-governed dialect spoken by American black youth, especially in inner-city areas; also spoken in rural areas and used in the casual, intimate speech of many adults; also known as *ebonics.*

blood feud: Feud between families, usually in a nonstate society.

bourgeoisie: One of Karl Marx's opposed classes; owners of the means of production (factories, mines, large farms, and other sources of subsistence).

brideprice: A customary gift before, at, or after marriage from the husband and his kin to the wife and her kin; a misleading term because people with the custom don't usually regard the exchange as a sale; see also *progeny price.*

bridewealth: A customary gift before, at, or after marriage from the husband and his kin to the wife and her kin; see also *progeny price.*

call systems: Vocal systems of communication used by nonhuman primates, composed of a limited number of sounds—calls—which are produced only when particular environmental stimuli are encountered.

candomblé: A syncretic "Afro-Brazilian" religion.

capital: Wealth or resources invested in business, with the intent of producing a profit.

capitalist world economy: The single world system, which emerged in the sixteenth century, committed to production for sale, with the object of maximizing profits rather than supplying domestic needs.

cargo cults: Postcolonial, acculturative, religious movements common in Melanesia that attempt to explain European domination and wealth and to achieve similar success magically by mimicking European behavior.

caste system: Closed, hereditary system of stratification, often dictated by religion; hierarchical social status is ascribed at birth, so that people are locked into their parents' social position.

ceremonial fund: Resources invested in ceremonial or ritual expenses or activity.

chiefdom: Form of sociopolitical organization intermediate between the tribe and the state; kin-based with differential access to resources and a permanent political structure.

clan: Unilineal descent group based on stipulated descent.

class consciousness: Recognition of collective interests and personal identification with one's economic group (particularly the proletariat); basic to Marx's view of class.

close-knit networks: Characteristic of rural communities and nonindustrial societies; many of one's friends, neighbors, and relatives know one another.

colonialism: The political, social, economic, and cultural domination of a territory and its people by a foreign power for an extended time.

communal religions: In Wallace's typology, these religions have—in addition to shamanic cults—communal cults in which people organize community rituals such as harvest ceremonies and rites of passage.

communitas: Intense community spirit, a feeling of great social solidarity, equality, and togetherness; characteristic of people experiencing liminality together.

community study: Anthropological method for studying complex societies. Small communities are studied ethnographically as being (partially) representative of regional culture or particular contrasts in national life.

complex societies: Nations; large and populous, with social stratification and central governments.

convergent cultural evolution: See *cultural convergence.*

copula deletion: Absence of the verb *to be;* featured in BEV and in diverse languages, including Hebrew and Russian.

core: Dominant structural position in the world system; consists of the strongest and most powerful states with advanced systems of production.

core values: Key, basic, or central values that integrate a culture and help distinguish it from others.

correlation: An association between two or more variables such that when one changes (varies), the other(s) also change(s) (covaries); for example, temperature and sweating.

creative opposition: Process in which people change their behavior as they consciously and actively avoid or spurn an external image or practice.

cultural anthropologist: (sociocultural anthropologist) A student of social life and culture, a practitioner of cultural anthropology, whether ethnology or ethnography.

cultural colonialism: Within a nation or empire, domination by one ethnic group or nationality and its culture/ideology over others—e.g., the dominance of Russian people, language, and culture in the former Soviet Union.

cultural consultant: Someone the ethnographer gets to know in the field, who teaches him or her about their society and culture.

cultural convergence: Development of similar traits, institutions, or behavior patterns as a result of adaptation to similar environments; parallel development without contact or mutual influence.

cultural determinists: Those who relate behavior and social organization to cultural or environmental factors. This view focuses on variation rather than universals and stresses learning and the role of culture in human adaptation.

cultural imperialism: The rapid spread or advance of one culture at the expense of others, or its imposition on other cultures, which it modifies, replaces, or destroys—usually because of differential economic or political influence.

cultural learning: Learning based on the human capacity to think symbolically.

cultural relativism: The position that the values and standards of cultures differ and deserve respect. Extreme relativism argues that cultures should be judged solely by their own standards.

cultural rights: Doctrine that certain rights are vested not in individuals but in identifiable groups, such as religious and ethnic minorities and indigenous societies.

culturally compatible economic development projects: Projects that harness traditional organizations and locally perceived needs for change and that have a culturally appropriate design and implementation strategy.

culture: Traditions and customs that govern behavior and beliefs; distinctly human; transmitted through learning.

curer: Specialized role acquired through a culturally appropriate process of selection, training, certification, and acquisition of a professional image; the curer is consulted by patients, who believe in his or her special powers, and receives some form of special consideration; a cultural universal.

daughter languages: Languages developing out of the same parent language; for example, French and Spanish are daughter languages of Latin.

demonstrated descent: Basis of the lineage; descent-group members cite the names of their forebears in each generation from the apical ancestor through the present.

descent: Rule assigning social identity on the basis of some aspect of one's ancestry.

descent group: A permanent social unit whose members claim common ancestry; fundamental to tribal society.

development anthropology: The branch of applied anthropology that focuses on social issues in, and the cultural dimension of, economic development.

diaspora: The offspring of an area who have spread to many lands.

differential access: Unequal access to resources; basic attribute of chiefdoms and states. Superordinates have favored access to such resources, while the access of subordinates is limited by superordinates.

diffusion: Borrowing between cultures either directly or through intermediaries.

diglossia: The existence of "high" (formal) and "low" (familial) dialects of a single language, such as German.

discourse: Talk, speeches, gestures, and actions.

discrimination: Policies and practices that harm a group and its members.

disease: An etic or scientifically identified health threat caused by a bacterium, virus, fungus, parasite, or other pathogen.

displacement: A basic feature of language; the ability to speak of things and events that are not present.

domestic: Within or pertaining to the home.

domestic system (of manufacture): Also known as "home handicraft production"; preindustrial manufacturing system in which organizer-entrepreneurs supplied raw materials to people who worked at home and collected finished products from them.

domestic-public dichotomy: Contrast between women's role in the home and men's role in public life, with a corresponding social devaluation of women's work and worth.

dowry: A marital exchange in which the wife's group provides substantial gifts to the husband's family.

ebonics: Another name for *Black English Vernacular;* derived from "ebony" and "phonics."

ecocide: Destruction of local ecosystems.

economic typology: Classification of societies based on their adaptive strategies, such as foraging, horticulture, pastoralism, agriculture.

economizing: The rational allocation of scarce means (or resources) to alternative ends (or uses); often considered the subject matter of economics.

economy: A population's system of production, distribution, and consumption of resources.

ego: Latin for "I". In kinship charts, the point from which one views an egocentric genealogy.

emic: The research strategy that focuses on native explanations and criteria of significance.

emotionalistic disease theories: Theories that assume that illness is caused by intense emotional experiences.

enculturation: The social process by which culture is learned and transmitted across the generations.

endogamy: Marriage between people of the same social group.

environmentalists: See *nurturists.*

equity, increased: A reduction in absolute poverty and a fairer (more even) distribution of wealth.

ethnic expulsion: A policy aimed at removing groups who are culturally different from a country.

ethnic group: Group distinguished by cultural similarities (shared among members of that group) and differences (between that group and others); ethnic group members share beliefs, values, habits, customs, and norms, and a common language, religion, history, geography, kinship, and/or race.

ethnicity: Identification with, and feeling part of, an ethnic group, and exclusion from certain other groups because of this affiliation.

ethnocentrism: The tendency to view one's own culture as best and to judge the behavior and beliefs of culturally different people by one's own standards.

ethnocide: Destruction by a dominant group of the culture of an ethnic group.

ethnography: Field work in a particular culture.

ethnology: The theoretical, comparative study of society and culture; compares cultures in time and space.

ethnoscience: See *ethnosemantics.*

ethnosemantics: The study of lexical (vocabulary) contrasts and classifications in various languages.

etic: The research strategy that emphasizes the observer's rather than the natives' explanations, categories, and criteria of significance.

Etoro: Papua New Guinea culture in which males are culturally trained to prefer homosexuality.

exogamy: Mating or marriage outside one's kin group; a cultural universal.

extended family: Expanded household including three or more generations.

extradomestic: Outside the home; within or pertaining to the public domain.

family of orientation: Nuclear family in which one is born and grows up.

family of procreation: Nuclear family established when one marries and has children.

fictive kinship: Personal relationships modeled on kinship, such as that between godparents and godchildren.

First World: The "democratic west"—traditionally conceived in opposition to a "Second World" ruled by "communism."

fiscal: Pertaining to finances and taxation.

focal vocabulary: A set of words and distinctions that are particularly important to certain groups (those with particular foci of experience or activity), such as types of snow to Eskimos or skiers.

food production: Plant cultivation and animal domestication.

foraging: Hunting and gathering.

forced assimilation: Use of force by a dominant group to compel a minority to adopt the dominant culture—for example, penalizing or banning the language and customs of an ethnic group.

gender roles: The tasks and activities that a culture assigns to each sex.

gender stereotypes: Oversimplified but strongly held ideas about the characteristics of males and females.

gender stratification: Unequal distribution of rewards (socially valued resources, power, prestige, and personal freedom) between men and women, reflecting their different positions in a social hierarchy.

genealogical method: Procedures by which ethnographers discover and record connections of kinship, descent, and marriage, using diagrams and symbols.

general anthropology: The field of anthropology as a whole, consisting of cultural, archaeological, biological, and linguistic anthropology.

generality: Culture pattern or trait that exists in some but not all societies.

generalized reciprocity: Principle that characterizes exchanges between closely related individuals: As social distance increases, reciprocity becomes balanced and finally negative.

genocide: The deliberate elimination of a group, e.g., through mass murder, warfare, or introduced diseases.

globalization: The accelerating interdependence of nations in a world system linked economically and through mass media and modern transportation systems.

green revolution: Agricultural development based on chemical fertilizers, pesticides, twentieth-century cultivation techniques, and new crop varieties such as IR-8 ("miracle rice").

head, village: A local leader in a tribal society who has limited authority, leads by example and persuasion, and must be generous.

health care systems: Beliefs, customs, and specialists concerned with ensuring health and preventing and curing illness; a cultural universal.

hegemonic reading (of a "text"): The reading or meaning that the creators intended, or the one the elites consider to be the intended or correct meaning.

hegemony: As used by Antonio Gramsci, a stratified social order in which subordinates comply with domination by internalizing its values and accepting its "naturalness."

hidden transcript: As used by James Scott, the critique of power by the oppressed that goes on offstage—in private—where the power holders can't see it.

historical linguistics: Subdivision of linguistics that studies languages over time.

holistic: Interested in the whole of the human condition: past, present, and future; biology, society, language, and culture.

homeostasis: Equilibrium, or a stable relationship, between a population and its resource base.

hominids: Members of the zoological family (*Hominidae*) that includes fossil and living humans.

homonyms: Words that sound the same but have different meanings; for example, *bare* and *bear*.

horticulture: Nonindustrial system of plant cultivation in which plots lie fallow for varying lengths of time.

human rights: Doctrine that invokes a realm of justice and morality beyond and superior to particular countries, cultures, and religions. Human rights, usually seen as vested in individuals, would include the right to speak freely, to hold religious beliefs without persecution, and not to be enslaved.

hypodescent: A rule that automatically places the children of a union or mating between members of different socioeconomic groups in the less privileged group.

ideal types: Labels that make contrasts seem more extreme than they really are (e.g., big and little). Instead of discrete categories, there is actually a continuum from one type to the next.

identity politics: Sociopolitical identities based on the perception of sharing a common culture, language, religion, or "race," rather than citizenship in a nation-state, which may contain diverse social groups.

illness: An emic condition of poor health felt by individual.

imperialism: A policy of extewnding the rule of a nation or empire over foreign nations and of taking and holding foreign colonies.

incest: Sexual relations with a close relative.

incest taboo: Universal prohibition against marrying or mating with a close relative.

income: Earnings from wages and salaries.

independent invention: Development of the same culture trait or pattern in separate cultures as a result of comparable needs and circumstances.

indigenized: Modified to fit the local culture.

indigenous peoples: The original inhabitants of particular territories; often descendants of tribespeople who live on as culturally distinct colonized peoples, many of whom aspire to autonomy.

individual situational learning: Type of learning in which animals learn from and base their future behavior on personal experience.

Industrial Revolution: The historical transformation (in Europe, after 1750) of "traditional" into "modern" societies through industrialization of the economy.

infanticide: Killing a baby; a form of population control in some societies.

international culture: Cultural traditions that extend beyond national boundaries.

intervention philosophy: Guiding principle of colonialism, conquest, missionization, or development; an ideological justification for outsiders to guide native peoples in specific directions.

interview schedule: Ethnographic tool for structuring a formal interview. A prepared form (usually printed or mimeographed) that guides interviews with households or individuals being compared systematically. Contrasts with a questionnaire because the researcher has personal contact and records people's answers.

IPR (intellectual property rights): Each society's cultural base—its core beliefs and principles. IPR is claimed as a group right—a cultural right, allowing indigenous groups to control who may know and use their collective knowledge and its applications.

Iroquois: Confederation of tribes in aboriginal New York State; matrilineal with communal longhouses and a prominent political, religious, and economic role for women.

key cultural consultant: An expert on a particular aspect of local life who helps the ethnographer understand that aspect.

kin terms: The words used for different relatives in a particular language, as opposed to actual genealogical relationships (biological kin types).

kin-based: Characteristic of many nonindustrial societies. People spend their lives almost exclusively with their relatives; principles of kinship, descent, and marriage organize social life.

kinesics: The study of communication through body movements, stances, gestures, and facial expressions.

kinship calculation: The system by which people in a particular society reckon kin relationships.

Kwakiutl: A potlatching society on the North Pacific Coast of North America.

lactation: Milk production.

language: Spoken (speech) and written (writing—which has existed for about 6,000 years); the primary human means of communication; key features of language include cultural transmission, displacement, and productivity.

law: A legal code, including trial and enforcement; characteristic of state-organized societies.

law of supply and demand: See *supply and demand, law of.*

LDC: A less developed country; by contrast with an industrial nation.

leveling mechanisms: Customs and social actions that operate to reduce differences in wealth and thus to bring standouts in line with community norms.

levirate: Custom by which a widow marries the brother of her deceased husband.

lexicon: Vocabulary; a dictionary containing all the morphemes in a language and their meaning.

life history: Of a cultural consultant; provides a personal cultural portrait of existence or change in a culture.

liminality: The critically important marginal or in-between phase of a rite of passage.

lineage: Unilineal descent group based on demonstrated descent.

linguistic anthropology: The branch of anthropology that studies linguistic variation in time and space, including interrelations between language and culture; includes *historical linguistics* and *sociolinguistics.*

linguistic relativity: Notion that all languages and dialects are equally effective as systems of communication.

linguistic uniformitarianism: The idea that the same forces that have produced large-scale linguistic changes over the centuries, working gradually, are still at work and can be observed in linguistic events (language use) taking place today.

linkages: Interconnections between small-scale and large-scale units and systems; political, economic, informational, and other cultural links between village, region, nation, and world.

liturgical order: A set sequence of words and actions invented prior to the current performance of the ritual in which it occurs.

local descent group: All the members of a particular descent group who live in the same place, such as the same village.

longitudinal research: Long-term study of a community, society, culture, or other unit, usually based on repeated visits.

loose-knit networks: Characteristic of urban and complex societies; people who know each other often don't know each other's friends, neighbors, and relatives.

magic: Use of supernatural techniques to accomplish specific aims.

majority groups: Superordinate, dominant, or controlling groups in a social-political hierarchy.

maladaptive: Harmful to survival and reproduction.

mana: Sacred impersonal force in Melanesian and Polynesian religions.

market principle: Profit-oriented principle of exchange that dominates in states, particularly industrial states. Goods and services are bought and sold, and values are determined by supply and demand.

marriage: Socially approved relationship between a socially recognized male (the husband) and a socially recognized female (the wife) such that the children born to the wife are accepted as the offspring of both husband and wife.

massification: Production and marketing aimed at a relatively undifferentiated mass market or audience (e.g., the advertising of McDonald's).

matriarchy: A society ruled by women; unknown to ethnography.

matrifocal: Mother-centered; often refers to a household with no resident husband-father.

matrilateral skewing: A preference for relatives on the mother's side.

matrilineal descent: Unilineal descent rule in which people join the mother's group automatically at birth and stay members throughout life.

matrilocality: Customary residence with the wife's relatives after marriage, so that children grow up in their mother's community.

matrons: Senior women, as among the Iroquois.

means (or factors) of production: Land, labor, technology, and capital—major productive resources.

medical anthropology: Unites biological and cultural anthropologists in the study of disease, health problems, health care systems, and theories about illness in different cultures and ethnic groups.

mestizo: Mixed. In Latin America, having a combination of European, African, and Native American ancestors. Mestizos speak the national language.

microenculturation: The process by which people learn particular roles in a limited social system; creates microcultures.

minimal pairs: Words that resemble each other in all but one sound; used to discover phonemes.

minority groups: Subordinate groups in a social-political hierarchy, with inferior power and less secure access to resources than majority groups have.

mode of production: Way of organizing production—a set of social relations through which labor is deployed to wrest energy from nature by means of tools, skills, and knowledge.

monocrop production: System of production, often on plantations, based on the cultivation of a single cash crop.

monograph: A report based on ethnographic field work.

monotheism: Worship of an eternal, omniscient, omnipotent, and omnipresent supreme being.

morpheme: Minimal linguistic form (usually a word) with meaning.

morphology: The study of form; used in linguistics (the study of morphemes and word construction) and for form in general—for example, biomorphology relates to physical form.

multicentric exchange system: Economy organized into different categories or spheres.

multiculturalism: The view of cultural diversity in a country as something good and desirable; a multicultural society socializes individuals not only into the dominant (national) culture, but also into an ethnic culture.

namesakes: People who share the same name; a form of fictive kinship among the San, who have a limited number of personal names.

nation: Once a synonym for "ethnic group," designating a single culture sharing a language, religion, history, territory, ancestry, and kinship; now usually a synonym for "state" or "nation-state."

nation-state: An autonomous political entity, a country like the United States or Canada.

national culture: Cultural experiences, beliefs, learned behavior patterns, and values shared by citizens of the same nation.

nationalities: Ethnic groups that once had, or wish to have or regain, autonomous political status (their own country).

naturalistic disease theories: Includes scientific medicine; theories that explain illness in impersonal systemic terms.

naturists: Those who argue that human behavior and social organization are biologically determined.

negative reciprocity: See *generalized reciprocity.*

négritude: African identity—developed by African intellectuals in Francophone (French-speaking) West Africa.

neocolonialism: A revival, or a new form, of colonialism—the political, social, economic, and cultural domination of a territory and its people by a foreign power, often justified by the assertion that foreigners are more enlightened at governing than are natives of the colonial area.

neolocality: Postmarital residence pattern in which a couple establishes a new place of residence rather than living with or near either set of parents.

network analysis: Technique developed by anthropologists to adapt ethnographic procedures to modern cities and nations. Focuses on types of contacts (networks of relationships) between people.

NGOS: Nongovernmental organizations.

Nilotic populations: Populations, including the Nuer, that inhabit the Upper Nile region of eastern Africa.

nomadism, pastoral: Movement throughout the year by the whole pastoral group (men, women, and children) with their animals. More generally, such constant movement in pursuit of strategic resources.

nuclear family: Kinship group consisting of parents and children.

nurturists: Those who link behavior and social organization to environmental factors. Nurturists focus on variation rather than universals and stress learning and the role of culture in human adaptation.

office: Permanent political position.

Olympian religions: In Wallace's typology, develop with state organization; have full-time religious specialists—professional priesthoods.

open class system: Stratification system that facilitates social mobility, with individual achievement and personal merit determining social rank.

overinnovation: Characteristic of development projects that require major changes in people's daily lives, especially ones that interfere with customary subsistence pursuits.

pantheon: A collection of supernatural beings in a particular religion.

pantribal sodality: A non-kin-based group that exists throughout a tribe, spanning several villages.

participant observation: A characteristic ethnographic technique; taking part in the events one is observing, describing, and analyzing.

particularity: Distinctive or unique culture trait, pattern, or integration.

pastoralists: People who use a food-producing strategy of adaptation based on care of herds of domesticated animals.

patriarchy: Political system ruled by men in which women have inferior social and political status, including basic human rights.

patrilineal descent: Unilineal descent rule in which people join the father's group automatically at birth and stay members throughout life.

patrilineal-patrilocal complex: An interrelated constellation of patrilineality, patrilocality, warfare, and male supremacy.

patrilocality: Customary residence with the husband's relatives after marriage, so that children grow up in their father's community.

peasant: Small-scale agriculturist living in a state, with rent fund obligations.

periphery: Weakest structural position in the world system.

personal network: Each person's particular set of relationships (economic, social, political, religious) with all others.

personalistic disease theories: Theories that attribute illness to sorcerers, witches, ghosts, or ancestral spirits.

phenotype: An organism's evident traits, its "manifest biology"—anatomy and physiology.

phone: Any speech sound.

phoneme: Significant sound contrast in a language that serves to distinguish meaning, as in minimal pairs.

phonemics: The study of the sound contrasts (phonemes) of a particular language.

phonetics: The study of speech sounds in general; what people actually say in various languages.

phonology: The study of sounds used in speech.

physical anthropology: See *biological anthropology.*

pidgins: Mixed languages that develop to ease communication between members of different cultures in contact, usually in situations of trade or colonial domination.

plural marriage: Marriage of a man to two or more women (polygyny) or marriage of a woman to two or more men (polyandry)— at the same time; see also *polygamy.*

plural society: A society that combines ethnic contrasts, ecological specialization (i.e., use of different environmental resources by each ethnic group), and the economic interdependence of those groups.

polity: The political order.

polyandry: Variety of plural marriage in which a woman has more than one husband.

polygamy: Marriage with three or more spouses, at the same time; see also *plural marriage.*

polygyny: Variety of plural marriage in which a man has more than one wife.

polytheism: Belief in several deities who control aspects of nature.

postmodern: In its most general sense, describes the blurring and breakdown of established canons (rules, standards), categories, distinctions, and boundaries.

postmodernism: A style and movement in architecture that succeeded modernism. Compared with modernism, postmodernism is less geometric, less functional, less austere, more playful, and more willing to include elements from diverse times and cultures; *postmodern* now describes comparable developments in music, literature, and visual art.

postmodernity: Condition of a world in flux, with people on-the-move, in which established groups, boundaries, identities, contrasts, and standards are reaching out and breaking down.

potlatch: Competitive feast among Indians on the North Pacific Coast of North America.

power: The ability to exercise one's will over others—to do what one wants; the basis of political status.

prejudice: Devaluing (looking down on) a group because of its assumed behavior, values, capabilities, or attributes.

prestige: Esteem, respect, or approval for acts, deeds, or qualities considered exemplary.

productivity: A basic feature of language; the ability to use the rules of one's language to create new expressions comprehensible to other native speakers.

progeny price: A gift from the husband and his kin to the wife and her kin before, at, or after marriage; legitimizes children born to the woman as members of the husband's descent group.

proletarianization: Separation of workers from the means of production through industrialism.

protolanguage: Language ancestral to several daughter languages.

public transcript: As used by James Scott, the open, public interactions between dominators and oppressed—the outer shell of power relations.

questionnaire: Form (usually printed) used by sociologists to obtain comparable information from respondents. Often mailed to and filled in by research subjects rather than by the researcher.

race: An ethnic group assumed to have a biological basis.

racism: Discrimination against an ethnic group assumed to have a biological basis.

random sample: A sample in which all members of the population have an equal statistical chance of being included.

reciprocity: One of the three principles of exchange. Governs exchange between social equals; major exchange mode in band and tribal societies.

redistribution: Major exchange mode of chiefdoms, many archaic states, and some states with managed economies.

refugees: People who have been forced (involuntary refugees) or who have chosen (voluntary refugees) to flee a country, to escape persecution or war.

regulation: The management of variables within a system of related and interacting variables. Regulation assures that variables stay within their normal ranges, corrects deviations from the norm, and thus maintains the system's integrity.

religion: Beliefs and rituals concerned with supernatural beings, powers, and forces.

rent fund: Scarce resources that a social inferior is required to render to an individual or agency that is superior politically or economically.

replacement fund: Scarce resources invested in technology and other items essential to production.

respondents: Subjects in survey research; people who answer or fill in questionnaires.

revitalization movements: Movements that occur in times of change, in which religious leaders emerge and undertake to alter or revitalize a society.

rites of passage: Culturally defined activities associated with the transition from one place or stage of life to another.

ritual: Behavior that is formal, stylized, repetitive, and stereotyped, performed earnestly as a social act; rituals are held at set times and places and have liturgical orders.

role: A set of expected (culturally "proper") behaviors, attitudes, rights, and obligations attached to a particular status.

sample: A smaller study group chosen to represent a larger population.

San: Foragers of southern Africa, also known as Bushmen; speakers of San languages.

Sapir-Whorf hypothesis: Theory that different languages produce different ways of thinking.

schistosomiasis: Disease caused by liver flukes transmitted by snails inhabiting ponds, lakes, and waterways, often created by irrigation projects.

scientific medicine: As distinguished from Western medicine, a health care system based on scientific knowledge and procedures, encompassing such fields as pathology, microbiology, biochemistry, surgery, diagnostic technology, and applications.

Second World: The Warsaw Pact nations, including the former Soviet Union, the Socialist and once-Socialist countries of eastern Europe and Asia.

secret societies: Sodalities, usually all-male or all-female, with secret initiation ceremonies.

segmental appeal: Production or marketing aimed at specific audiences, rather than at a mass audience. Also called "targeting."

semantics: A language's meaning system.

semiperiphery: Structural position in the world system intermediate between core and periphery.

serial monogamy: Marriage of a given individual to several spouses, but not at the same time.

settlement hierarchy: A ranked series of communities differing in size, function, and type of building.

sexual dimorphism: Marked differences in male and female biology besides the contrasts in breasts and genitals.

sexual orientation: A person's habitual sexual attraction to, and activities with: persons of the opposite sex, *heterosexuality,* the same sex, *homosexuality,* or both sexes, *bisexuality.*

shaman: A part-time religious practitioner who mediates between ordinary people and supernatural beings and forces.

slash and burn: Form of horticulture in which the forest cover of a plot is cut down and burned before planting to allow the ashes to fertilize the soil.

slavery: The most extreme, coercive, abusive, and inhumane form of legalized inequality; people are treated as property.

social fund: Scarce resources invested to assist friends, relatives, in-laws, and neighbors.

social race: A group assumed to have a biological basis but actually perceived and defined in a social context—by a particular culture rather than by scientific criteria.

society: Organized life in groups; typical of humans and other animals.

sociolinguistics: Study of relationships between social and linguistic variation; study of language in its social context.

sociopolitical typology: Classification scheme based on the scale and complexity of social organization and the effectiveness of political regulation; includes band, tribe, chiefdom, and state.

sodality: See *pantribal sodality.*

sororate: Custom by which a widower marries the sister of the deceased wife.

state (nation-state): Complex sociopolitical system that administers a territory and populace with substantial contrasts in occupation, wealth, prestige, and power. An independent, centrally organized political unit, a government.

status: Any position that determines where someone fits in society; may be ascribed or achieved.

stereotypes: Fixed ideas—often unfavorable—about what members of a group are like.

stimulus diffusion: The process by which a group modifies a custom by adopting images and behavior associated with an external practice, without borrowing the practice itself.

stipulated descent: Basis of the clan; members merely say they descend from their apical ancestor; they don't trace the actual genealogical links between themselves and that ancestor.

strategic resources: Resources necessary for life, such as food and space.

stratification: Characteristic of a system with socioeconomic strata; see also *stratum.*

stratified: Class-structured; stratified societies have marked differences in wealth, in prestige, and in power between social classes.

stratum: One of two or more groups that contrast in regard to social status and access to strategic resources. Each stratum includes people of both sexes and all ages.

structuralism: Structural analysis; technique developed by Lévi-Strauss not to explain sociocultural similarities and differences but to uncover themes, relations, and other cross-cultural connections.

style shifts: Variations in speech in different contexts.

subaltern: Lower in rank; subordinate; traditionally lacking an influential role in decision making.

subcultures: Different cultural symbol-based traditions associated with subgroups in the same complex society.

subgroups: Languages within a taxonomy of related languages that are most closely related.

subordinate: The lower, or underprivileged, group in a stratified system.

subsistence fund: Scarce resources invested to provide food in order to replace the calories expended in daily activity.

sumptuary goods: Items whose consumption is limited to the elite.

superordinate: The upper, or privileged, group in a stratified system.

supply and demand, law of: Economic rule that things cost more the scarcer they are and the more people want them.

survey research: Characteristic research procedure among social scientists other than anthropologists. Studies society through sampling, statistical analysis, and impersonal data collection.

symbiosis: An obligatory interaction between groups that is beneficial to each.

symbol: Something, verbal or nonverbal, that arbitrarily and by convention stands for something else, with which it has no necessary or natural connection.

syncretisms: Cultural blends or mixtures that emerge from acculturation, particularly under colonialism, such as African, Native American, and Roman Catholic saints and deities in Caribbean vodun, or "voodoo," cults.

syntax: The arrangement and order of words in phrases and sentences.

systemic perspective: View that changes have multiple consequences, some unforeseen.

taboo: Prohibition backed by supernatural sanctions.

terraforming: From science fiction, the use of technology to make other worlds as much like earth (*terra*) as possible;

applied by analogy to results of political and economic domination on earth.

text: Something that is creatively "read," interpreted, and assigned meaning by each person who receives it; includes any media-borne image, such as Carnival.

Third World: The "less-developed countries" (LDCs).

totem: An animal or plant apical ancestor of a clan.

transecting groups: Networks created through direct communication channels between groups that previously had, or otherwise have, trouble communicating—for example, physicians and patients.

transhumance: One of two variants of pastoralism; part of the population moves seasonally with the herds while the other part remains in home villages.

tribe: Form of sociopolitical organization usually based on horticulture or pastoralism. Socioeconomic stratification and centralized rule are absent in tribes, and there is no means of enforcing political decisions.

typology, economic: See *economic typology.*

typology, sociopolitical: See *sociopolitical typology.*

underdifferentiation: Planning fallacy of viewing less developed countries as an undifferentiated group; ignoring cultural diversity and adopting a uniform approach (often ethnocentric) for very different types of project beneficiaries.

unilineal descent: Matrilineal or patrilineal descent.

unilocal: Either patrilocal or matrilocal postmarital residence; requires that a married couple reside with the relatives of either the husband or the wife, depending on the society.

universal: Something that exists in every culture.

urban anthropology: The anthropological study of cities.

variables: Attributes (e.g., sex, age, height, weight) that differ from one person or case to the next.

vernacular: Ordinary, casual speech.

vertical mobility: Upward or downward change in a person's social status.

village head: Leadership position in a village (as among the Yanomami, where the head is always a man); has limited authority; leads by example and persuasion.

wealth: All a person's material assets, including income, land, and other types of property; the basis of economic status.

Westernization: The acculturative influence of Western expansion on other cultures.

working class (or proletariat): Those who must sell their labor to survive; the antithesis of the bourgeoisie in Marx's class analysis.

world-system perspective: Recognition that we live in a single world system, based on a capitalist world economy, which emerged in the sixteenth century, committed to production for sale, with the object of maximizing profits rather than supplying domestic needs.

Bibliography

ABELMANN, N., AND J. LIE
  1995 *Blue Dreams: Korean Americans and the Los Angeles Riots.* Cambridge, MA: Harvard University Press.
AHMED, A. S.
  1992 *Postmodernism and Islam: Predicament and Promise.* New York: Routledge.
AMADIUME, I.
  1987 *Male Daughters, Female Husbands.* Atlantic Highlands, NJ: Zed.
AMERICAN ALMANAC 1994–1995
  1994 (*Statistical Abstract of the United States,* 114th ed.) Austin, TX: Reference Press.
AMERICAN ALMANAC 1996–1997
  1996 (*Statistical Abstract of the United States,* 116th ed.) Austin, TX: Reference Press.
AMERICAN ANTHROPOLOGICAL ASSOCIATION
  Anthropology Newsletter. Published 9 times annually by the American Anthropological Association, Washington, DC.
ANDERSON, B.
  1991 *Imagined Communities: Reflections on the Origin and Spread of Nationalism,* rev. ed. London: Verso.
ANDERSON, R.
  1996 *Magic, Science, and Health: The Aims and Achievements of Medical Anthropology.* Fort Worth: Harcourt Brace.

AOKI, M. Y., AND M. B. DARDESS, EDS.
  1981 *As the Japanese See It: Past and Present.* Honolulu: The University Press of Hawaii.
APPADURAI, A.
  1990 Disjuncture and Difference in the Global Cultural Economy. *Public Culture* 2(2):1–24.
  1991 Global Ethnoscapes: Notes and Queries for a Transnational Anthropology. In *Recapturing Anthropology: Working in the Present,* R. G. Fox, ed., pp. 191–210. Santa Fe: School of American Research Advanced Seminar Series.
APPIAH, K. A.
  1990 Racisms. In *Anatomy of Racism,* David Theo Goldberg, ed., pp. 3–17. Minneapolis: University of Minnesota Press.
APPLEBOME, P.
  1996 English Unique to Blacks Is Officially Recognized. *New York Times,* December 20, www.nytimes.com.
  1997 Dispute over Ebonics Reflects a Volatile Mix. *New York Times,* March 1, www.nytimes.com.
ARCHER, M. S.
  1996 *Culture and Agency: The Place of Culture in Social Theory,* rev. ed. Cambridge: Cambridge University Press.

ARENS, W.
1981   Professional Football: An Amer-
        ican Symbol and Ritual. In *The
        American Dimension: Cultural
        Myths and Social Realities*, 2nd
        ed., W. Arens and S. P. Mon-
        tague, eds., pp. 1–10. Sherman
        Oaks, CA: Alfred.
ARENSBERG, C.
1987   Theoretical Contributions of In-
        dustrial and Development Stud-
        ies. In *Applied Anthropology in
        America*, 2nd ed., E. M. Eddy
        and W. L. Partridge, eds. New
        York: Columbia   University
        Press.
ARNOLD, B., AND B. GIBSON, EDS.
1995   *Celtic Chiefdom, Celtic State.*
        New York: Cambridge Univer-
        sity Press.
ARRIGHI, G.
1994   *The Long Twentieth Century;
        Money, Power, and the Origins of
        Our Times.* New York: Verso.
BAILEY, R. C.
1990   *The Behavioral Ecology of Efe
        Pygmy Men in the Ituri Forest,
        Zaire.* Ann Arbor: Anthropologi-
        cal Papers, Museum of Anthro-
        pology, University of Michigan,
        no. 86.
BAILEY, R. C., G. HEAD, M. JENIKE, B.
OWEN, R. RECHTMAN, AND E. ZECHENTER
1989   Hunting   and   Gathering   in
        Tropical Rain Forests: Is It
        Possible? *American Anthropolo-
        gist* 91:59–82.
BANTON, M.
1957   *West African City. A Study in
        Tribal Life in Freetown.* London:
        Oxford University Press.
BARNABY, F., ED.
1984   *Future War: Armed Conflict in
        the Next Decade.* London: M.
        Joseph.
BARNARD, A.
1979   Kalahari Settlement Patterns.
        In *Social and Ecological Sys-
        tems*, P. Burnham and R. Ellen,
        eds. New York: Academic Press.
BARRINGER, F.
1989   32 Million Lived in Poverty in
        '88, a Figure Unchanged. *New
        York Times,* October 19, p. 18.
1992   New Census Data Show More
        Children Living in Poverty. *New
        York Times,* May 29, pp. A1,
        A12, A13.
BARTH, F.
1968   (orig. 1958). Ecologic Relations
        of Ethnic Groups in Swat,
        North Pakistan. In *Man in
        Adaptation: The Cultural Pres-
        ent*, Yehudi Cohen, ed., pp.
        324–331. Chicago: Aldine.
1969   *Ethnic Groups and Boundaries:
        The Social Organization of Cul-
        tural Difference.* London: Allyn
        and Unwin.
BEEMAN, W.
1986   *Language, Status, and Power
        in Iran.* Bloomington: Indiana
        University Press.
BEHAR, R.
1993   *Translated Woman: Crossing the
        Border with Esperanza's Story.*
        Boston: Beacon.
BEHAR, R., AND D. A. GORDON, EDS.
1995   *Women Writing Culture.* Berke-
        ley: University of California
        Press.
BELL, W.
1981   Neocolonialism. In *Encyclope-
        dia of Sociology,* p. 193. Guil-
        ford, CT: DPG Publishing.
BELLAH, R. N.
1978   Religious Evolution. In *Reader
        in Comparative Religion: An An-
        thropoloogical Approach*, 4th
        ed., W.A. Lessa and E. Z. Vogt,
        eds., pp. 36–50. New York:
        Harper and Row.
BENNETT, J. W.
1969   *Northern Plainsmen: Adaptive
        Strategy   and   Agrarian   Life.*
        Chicago: Aldine.

BERLIN, B., AND P. KAY
1992 *Basic Color Terms: Their Universality and Evolution,* 2nd ed. Berkeley: University of California Press.

BERLIN, B. D., E. BREEDLOVE, AND P. H. RAVEN
1974 *Principles of Tzeltal Plant Classification: An Introduction to the Botanical Ethnography of a Mayan-Speaking People of Highland Chiapas.* New York: Academic Press.

BERNARD, H. R.
1994 *Research Methods in Cultural Anthropology, Qualitative and Quantitative Approaches,* 2nd ed. Thousand Oaks, CA: Sage.

BERNARD, H. R., ED.
1998 *Handbook of Methods in Cultural Anthropology,* Walnut Creek, CA: Altamira.

BERREMAN, G. D.
1962 Pahari Polyandry: A Comparison. *American Anthropologist* 64:60–75.
1975 Himalayan Polyandry and the Domestic Cycle. *American Ethnologist* 2:127–138.

BETTELHEIM, B.
1975 *The Uses of Enchantment: The Meaning and Importance of Fairy Tales.* New York: Vintage.

BIRD-DAVID, N.
1992 Beyond "The Original Affluent Society": A Culturalist Reformulation. *Current Anthropology* 33(1):25–47.

BJUREMALM, H.
1997 Rattvisa kan skippas i Rwanda: Folkmordet 1994 gar attt forklara och analysera pa samma satt som forintelsen av judarna. *Dagens Nyheter* [06-03-19777, p. B3].

BLACKWOOD, E., AND WIERINGA, S., EDS.
1999 *Female Desires: Same-Sex Relations and Transgender Practices across Cultures.* New York: Columbia University Press.

BLOCH, M., ED.
1975 *Political Language and Oratory in Traditional Societies.* London: Academic.

BOAS, F.
1966 (orig. 1940). *Race, Language, and Culture.* New York: Free Press.

BODLEY, J. H.
1985 *Anthropology and Contemporary Human Problems,* 2nd ed. Palo Alto, CA: Mayfield.

BODLEY, J. H., ED.
1988 *Tribal Peoples and Development Issues: A Global Overview.* Mountain View, CA: Mayfield.

BOGORAS, W.
1904 The Chukchee. In *The Jesup North Pacific Expedition,* F. Boas, ed. New York: Memoir of the American Museum of Natural History.

BOLINGER, D.
1975 *Aspects of Language,* 2nd ed. New York: Harcourt Brace Jovanovich.

BOLTON, R.
1981 Susto, Hostility, and Hypoglycemia. *Ethnology* 20(4):227–258.

BONVILLAIN, N.
1993 *Language, Culture, and Communication: The Meaning of Messages.* Englewood Cliffs, NJ: Prentice Hall.
2001 *Women and Men: Cultural Constructions of Gender,* 3rd ed. Upper Saddle River, NJ: Prentice Hall.

BOSERUP, E.
1970 *Women's Role in Economic Development.* London: Allen and Unwin.

BOURDIEU, P.
1977 *Outline of a Theory of Practice.* R. Nice (trans.). Cambridge: Cambridge University Press.

1982 *Ce Que Parler Veut Dire.* Paris: Fayard.

1984 *Distinction: A Social Critique of the Judgment of Taste.* R. Nice (trans.). Cambridge, MA: Harvard University Press.

BOURQUE, S. C., AND K. B. WARREN

1981 *Women of the Andes: Patriarchy and Social Change in Two Peruvian Villages.* Ann Arbor: University of Michigan Press.

1987 Technology, Gender and Development. *Daedalus* 116(4): 173–197.

BRAUDEL, F.

1973 *Capitalism and Material Life, 1400–1800.* M. Kochan (trans.). London: Weidenfeld and Nicolson.

1981 *Civilization and Capitalism, 15th–18th Century,* Volume I: *The Structure of Everyday Life: The Limits.* S. Reynolds (trans.). New York: Harper and Row.

1982 *Civilization and Capitalism, 15th–18th Century,* Volume II: *The Wheels of Commerce.* New York: Harper and Row.

1984 *Civilization and Capitalism 15th–18th Century,* Volume III: *The Perspective of the World.* New York: Harper and Row.

1992 *Civilization and Capitalism, 15th–18th Century,* Volume III: *The Perspective of the World.* Berkeley: University of California Press.

BRENNEIS, D.

1988 Language and Disputing. *Annual Review of Anthropology* 17:221–237.

BRONFENBRENNER, U.

1975 Nature with Nurture: A Reinterpretation of the Evidence. In *Race and IQ,* A. Montagu, ed., pp. 114–144. New York: Oxford University Press.

BROOKE, J.

1992 Rio's New Day in Sun Leaves Laplander Limp. *New York Times,* June 1, p. A7.

BROWN, D.

1991 *Human Universals.* New York: McGraw-Hill.

BROWN, J. K.

1975 Iroquois Women: An Ethnohistoric Note. In *Toward an Anthropology of Women,* R. Reiter, ed., pp. 235–251. New York: Monthly Review Press.

BROWN, P. J.

1998 *Understanding and Applying Medical Anthropology.* Mountain View, CA: Mayfield.

BROWN, R. W.

1958 *Words and Things.* Glencoe, IL: Free Press.

BRUMFIEL, E. M.

1980 Specialization, Market Exchange, and the Aztec State: A View from Huexotla. *Current Anthropology* 21(4):459–478.

BRYANT, B., AND P. MOHAI

1991 Race, Class, and Environmental Quality in the Detroit Area. In *Environmental Racism: Issues and Dilemmas,* B. Bryant and P. Mohai, eds. Ann Arbor: The University of Michigan Office of Minority Affairs.

BRYSON, K.

1996 Household and Family Characteristics: March 1995, P20-488, November 26. United States Department of Commerce, Bureau of Census, Public Information Office, CB96-195.

BURENHULT, G., ED.

1993 *People of the Stone Age: Hunters and Gatherers and Early Farmers.* San Francisco: HarperCollins.

BURLING, R.

1970 *Man's Many Voices: Language in Its Cultural Context.* New York: Holt, Rinehart & Winston.

BURNS, J. F.
1992a Bosnian Strife Cuts Old Bridges of Trust. *New York Times,* May 22, pp. A1, A6.
1992b A Serb, Fighting Serbs, Defends Sarajevo. *New York Times,* July 12, sec. 4, p. E3.
1997 A Year of Harsh Islamic Rule Weighs Heavily for Afghans. September 24, www.nytimes.com

BUVINIC, M.
1995 The Feminization of Poverty? Research and Policy Needs. In *Reducing Poverty through Labour Market Policies.* Geneva: International Institute for Labour Studies.

CARNEIRO, R. L.
1956 Slash-and-Burn Agriculture: A Closer Look at Its Implications for Settlement Patterns. In *Men and Cultures,* Selected Papers of the Fifth International Congress of Anthropological and Ethnological Sciences, pp. 229–234. Philadelphia: University of Pennsylvania Press.
1968 (orig. 1961). Slash-and-Burn Cultivation among the Kuikuru and Its Implications for Cultural Development in the Amazon Basin. In *Man in Adaptation: The Cultural Present,* Y. A. Cohen, ed., pp. 131–145. Chicago: Aldine.
1970 A Theory of the Origin of the State. *Science* 69:733–738.

CARVER, T.
1995 *Gender Is Not a Synonym for Women.* Boulder, CO: Lynne Reinner.

CASTELLI, J.
1984 *Twelve Rules for Mixing Religion and Politics,* Publication of People For the American Way, Washington, DC.

CERNEA, M., ED.
1991 *Putting People First: Sociological Variables in Rural Development,* 2nd ed. New York: Oxford University Press (published for The World Bank).

CHAGNON, N.
1992 *Yanomamo: The Fierce People,* 4th ed. New York: Harcourt Brace.
1997 *Yanomamo,* 5th ed. Fort Worth: Harcourt Brace.

CHAMBERS, E.
1987 Applied Anthropology in the Post-Vietnam Era: Anticipations and Ironies. *Annual Review of Anthropology* 16:309–337.

CHEATER, A. P., ED.
1999 *The Anthropology of Power: Empowerment and Disempowerment in Changing Structures.* New York: Routledge.

CHERLIN, A. J.
1992 *Marriage, Divorce, Remarriage.* Cambridge, MA: Harvard University Press.

CHILD, A. B., AND CHILD, I. L.
1993 *Religion and Magic in the Lives of Traditional Peoples.* Englewood Cliffs, NJ: Prentice Hall.

CHISERI-STRATER, E., AND B. S. SUNSTEIN.
2001 *Fieldworking: Reading and Writing Research,* 2nd ed. Upper Saddle River, NJ: Prentice Hall.

CHOMSKY, N.
1957 *Syntactic Structures,* The Hague: Mouton.

CLIFFORD, J.
1982 *Person and Myth: Maurice Leenhardt in the Melanesian World.* Berkeley: University of California Press.
1988 *The Predicament of Culture: Twentieth-Century Ethnography, Literature and Art.* Cambridge, MA: Harvard University Press.

COATES, J.
1986 *Women, Men, and Language.* London: Longman.

CODY, D.
1998 British Empire. http://www.stg.brown.edu/projects/hypertext/

landow/victorian/history/Empire.html, May 18.

COHEN, M.
1998 *Culture of Intolerance: Chauvinism, Class, and Racism.* New Haven: Yale University Press.

COHEN, M. N., AND ARMELAGOS, G., EDS.
1984 *Paleopathology at the Origins of Agriculture.* New York: Academic Press.

COHEN, R.
1995 Serbs Shift Opens a Chance for Peace, a U.S. Envoy Says. *New York Times,* September 1, pp. A1, A6.

COHEN, R.
1967 *The Kanuri of Bornu.* New York: Holt, Rinehart & Winston.

COHEN, Y.
1974 Culture as Adaptation. In *Man in Adaptation: The Cultural Present,* 2nd ed., Y. A. Cohen, ed., pp. 45–68. Chicago: Aldine.

COLLINS, T. W.
1989 Rural Economic Development in Two Tennessee Counties: A Racial Dimension. Paper presented at the annual meetings of the American Anthropological Association, Washington, DC.

COLSON, E., AND T. SCUDDER
1975 New Economic Relationships between the Gwembe Valley and the Line of Rail. In *Town and Country in Central and Eastern Africa,* David Parkin, ed., pp. 190–210. London: Oxford University Press.

1988 *For Prayer and Profit: The Ritual, Economic, and Social Importance of Beer in Gwembe District, Zambia, 1950–1982.* Stanford, CA: Stanford University Press.

CONKLIN, H. C.
1954 *The Relation of Hanunóo Culture to the Plant World.* Unpublished Ph.D. dissertation, Yale University.

CONNELL, R. W.
1995 *Masculinities.* Berkeley: University of California Press.

CONNOR, W.
1972 Nation-Building or Nation-Destroying. *World Politics* 24(3).

CROSBY, A. W., JR.
1972 *The Columbian Exchange: Biological and Cultural Consequences of 1492.* Westport, CT: Greenwood Press.

1986 *Ecological Imperialism: The Biological Expansion of Europe 900–1900.* Cambridge: Cambridge University Press.

CULTURAL SURVIVAL QUARTERLY
Quarterly journal. Cambridge, MA: Cultural Survival, Inc.

DALTON, G., ED.
1967 *Tribal and Peasant Economies.* Garden City, NY: The Natural History Press.

DaMATTA, R.
1991 *Carnivals, Rogues, and Heroes: An Interpretation of the Brazilian Dilemma.* Translated from the Portuguese by John Drury. Notre Dame, IN.: University of Notre Dame Press.

D'ANDRADE, R.
1984 Cultural Meaning Systems. In *Culture Theory: Essays on Mind, Self, and Emotion,* R. A. Shweder and R. A. Levine, eds., pp. 88–119. Cambridge: Cambridge University Press.

DAVIS, D. L., AND R. G. WHITTEN
1987 The Cross-Cultural Study of Human Sexuality. *Annual Review of Anthropology* 16:69–98.

DEGLER, C.
1970 *Neither Black or White: Slavery and Race Relations in Brazil and the United States.* New York: Macmillan.

DELAMONT, S.
1995 *Appetites and Identities: an Introduction to the Social Anthropology of Western Europe.* London: Routledge.

DENTAN, R. K.
  1979 *The Semai: A Nonviolent People of Malaya.* Fieldwork edition. New York: Harcourt Brace.

DE VOS, G. A., AND H. WAGATSUMA
  1966 *Japan's Invisible Race: Caste in Culture and Personality.* Berkeley: University of California Press.

DE VOS, G. A., W. O. WETHERALL, AND K. STEARMAN
  1983 *Japan's Minorities: Burakumin, Koreans, Ainu and Okinawans.* Report no. 3. London: Minority Rights Group.

DE WAAL, F. B. M.
  1997 *Bonobo: The Forgotten Ape.* Berkeley: University of California Press.

DI LEONARDO, M., ED.
  1991 *Toward an New Anthropology of Gender.* Berkeley: University of California Press.

DIAMOND, J. M.
  1997 *Guns, Germs, and Steel: The Fates of Human Societies.* New York: W. W. Norton.

DIVALE, W. T., AND M. HARRIS
  1976 Population, Warfare, and the Male Supremacist Complex. *American Anthropologist* 78:521–538.

DRAPER, P.
  1975 !Kung Women: Contrasts in Sexual Egalitarianism in Foraging and Sedentary Contexts. In *Toward an Anthropology of Women*, R. Reiter, ed., pp. 77–109. New York: Monthly Review Press.

DURKHEIM, E.
  1951 (orig. 1897). *Suicide: A Study in Sociology.* Glencoe, IL: Free Press.
  1961 (orig. 1912). *The Elementary Forms of the Religious Life.* New York: Collier Books.

DWYER, K.
  1982 *Moroccan Dialogues: Anthropology in Question.* Baltimore: Johns Hopkins University Press.

EAGLETON, T.
  1983 *Literary Theory: An Introduction.* Minneapolis: University of Minnesota Press.

EARLE, T. K.
  1987 Chiefdoms in Archaeological and Ethnohistorical Perspective. *Annual Review of Anthropology* 16:279–308.
  1991 *Chiefdoms: Power, Economy, and Ideology.* New York: Cambridge University Press.
  1997 *How Chiefs Come to Power: The Political Economy in Prehistory.* Stanford, CA: Stanford University Press.

EASTMAN, C. M.
  1975 *Aspects of Language and Culture.* San Francisco: Chandler and Sharp.

ECKERT, P.
  1989 *Jocks and Burnouts: Social Categories and Identity in the High School.* New York: Teachers College Press, Columbia University.
  2000 *Linguistic Variation as Social Practice: The Linguistic Construction of Identity in Belten High.* Malden, MA: Blackwell.

ERLANGER, S.
  1992 An Islamic Awakening in Central Asian Lands. *New York Times*, June 9, pp. A1, A7.

ERRINGTON, F., AND D. GEWERTZ
  1987 *Cultural Alternatives and a Feminist Anthropology: An Analysis of Culturally Constructed Gender Interests in Papua New Guinea.* New York: Cambridge University Press.

ESCOBAR, A.
  1991 Anthropology and the Development Encounter: The Making and Marketing of Development Anthropology. *American Ethnologist* 18:658–682.
  1994 Welcome to Cyberia: Notes on the Anthropology of Cyberculture. *Current Anthropology* 35(3):211–231.

1995   *Encountering Development: The Making and Unmaking of the Third World.* Princeton, NJ: Princeton University Press.

ESKRIDGE, W. N., JR.
1996   *The Case for Same-Sex Marriage: From Sexual Liberty to Civilized Commitment.* New York: Free Press.

EVANS-PRITCHARD, E. E.
1940   *The Nuer: A Description of the Modes of Livelihood and Political Institutions of a Nilotic People.* Oxford: Clarendon Press.
1970   Sexual Inversion among the Azande. *American Anthropologist* 72:1428–1433.

FAGAN, B. M.
1998   *World Prehistory: A Brief Introduction,* 4th ed. New York: Longman.

FAROOQ, M.
1966   Importance of Determining Transmission Sites in Planning Bilharziasis Control: Field Observations from the Egypt-49 Project Area. *American Journal of Epidemiology* 83:603–612.

FARR, D. M. L.
1980   British Empire. *Academic American Encyclopedia.* Princeton, NJ: Arete, volume 3, pp. 495–496.

FASOLD, R. W.
1990   *The Sociolinguistics of Language.* Oxford: Basil Blackwell.

FELD, S.
1991   Voices of the Rainforest. *Public Culture* 4(1):131–140.

FERGUSON, R. B.
1995   *Yanomami Warfare: A Political History.* Santa Fe, NM: School of American Research.

FERRARO, G. P.
2001   *The Cultural Dimension of International Business,* 4th ed. Upper Saddle River, NJ: Prentice Hall.

FIELDS, J.
       Current Population Reports: America's families and living arrangements, 2000. U.S. Census Bureau. P20–537, June. www.census.gov.

FINKLER, K.
1985   *Spiritualist Healers in Mexico: Successes and Failures of Alternative Therapeutics.* South Hadley, MA: Bergin and Garvey.

FINNSTROM, S.
1997   Postcoloniality and the Postcolony: Theories of the Global and the Local. http://www.stg.brown.edu/projects/hypertext/landow/post/poldiscourse/finnstrom/finnstrom1.html.

FISKE, J.
1989   *Understanding Popular Culture.* Boston: Unwin Hyman.

FLEISHER, M. L.
2000   *Kuria Cattle Raiders: Violence and Vigilantism on the Tanzania/Kenya Frontier.* Ann Arbor: University of Michigan Press.

FORD, C. S., AND F. A. BEACH
1951   *Patterns of Sexual Behavior.* New York: Harper Torchbooks.

FOSTER, G. M.
1965   Peasant Society and the Image of Limited Good. *American Anthropologist* 67:293–315.

FOSTER, G. M., AND B. G. ANDERSON
1978   *Medical Anthropology.* New York: McGraw-Hill.

FOUCAULT, M.
1979   *Discipline and Punish: The Birth of the Prison.* A. Sheridan (trans,). New York: Vintage Books.

FRAKE, C. O.
1961   The Diagnosis of Disease among the Subanun of Mindanao. *American Anthropologist* 63:113–132.

FRANKE, R.
1977   Miracle Seeds and Shattered Dreams in Java. In *Readings in Anthropology,* pp. 197–201. Guilford, CT: Dushkin.

FREEMAN, M.
1994 *Twelve Rules for Mixing Religion and Politics,* 1994 ed., Publication of People For the American Way, Washington, DC.

FRICKE, T.
1994 *Himalayan Households: Tamang Demography and Domestic Processes,* 2nd ed. New York: Columbia University Press.

FRIED, M. H.
1960 On the Evolution of Social Stratification and the State. In *Culture in History,* S. Diamond, ed. pp. 713–731. New York: Columbia University Press.
1967 *The Evolution of Political Society: An Essay in Political Anthropology.* New York: McGraw-Hill.

FRIEDAN, B.
1963 *The Feminine Mystique.* New York: Norton.

FRIEDL, E.
1975 *Women and Men: An Anthropologist's View.* New York: Holt, Rinehart & Winston.

GAL, S.
1989 Language and Political Economy. *Annual Review of Anthropology* 18:345–367.

GEERTZ, C.
1973 *The Interpretation of Cultures.* New York: Basic Books.

GEIS, M. L.
1987 *The Language of Politics..* New York: Springer-Verlag.

GELLNER, E.
1997 *Nationalism.* New York: New York University Press.

GIDDENS, A.
1973 *The Class Structure of the Advanced Societies.* New York: Cambridge University Press.

GILMORE, D.
1987 *Aggression and Community: Paradoxes of Andalusian Culture.* New Haven: Yale University Press.

1991 *Manhood in the Making: Cultural Concepts of Masculinity.* New Haven: Yale University Press.

GOLDEN, T.
1997 Oakland Revamps Plan to Teach Black English. *New York Times,* January 14, www.nytimes.com.

GOODENOUGH, W. H.
1953 *Native Astronomy in the Central Carolines,* Philadelphia: University of Pennsylvania Press.

GORDON, A. A.
1996 *Transforming Capitalism and Patriarchy: Gender and Development in Africa.* Boulder, CO: Lynne Reinner.

GOTTDIENER, M., ED.
2000 *New Forms of Consumption: Consumers, Culture, and Commodification.* Lanham, MD: Rowman and Littlefield.

GOUGH, E. K.
1959 The Nayars and the Definition of Marriage. *Journal of the Royal Anthropological Institute* 89:23–34.

GRAMSCI, A.
1971 *Selections from the Prison Notebooks.* Q. Hoare and G. N. Smith (ed. and trans.) London: Wishart.

GRASMUCK, S., AND P. PESSAR
1991 *Between Two Islands: Dominican International Migration.* Berkeley: University of California Press.

GRAY, J.
1986 With a Few Exceptions, Television in Africa Fails to Educate and Enlighten. *Ann Arbor News,* December 8.

GREAVES, T. C.
1995 Problems Facing Anthropologists: Cultural Rights and Ethnography. *General Anthropology* 1(2):1,3–6.

GREEN, E. C.
1992 (orig. 1987). The Integration of Modern and Traditional Health

Sectors in Swaziland. In *Applying Anthropology*, A. Podolefsky and P. J. Brown, eds., pp. 246–251. Mountain View, CA: Mayfield.

GRIFFIN, P. B., AND A. ESTIOKO-GRIFFIN, EDS.
1985 *The Agta of Northern Luzon: Recent Studies*. Cebu City, Philippines: University of San Carlos.

GUDEMAN, S., ED.
1999 *Economic Anthropology*. Northampton, MA: E. Elgar.

GUMPERZ, J. J., AND S. C. LEVINSON, EDS.
1996 *Rethinking Linguistic Relativity*. New York: Cambridge University Press.

HALL, T. D., ED.
1999 *A World-System Reader: New Perspectives on Gender, Urbanism, Cultures, Indigenous Peoples, and Ecology*. Lanham, MD: Rowman and Littlefield.

HANSEN, K. V., AND A. I. GAREY, EDS.
1998 *Families in the U.S.: Kinship and Domestic Politics*. Philadelphia: Temple University Press.

HARDING, S.
1975 Women and Words in a Spanish Village. In *Toward an Anthropology of Women*, R. Reiter, ed., pp. 283–308. New York: Monthly Review Press.

HARRIS, M.
1964 *Patterns of Race in the Americas*. New York: Walker.
1970 Referential Ambiguity in the Calculus of Brazilian Racial Identity. *Southwestern Journal of Anthropology* 26(1):1–14.
1974 *Cows, Pigs, Wars, and Witches: The Riddles of Culture*. New York: Random House.
1978 *Cannibals and Kings*. New York: Vintage.

HARRIS, M., AND C. P. KOTTAK
1963 The Structural Significance of Brazilian Racial Categories. *Sociologia* 25:203–209.

HART, C. W. M., AND A. R. PILLING
1960 *The Tiwi of North Australia*. New York: Holt, Rinehart & Winston.

HART, C. W. M., A. R. PILLING, AND J. C. GOODALE
1988 *The Tiwi of North Australia*, 3rd ed. Fort Worth: Harcourt Brace.

HARVEY, D. J.
1980 French Empire. *Academic American Encyclopedia*. Princeton, NJ: Arete, volume 8, pp. 309–310.

HARVEY, K.
1996 Online for the Ancestors: The Importance of Anthropological Sensibility in Information Superhighway Design. *Social Science Computing Review* 14(1):65–68.

HASTINGS, A.
1997 The *Construction of Nationhood: Ethnicity, Religion, and Nationalism*. New York: Cambridge University Press.

HAWKES, K., J. O'CONNELL, AND K. HILL
1982 Why Hunters Gather: Optimal Foraging and the Aché of Eastern Paraguay. *American Ethnologist* 9:379–398.

HEADLAND, T. N., AND L. A. REID
1989 Hunter-gatherers and Their Neighbors from Prehistory to the Present. *Current Anthropology* 30:43–66.

HEADLAND, T. N., ED.
1992 *The Tasaday Controversy: Assessing the Evidence*. Washington: American Anthropological Association.

HEDGES, C.
1992 Sudan Presses Its Campaign to Impose Islamic Law on Non-Muslims. *New York Times*, June 1, p. A7.

HELMAN, C.
2001 *Culture, Health, and Illness: an Introduction for Health Professionals*, 4th ed. Boston: Butterworth-Heinemann.

HENRY, J.
1955 Docility, or Giving Teacher What She Wants. *Journal of Social Issues* 2:33–41.

HERDT, G.
1981 *Guardians of the Flutes.* New York: McGraw-Hill.
1986 *The Sambia: Ritual and Gender in New Guinea.* Fort Worth: Harcourt Brace.

HERDT, G. H., ED.
1984 *Ritualized Homosexuality in Melanesia.* Berkeley: University of California Press.

HERRNSTEIN, R. J.
1971 I.Q. *The Atlantic* 228(3):43–64.

HERRNSTEIN, R. J., AND C. MURRAY
1994 *The Bell Curve: Intelligence and Class Structure in American Life.* New York: Free Press.

HESS, D. J.
1995 A Democratic Research Agenda in the Social Studies of the National Information Infrastructure. Paper prepared for the National Science Foundation Workshop on Culture, Society, and Advanced Information Technology. Washington, DC: May 31–June 1.

HEYNEMAN, D.
1984 Development and Disease: A Dual Dilemma. *Journal of Parasitology* 70:3–17.

HICKS, D., ED.
1999 *Ritual and Belief: Readings in the Anthropology of Religion.* New York: McGraw-Hill.

HILL, K., H. KAPLAN, K. HAWKES, AND A. HURTADO
1987 Foraging Decisions among Aché Hunter-gatherers: New Data and Implications for Optimal Foraging Models. *Ethology and Sociobiology* 8:1–36.

HILL-BURNETT, J.
1978 Developing Anthropological Knowledge through Application. In *Applied Anthropology in America,* E. M. Eddy and W. L. Partridge, eds., pp. 112–128. New York: Columbia University Press.

HOEBEL, E. A.
1954 *The Law of Primitive Man.* Cambridge, MA: Harvard University Press.
1968 (orig. 1954). The Eskimo: Rudimentary Law in a Primitive Anarchy. In *Studies in Social and Cultural Anthropology,* J. Middleton, ed., pp. 93–127. New York: Crowell.

HOPKINS, T., AND I. WALLERSTEIN
1982 Patterns of Development of the Modern World System. In *World System Analysis: Theory and Methodology,* by T. Hopkins, I. Wallerstein, R. Bach, C. Chase-Dunn, and R. Mukherjee, pp. 121–141. Thousand Oaks, CA: Sage.

INHORN, M. C., AND P. J. BROWN
1990 The Anthropology of Infectious Disease. *Annual Review of Anthropology* 19:89–117.

JENSEN, A.
1969 How Much Can We Boost I.Q. and Scholastic Achievement? *Harvard Educational Review* 29:1–123.

JOHNSON, A. W.
1978 *Quantification in Cultural Anthropology: An Introduction to Research Design.* Stanford, CA: Stanford University Press.

JOHNSON, A. W., AND T. K. EARLE
1987 *The Evolution of Human Societies: From Foraging Group to Agrarian State.* Stanford, CA: Stanford University Press.
2000 *The Evolution of Human Societies: from Foraging Group to Agrarian State,* 2nd ed. Stanford, CA: Stanford University Press.

JONES, D.
1999 Hot Asset in Corporate: Anthropology Degrees. In *USA Today,* February 18, p. B1.

JORALEMON, D.
   1999 *Exploring Medical Anthropology.*
         Boston: Allyn and Bacon.
KAN, S.
   1986 The 19th-Century Tlingit Pot-
         latch: A New Perspective. *Amer-
         ican Ethnologist* 13 191–212.
   1989 *Symbolic Immortality: The Tlin-
         git Potlatch of the Nineteenth
         Century.* Washington: Smith-
         sonian Institution Press.
KANTOR, P.
   1996 Domestic   Violence   against
         Women: A Global Issue. http://
         metalab.unc.edu/ucis/pubs/Caro
         lina_Papers/Abuse/figure1.html.
KAPLAN, R. D.
   1994 The Coming Anarchy: How
         Scarcity, Crime, Overpopula-
         tion, and Disease Are Rapidly
         Destroying the Social Fabric of
         Our Planet. *Atlantic Monthly,*
         February, pp. 44–76.
KARDULIAS, P. N.
   1999 *World-Systems Theory in Prac-
         tice: Leadership, Production, and
         Exchange.* Lanham, MD: Row-
         man and Littlefield.
KEARNEY, M.
   1996 *Reconceptualizing the Peasantry:
         Anthropology in Global Perspec-
         tive.* Boulder, CO: Westview.
KELLY, R. C.
   1976 Witchcraft and Sexual Rela-
         tions: An Exploration in the So-
         cial and Semantic Implications
         of the Structure of Belief. In
         *Man and Woman in the New
         Guinea Highlands,* P. Brown
         and G. Buchbinder, eds., pp.
         36–53. Special Publication, no.
         8. Washington, DC: American
         Anthropological Association.
   2000 *Warless Societies and the Origin
         of War.* Ann Arbor: University of
         Michigan Press.
KENT, S.
   1992 The Current Forager Contro-
         versy: Real versus Ideal Views of
         Hunter-gatherers. *Man* 27:45–70.

   1996 *Cultural   Diversity   among
         Twentieth-Century Foragers: An
         African Perspective.* New York:
         Cambridge University Press.
KENT, S., AND H. VIERICH
   1989 The Myth of Ecological Deter-
         minism: Anticipated Mobility
         and Site Organization of Space.
         In *Farmers as Hunters: The Im-
         plications of Sedentism,* S.
         Kent, ed., pp. 96–130. New
         York: Cambridge University
         Press.
KIMMEL, M. S., AND M. A. MESSNER, EDS.
   1995 *Men's Lives,* 3rd ed. Needham
         Heights, MA: Allyn and Bacon.
KINSEY, A. C., W. B. POMEROY, AND C. E.
MARTIN
   1948 *Sexual Behavior in the Human
         Male.* Philadelphia: W. B. Saun-
         ders.
KIRCH, P.V.
   1984 *The Evolution of the Polynesian
         Chiefdoms.* Cambridge: Cam-
         bridge University Press.
KLASS, M.
   1995 *Ordered Universes: Approaches
         to the Anthropology of Religion.*
         Boulder, CO: Westview.
KLASS, M., AND M. WEISGRAU, EDS.
   1999 *Across the Boundaries of Belief:
         Contemporary Issues in the An-
         thropology of Religion.* Boulder,
         CO: Westview.
KLEINFELD, J.
   1975 Positive Stereotyping: The Cul-
         tural Relativist in the Class-
         room. *Human Organization*
         34:269–274.
KLINEBERG, O.
   1951 Race and Psychology. In *The
         Race Question in Modern Sci-
         ence.* Paris: UNESCO.
KLING, R.
   1996 Synergies and Competition be-
         tween Life in Cyberspace and
         Face-to-Face Communities. *So-
         cial Science Computing Review*
         14(1):50–54.

KLUCKHOHN, C.

1944 *Mirror for Man: A Survey of Human Behavior and Social Attitudes.* Greenwich, CT: Fawcett.

KOTTAK, C. P.

1980 *The Past in the Present: History, Ecology, and Social Organization in Highland Madagascar.* Ann Arbor: University of Michigan Press.

1990a Culture and "Economic Development." *American Anthropologist* 93(3):723–731.

1990b *Prime-Time Society: An Anthropological Analysis of Television and Culture.* Belmont, CA: Wadsworth.

1991 When People Don't Come First: Some Lessons from Completed Projects. In *Putting People First: Sociological Variables in Rural Development,* 2nd ed., M. Cernea, ed., pp. 429–464. New York: Oxford University Press.

1999 *Assault on Paradise: Social Change in a Brazilian Village,* 3rd ed. New York: McGraw-Hill.

KOTTAK, C. P., AND K. A. KOZAITIS

1999 *On Being Different: Diversity and Multiculturalism in the North American Mainstream.* New York: McGraw-Hill.

KUNITZ, S. J.

1994 *Disease and Social Diversity: The European Impact on the Health of Non-Europeans.* New York: Oxford University Press.

KURTZ, D. V.

2001 *Political Anthropology: Power and Paradigms.* Boulder, CO: Westview.

KUTSCHE, P.

1998 *Field Ethnography: A Manual for Doing Cultural Anthropology.* Upper Saddle River, NJ: Prentice Hall.

LABOV, W.

1972a *Language in the Inner City: Studies in the Black English Vernacular.* Philadelphia: University of Pennsylvania Press.

1972b *Sociolinguistic Patterns.* Philadelphia: University of Pennsylvania Press.

LAGUERRE, M.

1984 *American Odyssey: Haitians in New York.* Ithaca, NY: Cornell University Press.

LAKOFF, R. T.

1975 *Language and Woman's Place.* New York: Harper and Row.

2000 *The Language War.* Berkeley: University of California Press.

LANCASTER, R. N., AND M. DI LEONARDO, EDS.

1997 *The Gender/Sexuality Reader: Culture, History, Political Economy.* New York: Routledge.

LANCE, L. M., AND E. E. MCKENNA

1975 Analysis of Cases Pertaining to the Impact of Western Technology on the Non-Western World. *Human Organization* 34:87–94.

LARSON, A.

1989 Social Context of Human Immunodeficiency Virus Transmission in Africa: Historical and Cultural Bases of East and Central African Sexual Relations. *Review of Infectious Diseases* 11:716–31.

LASSITER, L. E.

1998 *The Power of Kiowa Song: A Collaborative Ethnography.* Tucson: University of Arizona Press.

LEACH, E .R.

1955 Polyandry, Inheritance and the Definition of Marriage. *Man* 55:182–186.

1961 *Rethinking Anthropology.* London: Athlone Press.

LEE, R. B.

1974 (orig. 1968). What Hunters Do for a Living, or, How to Make Out on Scarce Resources. In *Man in Adaptation: The Cultural Present,* 2nd ed., Y. A. Cohen, ed., pp. 87–100. Chicago: Aldine.

1979 *The !Kung San: Men, Women, and Work in a Foraging Society.* New York: Cambridge University Press.

1984 *The Dobe !Kung.* New York: Harcourt Brace.

1993 *The Dobe Ju/'hoansi,* 2nd ed. Fort Worth: Harcourt Brace.

LEE, R. B., AND R. H. DALY

1999 *The Cambridge Encyclopedia of Hunters and Gatherers.* New York: Cambridge University Press.

LEE, R. B., AND I. DEVORE, EDS.

1977 *Kalahari Hunter-Gatherers: Studies of the !Kung San and Their Neighbors.* Cambridge, MA: Harvard University Press.

LEHMANN, A. C., AND J. E. MEYERS, EDS.

1997 *Magic, Witchcraft, and Religion: An Anthropological Study of the Supernatural,* 4th ed. Mountain View, CA: Mayfield.

LENSKI, G.

1966 *Power and Privilege: A Theory of Social Stratification.* New York: McGraw-Hill.

LÉVI-STRAUSS, C.

1963 *Totemism.* R. Needham (trans.). Boston: Beacon Press.

1967 *Structural Anthropology.* New York: Doubleday.

1969 (orig. 1949). *The Elementary Structures of Kinship.* Boston: Beacon Press.

LEWIS, P.

1992 U.N. Sees a Crisis in Overpopulation. *The New York Times,* p. A6.

LIEBAN, R. W.

1977 The Field of Medical Anthropology. In *Culture, Disease, and Healing: Studies in Medical Anthropology,* D. Landy, ed., pp. 13–31. New York: Macmillan.

LIGHT, D., S. KELLER, AND C. CALHOUN

1997 *Sociology,* 7th ed. New York: McGraw-Hill.

LINDENBAUM, S.

1972 Sorcerers, Ghosts, and Polluting Women: An Analysis of Religious Belief and Population Control. *Ethnology* 11:241–253.

LINDHOLM, C.

2001 *Culture and Identity: The History, Theory, and Practice of Psychological Anthropology.* Boston: McGraw-Hill.

LINTON, R.

1943 Nativistic Movements. *American Anthropologist* 45:230–240.

LITTLE, K.

1965 *West African Urbanization: A Study of Voluntary Associations in Social Change.* Cambridge: Cambridge University Press.

1971 Some Aspects of African Urbanization South of the Sahara. Reading, MA: Addison-Wesley, McCaleb Modules in Anthropology.

LOCKWOOD, W. G.

1975 *European Moslems: Economy and Ethnicity in Western Bosnia.* New York: Academic Press.

LOWIE, R. H.

1935 *The Crow Indians.* New York: Farrar and Rinehart.

LUGAILA, T.

1999 Married Adults Still in the Majority, Census Bureau Reports. http://www.census.gov/ Press-Release/www/1999/ cb99-03.html.

MALINOWSKI, B.

1929 Practical Anthropology. *Africa* 2:23–38.

1961 (orig. 1922). *Argonauts of the Western Pacific.* New York: Dutton.

1978 (orig. 1931). The Role of Magic and Religion. In *Reader in Comparative Religion: An Anthropological Approach,* 4th ed., W. A. Lessa and E. Z. Vogt, eds., pp. 37–46. New York: Harper and Row.

MALKKI, LIISA H.

1995 *Purity and Exile: Violence, Memory, and National Cosmology among Hutu Refugees in*

Tanzania. Chicago: University of Chicago Press.

MANNERS, R.
1973 (orig. 1956). Functionalism, Realpolitik and Anthropology in Underdeveloped Areas. *America Indigena* 16 (also in T. Weaver, gen. ed., pp. 113–126).

MAQUET, J.
1964 Objectivity in Anthropology. *Current Anthropology* 5:47–55.

MAR, M. E.
1997 Secondary Colors: The Multiracial Option. *Harvard Magazine,* May–June, pp. 19–20.

MARCUS, G. E., AND CUSHMAN, D.
1982 Ethnographies as Texts. *Annual Review of Anthropology* 11:25–69.

MARCUS, G. E., AND FISCHER, M. M. J.
1986 *Anthropology as Cultural Critique: an Experimental Moment in the Human Sciences.* Chicago: University of Chicago Press.
1999 *Anthropology as Cultural Critique: an Experimental Moment in the Human Sciences,* 2nd ed. Chicago: University of Chicago Press.

MARCUS, G. E., AND MYERS, F. R. EDS.
1995 *The Traffic in Culture: Refiguring Art and Anthropology.* Berkeley: University of California Press.

MARGOLIS, M.
1984 *Mothers and Such: American Views of Women and How They Changed.* Berkeley: University of California Press.
1994 *Little Brazil: An Ethnography of Brazilian Immigrants in New York City.* Princeton, NJ: Princeton University Press.
2000 *True to Her Nature: Changing Advice to American Women.* Prospect Heights, IL: Waveland.

MARTIN, E.
1987 *The Woman in the Body: A Cultural Analysis of Reproduction.* Boston: Beacon Press.
1992 The End of the Body? *American Ethnologist* 19:121–140.

MARTIN, K., AND B. VOORHIES
1975 *Female of the Species.* New York: Columbia University Press.

MARX, K., AND F. ENGELS
1976 (orig. 1948). *Communist Manifesto.* New York: Pantheon.

MCDONALD, G.
1984 *Carioca Fletch.* New York: Warner Books.

MCELROY, A., AND P. K. TOWNSEND
1996 *Medical Anthropology in Ecological Perspective,* 3rd ed. Boulder, CO: Westview.

MCKINLEY, J.
1996 Board's Decision on Black English Stirs Debate. *New York Times,* December 21, www.nytimes.com.

MEAD, M.
1950 (orig. 1935). *Sex and Temperament in Three Primitive Societies.* New York: New American Library.

MICHAELS, E.
1986 Aboriginal Content. Paper presented at the meeting of the Australian Screen Studies Association. Sydney, December.

MICHAELSON, K.
1996 Information, Community, and Access. *Social Science Computing Review* 14(1):57–59.

MILLER, B. D.
1997 *The Endangered Sex: Neglect of Female Children in Rural North India.* New York: Oxford University Press.

MILLER, B. D., ED.
1993 *Sex and Gender Hierarchies.* New York: Cambridge University Press.

MILLER, N., AND R. C. ROCKWELL, EDS.
1988 *AIDS in Africa: The Social and Policy Impact.* Lewiston: Edwin Mellen.

MINTZ, S.
1985 *Sweetness and Power: The Place of Sugar in Modern History.* New York: Viking Penguin.

MITCHELL, J. C.
   1966 Theoretical Orientations in African Urban Studies. In *The Social Anthropology of Complex Societies*, M. Banton, ed., pp. 37–68. London: Tavistock.

MOERMAN, M.
   1965 Ethnic Identification in a Complex Civilization: Who Are the Lue? *American Anthropologist* 67(5 Part I):1215–1230.

MONTAGU, A., ED.
   1997 *Man's Most Dangerous Myth: The Fallacy of Race*. Walnut Creek, CA: AltaMira.

MORGEN, S., ED.
   1989 *Gender and Anthropology: Critical Reviews for Research and Teaching*. Washington: American Anthropological Association.

MUKHOPADHYAY, C., AND P. HIGGINS
   1988 Anthropological Studies of Women's Status Revisited: 1977–1987. *Annual Review of Anthropology* 17:461–495.

MULLINGS, L., ED.
   1987 *Cities of the United States: Studies in Urban Anthropology*. New York: Columbia University Press.

MURDOCK, G. P.
   1934 *Our Primitive Contemporaries*. New York: Macmillan.
   1949 *Social Structure*. New York: Macmillan.
   1957 World Ethnographic Sample. *American Anthropologist* 59:664–687.

MURPHY, R. F., AND L. KASDAN
   1959 The Structure of Parallel Cousin Marriage. *American Anthropologist* 61:17–29.

MURRAY, S. O., AND W. ROSCOE, EDS.
   1998 *Boy-wives and Female Husbands: Studies in African Homosexualities*. New York: St. Martin's.

MYDANS, S.
   1992a Criticism Grows over Aliens Seized during Riots. *New York Times*, May 29, p. A8.

   1992b Judge Dismisses Case in Shooting by Officer. *New York Times*, June 4, p. A8.

NAGEL, J.
   1996 *American Indian Ethnic Renewal: Red Power and the Resurgence of Identity and Culture*. New York: Oxford University Press.

NASH, J., AND H. SAFA, EDS.
   1986 *Women and Change in Latin America*. South Hadley, MA: Bergin and Garvey.

NAYLOR, L. L.
   1996 *Culture and Change: An Introduction*. Westport, CT: Bergin and Garvey.

NEVID, J. S., AND S. A. RATHUS
   1995 *Human Sexuality in a World of Diversity*, 2nd ed. Needham Heights, MA: Allyn and Bacon.

NEWMAN, M.
   1992 Riots Bring Attention to Growing Hispanic Presence in South-Central Area. *New York Times*, May 11, p. A10.

NEW YORK TIMES
   1992 Alexandria Journal: TV Program for Somalis Is a Rare Unifying Force. December 18.

NIELSSON, G. P.
   1985 States and Nation-Groups: A Global Taxonomy. In *New Nationalisms of the Developed World*, E. A. Tiryakian and R. Rogowski, eds., pp. 27–56. Boston: Allen and Unwin.

NUSSBAUM, M., AND J. GLOVER, EDS.
   1995 *Women, Culture, and Development: A Study of Human Capabilities*. New York: Oxford University Press.

O'LEARY, C.
   2002 *Class Formation, Diet and Economic Transformation in Two Brazilian Fishing Communities*. Unpublished Ph.D. dissertation, University of Michigan, Ann Arbor.

ONG, A.
   1987 *Spirits of Resistance and Capitalist Discipline: Factory Women*

in Malaysia. Albany: State University of New York Press.

1989 Center, Periphery, and Hierarchy: Gender in Southeast Asia. In *Gender and Anthropology: Critical Reviews for Research and Teaching,* S. Morgen, ed., pp. 294–312. Washington: American Anthropological Association.

ONTARIO CONSULTANTS ON RELIGIOUS TOLERANCE

1996 Religious Access Dispute Resolved. Internet Mailing List, April 12, http://www.religious-tolerance.org/news_694.htm.

PELETZ, M.

1988 *A Share of the Harvest: Kinship, Property, and Social History among the Malays of Rembau.* Berkeley: University of California Press.

PELTO, P.

1973 *The Snowmobile Revolution: Technology and Social Change in the Arctic.* Menlo Park, CA: Cummings.

PEPLAU, L. A., ED.

1999 *Gender, Culture, and Ethnicity: Current Research about Women and Men.* Mountain View, CA: Mayfield.

PETERS-GOLDEN, H.

2002 *Culture Sketches: Case Studies in Anthropology,* 3rd ed. New York: McGraw-Hill.

PIDDOCKE, S.

1969 The Potlatch System of the Southern Kwakiutl: A New Perspective. In *Environment and Cultural Behavior,* A. P. Vayda, ed., pp. 130–156. Garden City, NY: Natural History Press.

PLATTNER, S., ED.

1989 *Economic Anthropology.* Stanford, CA: Stanford University Press.

POLANYI, K.

1968 *Primitive, Archaic and Modern Economies: Essays of Karl Polanyi,* G. Dalton, ed., Garden City, NY: Anchor Books.

POSPISIL, L.

1963 *The Kapauku Papuans of West New Guinea.* New York: Holt, Rinehart & Winston.

POTASH, B., ED.

1986 *Widows in African Societies: Choices and Constraints.* Stanford, CA: Stanford University Press.

PRICE, R., ED.

1973 *Maroon Societies.* New York: Anchor Press/Doubleday.

RADCLIFFE-BROWN, A.R.

1965 (orig. 1962). *Structure and Function in Primitive Society.* New York: Free Press.

RANGER, T. O.

1996 Postscript. In *Postcolonial Identities,* R. Werbner and T. O. Ranger, eds., London: Zed.

RAPPAPORT, R. A.

1974 Obvious Aspects of Ritual. *Cambridge Anthropology* 2:2–60.

1999 *Holiness and Humanity: Ritual in the Making of Religious Life.* New York: Cambridge University Press.

RATHUS, S. A., J. S. NEVID, AND J. FICHNER-RATHUS

2000 *Human Sexuality in a World of Diversity,* 4th ed. Boston: Allyn and Bacon.

REDFIELD, R.

1941 *The Folk Culture of Yucatan.* Chicago: University of Chicago Press.

REDFIELD, R., R. LINTON, AND M. HERSKOVITS

1936 Memorandum on the Study of Acculturation. *American Anthropologist* 38:149–152.

REITER, R.

1975 Men and Women in the South of France: Public and Private Domains. In *Toward an Anthropology of Women,* R. Reiter, ed., pp. 252–282. New York: Monthly Review Press.

RICKFORD, J. R.

1999 *African American Vernacular English: Features, Evolution,*

Educational Implications. Malden, MA: Blackwell.

RICKFORD, J. R., AND R. J. RICKFORD
2000 *Spoken Soul: The Story of Black English.* New York: Wiley.

ROBERTSON, A. F.
1995 *The Big Catch: A Practical Intro-duction to Development.* Boulder, CO: Westview.

ROBERTSON, J.
1992 Koreans in Japan. Paper presented at the University of Michigan Department of Anthropology, Martin Luther King Jr. Day Panel, January. Ann Arbor: University of Michigan Department of Anthropology (unpublished).

ROMAINE, S.
1999 *Communicating Gender.* Mahwah, NJ: L. Erlbaum.

ROOT, D.
1996 *Cannibal Culture: Art, Appropriation, and the Commodification of Difference.* Boulder, CO: Westview.

ROSALDO, M. Z.
1980a *Knowledge and Passion: Notions of Self and Social Life.* Stanford, CA: Stanford University Press.
1980b The Use and Abuse of Anthropology: Reflections on Feminism and Cross-Cultural Understanding. *Signs* 5(3):389–417.

ROUSE, R.
1991 Mexican Migration and the Social Space of Postmodernism. *Diaspora* 1(1):8–23.

ROYAL ANTHROPOLOGICAL INSTITUTE
1951 *Notes and Queries on Anthropology,* 6th ed. London: Routledge and Kegan Paul.

RYAN, S.
1990 *Ethnic Conflict and International Relations.* Brookfield, MA: Dartmouth.
1995 *Ethnic Conflict and International Relations,* 2nd ed. Brookfield, MA: Dartmouth.

SACHS, C. E.
1996 *Gendered Fields: Rural Women, Agriculture, and Environment.* Boulder, CO: Westview.

SAHLINS, M. D.
1961 The Segmentary Lineage: An Organization of Predatory Expansion. *American Anthropologist* 63:322–345.
1968 *Tribesmen.* Englewood Cliffs, NJ: Prentice Hall.
1972 *Stone Age Economics.* Chicago: Aldine.

SALUTER, A.
1996 Marital Status and Living Arrangements: March 1994, P20-484, U.S. Census Bureau, press release, March 13, 1996, CB96-33.

SALZMAN, P. C.
1974 Political Organization among Nomadic Peoples. In *Man in Adaptation: The Cultural Present,* 2nd ed., Y. A. Cohen, ed., pp. 267–284. Chicago: Aldine.

SANDAY, P. R.
1974 Female Status in the Public Domain. In *Woman, Culture, and Society,* M. Z. Rosaldo and L. Lamphere, eds., pp. 189–206. Stanford, CA: Stanford University Press.

SAPIR, E.
1931 Conceptual Categories in Primitive Languages. *Science* 74:578–584.

SARGENT, C. F., AND C. B. BRETTELL
1996 *Gender and Health: An International Perspective.* Englewood Cliffs, NJ: Prentice Hall.

SCHAEFER, R., AND R. P. LAMM
1992 *Sociology,* 4th ed. New York: McGraw-Hill.

SCHEINMAN, M.
1980 Imperialism. *Academic American Encyclopedia.* Princeton, NJ: Arete, volume 11, pp. 61–62.

SCHIEFFELIN, E.
1976 *The Sorrow of the Lonely and the Burning of the Dancers.* New York: St. Martin's.

SCHOLTE, J. A.
2000 *Globalization: A Critical Intro-duction.* New York: St. Martin's.

SCOTT, J. C.
1985 *Weapons of the Weak.* New Haven: Yale University Press.
1990 *Domination and the Arts of Re-sistance.* New Haven: Yale University Press.

SCUDDER, T., AND E. COLSON
1980 *Secondary Education and the For-mation of an Elite: The Impact of Education on Gwembe District, Zambia.* London: Academic Press.

SERVICE, E. R.
1962 *Primitive Social Organization: An Evolutionary Perspective.* New York: McGraw-Hill.
1966 *The Hunters.* Englewood Cliffs, NJ: Prentice Hall.

SHANKLIN, E.
1995 *Anthropology and Race.* Belmont, CA: Wadsworth.

SHANNON, T. R.
1989 *An Introduction to the World-System Perspective.* Boulder, CO: Westview.
1996 *An Introduction to the World-System Perspective,* 2nd ed. Boulder, CO: Westview.

SHIVARAM, C.
1996 Where Women Wore the Crown: Kerala's Dissolving Matriarchies Leave a Rich Legacy of Compassionate Family Culture. *Hinduism Today,* http://www.spiritweb.org/Hinduism Today/96_02_Women_Wore_Crown.html.

SHOSTAK, M.
1981 *Nisa: The Life and Words of a !Kung Woman.* Cambridge, MA: Harvard University Press.

SILBERBAUER, G.
1981 *Hunter and Habitat in the Cen-tral Kalahari Desert.* New York: Cambridge University Press.

SIMONS, A.
1995 *Networks of Dissolution: Somalia Undone.* Boulder, CO: Westview.

SIMPSON, B.
1998 *Changing Families: a Ethno-graphic Approach to Divorce and Separation.* New York: Berg.

SLADE, M.
1984 Displaying Affection in Public. *New York Times,* December 17.

SMITHERMAN, G.
1986 (orig. 1977) *Talkin and Testifyin: The Language of Black America.* Detroit: Wayne State University Press.

SOLWAY, J., AND R. LEE
1990 Foragers, Genuine and Spuri-ous: Situating the Kalahari San in History (with CA treat-ment). *Current Anthropology* 31(2):109–146.

SPINDLER, G. D., ED.
2000 *Fifty Years of Anthropology and Education, 1950-2000: A Spindler Anthology.* Mahwah, NJ: L. Erlbaum.

STACK, C. B.
1975 *All Our Kin: Strategies for Sur-vival in a Black Community.* New York: Harper Torchbooks.

STATISTICAL ABSTRACT OF THE UNITED STATES
1991 111th ed. Washington, DC: U.S. Bureau of the Census, U.S. Government Printing Office.
1996 116th ed. Washington, DC: U.S. Bureau of the Census, U.S. Government Printing Office.
1999 119th ed. Washington, DC: U.S. Bureau of the Census, U.S. Government Printing Office.

STEINFELS, P.
1997 Beliefs: Cloning, as Seen by Buddhists and Humanists. *New York Times,* July 12 www.nytimes.com.

STEVENS, W. K.
1992 Humanity Confronts Its Handi-work: An Altered Planet. *New York Times,* May 5, pp. B5–B7.

STEWARD, J. H.
1955 *Theory of Culture Change.* Ur-bana: University of Illinois Press.

STOLER, A.
1977   Class Structure and Female Autonomy in Rural Java. *Signs* 3:74–89.

STRATHERN, M.
1988   *The Gender of the Gift: Problems with Women and Problems with Society in Melanesia.* Berkeley: University of California Press.

STRATHERN, A., AND P. J. STEWART
1999   *Curing and Healing: Medical Anthropology in Global Perspective.* Durham, NC: Carolina Academic Press.

SUTTLES, W.
1960   Affinal Ties, Subsistence, and Prestige among the Coast Salish. *American Anthropologist* 62:296–305.

SWIFT, M.
1963   Men and Women in Malay Society. In *Women in the New Asia,* B. Ward, ed., pp. 268–286. Paris: UNESCO.

TANAKA, J.
1980   *The San Hunter-Gatherers of the Kalahari.* Tokyo: University of Tokyo Press.

TANNEN, D.
1986   *That's Not What I Meant! How Conversational Style Makes or Breaks Your Relations with Others.* New York: William Morrow.
1990   *You Just Don't Understand: Women and Men in Conversation.* New York: Ballantine.

TANNEN, D., ED.
1993   *Gender and Conversational Interaction.* New York: Oxford University Press.

TANNER, N.
1974   Matrifocality in Indonesia and Africa and among Black Americans. In *Women, Culture, and Society,* M. Z. Rosaldo and L. Lamphere, eds., pp. 129–156. Stanford, CA: Stanford University Press.

TAYLOR, C.
1987   Anthropologist-in-Residence. In *Applied Anthropology in America,* 2nd ed., E. M. Eddy and W. L. Partridge, eds., New York: Columbia University Press.

THOMAS, L.
1999   *Language, Society and Power.* New York: Routledge.

THOMPSON, W.
1983   Introduction: World System with and without the Hyphen. In *Contending Approaches to World System Analysis,* W. Thompson, ed., pp. 7–26. Thousand Oaks, CA: Sage.

TOFFLER, A.
1980   *The Third Wave.* New York: William Morrow.

TICE, K.
1997   Reflections on Teaching Anthropology for Use in the Public and Private Sector. In *The Teaching of Anthropology: Problems, Issues, and Decisions,* C. P. Kottak, J. J. White, R. H. Furlow, and P. C. Rice, eds., pp. 273–284. Mountain View, CA: Mayfield.

TONER, R.
1992   Los Angeles Riots Are a Warning, Americans Fear. *New York Times,* May 11, pp. A1, A11.

TRIGGER, B. G.
1995   *Early Civilizations: Ancient Egypt in Context.* New York: Columbia University Press.

VAN WILLINGEN, J.
1993   *Applied Anthropology: An Introduction,* 2nd ed. South Hadley, MA: Bergin and Garvey.

TURNBULL, C.
1965   *Wayward Servants: The Two Worlds of the African Pygmies.* Garden City, NY: Natural History Press.

TURNER, V. W.
1974   (orig. 1969). *The Ritual Process.* Harmondsworth, England: Penguin.

TYLOR, E. B.
1889   On a Method of Investigating the Development of Institutions: Applied to Laws of Mar-

riage and Descent. *Journal of the Royal Anthropological Institute* 18:245–269.

1958 (orig. 1871). *Primitive Culture.* New York: Harper Torchbooks.

U.S. CENSUS BUREAU

2000 www.census.gov.

VAYDA, A. P.

1968 (orig. 1961). Economic Systems in Ecological Perspective: The Case of the Northwest Coast. In *Readings in Anthropology,* 2nd ed., volume 2, M. H. Fried, ed., pp. 172–178. New York: Crowell.

VEBLEN, T.

1934 *The Theory of the Leisure Class: An Economic Study of Institutions.* New York: The Modern Library.

VIETNAM LABOR WATCH

1997 Nike Labor Practices in Vietnam, March 20, http://www.saigon.com/~nike/reports/report1.html.

VIOLA, H. J. AND C. MARGOLIS

1991 *Seeds of Change: Five Hundred Years since Columbus, a Quincentennial Commemoration.* Washington: Smithsonian Institution Press.

WAGLEY, C. W.

1968 (orig. 1959). The Concept of Social Race in the Americas. In *The Latin American Tradition,* by C. Wagley, pp. 155–174. New York: Columbia University Press.

WALLACE, A. F. C.

1956 Revitalization Movements. *American Anthropologist* 58:264–281.

1966 *Religion: An Anthropological View.* New York: McGraw-Hill.

1969 *The Death and Rebirth of the Seneca.* New York: Knopf.

WALLERSTEIN, I. M.

1982 The Rise and Future Demise of the World Capitalist System: Concepts for Comparative Analysis. In *Introduction to the Sociology of "Developing Societies,"* H. Alavi and T. Shanin, eds., pp. 29–53. New York: Monthly Review Press.

2000 *The Essential Wallerstein.* New York: New Press, W. W. Norton.

WARD, M. C.

1999 *A World Full of Women,* 2nd ed. Boston: Allyn and Bacon.

WATSON, P.

1972 Can Racial Discrimination Affect IQ? In *Race and Intelligence; The Fallacies behind the Race-IQ Controversy,* K. Richardson and D. Spears, eds., pp. 56–67. Baltimore: Penguin.

WEBER, M.

1958 (orig. 1904). *The Protestant Ethic and the Spirit of Capitalism.* New York: Scribner's.

1968 (orig. 1922). *Economy and Society.* E. Fischoff et al. (trans.). New York: Bedminster Press.

WEBSTER'S NEW WORLD ENCYCLOPEDIA

1993 College Edition. Englewood Cliffs, NJ: Prentice Hall.

WEINBERG, D.

1996 Press Briefing on 1995 Income, Poverty, and Health Insurance Estimates. Housing and Household Economic Statistics Division, U.S. Bureau of the Census. Washington, DC, September 26, www.census.gov/Press-Release/speech1.html.

WESTON, K.

1991 *Families We Choose: Lesbians, Gays, Kinship.* New York: Columbia University Press.

WHITE, L. A.

1959 *The Evolution of Culture: The Development of Civilization to the Fall of Rome.* New York: McGraw-Hill.

WHORF, B .L.

1956 A Linguistic Consideration of Thinking in Primitive Communities. In *Language, Thought, and Reality: Selected Writings of Benjamin Lee Whorf,* J. B. Carroll, ed., pp. 65–86. Cambridge, MA: MIT Press.

WILK, R. R.
   1996   *Economies and Cultures: An Introduction to Economic Anthropology.* Boulder, CO: Westview.
WILLIAMS, B.
   1989   A Class Act: Anthropology and the Race to Nation across Ethnic Terrain. *Annual Review of Anthropology* 18:401–444.
WILLIAMS, J.
   1985   What They Say, Home? English Dialects Are Adding to Racial Misunderstandings. *Washington Post National Weekly Edition,* May 6, p. 10.
WILMSEN, E. N.
   1989   *Land Filled with Flies: A Political Economy of the Kalahari.* Chicago: University of Chicago Press.
WILMSEN, E. N., AND P. MCALLISTER, EDS.
   1996   *The Politics of Difference: Ethnic Premises in a World of Power.* Chicago: University of Chicago Press.
WILSON, R., ED.
   1996   *Human Rights: Culture and Context: Anthropological Perspectives.* Chicago: Pluto.

WOLF, E. R.
   1966   *Peasants.* Englewood Cliffs, NJ: Prentice Hall.
   1982   *Europe and the People without History.* Berkeley: University of California Press.
WOLF, E. R., WITH S. SILVERMAN
   2001   *Pathways of Power: Building an Anthropology of the Modern World.* Berkeley: University of California Press.
WORLD ALMANAC AND BOOK OF FACTS
   1992   New York: Newspaper Enterprise Association.
WORSLEY, P.
   1985   (orig. 1959). Cargo Cults. In *Readings in Anthropology* 85/86. Guilford, CT: Dushkin.
YETMAN, N., ED.
   1991   *Majority and Minority: The Dynamics of Race and Ethnicity in American Life,* 5th ed. Boston: Allyn and Bacon.

Acknowledgments

Photo Credits

4: Diana Seaward/Photo Researchers. **7:** British Library of Political & Economic Science, London School of Economics and Political Science. **11:** Mark Edwards/Still Pictures/Peter Arnold, Inc. **14:** Christopher M. O'Leary. **21:** Jason Homa/The Image Bank/Getty Images (top); Ted Spiegel/Corbis (bottom). **25:** H. Armstrong Roberts (top); Mark Foley/AP/Wide World Photos (bottom). **28:** Kim Newton/Woodfin Camp & Assoc. **40:** Alex Webb/Magnum. **46:** J.P. Griffiths/Magnum. **54:** Alain Buu/Liaison/Getty Images. **63:** Jean-Philippe/AFP/Corbis. **71:** Lonny Shavelson. **73:** Reuters NewMedia Inc./Corbis. **75:** Burt Glinn/Magnum. **78:** James Nachtwey/Magnum. **90:** D. Halleux/Bios/Peter Arnold, Inc. **92:** Chin Ki Au/UNEP/Peter Arnold, Inc. **96:** T. Ketkaew/UNEP/Peter Arnold. **104:** Elbridge W. Merrill Collection/Alaska State Library and Archives, # PCA57-028. **111:** James L. Stanfield/National Geographic Society. **114:** Najlah Feanny/Stock, Boston. **120:** Donna Binder. **130:** Thomas L. Kelly. **135:** Ken Lambert/Liaison/Getty Images. **141:** Burt Glinn/Magnum. **144:** Douglas Kirkland/Image Bank/Getty Images. **148:** R.H. Beck/American Museum of Natural History. **150:** L. Schwartzwald/Corbis Sygma. **161:** Steve McCurry/Magnum. **167:** George Holton/Photo Researchers. **171:** Martha Cooper/Peter Arnold, Inc. **174:** Norman Rockwell Family Trust Copyright © 1943 the Norman Rockwell Family Trust. **184:** Duane Burleson/AP/Wide World Photos. **187:** David Maybury-Lewis/Anthro-Photo. **191:** Shabbir Hussain Imam/AP/Wide World Photos. **196:** Kal Muller/Woodfin Camp & Assoc. **203:** Hiroji Kubota/Magnum. **205:** Mercury Archives/Image Bank/Getty Images. **211:** General Research Division, The New York Public Library, Astor, Lenox and Tilden Foundation. **215:** U. Emerole/UNEP/Peter Arnold, Inc. **221:** Roger Viollet/Liaison/Getty Images. **229:** Marc & Evelyn Bernheim/Woodfin Camp & Assoc. **231:** Noorani/Still Pictures/Peter Arnold, Inc. **241:** Rob Crandall/Stock, Boston. **244:** Andres Hernandez/Liaison/Getty Images. **246:** H. Schwarzbach/Still Pictures/Peter Arnold, Inc. **248:** Ricardo Funari. **255:** Ron Giling/Peter Arnold, Inc. **258:** Alon Reininger/Woodfin Camp & Assoc. **261:** Photo Researchers. **262:** Professor Marietta Baba, Michigan State University.

Illustration Credits

Figure 3-3: Adapted from Philip Martin and Elizabeth Midgley, "Immigration to the United States: Journey to an Uncertain Destination." *Population Bulletin* 49:2, Sept. 1994. Washington, DC: Population Reference Bureau. Copyright 1994. **Figure 4-1:** From *Aspects of Language,* 3rd edition, by Dwight L. Bolinger and Donald A. Sears © 1981. Reprinted with permission of Heinle & Heinle a division of Thomson Learning. Fax 800-730-2215. **Box (Using Modern Technology to Preserve Linguistic Diversity):** John Noble Wilford, "In a Publishing Coup, Books in 'Unwritten' Languages," *The New York Times,* December 31, 1991, C1, C7. Copyright © 1991 by the New York Times Co. Reprinted by permission. **Figure 5-1:** From *People of the Stone Age* (The Illustrated History of Humankind Series, Volume 2) by Göran Burenhult, General Editor, p. 193. Copyright © 1993 by Weldon Owen Pty Limited/Bra Böcker AB. Reprinted by permission of Harper-Collins Publishers Inc. and Weldon Owen Pty Limited. **Box (Love and Marriage):** Daniel Goleman, "After Kinship and Marriage, Anthropology Discovers Love," *The New York Times,* November 24, 1992, C1, C12. Copyright © 1992 by the New York Times Co. Reprinted by permission. **Table 8-1:** From *Female of the Species* by Kay Martin and Barbara Voorhies. Copyright © 1975, Columbia University Press. Reprinted with permission of publisher. **Table 9-1:** Reprinted with permission from Victor Turner. *The Ritual Process: Structure and Anti-Structure* (New York: Aldine de Gruyter) Copyright © 1969 Victor W. Turner. **Figure 10-1:** From Thomas Richard Shannon. *An Introduction to the World-System Perspective.* Westview Press, 1989, p. 130. Reprinted by permission of the author. **Table 10-2:** From John H. Bodley, *Anthropology and Contemporary Human Problems.* Mayfield Publishing, 1985. Reprinted by permission of The McGraw-Hill Companies, Inc. **Figure 11-1:** From the *Academic American Encyclopedia,* 1998 Edition. Copyright 1998 by Grolier Incorporated. Reprinted by permission. **Figure 11-2:** From the *Academic American Encyclopedia,* 1998 Edition. Copyright 1998 by Grolier Incorporated. Reprinted by permission. **Box (Hot Asset in Corporate: Anthropology Degrees):** Del Jones, *"Hot Asset in Corporate: Anthropology Degrees,"* USA Today, February 18, 1999, B1. © 1999 USA Today, a division of Gannett Co., Inc. Reprinted by permission.

Index